DESKTOP
PUBLISHING
SUCCESS

Here are the full texts and IDs of the back cover quotes:

If ever a book should be called The Bible of the Desktop Publishing Biz, this is it. Kramer and Lovaas walk the reader through every step of establishing and growing a business, from practical marketing and salesmanship to keeping the books, from bidding on a project to dropping an unprofitable client, from finding customers to expanding revenues, with stops along the way for setting up a publishing system, writing contracts, learning how others solve problems. It's all here, told by people who have done it all and genuinely know what they're talking about. **—Sandra Rosenzweig, Editor-in-Chief, _Publish_ magazine**

I approached this book more than a little distracted—I had articles to edit, pages to approve, deadlines to meet. Halfway through, I felt excited and re-energized. This book recognizes electronic publishers' struggles and gives practical advice to make technology work in business, whether you're a freelance designer or an editor at a large corporation. As the one responsible to get each issue out the door, this book inspires me to keep going. **—Nancy McCarthy, Managing Editor, _Personal Publishing_ magazine**

There's nothing like this book. It raises and answers the main questions for us all. It's written for people with their own firms, people in corporations—and those who dream of working for themselves. Read it carefully before you strike out on your own. **—Barry Harrigan, Chairman, National Association of Desktop Publishers**

This is not a techie document. It is a human one. Its sly humor is a breath of fresh air. Never have I seen such an all-encompassing collection of accessible sophisticated computer wisdom coupled with so much common sense on running your own show (DTP or anything else). Rather than getting deep into design or typography, the book concentrates on aspects that no one else to my knowledge has covered. It pulls together strands that had previously been disassociated, and can now be seen in perspective. What a treasure-trove of practical tips to rely on, give you confidence, and make you realize you're not alone. **—Jan V. White, communications design consultant; author, _Editing by Design_, _Xerox Publication Standards_, _Graphic Design for the Electronic Age_**

This book is a deep well of common sense and practical guidance for those involved in the business of desktop publishing. Despite all the excitement, the claims of revelation, revolution and transformation … desktop publishing _is_ a business. And this is the best reality check I've seen. **—Michael Gosney, Publisher, _Verbum_ magazine; author, _The Verbum Electronic Art and Design_ book series; founding editor, _Step-By-Step Electronic Design_ newsletter**

Desktop Publishing Success is a comprehensive, detailed overview of how to make a go of this business. I recommend it for start-ups—and for seasoned pros.

**—Steve Roth, co-author, *Real World PageMaker*, *Real World PostScript*;
former editor, *Personal Publishing* magazine**

With the software available, enterprises and individuals needed only direction to build new businesses and effective organizations using desktop publishing. This well-timed book effectively brings together creative ideas, solid direction, and product understanding.

—Larry Gerhard, President & CEO, Xerox Ventura Software

While you can't expect to go from 0 to 60 in desktop publishing in a matter of seconds, this book will let new DTP entrepreneurs hit the ground running. I wish some of the service bureaus I've encountered had read—and put into practice—all the ideas and worthwhile information it contains.

**—Roger Black, President, Roger Black Incorporated, publication designer for *Smart*,
The New York Times, *San Francisco Examiner*, *Newsweek*, *Rolling Stone***

Desktop Publishing Success should be required reading for every desktop publishing entrepreneur—newcomer or experienced. Just one idea or warning can save you hours of frustration or earn you thousands of dollars of extra income over the coming months. This book reads like a conversation over lunch. Unique in concept and execution, it combines a friendly style with a wealth of techniques to enhance your professionalism and your income. It will help you avoid expensive mistakes, identify markets, run a more efficient service firm, and establish pleasurable, profitable and lasting relationships with clients, vendors and subcontractors. **—Roger C. Parker, author, *Looking Good in Print*,
The Makeover Book, *Newsletters from the Desktop***

As the "father" of desktop publishing I am pleased to see a book that addresses the needs of someone starting a desktop publishing business. Wherever I travel in the world today I can see the impact of desktop publishing—from the dark horse political candidate getting a message out, to the mother in San Francisco creating hand-illustrated books for children; from the manufacturer in Italy producing the Ferrari owner's manual, to the fledgling government in Eastern Europe building democracy through better information. *Desktop Publishing Success* offers straightforward, practical advice from authors who know the ropes and communicate this knowledge in a conversational style. The book is an excellent resource for anyone involved in desktop publishing.

—Paul Brainerd, President, Aldus Corporation (creators of PageMaker)

BUSINESS ONE IRWIN
Desktop Publishing Library

DESKTOP PUBLISHING SUCCESS

HOW TO START AND RUN A DESKTOP PUBLISHING BUSINESS

FELIX KRAMER   MAGGIE LOVAAS

BUSINESS ONE IRWIN
Homewood, Illinois 60430

Senior editor: Susan Glinert Stevens, Ph.D.
Project editor: Karen J. Nelson
Production manager: Ann Cassady
Cover Design: Renee Klyczek-Nordstrom
Printer: R. R. Donnelley & Sons Company

Library of Congress Cataloging-in-Publication Data

Kramer, Felix.
    Desktop publishing success : how to start and run a desktop publishing business / by Felix Kramer and Maggie Lovaas.
      p.   cm.
    ISBN 1–55623–424–4
    1. Desktop publishing. 2. New business enterprises. I. Lovaas, Maggie. II. Title.
    Z286.D47K73 1991
    686.2′2544 — dc20   90–19933

Printed in the United States of America

1 2 3 4 5 6 7 8 9 0 DOC 8 7 6 5 4 3 2 1

CONTENTS

PREFACE

Who this book is for

If you want to make a living in desktop publishing—or if you're already doing it and want to sharpen your skills and enjoy your work more—you're our main audience.

You want to start your own business
- As a one-person desktop publishing enterprise offering production, consulting, training or systems support services based in your own office or at home;
- As a freelance production employee, occasionally working part- or full-time through temporary agencies;
- As an employee or manager in a small desktop publishing business.

You want to integrate desktop publishing into what you already do
- As a writer who wants to take your work one step further;
- As a generalist who knows something about writing, design, illustration, and photography;
- As a designer who wants to produce sketches and prototypes electronically;
- As a professional typesetter who wants to go out on your own;
- As a graphics production manager who wants to open a one-stop business providing type, photostats, design, and art.

For all of you in transition, we hope to help you sort out whether this kind of work suits you, and, if so, to save you time, trouble, and money as you become a desktop publisher. Whether you're starting out, working at home with a small child, or changing careers, desktop publishing may be the right choice for you. It's a highly demanding job that will take your full attention. We'll let you know what you need to learn, and the tools you need to get, to be a full-service desktop publisher.

If you're among the many people already working in this field, we hope to help you look at your work differently and give you new ways to approach old problems. In short, we aim to improve the quality and productivity of your working life.

You are a corporate or institutional desktop publisher

- Employed in or managing a desktop publishing department;
- Responsible for hiring desktop publishing employees or consultants;
- Charged with establishing or expanding in-house publishing capability;
- Consulting with corporations about their publishing needs;
- Responsible for internal or external corporate communications.

Of course, corporate managers or employees may not be quite as concerned with writing contracts and collecting your invoices as people starting small businesses. Still, most of this book, about tools, production, and customers, will apply to you. We've written one section, **Appendix 1. Corporate Desktop Publishing**, especially for people like you.

Or you just need to know more about the field

Finally, we also wrote this book for people working with desktop publishers, who are employed by service bureaus, employment agencies, training facilities, and printing and publishing houses.

A different kind of computer book

At computer user group meetings, more and more of the questions we get from people coming into this field are about the business side of desktop publishing. Everyone always perks up when we talk about how to find clients, how much to charge, and how to get the work done quickly and well. Noticing those kinds of questions gave us the idea for this book.

We concentrate on the human relationships and work processes of desktop publishing. The key to doing any job well is to recognize who is involved and how to treat them. And the key to higher productivity is to improve the way work is organized and conducted.

Although we do offer tips and suggestions for choosing, using, or understanding different types and brands of hardware or software, we don't go into detailed explanations about how certain tools work or about features of particular products. The best way for you to find that out is to read other, more basic books and product reviews in magazines, plus the manuals that come with the products. Then try out the tools themselves.

We do give our opinions about what you should buy, because there's no getting away from those decisions, and sometimes we want to illustrate our approach. We concentrate our recommendations on the basic tools you'll need to get started. We hope you'll check out the books, magazines, and other resources we cite in the text and in **Appendix 2** for more details and depth.

In the end, we hope that as you make decisions about the tools you buy, you *don't* rely on any advice written by someone who has never met you. To make decisions about the tools to use, there's no substitute for sitting down and trying out a screen, keyboard, operating system, user interface, or software approach.

Using this book

We've assumed you know something about computers and publishing, but have tried to define arcane terms the first time they're used. When subjects have been handled well by others, instead of long paraphrases, we don't hesitate to refer you to those sources.

When we refer you to another part of the book, to help you find a particular citation, we usually mention the **chapter number** and then the **subhead name** rather than the **chapter title**. You'll find our figures included in italics within the table of contents.

We've included addresses and phone numbers only for product vendors and small presses that may be hard to find through large retailers or mail order companies.

In **7. Working Efficiently**, we've included a section of tips and suggestions for improving your efficiency. It comes way back in the book, not because it's less important than other subjects, but because there are six chapters of information you need to think about first.

At the end we include **15. Profiles of Desktop Publishers** to give you a taste of what the work is like, and what these professionals think about. We close with **16. Authors' Profiles**.

We've also sprinkled the text with comments from the people we've profiled and others. Since we've been picking other people's brains while we've been doing this work, some of the suggestions are too useful to share without credit. We've included both amplifications and viewpoints differing from ours. At a person's first appearance, which you can track down through the **Index**, we've included a short identification of the people who are not profiled.

Desktop publishing for fun and profit

That's what we planned to call this book—until our publisher pointed out that it might deter some serious people. Nevertheless, desktop publishing can offer you a way to make a comfortable living *and* enjoy yourself. Most of this book concentrates on the living part of it:

- Unlike most businesses, you don't have to lose money the first year;
- You'll need to invest relatively small sums to start your business;
- You can work out of your home, if you choose.

The satisfying part comes from taking what you enjoy doing and getting it to occupy an increasing part of your worklife. Most desktop publishers we know confess to having a great deal of difficulty seeing what they do as work—they enjoy it too much! That feeling can get in the way of being a hard-nosed businessperson when it comes to bidding and invoicing jobs, but it's a problem most people would love to face.

Here are some reasons we see our work as enjoyable. We love:

- Admiring our creative leaps in design, on the screen and on paper;
- Finding new ways to do things and inventing technical workarounds;
- Not having to apologize—at last—for wanting the latest gadgets;
- Feeling virtuous when we experiment with software;
- Dropping our jaws at what software developers come up with next;
- Passing our discoveries and tips back to people at software companies;
- Being treated as equals, allies, and sometimes friends, by clients;
- Surprising our clients and, occasionally, thrilling them by solving a difficult problem or beating a major deadline;
- Working with and helping our fellow desktop publishers;
- Getting a kick out of pet projects, party announcements, parodies, and résumés for friends.

If this sounds like fun, you, too, could begin counting as work untold hours spent in these pursuits.

Our philosophy

From our experiences and a perusal of the classic books on starting and running successful businesses, we've culled some basic principles:

- Concentrate on what you enjoy doing;
- Pay attention to what your customers tell you;
- Treat your customers and employees well;
- Don't get stuck in a rut—keep your eyes open and take risks.

To that advice, we add lots of specifics about desktop publishing. Plus the general suggestion that in running your own business, you'll need a particular kind of mindset. You're truly on your own. You can't let a moment go by without being ready to apply every part of your imagination, analytic ability, and experience to every problem and event, first as you encounter and understand it, then as you plan and execute its solution.

If you pay attention to all the advice in the business books and remain conscious of your own evolution, you'll have a good chance at success. And hopefully you'll enjoy what you do, and not end up embittered by your life, hating your job, resenting your clients, or sorry you never tried your wings.

Too much to know and remember

Just as you can't expect to understand every technical term or explanation in articles or at user group meetings, don't expect to absorb and recall everything covered in this book. Just keep track of what you need to know now and where to find information you'll need as you progress.

We wrote the book by watching how we work, and thinking about the implications of each thing we do. For months, we took notes as we worked on jobs and with people, gradually adding more points and tips. A note on our advice: It's just that. We have lots of suggestions about how to set up your business and work methods. Some are the product of hindsight—or painfully learned lessons. There's always a more logical way to plan, do, and track work. No one is as efficient and well-organized as they would wish; that includes us.

It's often easier to do more work rather than stop while you improve your methods. But sometimes you'll find yourself in the mood to tidy up your computer files, or write some macros to automate repetitious tasks, or fine-tune your billing sheets. Don't let these impulses go unfulfilled. The rest of the time, don't be too hard on yourself for not meeting an ideal. Even if you're behind on your goals of getting organized, you can still make money.

As for technology, everyone we've met—from computer novice to power user, expert consultant, professional trainer, or expert—feels behind the times. All confess to shelving a manual, being intimidated by someone else who knows more, not taking the time to improve their methods, leaving new, exciting software sitting unopened on the shelf, and letting trade magazines pile up unread on the floor. No one can ever reach computer nirvana. Besides, there's no such state, because the technology is always advancing.

About producing, revising, and distributing this book

We wrote this book using Microsoft Word as a document that gradually emerged from an outline structure. Most of the time, to facilitate editing and reorganizations, we kept the entire book in one large file. It got as large as 750K, and we took elaborate precautions when saving and backing up. Felix produced the pages using Aldus PageMaker. We decided to take our own advice about not venturing into uncharted waters when on deadline, and had the index created conventionally. For the typefaces and styles used, see **Fig. 7.6**.

Because we like to hear from readers and may one day revise this book, we welcome your comments, suggestions, war stories, or tips that illustrate points we made or should have made. Please send them to us at the address below.

This book is available at many bookstores. You can order copies from anywhere in the U.S. or Canada by calling (800) 541-2318. If you want to order individual or gift copies, or you're interested in multiple copies for training programs or institutional use, you can order from the address below. (Write, or call us at (212) 529-6110, for information on special prices for members of user groups and associations.)

c/o Kramer Communications
PO Box 844 Cathedral Station
New York, NY 10025

ACKNOWLEDGMENTS

Maggie came up with the idea for this book; Felix wrote the successive drafts. Maggie conducted the interviews and wrote the first drafts of the profiles. Both Felix and Maggie conducted the research and designed the book, and Felix produced the camera-ready pages.

We thank our colleagues who gave us ideas and suggestions, helped us find key sources, and reviewed all or part of the work in progress. They include: Peter Brooks, Ann Raszmann Brown, Sandy Chelnov, Bonnie Cohen, Laurie Kramer, Ron Lockhart, Richard Metter, Luther Sperberg, Margaret Styne, Earl Wilken, as well as many of the people profiled or quoted in the book. Thanks to Franklin Moss for legal review. We thank Geraldine Albert and John Beattie for copy editing, Sarah Sills for help with production, Chris Holme for design ideas, Renee Klyczek Nordstrom for cover design, Maro Riofrancos for indexing, and Ray Noonan of ParaGraphic Artists, NYC, for camera-ready printing.

We thank the inspired and amorphous computer user group community who have been so important to us as desktop publishers. The authors met at an early 1985 user group meeting. We owe much to our friends in the New York Macintosh Users' Group and the New York Personal Computer Corporation (the PC user group); especially to their respective Desktop Publishing Special Interest Groups. We also want to acknowledge the generous and creative people we encountered through these groups, who motivated us to write this book.

We also owe many thanks to the people at other important institutions, including the NY Professional PostScript Users Group, the Nonprofit Computer Exchange, Wheeler-Hawkins (formerly Electronic Directions), the Computers for Social Change Conference, and Computer Professionals for Social Responsibility.

Thanks to our enthusiastic and entertaining editor, Susan Glinert Stevens, our contract attorney, Bob Stein, and our agent, Bill Gladstone of Waterside Productions. Thanks to colleagues at the National Writers Union who helped us find our attorney and agent and advised us on negotiations.

Felix thanks his wife, Rochelle, who helped out with a book project that came along at an inopportune time, for her and for then-brand-new Joshua Ethan Kramer. Thanks also to Thomas J. Connolly, a general contractor who knows how to keep customers happy, and Arthur Naething, Walter Schneller, Alan Snitow, and Mim Kelber for encouraging him to think of himself as a writer.

Maggie thanks her husband, Tom, for his help, patience and good humor. Thanks also to Rich Arends, Charley McCourt, Steve Stone, Joe Cornacchia, Karen Randlev, Joan Hochman and Chris Reid, and the crew at Fintec Corporation for support and encouragement. A special thanks to On Far Tse for his unfailing cooperation.

Of course, without our clients we would never have had the chance to get the experience, to make mistakes and enjoy stunning succcesses, producing more published materials in a year than anyone used to do in a lifetime. We've learned from them, laughed with them, crossed our fingers with them, and sometimes grumbled about them. But they've made it all possible—and we thank them.

INTRODUCTION: SO YOU WANT TO BE A DESKTOP PUBLISHER

What is desktop publishing?

Desktop publishing, simply defined, is the process of creating pages of text and graphics using a personal computer, page layout and other software, and a printer that produces a minimum resolution of 300 by 300 dots per inch (dpi). That's the starting point, though, of course, the hardware and software can get more elaborate.

Desktop publishing is actually a misleading name. True, it's often on a desktop, though it can be a tight fit, but it isn't really publishing. It's understood to mean a process that ends with original pages to be reproduced and distributed by conventional means. Publishing, on the other hand, usually produces multiples of two-sided, bound pages or volumes and gets them into the hands of wholesalers, newsstands, bookstores, subscribers, and buyers.

But thanks to the ads and hype that accompanied a dazzling torrent of software back in 1985-88, the phrase caught on over computer typography, electronic pagination, and other less flashy names.

Throughout this book, we use the shorthand DTP to refer to the entire constellation of electronic publishing technologies, techniques, and products. Not that we're any happier with the acronym than anyone else—but it's convenient. (Don't confuse it with the infant Diphtheria, Tetanus, and Pertussis shot.) We include in DTP:

- Creation of original pages of text and graphics for one-time use, or for photocopying or printing—for stationery, flyers, awards, menus, brochures, proposals, reports, newsletters, catalogs, annual reports, directories, magazines, books, tabloids and newspapers ;

- Typesetting for other purposes, such as signs, labels, tickets, maps, and packages;
- Presentation graphics for slides and overheads;
- Graphics for transfer to videotape or film;
- Preparing computer files for transfer to high-end color prepress systems;
- The emerging area of desktop multimedia—incorporating text, graphics, video, and sound into animations. This is a field with its origins in video and film, but many people who began in DTP now use DTP tools for multimedia; many overlap the two fields.

Our discussion of DTP applies to projects undertaken on every kind of computer, from the lowly 8-bit computer and dot-matrix printer to the 32-bit networked workstation or minicomputer connected directly to imagesetters (high-resolution laser printers). However, to the extent we mention specific tools, we concentrate on the computer types—what industry insiders call platforms—of interest to people who want to make a living as DTPers.

During its first years, DTP came under heavy fire from people who felt it was usurping a quality level that only true typesetting could achieve. That criticism has now died down as even the most exacting graphic designers and publishers are finding uses for the technology. Increasingly, too, typesetters have realized they'll be left behind unless they can work with DTP-oriented clients and use DTP when it outshines other technologies. Nowadays, whether or not they realize it, DTP's detractors are not really criticizing the tools, but rather their use by people who have inadequate talent, training, or skills.

A rapidly growing and evolving industry

The business of printed communications, broadly viewed, may be the nation's largest industry. Practically every institution in America relies heavily on printed material. Nowadays, every neighborhood in every city and every small town has a couple of copy shops. And you'll be seeing more people hanging out their DTP shingles.

How many people are desktop publishing in some way or other? Looking at the two main microcomputer desktop publishing software packages, Aldus Corporation has an installed base over 500,000 for PageMaker, and Xerox Ventura Software records over 225,000 registered owners of Ventura Publisher.

Looking at those intensely involved with the technology, the two dominant monthly magazines had these circulations as of October, 1990:

Publish 125,000
Personal Publishing 75,000

In 1990, the *rate* of growth in the sale of DTP software slowed for the first time (probably because the first wave of users had stocked up on what they needed), but sales continued at a rapid pace. Market researchers Desktop Presentations, Inc. projects a worldwide market for DTP tools growing from $2.4 billion in 1987 to $6.9 billion by 1992. This is an industry that keeps growing because people will always need to have better looking documents. And it's one that keeps changing, as more and more capabilities migrate down from the $100,000 professional machines to the affordable and easy-to-use desktop computers.

The growth of DTP also depends, in part, on the general growth of the use of computers in society as a whole. Computers have penetrated some parts of society less than you might assume. Market research firm Biz Cap International estimates that only 46% of companies with fewer than 10 employees currently have a PC. And only 31% of the growing number of households with income-generating home offices are computerized. As these numbers rise, many people who are aware of DTP's potential probably won't want to do it themselves and are likely give DTPers text files on disk.

Windows of opportunity

DTP tools are changing the world of written communications—and creating some extraordinary opportunities for thousands of people to redefine their work lives.

What stage has DTP reached? As we write, the first commercial DTP products are five years old. It's about three years since we began getting version 2.0 of the first software packages, and about four years since everyone in the field felt like a pioneer.

DTP is still a young enough industry to have an entrepreneurial flavor to it. And opportunities abound—for freelancers, people starting their own businesses, and people looking for good jobs in DTP centers at corporations. In

September 1990, *Home Office Computing* magazine called DTP one of the 10 best business opportunities for the 1990s.

There's plenty of room for new people in the field. For one thing, some of the veterans have left hands-on production, moving on to related pursuits: high-end color, multimedia, managing DTP centers, training, and consulting. For another, it's still safe to say that most typography in this country and the overwhelming majority of graphics continue to be produced without desktop computers. The countless publications distributed in typewritten form are also candidates for DTP. The shift of increasing amounts of this work will offer employment to many more DTPers than currently exist.

Today, we only rarely hear of any DTPer mentioning competition from other DTPers or a glut on the market as obstacles to finding work. So far, the growing availability of DTP services has led to an expansion of the marketplace and more interest in DTP services by people shopping for type and graphics services.

What happens when there are tens of thousands more DTPers? As an emerging industry matures and becomes more competitive, the people who have the most to offer will prosper. The others—less capable, imaginative, or resource-ful—will struggle or abandon the field.

What happens when every computer user has a laser, inkjet, or bubblejet printer and can buy for $100 moderately capable DTP software that can run on a typical home machine? That day is not far off.

To reassure aspiring DTPers, Felix likes to use a parallel from photography. After all, for the past 30 years practically anyone could afford a quality 35-millimeter camera that produces magazine-quality results. But the availability of affordable and easy-to-use tools hasn't cut into the demand for professional photographers. Many people own the equipment, but when they need to know the job will be done right they hire a pro. In fact, as occasional amateur photographers, they're more likely both to appreciate the value they receive when they pay someone else, and to be able to discuss what they want in a useful and informed manner.

Most people concentrate on their specialties and on what they do best. They find an expert when they need help. That expert will continue to be the experienced DTPer.

A mini-inventory for prospective DTPers

Your answers to these questions won't give you a score you can use to decide whether to become a DTPer. But your answers will help you decide whether DTP is for you.

- What are my personal goals?
- What do I enjoy doing?
- Am I willing to spend a lot of time sitting?
- Am I willing to work 'round the clock at the start?
- Do I expect to work normal hours once I'm established?
- Can I live through spells when the work dries up or my enthusiasm flags?
- Will I enjoy always expecting to learn something new?
- Will I mind always feeling behind?
- Do I relish or dread the idea of working alone, without a water cooler?
- Will I enjoy working with a client peering over my shoulder?
- Can I face admitting my shortcomings and ask for help?
- Do I mind typing boring material?
- Am I detail oriented?
- Do I enjoy going over finished projects for one last round of improvements?
- Can I be relaxed and creative under deadline pressures?

1. BECOMING A DESKTOP PUBLISHER

Chances are you've been reading about desktop publishing, which we call DTP for short. Maybe you know someone who is happily and profitably mousing away. Yes, you'll need one of those strange pointing devices, and someone is likely to get a laugh out of giving you one of those cute cloth covers in the shape of a real mouse. But how can you judge whether DTP can be a promising career for you?

You can start by matching your temperament and expectations to our picture of the reality of DTP work. Next, see how you do with the checklist of qualifications and skills, and your options for filling in the missing pieces.

What's DTP production work like?

As a self-employed DTPer, you'll probably start in production work. You're not likely to know enough at first to be a consultant or trainer. That means you'll spend up to half your working hours staring at screens and papers. For the most part, unless you end up constantly working against tight deadlines, you'll enjoy production work. When all goes well, the hard disk hums and clicks reassuringly, the software obliges, the display responds to your every command, the columns snap in and flow out—and the pages roll right out of the printer. No problem!

The stress level for production work is usually not high. If the machine turns on and the screen comes up in the morning—and you know what you're doing— you'll feel like a seasoned high-tech craftsperson, using just the right array of skills and shortcuts to create fitting pages.

Unlike the writer, who wakes up every day wondering if there's anything more to say, or the business professional enmeshed in an office hierarchy that watches and judges every move, as a DTPer you'll usually be pretty confident you can complete every project successfully. All you have to do is take the time to set up your job carefully, get help when you need it, and budget your time well!

Of course, sometimes everything goes wrong. You'll have days when you get no work done. You'll be on a deadline, but you'll run into an intractable technical problem: a software glitch or some crucial part of hardware goes haywire. First you'll think there's an easy solution, so you'll stop everything to find or work on the problem. Much later, you'll look up and find your day gone. And maybe you solved the problem, or maybe you gave up and called for help, or just found a workaround.

What's the rest of your day going to be like?

During the other half of your workday, you'll be a computer businessperson, on the buy and sell sides of every kind of transaction, planning and accounting for jobs, shopping for tools and learning technology. Every day you'll make countless choices.

You'll either love or hate this part; here you'll have to find your own way. No one could write a manual accounting for every way you'll run the small business you create based on your style and idiosyncrasies.

You'll have no boss—and no mentor. You'll have to face every day deciding whether to spend your time working, learning, or marketing, and whether to choose high-paid work with little challenge or lower-paid work with growth opportunities.

More than in many businesses, your DTP environment is dynamic. As you gain knowledge, experience, contacts and options, and as the technology evolves, you'll increase your range of choices:

- What kind of projects should you try for?
- Can you say no to a tempting, but possibly diverting, offer?
- Will you work for other DTPers or have them work for you?
- For a new kind of special effect, is it worth it to you to learn how to do it yourself or hire your colleague in the user group who can handle it in a flash?
- Should you branch out into training or a related field like presentation graphics?
- Should you hire a part-time bookkeeper, salesperson, or assistant? How big do you want to grow your business?

The special nature of technology-based skills complicates the dilemmas that are common to any small business. Unlike traditional craftspeople—cabinet-makers, potters, shoemakers, or tailors, who may use almost the same materials and techniques as their 19th century predecessors—as a DTPer you can be certain that a year from now you'll be doing almost nothing in the same way as you now do it! Even the tools you have don't stay the same. You'll be reconfiguring, upgrading, and replacing your equipment frequently. (The impermanence is hard for some people we know.)

Improving your chances for success and satisfaction

Personal characteristics

By definition, when you're starting a business you need an entrepreneurial temperament. That includes self-confidence and enthusiasm for the project; excitement, curiosity, and confidence about the future; high energy and tenacity for the long and demanding journey; and realism mixed with imagination to take full advantage of every opportunity.

You'll need to be self-reliant and happy working by yourself; productive when no one is cracking the whip; and content when you can't get angry at the boss. You'll also need to be a good judge of people because you'll be choosing clients, vendors, collaborators, and part- or full-time employees. If you expect to become a consultant or trainer, you'll need to be a good communicator—beyond the good communication essential to any business.

You'll need to be able to handle pressure: Most clients come to you when they had expected to be at the printer, so they expect instant turnaround. Finally, you'll need to be meticulous. Publishing is often a matter of rigid exactitude and consistency. There's no room for casual inattention or inaccuracy.

For any job, particularly where you're the owner, boss, and principal employee, you need to get to work early, make list after list, and be disciplined about getting to your priorities.

Business experience

If you don't have a background in business, prepare to learn fast. You'll find some of what you need to know here, and some suggestions for further reading in **Appendix 2**. Developing systems and approaches that work for you is, on the one hand, a matter of common sense. On the other hand, DTP is just one type of service business. By now the professionals have discovered and set down all the rules for bidding, contracting, delivering, analyzing, and billing work. If you've been through this before, you'll be ahead of the game. If not, there's no inherent reason you can't succeed despite some false starts, slipups, hard knocks, and quick saves and rebounds along the way.

Similarly, some experience with (or at least a low anxiety level about) the prospect of marketing and selling will help. But don't worry too much about this. Many people who thought they hated selling discover it feels completely different when they're selling something they believe in: their own capabilities and services.

Other work-related experience can come in handy. For example, a familiarity with some industry or product might be the source of your first clients. Experience in teaching and an appreciation for how people connect to technology could pave the way later to your becoming a DTP trainer.

Incidentally, experience with working in or managing nonprofit organizations can count just as well as for-profit business experience. Felix has found that the common wisdom exaggerates the differences between the two.

Resources

If you already have most of the computer hardware you need, you'll be able to start up much more quickly than if you have to go out and buy it. If you have an established workspace (in your home, or in the corner of someone else's office) that's one less problem. And a longstanding, trusting relationship with an accountant and a lawyer will take two major items off your startup checklist.

But most important is working capital. Ideally, you should have enough working capital to cover your startup, living, and operating costs for six months to a year. That way you can get the right tools, take time to learn them, and start your business without too much pressure. If you don't have that much, try to put aside at least $15,000 in addition to $10,000 for startup costs. That way you won't have to worry all the time about folding prematurely because of a cash flow crunch. If you can't come up with that minimum amount, plan to start your DTP business on the side of a full-time job for as long as you need to get a solid foothold. Of course, many people go ahead without these kinds of reserves, build their arsenal of equipment carefully and gradually, and succeed.

Skills

Touch-typing is a necessity. If you aren't a fast typist yet, add a typing program to your software list. Unless you intend to use the computer exclusively for graphic design, if you don't learn to type, you'll regret every hunt and peck. Even if you hire typists, or use a scanner to input text, you'll still be making lots of last-minute text changes—and using software with keyboard shortcuts that assume you're a touch typist.

If you have good communications skills, you'll have a much easier time finding DTP clients. Before DTP, no one expected typesetters to be writers, copy editors, or proofreaders. With the expansion of the client base for typesetting that has accompanied DTP, these are often valued services a DTPer can offer to customers. Any expertise in direct mail, advertising, and public relations can also help you find and advise clients.

Talents

Though you'll be a businessperson and an entrepreneur, you'll also be an artist. As a DTPer, you'll often be able to express your creativity through your business.

If you don't already know the concepts and terminology of typography, graphic design, photography, and printing, you'll need to *start* learning them. What if DTP attracts you but you're not satisfied with your existing design skills? If, as you begin in DTP, you feel your graphic instincts improve, you'll probably continue to get better. You'll become sensitized to the basics of design: unity, proportion, balance, contrast, rhythm, and restraint, and to the ins and outs of typographic choices, grids, and the interplay between type and graphics.

Meanwhile, you can hook up with a DTP colleague with a graphic design background, read up on the subject, hire an advisor, or take evening courses. Or you can accept only those jobs that include a budget for a professional graphic designer (you'll learn lots working closely with a pro).

Still, if you really have *no eye* for what looks good, no matter how well you learn how to use DTP software, you'll keep running into trouble. Your pages, even if competently produced, may look wrong or lifeless to you and to clients, and you should think twice about this career.

> DTP does not make you more creative. It makes you faster. It makes your comps look better. But ideas are ideas—whether you put them down on paper or mouse around with them.
>
> —*Ann Raszmann Brown, graphic designer, Buffalo, NY*

What you need to learn

Launching your DTP career will take every minute you've got. However smooth the startup, once you're established you'll still never be able to put the business on automatic pilot. That's one of the less charming consequences of a technology-based enterprise.

DTP abounds in hidden costs—especially time, your most precious resource. The most time-consuming part of DTP is the hours you'll spend learning how to do it—and then keeping your expertise up to date. You can't charge your clients directly for this time. Though part of your workday, these are unbillable hours, and you'll have to find a way to cover their cost as you structure your fees.

> Years ago, I took a hand-lettering course with Ed Benguiat, a world-renowned type designer. The first day in class he looked around the room and pointed to a person wearing a baseball jacket. He asked him some baseball statistics. The person rattled off answers to all the questions. Then Ed asked what was the difference between the letter "T" in Tiffany and Souvenir, and then Garamond. The person didn't know. Ed commented that most of us know more about our hobbies than we do about our professions. If we want to do well as a professional, it behooves us to know inside out what we spend most of our day doing.
>
> *—Lawrence Kaplan*

First you'll need basic **computer literacy**. Chances are you're already comfortable with your computer's general capabilities. Being able to handle your computer may mean recognizing a few unexpected mechanical idiosyncrasies. Some computers are finicky about humidity and heat; some cables and peripherals need a tap once in a while to get unglued; some disk drives are sticky or don't work reliably until they've warmed up; some software combinations make the machine freeze up.

Before you'll have a clear shot at learning DTP, you'll need to know more about your computer's **operating system**, the way it organizes and accesses applications and data. You'll need to know your way around your **network**, even if this is just a fancy name for the connection between computer and printer. And you'll need a ready familiarity with the key **utility software** you'll use to keep your files organized and backed up.

Next is **publishing literacy**. If you think pica is like elite, mechanicals are for engineers, hairlines recede, carets are jewels, and imposition is impolite, you probably have a business, or editorial background. You'll need to learn the specialized vocabulary and concepts essential to typography, graphic design, and printing. Many page layout software packages include a separate book or a section in their manual explaining DTP and typesetting concepts. That's a start, as is *Pocket Pal,* International Paper Company's frequently updated and reasonably priced graphic arts production handbook. (See **Appendix 2. Books on DTP and graphic design**.) Learn standard proofreading marks: you'll find them in most dictionaries and all manuals of style (see **5. Accessories, Peripherals, and Supplies**).

Finally, you'll need some basic understanding of **design concepts**: an appreciation of what looks good and what doesn't work on a page. Don't confuse the mastery of software tools with the ability to use those tools to produce well-designed pages. We can't repeat enough that if you have no intuitive feeling for graphic design, you might consider another career. Otherwise, start learning more by looking carefully at every publication and document you encounter; read up on the subject; and consider getting some formal training.

> If you don't have familiarity with text, typography, composition, or design, you're not going to do a particularly good job at putting together a page of text. The same holds true for color work. You need to know the basics before you can effectively utilize the tools on a microcomputer platform. I recommend taking a course in traditional methodologies that have nothing to do with computers: basic typography, text, type, color; how it works; what's good, what's not; basic design philosophy. Learn these from someone who is not using computer technology. The computer is just a tool. It doesn't teach these to you; you first have to know the basics.
> —*Paul Constantine*

Ways to learn it

Now you're ready to begin mastering DTP. Of course, everyone learns differently—some learn best from books, others from people, still others from electronic tutorials. Developing a new skill can be a pleasure or an anxious nightmare; find what's right for you. Don't be in a hurry; encourage your curiosity. Avoid or at least cut short any experience that makes you feel dumb.

You can consider going **back to school** (it's also a good way to take extended test drives of hardware or software). These days, courses in DTP abound. You'll find them in the computer or arts programs of many college extension departments. Many computer user groups sponsor courses, or you may find an individual trainer through these groups. Some training centers and individual consultants get official stamps of approval from leading software publishers.

Though you'll get what you pay for, check out those for-profit singles- and career-oriented learning centers in major cities; you can usually pick up their desktop published catalogs in street newspaper boxes. Lately, we've seen some DTP programs offered through magazine ads by correspondence schools. One of these entices hopeful readers with promises that "you can earn top dollar as creative master of one of today's hottest computer technologies: desktop publishing." For $1,895, you get study materials, reviews of your work, an underpowered PC-XT clone, introductory software, and a nine-pin dot-matrix printer. Clearly, you can do better almost anywhere else.

Another alternative is an **electronic tutorial**. Videocassettes make sense for complex illustration software, but most people prefer audiocassettes, run simultaneously with disk-based tutorial and resource files. They usually cost from $75-$500, and some are multi-part. Personal Training Systems, (800) TEACH-99, produces an excellent line for the Macintosh; Fliptrack, (800) 222-FLIP, is for the PC. You can often review these cassettes along with hourly rentals of computer time at training centers and laser printing service bureaus.

Don't rule out **reading the manual** that comes with the software. In some cases, the publisher's material is outstanding; in other cases, supplement it with an independently published book.

We like to start off by **tinkering**. Especially when we know a little bit about what's in a program, we enjoy launching the application and seeing how far we can get on our own. This kind of exploring appeals to our inventive and detective sides; it also allows us to admire the ingenuity of the software designers without intermediaries or commentators. If there's on-line help—where a computerized advisor system is part of the program—we see whether we can progress further. Finally we return to the documentation and any accompanying tutorial.

> There's a lot to learn and even though the computer is user-friendly, I have spent *many hours* in front of the computer to learn all the programs I now use daily. I spent close to 45 minutes a day for two weeks just to learn where to place the points in Illustrator.   —*Lawrence Kaplan*

Perhaps you can **watch a seasoned DTPer at work**. That way you can see how an expert uses the software. At any stage when you become a silent observer, you're likely to pick up many insights.

Once you've gotten pretty far into a package, consider **hiring a pro** to look over your files and give you tips on ways to do things faster and more elegantly. When you bring in an expert who will casually suggest a solution to a problem that had you stumped, you'll realize you never would have thought of it. And you'll pat yourself on the back for saving hours of wasted effort on future jobs. Next time you set out to learn a package, you may even consider hiring a pro to give you the big picture before you try to master the details yourself.

A couple of months after you've become comfortable using a program, go back and look over the manual. You'll be surprised at the subtle techniques and shortcuts you missed the first time through.

Pressure and anxiety are the enemies of in-depth and satisfying learning. The only time you should ever agree to start a job using software that's still shrink-wrapped is when the client understands the situation and doesn't care how long you take to do it or what it will cost.

Which software to learn first

It's like learning scales on the piano before you can play the tunes: Start with the basics of the operating system and network software. For instance, learn how to install and remove fonts, a confusing and often highly technical issue to get out of the way at the start. Maggie has gotten desperate calls from clients who knew enough to get their work done—until a job came in requiring the installation of new fonts.

If you already know your way around a word processor, try out its DTP features. That will give you an easy introduction to such concepts as type specifications, leading, columns, and sidebars. You could buy one of those books about desktop publishing using WordPerfect or Microsoft Word.

Next, head straight for your core page layout application. If you're taking a course where you have a choice, pick one of the leading brands, and get started. After you've mastered that, you'll have a better perspective from which to make decisions about what other DTP software to learn.

As soon as you're done with the canned tutorials, try a small project. Whenever you're trying to master a new package, it's always a good idea to experiment on yourself. Avoid the stress you'd get from the combination of coping with the unfamiliar along with outside deadline pressures. What could be better than a one-page flyer for your own DTP services? Or a user's manual for the office you're setting up? Play around; try several looks. You'll exercise the software and improve your design skills.

> To use a computer efficiently, a person has to learn a program and stay with it. A good idea these days is not to attempt to learn too many programs. There are so many out there that people are barraged with new ones and new things to do from all sides. It dilutes your ability to concentrate on one area and to learn to think well. My advice to a beginner at this stage might be to settle on one program and learn that one really well; then go to another program, and so forth.   —*David Doty*

Leave yourself time to experiment with your tools. It's the only way you'll learn them fully. While you can learn most software packages in a week or two, you'll find it takes many months of using the software frequently to become an in-depth expert. In particular, the only way to learn the graphics tools is by using them on actual projects. Whether as a labor of love, a self-promotion piece, or a project for a low-budget client willing to be your guinea pig, you owe it to yourself and your clients to take that kind of learning time.

> I began my desktop publishing career as a volunteer. In 1984, I began using a Kaypro CP/M computer to generate coded text that I sent on disk to a typesetter for the New York Peace Calendar, a new monthly tabloid listing events of interest to peace, environmental, and social activists in New York City. With the arrival of ReadySetGo!, the first usable micro-computer page layout software, in January 1986 I switched to DTP—trimming several days off a production schedule and permitting up-to-deadline changes.

> From 1986 to 1990, I used the publication as my DTP laboratory, experimenting with alternative graphic designs and trying out (and at times beta-testing) new tools as they appeared: downloadable fonts, advanced word processing, illustration, special effects, and page layout software. At each stage, before offering a technique or feature to my regular clients, I fully tested it on a job over which I had control. When I said I could produce a tabloid newspaper, or run text around a complex path, or use type as a transparent mask for a scanned image behind it, I wasn't talking about a theoretical capability: I had a sample I could show, and I knew how long it would take.   —*Felix*

Staying on top takes time

What we're about to tell you might discourage you from pursuing a DTP career. Managing a business takes enormous amounts of time. Here's an idea of how much time to allocate for each unbillable but essential task.

On the computer side: 14 hours a week

- **Information:** Reading the magazines, attending one or two user group meetings, and keeping track of the latest products shortcuts and pitfalls. At least five hours, some of which you'll do at night.
- **Software upgrades and new hardware:** Contacting vendors, ordering, installing and setting up. One hour.
- **Disk housekeeping:** Organizing files, archiving completed jobs (storing compressed versions of final files, deleting outdated intermediate files, and documenting it all so you can remember what you did next time you want to revise the files). Three hours.
- **Client housekeeping:** Updating, compiling and filing notes, time sheets, and hard-copy proofs of jobs completed and in progress. Two hours.
- **Learning new software and getting up to speed on major upgrades:** This will take many hours several times during the year—but figure 15-30 hours for two or three software packages a year. One hour.
- **Unbillable work on client jobs:** Reconstructing a file that a client expects you to have, but you forgot to put in your archive. Undoing suggestions you made that the client didn't like and shouldn't have to pay for. Trying out some technique you suspect might be faster but that will take you some time to learn. Updating a file so it works with the latest version of your page layout software. Together, these could amount to two hours.

On the business side: 11 hours a week

These numbers will vary depending on your background, meticulousness, and whether you have an MBA.

- **Client contact, bids, and unbillable meetings:** No matter how easy it is for you to get clients, up to five hours.
- **Tracking:** Recording and analyzing your work process, profit margins, client profiles. One hour.
- **Billing:** The sooner after you finish a job you do it, the less time it will take you. But even if you do it as you go along, with some job-tracking software or custom database, it still takes time to update your data and produce the final invoices. One hour minimum.
- **Professional consultations:** Accounting, tax preparation, legal and other consultations. One hour.
- **Vendor contacts:** Some of this, like talking with printers and delivery services, or sending faxes, can be billed directly to clients; keeping office

supplies in stock cannot. And little of your time managing subcontractors can be billed. Two hours.

- **Interviewing**: Checking out prospective typists, temporary (or permanent, if and when you get to that stage) employees, collaborators on large projects, subcontractors for overflow work, a backup person to keep your clients happy when you're sick or on vacation, specialists in graphics or business applications to help you on single projects, and perhaps someone to train you in an application or write custom macros or a business management template for you. At least one hour.

Whew! This all adds up to 25 hours a week. Even if we've been overly conservative, it won't be easy to get it much under 20 hours a week. Most of these are tasks that you'll have a great deal of difficulty delegating or hiring an assistant to handle. These numbers set a serious limitation on the number of hours you can bill clients for.

How do many DTPers still make a good living? Some narrow their focus or are so efficient they can get away with 10-15 unbillable hours per week. Some live within these constraints, but charge high rates for their billable hours.

How much money can you make in DTP?

You *can* make a good living as a DTPer, but let's get one thing straight: On your own, you can't get rich. However you bill your client, as a DTPer you're essentially selling your time—in chunks of minutes, hours, days, or weeks. No matter how many hours you work, you'll probably be able to bill clients for only 20-30 hours/week. That puts an upper limit on your net income. That ceiling may be considerably higher than you are now making—but it won't get you into six figures.

You should be able to *gross* $50,000–$100,000 per year. Your challenge is to keep your billable hours up, your rates high, and your expenses down, so you end up with respectable take-home pay. To learn more about these numbers see **10. Pricing and Bidding.** For other strategies see **11. Expanding Revenues.**

Here's a preview:

- Keep your office at home, reducing your business expenses and improving your tax picture.
- Increase your billable hours—though if you push too far, you could end up hating your work life.

- Increase your productivity; become more skilled. One of the easiest ways to do this is to upgrade your tools, so you deliver more to the client in each billed hour.
- Freelance at corporate DTP centers or at other DTPers' offices, thereby gaining many of the same savings as a home office.
- Market some special skills to increase your effective hourly rates. For instance, if you can sell yourself as a hot-shot editor, a newsletter startup consultant, or as a graphic designer, you may be able to bill many projects by the job. Therefore, some of your intensive, creative hours will bring you many times your normal hourly rate.
- Start a DTP business with other employees, hiring other DTPers to do the work. If this is your ambition, be prepared for the enormous pressures to abandon hands-on work. If you most enjoy design or production work, be cautious about turning into a salesperson, manager, and number-cruncher, with all the attendant worries. Maggie has succeeded by concentrating on consulting, sales, and management. Felix has been content to remain on his own, augmenting his solo practice with a loose confederacy of other self-sufficient, capable, and reliable DTPers—each with a fully-equipped electronic cottage.

If you're a traditional graphic designer or typesetter making the switch to DTP, you'll improve your profit margins by reducing your needs to purchase and pick up or pay for delivery of outside services like typesetting or photostats. You'll find an extended treatment of cost and time savings as well as creative benefits for people in graphics trades in *Making Your Computer a Design and Business Partner.* (See **Appendix 2: Books on the business of graphics and DTP.**)

You don't have to be a perfect 10

Start with a good appreciation of your strengths and weaknesses, take care not to oversell yourself, get help with your deficiencies—and look for a partner who is strong in those areas where you fall short.

2. STARTING YOUR BUSINESS

Take yourself and your business seriously

At user group meetings, we often meet people who dislike their jobs, and are trying to switch to a DTP business. Yet all too frequently, they're doing it on the cheap—and giving themselves a hard time. They don't want to risk too much until they're sure they can succeed in DTP. Often they hobble along with an underpowered computer, and spend anxious hours watching the clock tick off the dollars at a laser printing output service.

They're spread too thin. They try to learn too much (sometimes with "borrowed" software and no documentation). They worry about how to bid on work and about how much they can take on. And they're scared of losing money on their first jobs. Like kids going out on the ice for the first time with a rusty pair of hand-me-down skates, they're not giving themselves a fair chance.

If you're just exploring options, it makes sense not to take out a second mortgage on your house to finance a career you're not sure you'll like. But as soon as you know you want to give DTP your best shot, make sure you're prepared to make a serious effort. The right mindset can maximize your chances for success and satisfaction.

> I waited too long to buy a color workstation because I was afraid of spending all that money. But the minute I bit the bullet, I added an entire dimension to my business that I hadn't anticipated. It's all about taking a risk—but making sure it's the right risk.
> —*Steven Gorney, computer illustrator and trainer, NYC*

Fortunately, DTP is a business with relatively low startup costs. Many traditional small businesses (especially retail ones) require signing a lease for office space, and assembling up to $100,000 in startup capital. Then the owners expect to lose money for a while. In contrast, you can launch your DTP business from your home, with under $10,000 for tools plus about $15,000 to live on for a few months while you get started. You should see a positive cash flow pretty quickly. And if it doesn't work out, you can sell your equipment, recouping some of your initial investment.

What kind of business plan do you need?

If you're borrowing money, you'll need a business plan. If you're applying to a bank or another commercial source, you may need the traditional kind—described in any number of books in the business section of your library or bookstore. (See **Appendix 2** for specific titles.)

If you're financing the startup yourself or through family or close friends, you still owe it to your backers to go through the questions and analysis involved in preparing a business plan—but you may skip preparing the polished formal proposal.

Define your starting points
- Who constitutes the business (a one-person operation or a partnership; production and support staff);
- The services you intend to provide;
- Your market or markets;
- The location of your business and your markets;
- Technical advisors, legal, and accounting resources.

Estimate your potential and your risks
- The total size of target markets and related markets;
- The nature of your competition;
- How you will differentiate your services from competitors;
- Major hurdles to overcome;
- Strategies for expansion, if any;
- Timetables and milestones to determine success or failure.

Project your dollars and cents
- Initial and future capital needs;
- Growth objectives;
- Income and expenses.

As you develop your business plan, it's a good idea to get some objective opinions of your strategies and expectations. Don't restrict yourself to people in

DTP. Practically anyone with business experience will be helpful. Check around for programs sponsored by local government or nonprofit organizations that hook up retired executives or other mentors with people just starting up. (See **Appendix 2. Small business resources.**) Of course, you're best off if you can run your ideas and preliminary cash flow projections by an accountant, financial planner, or someone with experience in business startups.

Don't put your business plan into cold storage

It's a good idea to revisit your plan at least twice a year, to take stock of your progress, pat yourself on the back for your initiative and prescience, and plan your next moves.

This periodic self-audit and mental tune-up is crucial. In this fast-changing field, to ensure your long-term success, you need to find a way to differentiate yourself from other DTPers. You may start out doing generic DTP work. But unless you have very loyal customers or the lowest overhead around, you'll have to work toward finding some unique niche.

Naming your company

As your desktop publishing business comes to life, it shares some features with any newborn: It gets a name, takes up some space, and needs lots of attention.

Yes, you need a company name. No one will take you seriously if your invoice and business card don't establish your business identity. In an earlier incarnation as a promotional writer, Felix began using Kramer Communications before he was a DTPer and never changed it. Maggie's Acanthus Associates takes its unusual name from a plant whose leaf is used to decorate a Corinthian column, which conjures up images of growth and stability.

A nondescript name won't hurt you, but it won't reinforce the image you've already transmitted in person or in verbal or written form. A memorable name will help you answer the phone with enthusiasm. A name with a flair will jump out of the pack at potential customers, making it easier for people who hear about you to remember you.

Some names are so good they become major assets. Companies have been bought out by people who simply wanted to take over an inspired name. You can be clever, but try not to be silly. Not everyone will share your sense of humor. Whatever you choose, try it out on people who don't know you or your business idea.

Pick a name that rolls off your tongue—and can't be misunderstood—when you answer the phone. We know one firm that answers its phone with partners' names that sound just as if the receptionist were saying, "Hold for a minute."

Aim for a memorable name—one that communicates energy and effectiveness. All else being equal, use a name starting early in the alphabet, so you'll come up at the top of directories and resource lists. Stay away from initials. Until you can afford an ad budget like AT&T, initials mean nothing to anyone else. As you brainstorm, consider possible interpretations of the name as a logo. If you're a designer, you might start with an image or logo, then choose a name.

In most states, you can simply start using a business name. You don't have to incorporate, though a lawyer will recommend you conduct a search at City Hall or the appropriate government office. If, as is most likely, you're in a sole proprietorship (an individually-owned business with no separate legal corporate identity), to open a checking account in the company name, you'll need to file a "doing business as" (DBA) form with the proper government agency. If you come up with a unique name, you can protect it by registering it, and trademarking your logo. If you incorporate, you are automatically reserving its use at least in your state.

Before you decide on your name, check the telephone book and directory assistance to make sure no one else has the same name or something too similar. If you choose to incorporate (see **13. Incorporating and Accounting**) you'll do a search of this sort as part of the legal process. You're not allowed to use a name similar to an incorporated name or one registered as a DBA. Even if you're legally entitled to use a name, you won't want to complicate your life or confuse callers.

Your home or business office

We know DTPers who literally clear off the breakfast plates and use their kitchen tables as desktops every day. Indeed, a friend of Felix teased him about being a stovetop publisher when he started out. Some DTPers carve out corners of their living rooms or bedrooms. But if you take yourself seriously—and you can afford it—give yourself a room of your own and a door you can close.

How much space do you need?

Consider your work flow. Ideally you'll want everything at your fingertips. Put the computer on a desktop. We favor fancy workstation furniture with room for swiveling monitors, easy access to the backs of equipment for trouble-shooting and cabling, and an adjustable height surface for keyboards. That, plus a good adjustable chair, will save your back and your wrists. If possible, get another desk or table, perpendicular to your computer station, for spreading out papers, pasteups, meeting with clients, and paying bills. Add two large file cabinets, some bookshelves, your work chair, and two fixed or folding chairs for guests. You may need other furniture, such as a base for a laser printer, phone, answering machine, and perhaps for your scanner, fax, and photocopier. If you have less than 100 square feet, you're likely to feel cramped. Consider your choices of lighting, chairs, and table heights from an ergonomic (human engineering) perspective. (See **6. Remember to protect your health.**)

Make sure the space is adequately wired with at least two separate electrical circuits, and capability for at least two telephone lines. You'll need an electrician if you need extra power lines.

Take some time to plan your layout. The basic possibilities boil down to these four: a single long strip, an L shape, a galley with two back-to-back strips, or a U. We think the U makes the most sense if you have the space. You can put your computer on the table in front of you. Depending on whether you're left- or right-handed, on one side are your phone, business and office paraphernalia; on the other is a paste-up table or its equivalent, where you keep your projects and manuscripts. For more ideas on office layout see **Appendix 2. Books on small business and working at home.**

Keep all your cables and the backs of your equipment easily accessible. You don't under any circumstances want to make your setup so inconvenient that you're reluctant to pull a suspected component or wire when trouble first appears. Label both ends of each cable with white plastic tape.

Can you be respectable without a business address?

These days, people don't get as excited as they used to about deciding whether or not to work at home. With all the new technology, there's not much you can't do from home. So many people are doing it that it's no longer such a big deal. Link Resources, a New York-based research firm, says that in 1990, 35 million Americans were part- or full-time home-based workers.

Why do so many people work at home? To avoid a commute, to make part-time work easier, to spend time with loved ones, to eat healthier lunches and get regular exercise, to keep expenses down, and because they like their homes. It's also easier to work at odd hours at home—for better and for worse. The importance of these and other reasons will vary for each person. Always keep in mind what's important to you: why you're starting your own business and how you envision your worklife.

For the pros and cons of working at home, the Roper Organization, in a 1989 survey commissioned by the *Wall Street Journal*, asked 2,000 adults: 27% said the advantages outweighed the drawbacks, 49% said the drawbacks outweighed the benefits. Though the survey compared working at home with work in a conventional office, the findings shed light both on the pluses and minuses of working for yourself or for a boss, and of working in your own one-person office or in a room at your home.

Among the benefits are more control over one's work schedule (53%); wearing more comfortable clothes (36%); avoiding a commute (35%); not having a boss close by (28%); being able to care for children (20%); no interruptions from co-workers (20%); job seems less like work (20%); not minding overtime as much (15%).

Among the drawbacks are not having the necessary supplies or equipment (51%); too many family interruptions (38%); mixing work with family life too much (35%); being distracted by household chores (32%); lack of interaction with co-workers (27%); lack of regular routine (23%); having trouble quitting after a full day (16%); feeling work is less important if done at home (14%).

Before you make your final plans, make sure no municipal ordinances, lease clauses, neighborhood homeowners' rules (or, in rare cases, restrictive covenants on your deed) prohibit you from establishing your business. If they do, see about getting a variance or dispensation by arguing that your business will not inconvenience, offend, or endanger anyone.

Make sure you'll get support from your co-habitants for your efforts to be productive. Expect to have to discipline your friends: If chums assume they can call you anytime they feel like chatting, make clear that you're on deadline, and ask them to call you at lunchtime or at night—on your personal line. On the other hand, don't turn your home office into a prison: Try to get outside at least once a day. When Felix worked at home, he turned the pilgrimage to his nearby post office box into a morning expedition.

Do try to get your clients to understand that you keep regular business hours, and would rather hear from them then. (The worst part is when your clients call you at 10:30 a.m. and innocently ask, "Did I wake you?" Or maybe the worst part is when they call at 10:30 p.m. with the same question.)

> It doesn't matter when I start a job; when I finish it, I can hear the garbage trucks outside making their morning rounds.   —*Rick Barry*

If you're at all tempted to work at home—if you have the space, and if you think you'll get enough cooperation from your co-habitants—try it. It's certainly easier to start there. The worst that will happen is you'll end up hating it, or liking it but find you're unable to get enough work done, and then move your office out.

If you have a good reason for staying there, don't be strong-armed into leaving home. Some people won't think you're serious or successful until you have an office, but you don't need to worry about them. Whatever your decision, if you aren't happy with the way it works out, don't hesitate to reconsider and re-establish the business style, location, and rhythm you preferred from the start.

Location, location, location

Any good real estate broker will tell you those are the three most important words for business. As a new DTPer, you probably have a narrow range of options—you can't exactly commission an architect to build your company headquarters. If you plan to be home-based, you've already made your decision. But if you will be deciding among several shared spaces, or intend to rent an office, we suggest you go for amenities over prestige.

First, make your life easier. You're the boss, so keep your commute short. Make sure you have 24-hour, seven-days-a-week access to your office. That means a neighborhood where you feel safe day and night. It also means a spot where you and your equipment are not visible and tempting to the criminally inclined passerby. Wherever you locate, make sure your office is insurable.

Then there's the convenience of your business operations. If you expect to use a service bureau or printer frequently, try for a space in their neighborhood. (If you're just down the block, you might get referrals from these vendors.) And, in these days of messengers and overnight delivery services, you'll be crippled without an easy way to get dropoffs and leave pickups day and night. If you can't find a person to fill this role, you could attach a lock box to the outside wall or door of your business. You've seen these at banks: Your customers get keys, and can pick up or leave off work when you're not there.

Of course, there's your customers' convenience. Unless you're depending on a brisk walk-in trade, you don't need a storefront, or even a second-floor window on Main Street. But it helps to be in an elevator building, not a walkup, accessible to mass transit and parking, and near a familiar landmark so you don't have to give complex directions. If you're on the low floor of an office building, put a sign in your window, unless you worry about attracting burglars. If you're at home, post an attractive shingle with your company name (zoning regulations permitting), with your street number plainly visible to help customers find you.

These factors are more important than your name in lights on a power block. If you hope to reassure your first clients with a fancy address, think hard about how much it will cost you each month, then consider what you could buy instead: tools, learning time, or consultant time. These will contribute far more to the skills and capabilities you'll need most to succeed in business.

Control your business image

Once you have a good name, address, and phone number, pay some attention to style as well as substance. Make sure you have professional-looking letterhead, with envelopes and business cards to match. Use your logo, if you have one—but don't give in to the temptation to show off all your skills with an overstated letterhead. Do spend the time and money necessary so your stationery embodies the care, competence, and reassurance that you will provide.

Be sure to be accessible to your clients by phone at all times. An answering machine is better than an answering service, especially with the kinds of messages people are likely to leave you: "Make the fourth word in the second 'graph on the third proof upper case." You need a machine that can accurately record long messages and allows you to call in to retrieve them. Make sure you have a straightforward, no-nonsense recorded message. Your home machine is the place to play around with Humphrey Bogart imitations.

Try to feel and sound happy when you answer the phone. If you're comfortable enough to crack a joke, you're communicating confidence and pleasure to your potential clients.

Separating your home and business phone lines will improve your personal life. It will also give you a record of all your business phone expenses. You'll need at least two phone lines, so your clients can always reach you. If you're working out of your home, and you stick with personal phone service, which tends to be cheaper for installation and per call than business service, you'll have trouble being listed as a business in the phone company's directory.

Think about getting two business lines, a second one to pick up calls that jump from the busy first one (the phone company calls it a hunt line). What about call waiting? Modems and faxes don't mix well with call-waiting, and you don't get the conference calling capability that two lines offer. If you're getting a fax, and don't feel you can afford a third phone line, you can use what's called a **smart switch**. It sells for about $100, and is built into some fax machines, so voice calls can still jump to your second line, and fax calls can be dialed intentionally to that line. Its often unmentioned drawback is the switch must be wired in front of any extension phones on the second line.

Plan to succeed

At the start, be prepared to deal with skeptical friends and relatives. If you're not getting support from people you care about, or people who depend on you, that's all the more reason for planning your launch carefully and realistically. That will do you much more good than some variant on the power of positive thinking.

Later on, if you succeed, you'll be saddled with envious and unrealistic people who will presume you got a few lucky breaks and are sure that your life as an entrepreneur is now carefree.

3. FINDING CUSTOMERS

You can do everything right in starting your venture—find a great location, create sophisticated management systems, learn your tools backward and forward—yet be short of customers. A few lucky DTPers, after their first few jobs, sail along on word-of-mouth referrals and random encounters. But even the most successful ones sometimes have to drum up business.

Everything starts with a sale. If you don't have a sale, you don't have a business. The prospect of selling your DTP services may frighten you, particularly if you're more comfortable at a drafting table or in front of a computer than calling people you've never met. Yet unless you have guaranteed sources of work, or a partner who is a sales whiz, you'll need to get almost as good at selling as you are at DTP. To do this, you first need to know who your potential customers are, and what they're looking for.

Marketing fundamentals

Marketing and sales are the bugaboos of small businesspeople who have to do a little bit of everything. Along with securing financing, hiring, managing, and pricing, they are crucial skills. For those of you who never had the nerve to ask, here's the difference between the two. Marketing includes where you go to find clients and how you reach them through advertising, public relations, and direct-mail promotion. Sales is direct, person-to-person contacts with the goal of signing up individual buyers of your services.

Though we'll touch on some of the important points, we list some of the best reading materials in **Appendix 2. Books on marketing and selling.** The principles are similar for almost any small service business.

Whether you're selling fast food or DTP, your marketing needs to address the four P's: product, planning, promotion, and pricing.

Product

Know *exactly* what you're selling—which services and skills. Are you strictly a page layout production type? Or do you offer one or more unusual or valuable specialties? Next develop your 50 words about the business, encapsulating what you're about and why someone should be interested in you. You'll say these words over and over as you meet people at parties, or present yourself to prospective clients on the phone, or talk with friends.

For example,

> Kramer Communications has been doing one-stop desktop publishing since 1985. We work with you from start to finish—writing, editing, designing, producing camera-ready copy, and handling printing. We can also help you buy equipment and train you to run your own in-house system.
>
> Acanthus is a production and consulting company using DTP to support corporate clients. We set up and maintain corporate centers. Once up and running, we provide ongoing systems support, which can take the form of DTP support or information management support, including database systems for managing work.

The crispness with which you state your business will come across to potential clients as confidence and expertise.

Planning

Figure out how you'll market yourself, how much time you'll spend on it, and how you'll track your results. You may discover that sales calls work better for some markets, letters for others, or that nothing except personal referrals works for you in still other markets. The more aware you are of trends, the better you're able to target your efforts to productive markets. Of course, it will take some time to accumulate enough information to say confidently that you're looking at trends, not random results. Always find out where callers and new clients heard about you, so you can determine what marketing strategies work best.

Develop a system for prospecting for clients, with things to do during slow periods, and tasks to do every day. Use a combination of file folders or trays plus a tickler file. You may organize names into categories like: call in future; send literature; call on DATE; call again if I don't hear by DATE; give up. Maggie uses Acius Fourth Dimension to track her efforts. Chang Laboratories C•A•T is the leading client tracking package for the Macintosh; Contact Software Act and Richmond Technologies Maximizer are packages for the PC.

Promotion

You'll do **informal promotion** all the time—your 50-word spiel will start that process. Visibility is the other part. Any time you have the opportunity to speak, give a seminar, or write an article that will reach an audience you'd like to work for, jump for the chance. We've both had the experience of being contacted by prospective customers who tell us "Joe sent me"—and we've never heard of Joe. Chances are Joe ran into us at some event, or in print, and passed our name on to someone else. Though you often can't trace back a referral, visibility can never hurt. Most of the inquiries Felix and Maggie get—and a *substantial chunk* of new business—come from referrals and networking.

Formal promotion takes the form of brochures and flyers describing your business and showing off your DTP skill. Start with mailings to your all-important house list: your database of all your present and past customers, as well as all the potential customers you've ever met or talked to on the phone, plus your valued vendors. Use direct mail to update your house list on your activities, remind them you exist, and return to you information about address changes. For more on the database, see **12. Make a smart invoice**.

If you're expecting to **advertise**, start with the lowest cost forms. Take advantage of local bulletin boards in stores and public buildings. Try your local community weekly or PennySaver. Often the ad rates are very low, and some of these throwaways are well read.

Don't overlook your computer user groups as promotion targets. A high proportion of members use computers for business—and read their user group newsletters from cover to cover. As a member, you're often entitled to a free ad. How good a source of business are computer users? A recent survey of the members of the NY Macintosh Users' Group found that 58% used DTP software, and 51% used graphics software (764 people, 40% of the membership, responded). *Macworld*'s December 1990 survey found 80% of respondents doing some kind of DTP, but fewer than 25% even close to full-time DTP (more than 50 hours a month). The numbers for PC users would be lower. While you might assume many computer users are people who do their own DTP rather than paying professionals, they're also all potential customers for big or tough projects. And when they come to you, the ones with rudimentary DTP experience will know what you're talking about.

> There's an old saw about advertising: A high frequency of reader impressions makes advertising pay. My free classified ad in my user group publication, which I've run for more than four years, regularly results in inquiries. Some turn into business—each ad keeps my name in front of all the other readers of the magazine, many of whom refer work to me.
>
> —*Felix*

Check to see if your Yellow Pages has a DTP section. Make sure you find out the closing deadline for copy before you make big plans that rely heavily on exposure through the Yellow Pages. Remember that you'll need a business telephone number, and you'll be charged monthly. If you're in a small town or city, it may be worth your while to pay for Yellow Pages advertising. But in a large city, most of the responses you're likely to get will come from shoppers who don't know what they want, and will be insulted if you don't offer a bargain price for sight-unseen jobs.

Then there's **cold promotion** to people you've never met. Think about who might use your services, what you offer, and make a list of prospects. Get their names, addresses, and numbers from directories, ads, or the phone book. Put all these names into your houselist database, coded by source. (Keep in mind that over the years, this list will become one of your business's most valuable assets.) Then start contacting them.

You can also rent lists. Look in the Mailing Lists category in your business yellow pages or the AT&T 800 Toll-Free Directory, or look at the publication *Direct Mail Lists* in the Standard Rates and Data Services (SRDS) series in your library's reference department. If you're looking for lots of names—for instance, every toy store with more than five employees in the Southwest—you may find Lotus Development MarketPlace cheaper. It contains seven million businesses by category and location, supplied on CD-ROM disks. For $695 you can unlock 5,000 companies, addresses, contact names and phone numbers selected by Standard Industry Code classification, zip code, size, and other categories you choose. So far, it's available only for the Macintosh.

If you're sending out a cold letter, explain the solutions you offer and the benefits of working with you—quality, quick turnaround, and lower cost. Be sure to include a postal reply card. (So you don't waste stamps on the return card, you'll need to get a business reply permit from the U.S. Postal Service.)

If you hate collating, folding, and stuffing, this is an ideal time to hire a neighborhood kid. Make sure you demonstrate how to fold so the letter opens right side up and print side in. If you produce large mailings out of your laser printer, consider buying an Execufold, which turns one to three 8 ½-by-11-inch letters into a #10 envelope in one and a half seconds. It's available from MicroBusiness Solutions Analysis for under $300, (415) 581-9204.

You may want to offer something to those you contact—most likely a free consultation. If you're writing to people you think may not themselves need your services, but could be in a position to refer work, you could help them do a favor for customers they refer to you by offering a 10% discount for mentioning where they got your name. That way, you'll know where the client came from.

If you're cold calling, to unearth good prospects, use questions like, "May I speak to the person who makes decisions about your typesetting needs?" Anticipate possible concerns others may have about using an unfamiliar vendor. To: "You sound all right, but how do I know your work is good?" you can answer, "I'd like a chance to show you my work; can we set up a meeting? How's next Tuesday at 10?" It also helps if you can reassuringly say, "I've worked for many people in your industry," or "I've done some projects that sound very much like what you need." For many new business owners, cold calls prompt knots in the stomach. Try not to sound stiff or defensive. Remember, you're offering a quality service.

Pricing

We give guidelines in **10. Pricing and Bidding**. But for marketing, you need to know something about your competition. How much does conventional typography cost? The usual estimates are up to $50-100 per page for type-setting and layout; $1,000 to $2,000 for an eight-to-16 page corporate newsletter. But these numbers vary widely geographically, by customer, and by kind of typesetting business. To improve your marketing expertise and confidence, research your market carefully. Ask people you know what they're spending for conventional typesetting, and how long it takes. Once you're comfortable with your own clients, ask them what they used to pay. Or shop around yourself among the competition (people do that all the time); then you'll have something to which you can compare your pricing.

Finding your first customers

You're in the communications business. Broadly defined, it's one of the largest sectors of human enterprise. Most of the people you meet have some information that they routinely communicate to others—or would like to. You can help them. Practically everyone has a need to communicate on paper and is a potential source of clients.

You can integrate finding clients into almost all your activities: Every time you walk down the street, enter a business establishment, or attend a public event, you're seeing potential customers. Carry your business card, brochure, or latest flyer with you wherever you go. Hand them out at the slightest opportunity. If this seems a little narcissistic, be reassured that you'll be able to be more subtle once you're established. For now, you're at your most enthusiastic and aggressive.

To find clients, build on what you know. Look at the work world you're now moving out of. List the typeset materials you encounter and use all your contacts to track down who is responsible for buying type. Approach them with an offer they can't refuse. If they give you the job, they'll benefit by working with someone who knows what they're about. And unless they're already using DTP, you can safely promise to match or beat their current quality, costs, or production timetables. If they take you up on the offer, you won't be risking much, because you probably can find a way to improve on their current vendor's services. Of course, at this point, you're entitled to see their old invoices.

Start accumulating a list of possible clients. Ask everyone you know for names of contacts. If you're not already involved, see if there's a business networking group in your area; see if the local Chamber of Commerce sponsors any programs; go to local trade shows for industries that interest you. When you find the type of client you're interested in working with, according to your unique criteria, do some library research and look at trade publications.

Other sources of new clients include new businesses (get acquainted with real estate brokers), retail stores, restaurants, caterers, theaters, and auditoriums. Make friends with printers, stationers, and copy shop proprietors to get referrals.

Don't forget to look at all those hand-lettered, typed, and word processed pages, announcements, signs, flyers, reports, and manuals you'll find in every office, factory, and school. Here you're not competing with conventional typesetting— you're trying to show a potential client it's worth their while to upgrade their materials. Slip some samples into sturdy frames and walk them around.

Another way to find clients is to become an arms-length partner or share space with someone in a related business: a printer, direct-mail house, word processing business, public relations or advertising agency, or even a copy shop. You'll be able to refer clients to each other. You can offer to send an advertisement for the associated company with your mailings. And you can arrange subcontracts so one of you becomes a one-stop service center.

For your first jobs, stick to the familiar. Take on projects you know you can handle. If a large, complex, and expensive job comes your way, be humble. Get expert help immediately in figuring out how to bid, schedule, and complete the work. If you can get some free advice, fine—otherwise, build into your bid the time to pay another DTPer for professional consulting.

Finding a market niche

Once you're beyond your work universe, there's the rest of the world. Start with your neighborhood. Half the stores you patronize could probably use a price sheet, counter advertisement, or a window sign. Many people are too intimidated to even consider walking into a typesetter's shop and facing the entire world of typography and design. You can make it easy for them, though try not to get in over your head on specialized jobs.

> Warning: The typography involved in supermarket flyers can be quite complicated, demanding, and not worth the effort. Many aspects of typography and design are difficult for people who are learning it themselves.   —*Ann Raszmann Brown*

Every second you're traveling or reading a newspaper or magazine, scan your environment for ways and places to market yourself. Soon you'll find one that appeals to you, or that seems in need of your services. Start on a small project to get your foot in the door. Produce one restaurant menu, video store ad, or community meeting announcement and you're on your way. You can take that sample to another business or community group and offer to help them, too.

Some DTPers carve out one or two comfortable niches and never leave them. This can be the key to your financial success. If you can latch on to producing product descriptions for the hardware industry, in-house newsletters, college catalogs, or real estate listings, and you enjoy it, you need look no further—until you start worrying about how long you'll be able to mine this vein.

Selling fundamentals

The more DTP work you do, and the more enthusiastic you become about it, the easier selling your services should become. Ever since Dale Carnegie, selling has been a subject for pep talks and inspirational writing. All the books say the same thing, but some say it better, or give you more details. (See **Appendix 2. Books on marketing and selling.**) We'll just give you a few basic pointers. We owe thanks for some of these tips to Jeff Baker, a NYC consultant and trainer in sales techniques, whose workshops have helped many computer consultants get over their hesitations about selling.

As a precondition for selling, you need to feel good about yourself and your services and willing to connect visually and verbally with your potential customer. Wait until you have your buyer's full attention; then communicate your enthusiasm and confidence.

Every relationship you have with a potential client is part of a *sales cycle:*

Initial contact: If you establish a positive tone, in person, on the phone, or by letter, the good impression you start with will set the stage for an easy sale.

If you're calling, make sure it's at a good time. Felix notes that Maggie has charmed him and everyone else for years by automatically starting every conversation with "Is this a good time to talk?" If it's not, once you've gotten the potential client's attention, arrange to talk at a better time.

Establish credibility: You need to make yourself real in your customer's eyes, by mentioning names the client knows, showing an account list or testimonial letters, or describing your experience filling needs similar to the client's.

Clients are looking for experts. Don't act overwhelmed, even if you feel uneasy. At your first meeting, assume you can handle the job and communicate that assurance. If you decide later it's over your head, you can get help, or refer the job. But be open in communicating any potential problems you may see in the project. As in any sale, the buyer wants to know you are reliable, honest, sincere, knowledgeable, and will be a pleasure to work with.

Create interest: Find out what's important to your potential customers and show them how you can give them what they want. Emphasize the benefits for them, not the mechanics for you, of your DTP services. Many clients won't care about how you do the work. Keep your eye out for peoples' hot buttons, whatever they may be.

Before you meet a client face-to-face, ask questions over the phone to increase your understanding of the client and the job. Prepare for your meeting by researching any facet of a project you may feel unsure about: a technical problem, finding the right designer, or getting a handle on printing costs.

In the meeting, focus on the customer's need by *listening*. Try to understand the situation from the customer's point of view. Then ask plenty of questions—and take copious notes. Before leaving, review your notes with the client to make sure you are in synch. Then ask, "Is there anything else I should know about?"

Qualify and gather information: You can waste lots of time becoming chummy with potential clients—but when it's time to nail down the business, your new pals may not have the authority to contract with you or to authorize payment. In an institution, save valuable hours by finding the decision-makers, the ones with the money and the authority to spend it. When you find them, talk to them to see if they are open to what you're offering. Meet with and sell to the highest level person involved—the one with the checkbook.

Transfer ownership: Define the features and benefits of what you're offering. Establish and obtain your new client's agreement that your services are what they need.

Close: At any time in the cycle, you can ask, "When do we start?" or "Shall we begin on Tuesday or Friday?" or, after dispensing with a problem, "So, can we go ahead?" Whenever you ask this kind of question, give the client as much time as needed to answer. Don't jump in to fill the silence—wait. What you hear will always be helpful information.

You can ask for the job any time. It can be a tool to identify any remaining obstacles. Sometimes they say yes, and you won't need to hang around, going through every step.

Resistance: You'll sometimes encounter resistance—everyone feels that making certain decisions is risky. Before meeting with a prospective client, imagine possible objections. In your presentation, address the ones you can anticipate, and expect to handle others as they come up. Each time a potential customer voices an objection and you meet it, you're moving toward the close. You can empathize with an *objection;* probe for hidden problems; isolate a problem and set conditions for meeting it.

You may also encounter *conditions*. A potential customer saying "I'm not interested," "I want to think about it," or "Your price is too high," often needs more information from you. If you persist, you can often meet their conditions on the spot.

For big projects you've been discussing with a prospective client for some time, you can say, "Look, it seems we both want to do this work, but it's taking a long time for a decision. Why don't we draw up a list of outstanding issues? If we can resolve them satisfactorily, then let's begin."

Relationship selling: You're working to make your clients more successful in their jobs by helping them save time, money, and communicating their organization's message and image most effectively. The partnership you form with your client is paramount. Your goal is to act in your clients' interests—as if you were their special ally and secret weapon.

If your clients don't have that sense, your DTP services will become just another commodity. They'll inevitably look for someone else to give them what they need, or, failing that, at least save them money. If you treat your clients loyally, and never lose touch with them for long, they'll see you as terrific and irreplaceable—not just another vendor. (See **9. Treating Your Clients Right.**)

Once you've established your relationship with a client with any one project, the door is open for you to meet more of their publishing needs. Maggie has found it's five times more expensive to develop a new client than to maintain an existing account. Take the time to develop good relationships and treat every client as well as your first client. Maintain them as the basis for your business and as the source of confidence for you to tap into new opportunities.

> Offer various skills to a client. Even if you're extremely proficient in, for example, Ventura, having other options such as editing and copy editing or a little bit of design, really does help. For example, my first project with a particular client was a newsletter. In the initial meeting, we were discussing my background and I mentioned I did editing. The client said, "Good, I have a need for that." Getting our foot in the door this way led to our doing editing, layout, and illustration of a large quarterly magazine, as well as several other projects. So offer an extra task to add more value, such as copy editing, or tactfully suggest a design improvement. That's what makes the client happy and come back to you.   —*Lynn Walterick*

DTP's specific selling points

You're selling the benefits of using DTP technology to meet a client's communications needs.

Some potential customers are new to typesetting—whether it's DTP or its traditional predecessor technologies. For this group, you can cite four very persuasive benefits:

- **Presentation:** Typography has flourished because every reader has an aesthetic sense, and every document has a graphic interest level. If you make a page more attractive; if you turn a gray, single-column sheet into well-organized columns, using a range of formatting and graphic techniques to highlight what's most important, readers will give the page their attention. To keep their attention, you can explain, single-spaced proportional laser printer type is far more readable than the double-spaced monospaced type most people produce with typewriters, dot-matrix, and letter-quality computer printers. Prospective customers using laser printers may already have made the switch to proportionally spaced type, but they may have an extremely limited or unattractive typeface, and you can offer them more choices in layout, white space, headline styles, and graphic embellishments. One way to illustrate proportional spacing to a client is to show them proportional and monospaced series of mmmmmnnnnniiiii and `mmmmmmnnnnniiiii`.
- **Consistency:** You can help a client establish a set of formats, typestyles, and graphic elements that will give a uniform look, and therefore, a greater recognition value and ease of use, to all the client's published materials. Of course, DTP is not unique in offering this service. But the style sheets, templates, and graphic libraries built into software make it more affordable, convenient, flexible, and expandable than with conventional graphics, illustration, and typesetting.
- **Economy:** You can comfortably fit 50-100% more words on a typeset page than on a typewritten page—and maintain a high readability level. As a result, for any publication destined for photocopying or volume printing, anything you can do to shorten a publication's length will significantly reduce a client's costs. The same principle applies to shipping costs. The 20¢ postage difference between a one-ounce and a two-ounce letter sent first-class comes to $200 for a mailing to 1,000 people. That's money a client can spend to upgrade a document's look instead. In general, as print or photocopy runs exceed 500, the cost for the design, graphics, and type on the camera-ready original becomes a small fraction of the total production cost. And the overall cost savings from typesetting rise as the print run increases.
- **Turnaround:** You can confidently tell clients that for all but the largest jobs, if they schedule the work in advance, *most* of the time spent on the job after they get the first proofs will be on their end, as they review proofs and make changes. You should structure your workload and workflow to

be able to fit in the hours to make changes within a day or two of receiving each proof from the customer.

Potential customers may have been using conventional hot or cold type, and are interested in switching to DTP. For this group, you can emphasize:

- **Time and accuracy:** When clients give you text on disk, they don't have to allow for the time (or pay you) for the effort re-key it; and they don't have to worry about new typos creeping in when they make revisions.
- **Long-term dollar savings:** Be wary of making bold promises about major cost savings over traditional typesetting. For any publication that will be updated or periodical that will appear regularly, you'll be creating templates that will reduce future work in setting up the publication. DTP's savings over conventional typography mushroom the more frequently a document is revised and re-used. Of course, if you can find out the cost per job or page the client is paying now, you may also be able to quote a better rate giving short-term dollar savings.
- **Less quantifiable benefits:** DTP is an interactive process, giving the client the option to watch the publication being created. This makes communications between the client and the DTPer much simpler and often more enjoyable. It also helps that at any stage of production, proofs with type and graphics in place provide a close representation of the final product, and that changes can be incorporated at any time.
- **Flexibility in design:** Computers automate and facilitate global changes to text and typestyles. The client can rapidly try out many variants or looks at a relatively low cost.
- **Special looks:** All sorts of effects that used to require costly hours at the paste-up table, multiple proofs from the typesetter, special efforts by the printer—and some that were essentially unachievable—can now be easily accomplished on the desktop. These include type following a curve or irregular path; type enclosed or wrapped around a shape; skewed type; type filled with images or graphic elements; proportional and nonproportional scaling of type and graphics; ramps and gradations of tints and colors; one shape evolving into another; cutouts of graphics and type; montages of photos and art; colorization, retouching, and other special effects on photographs.

Building up and using a sample collection

Nothing bolsters your confidence more than a bulging sample book. Think of samples as a critical part of your toolkit for the business of DTP. Samples are like the letters of reference people in many occupations collect because the nature of their work doesn't allow them to amass physical samples.

Showing your portfolio will reassure prospective clients. You'll never find a better way to talk about a project than to pull out an old job and say, "So you had something like this in mind?" Seeing a sample book with appropriate examples is the closest clients can come to asking you to do the work on spec, and paying you only if they are satisfied.

Looking at your samples along with any of the client's publications or models helps you think together. It helps clients communicate. Their reactions to what you show them clarifies what they want and what they don't like—especially since many people you'll work with start out with a limited visual vocabulary.

However you begin, keep collecting samples of your work. Hang on to intermediate and final proofs to simplify explaining the DTP process to clients. Whatever it takes, get at least five or 10 copies of important projects so you can give them out to people without worrying about whether to believe their promises that they'll return everything to you. For splashy projects, make sure your client's print run allows for enough extras for you. That may be 20 copies, 100, or more depending on what use you plan to make of the samples. Before you use or distribute any client's samples, clear it with them: Some people don't like having their work shown around.

Even after you have a great sample book, continue getting multiple copies of all DTP work you complete.

Package your samples professionally, in a three-ring binder with a high-quality cover and clear sheets each holding one sample, or in a designer's case that opens and folds flat to hold manuals and odd-sized pieces. Include samples of the kinds of text and graphics you can produce. Slide into the binder pocket a pica measure and type ruler so you can point out type sizes.

Be prepared to explain each sample to potential customers. Maggie's pitch book includes:

- Before and after pages showing how much more type you get per page with proportional type;

- The same page printed at 300, 1,270 and 2,540 dots per inch to demonstrate the difference;
- A price sheet for the different resolutions of final pages;
- Pages showing images scanned for position only and the resulting final pages;
- Samples of bar, line, and pie charts;
- Illustrations of scanned logos;
- Catalogs of typefaces available.

Eventually, you'll be especially satisfied with a project, and you'll feel it shows off your capabilities. Before the job is printed, negotiate with the client to increase the print run by 100-500 copies, with you paying the incremental cost. Send your sample to everyone on your house list.

By this time, you should have managed to put together a personal and business database, or, using client contact software, you'll have developed a database that way, so you can generate a set of mailing labels. Take your samples, add a cover letter and a promotional piece if you have one, and get them to your list of potential clients, and to your friends and relatives.

Don't expect the business to come pouring in. But you'll probably get a few inquiries. Now you've set the stage to start making some calls yourself. Of course, without any followup, mailings may be of marginal value.

Making samples to sell your services

To focus more directly on your special strengths, you could produce dummy samples: fictitious brochures, newsletters, and other pieces that demonstrate your range of design skills, typefaces, tools, and effects. Yet though graphic designers produce these imaginary publications all the time, it still seems a shame to go to all that trouble for something that will never see a printer's ink. Perhaps you could eventually use some of them as templates for actual jobs.

You could also put special efforts into self-promotion. In late 1987, when DTP was still relatively unfamiliar, but the tools were starting to match those of conventional typesetting, Felix combined a series of handouts he had produced into a 12-page booklet called *Make Your Words Count*. It included a write-up on the benefits of DTP, illustrations of the graphic resources available in three software packages, a typeface sampler, instructions for preparing text on disk, a DTP reading list, a client list, an ad for the Peace Calendar he produced, a large version of the new Kramer Communications logo, mini-pages of previous Kramer Communications projects, and an explanation of how the booklet was produced. Felix distributed the brochure at conferences, workshops, and user group events, and sent it out to people requesting work samples or information about his services. He printed it in two colors on prosperous-looking glossy stock. He estimates that the direct production costs of about $1,000 came back within a few months in new business. Doing it, he also learned a lot about pushing his software to its limits.

In some geographic localities or market segments where potential clients are less familiar with DTP technology, this kind of educational brochure may still serve an important function. You could even do a regular quarterly or semi-annual newsletter, listing your clients and showing off your new capabilities. Tailor your presentation to the familiarity and publishing vocabulary of your potential clients.

As his potential client base has become more informed, Felix hasn't updated his now antiquated booklet. But he has continued to produce postcards, flyers, tip sheets, and other small-scale promotional material. In these pieces, he presents his selling points and client list—while using the production opportunity to demonstrate some tool, such as scanning or imagesetting to film. He's even done a page with a scanned photo of him in front of his workstation and a caption inventorying all his equipment—for use when he's approaching those clients who want to know specifics about his resources. See **Figs. 3.1** and **3.2** for excerpts from Felix's and Maggie's past promotional material.

All kinds of businesses send out holiday greetings and other cards on special occasions. You have even more reason to do so, since the mailings illustrate your capabilities and services. You don't have to wait until you can handle, or afford, a four-color glossy piece. Spread goodwill and gain regular attention with low-cost, routine promotional mailings.

Promotional flyers can help you get clients. But unless you've found a niche with a standardized product, such as personalizing greeting cards, we don't think it makes sense to put your prices down on a sheet of paper. Most of DTP is too complex to summarize in a simple rate sheet. You would need to add all sorts of qualifications. Most price lists won't get you business you wouldn't get otherwise.

ONE-STOP DESKTOP PUBLISHING SINCE 1985

■ **We work with you from start-to-finish.** Because we write, edit, design and handle printing, when Kramer Communications spots a way to improve the content or format of your job, we tell you about it.

■ **We started doing desktop publishing before most people had heard the term.** We have the experience to accurately bid your job and meet your deadlines. We've done tabloid newspapers and 400-page books. We use the fastest, most powerful hardware — and the most advanced fourth-generation (sometimes not yet released) software.

■ **You'll enjoy working with us.** Our network of technical experts, designers, illustrators and printers gives you enthusiastic, literate, imaginative and savvy partners.

■ **Felix Kramer's experience** can help you create and deliver effective messages. He has spent over 20 years in communications, editing newsletters, magazines and newspapers, and writing investigative books, analytical articles, business plans and successful foundation grants. He has worked with computers since 1979. Plus he has managed staffs and large budgets, run special events and been a Congressional aide.

■ **What you get:** the flexibility of a computer-based system facilitates late changes; mechanicals at 300 dots per inch (on paper) or super-crisp 1,270 or 2,540 dots per inch quality (on RC paper or film); over 100 distinct type families; special effects with type, illustrations and digitized clip art; your art scanned to help visualize layouts; fax for rapid turnaround; MS-DOS compatibility (send us your word processor files on disk).

■ **Kramer Communications** can be your service bureau—or we can help you buy equipment and train your staff to run your own in-house system. Take advantage of our resources.

■ **Ask for a free estimate:** we'll often quote a maximum top rate, with a guaranteed price cut if the job takes less time than expected. (We offer sliding scale rates for small businesses and nonprofit organizations.)

Kramer Communications
212/866-4864

Systems Consulting ■ Training ■ Production

Figs 3.1 and 3.2 Sample promotional material

The original 8 ½- by 11-inch sheet includes a client list and photo.

EXPERTS IN DESKTOP PUBLISHING

The good news is desktop publishing can mean big savings for your company by cutting typesetting costs and making your publishing operations faster and more efficient.

The bad news is it can also mean big headaches, as many companies are finding out. But you can't afford to ignore desktop publishing. The question is, "How do you bring these systems into your company without losing control?"

The best news is Acanthus Associates. They answer this question by offering you a complete range of management and planning services for desktop publishing operations.

Acanthus Associates provides the services of developing, maintaining, and enhancing desktop publishing facilities in business locations. Acanthus will guide you through all phases of developing a desktop publishing center: detailed consultation, selection, installation of equipment and software, training, and ongoing support. For production of documents, Acanthus offers a talented, professional production department.

How Acanthus is helping companies take control:

Problem: Authors were submitting manuscripts to a small book publishing house on PC and Macintosh disks. Then the manuscripts were sent to be typeset. The publishers wanted to save production time and money by laser printing the books directly from the authors' disks, but it had to be done without disrupting day-to-day operations or lowering book design standards.

Solution: Desktop publishing systems with laser printers were installed. During the transition to the new system, Acanthus assumed the production of the books using the capabilities of the desktop publishing system. Acanthus created layout templates for efficient and consistent book design. The in-house staff was trained to use the templates.

Result: Dramatic cost savings without disruption of daily operations and confidence that Acanthus can back them up during busy times.

Problem: A restaurant chain was spending a small fortune on typesetting menus. The menus were constantly changing to reflect the latest food fads and price changes.

Solution: Acanthus introduced desktop publishing technology by providing consultation, training, and support on a complete DTP system.

Result: Immediate savings in typesetting costs, plus faster turnaround time and better looking menus.

Problem: A financial consulting firm was creating their financial planning reports on PCs and low-quality matrix printers and plotters. They wanted to upgrade the design and output quality of the reports in a short amount of time without investing in a whole new system.

Solution: A laser printer and DTP software were added to the existing PC network. Acanthus redesigned the reports. The in-house staff was trained to create their own great looking reports.

Result: First class reports at a reasonable cost.

Acanthus Associates, 212/529-6110

Getting samples: on your time

If you're raring to go, but have no established clients, then you'll have either some cash reserves or a regular paycheck from the other work you do. Consider yourself lucky. You can enjoy building your portfolio, in effect training yourself on the job without feeling the pressure of clients' demands. By the time you hunt for clients, you'll be in a better position to give realistic estimates for time and charges.

If you're starting without paying clients, you're also fortunate because you have time to donate your skills. Pick a social or political cause you identify with or an educational, religious, or community institution you like, and volunteer as their desktop publisher. If you're wary of an open-ended commitment, limit the offer in time or scope. Everyone will win: The group will save money, its audience will appreciate the upgraded publications, and you'll start filling your portfolio. You'll also have the satisfaction of furthering the goals of a group you care about.

If you don't find the right cause to work with, you can experiment on a friend or associate. Find someone with some small enterprise and offer to create a brochure. Tell your friend you'll do it for free, or leave that question open, by saying that if it turns out to benefit the enterprise, you'd be happy to be paid appropriately at some future time. As with a donated service to a nonprofit group, limit your offer's time and scope, and be as clear as you can about a possible price and any outside expenses, so as to avoid ending up resenting the project or jeopardizing your friendship.

Putting your name on your samples

You also gain other benefits from donating your work. Remember that among the readers of *any* publication are many potential customers. Each DTP project you complete has the potential to automatically promote your business. If you continue to volunteer and readers see your work over and over again, we guarantee you'll eventually get at least one paid client through your efforts.

Try to increase the visibility of your work. Sometimes a grateful group will thank you in a newsletter. That one-time notice is great, but if possible, arrange for a regular credit in the masthead, or in a small type size on a separate line, rotated 90 degrees from the text. Felix has persuaded many of his paying nonprofit clients to allow him to place a credit *and his firm's phone number* on the pages of newsletters, flyers, and posters, with good results.

Even some of Felix's corporate clients agree to give him a prominent credit. Your customers may agree to this in exchange for a reduced rate, for rush service— or simply out of appreciation. But whether or not your name appears on the publication, let the people you did the work for know that you're eager to get referrals from them.

Getting samples: on someone else's time

You can also accumulate samples by becoming a publisher's apprentice: Hire yourself out to an individual, a DTP company, or a corporate DTP department. Then you'll be able to show the work you do for another DTPer as your own. This can be tricky. Who was responsible for what may not be as clear. Of course, you could also have fuzzy credits in volunteer work, when you might collaborate with a *pro bono* graphic designer or illustrator.

There's a lot to be said for finding a DTP mentor. Even if you can't claim all the credit, you'll get a substantial volume of samples quicker than if you work by yourself. And you'll become familiar with a greater range of tools than you would on your own. If your boss is not threatened by you and shares lots of tips and advice, you could reduce time trying to do things the wrong way.

You could work out an apprenticeship arrangement where you concentrate more on learning than on making a good living from the work. This might mean you would agree to do a job for a low fixed price, which will include some training. With an expert as your supervisor and safety net, you'll reduce your worries as you produce work. You won't have to spend time looking for clients. You might complete the first DTP jobs you bring in yourself under your mentor's wing. And as you become more experienced, you'll be able to renegotiate your arrangement, so you earn a respectable amount for work you do for your mentor.

Collecting letters of reference

Our focus on DTP samples shouldn't eclipse the value of more traditional endorsements from satisfied clients. When people praise your work, ask them to put it in writing. These letters can attest not to only to the quality of your work, as do your samples, but also to the quality of your services, about which your samples are mute. Treasure these letters. Frame the best ones and put them on your office walls.

Your sales toolbox can include photocopies of these letters, a client list, and some names and phone numbers of a range of clients who are willing to be called by potential customers.

4. STAYING ON TOP OF THE BUSINESS

You can't stand still

As you gain skills, experience, and confidence, you'll evolve into a DTP pro. Once you've mastered the operating system, printer, plus one software package, you can start selling your services. From then on, you'll gradually trade in your learner's permit on each piece of hardware and software.

For better or worse, though, as a DTPer you'll never reach a pinnacle where you can survey the scene and just coast along. In traditional crafts and trades, people used their tools until they wore out. Now we use software until the manufacturer announces an improved version. It promises so much more speed, capacity, and reliability that we can't resist. Or a competing product sounds so much better we decide to switch (or use both). Either way, we must interrupt our work, buy the upgrade, retool, and learn more. That's the price we pay in a fast-changing field for new features and greater productivity.

Your first job is to keep tabs on your hardware. Unlike automotive safety recalls, no government agency makes sure that computer manufacturers notify their customers about problems. Felix once ordered an advanced monitor, only to find it inoperable until he took the computer in for an "optional" read-only memory (ROM) upgrade he knew about but thought unnecessary. You may be registered every way possible, but unless you read the trade weeklies or see the bulletins sent to developers and service technicians, you still may not hear that all owners of computer X with particular serial numbers are likely to run into trouble, and are eligible for a free replacement part. When you have a problem, it may be too late to save your data or your peace of mind.

You also have to keep up with operating system upgrades. Try phoning a company's tech support line sometime with a problem in a new program and say you're working with last year's system software. You're a setup for, "Our software works best with the latest system. Otherwise, no guarantees." Unless the computer company specifies that system 9.1 became 9.2 only to meet one specific problem, assume the upgrades are meant for you. Sometimes you'll get the newest system, or a subset of it, as part of an applications software package. But usually the best way to get the newest system is through a friend or consultant, user group, or a computer retailer. If the system is free, user groups will sell it for a dollar or two more than the cost of the blank floppy disks, and some dealers will let you copy it onto disks you provide.

As a precaution, keep a copy of the old system on a floppy disk, or on a spare or removable hard disk. At times, we've found that returning to an older operating system was the best or only way to use an old application.

Next are all the other upgrades. Computer programmers never sleep, they just keep tinkering. Companies release new software not simply to add features, but also to fix undisclosed, but potentially dangerous bugs that have so far, they hope, passed *you* by. All types of software, from utilities to data security to applications, get changed. Even typefaces: You'd think that once a font is designed and released that would be it. But in fact, typefaces continue to be refined and produced in new formats.

Expect a major upgrade of each application once a year, with one or two minor upgrades in between. Upgrades for brand-new software, from 1.0 to 1.1 to 1.11 to 1.2, are often more frequent—so some veteran DTPers make it a rule never to use version 1.0 of *any* product seriously. Most mainstream DTP software is now far beyond that, at versions 3.0 or 4.0.

If you start mastering and using many applications, keeping up can become a major chore. You can spend considerable time installing and trying out upgrades—but you really have no choice. Be sure to send in your registration form (keep a photocopy in a folder or inside the manual). As with hardware troubleshooting, be sure to install upgrades *after working hours* or on weekends in case you bite off more than you can chew. And as with system software, stow the old applications and fonts on a floppy disk somewhere, in case you need to go back to tap the resources used to create an old file. Maggie has begun to update clients' old files, only to discover that she needed to install older versions of applications and fonts before the files would look right. In general, when you need to print out a document a year or two after you created it, you'll usually be much better off running it with the old version that created it, rather than converting it and then facing minor or major adjustments throughout the document.

For your core applications—page layout and perhaps word processor or main graphics program—take advantage of any Extended Technical Support program offered by the software publisher. Usually, you get free calls to the technicians, technical bulletins, early shipments of upgrades, and discounts on other products. It's worth the $100 or so not to have to worry about the software you depend on every day. For the rest of your software, keep up with other upgrades as well as you can.

For your software and hardware, we suggest you extract from all your manuals and registration forms your product date of purchase, serial number, shipping address, latest software version, and the dates, phone number, and names of technical support people you speak with. Put these in a notebook, or make it a word processor, database, or spreadsheet document and keep it updated and accessible. This is such a good idea, we'll try to find the time to do it too!

Being nimble

Expect surprises. Nothing will go exactly according to plan. Cultivate flexibility as a state of mind—and as a way to react to unpredictable developments. You need to be ready, for example, if:

- **One day your computer simply won't turn on.** Though it's not likely to happen, it's still a good idea, at a minimum, to have an alternate location (a friend/colleague/competitor/service bureau) less than half an hour away where you can set up and continue working. We found we never felt safe until we had a small-scale version of those fault-tolerant installations typical of stock exchanges, the airlines, and the military: a complete duplicate setup at the same location, with the same configuration of systems, applications software, fonts, and data on a hard disk. Now at that heart-stopping moment, we can simply switch over, and spend as long as it takes to deal with a breakdown after hours, without deadline pressures.
- **Your hard disk crashes.** You probably won't take steps to be fully protected until you've learned a painful, but we hope not disastrous, lesson. You need to find a way to keep up-to-date copies of all your current application and data files—one in your office and one somewhere else. And you should have at least one or more hard disk recovery utilities at hand. (See **6. Rescuing data.**)

- **You're out of commission.** Carry with you a notebook with a database printout of all your clients' names and phone numbers so you can reach them if you're stuck somewhere. Cover yourself for getting the work done too. Keep your subcontractors' numbers there—including the one person you most trust, who has a key to your office and your OK to use good judgment in taking over if you become sick or incapacitated.
- **No work comes in.** Until you're confident you can weather a dry spell, keep your antennae out for freelance work at clients' offices, from other DTPers, and at temporary agencies (where, these days, a fast and skilled DTPer can net $15-$30 per hour).
- **Expected work doesn't come in as scheduled.** Maggie always keeps a running list of things to do (beyond the continuous task of marketing) at the first opportunity that work slows down. Tasks might include interviewing prospective freelancers or subcontractors, or checking in with friends and colleagues to find out what's going on. This relieves anxiety and enables you to project a sense of confidence to the delayed client.
- **Unexpected work comes in—more than you can handle.** That's where your colleagues and competitors can help. We practically never turn away work from clients we feel good about. If we can't do it ourselves, we subcontract it, or refer it and collect a finder's fee.
- **Your clients decide to do it themselves.** One or more major clients may decide to assign their staff to do the job, taking away your bread and butter. It happens. Offer consulting and training to help them make the transition. If they take you up on it, you'll keep them as a revenue source for a while, and perhaps still get their more challenging jobs. Three years after he began doing a bank's internal newsletter, and two years after he trained their editor in DTP, Felix still works occasionally for this client. If you help, the client will come back to you—and appreciate and refer you to others. A variant on this scenario came for Felix with another corporate client, who decided to bring the work in house, hiring a person they soon realized couldn't do the job. Of course, they could have looked for a replacement, but having just been burned, they decided it was easier to hand the entire monthly job right back to Felix.
- **You regret a decision to buy a piece of hardware.** Try to buy from places that will refund your money. Otherwise, sell it immediately. Advertise in your user group newsletter or sell it through a broker listed in **Appendix 2. Resources for buying and selling used computers**. Get rid of it soon.

An old computer or circuit board has no antique value. The longer you wait, the less it's worth.

- **Your original plan for doing business proves to be misdirected.** For example, suppose you have the idea that all your clients will telecommunicate work back and forth to you—then discover most of them can't master a modem. Quickly establish another way to handle receiving, transmitting, and proofing documents, such as faxes, messengers, and overnight services.

- **Worst case: You decide the life of an independent DTPer isn't for you.** Don't give up. Maybe you can find a way to turn what you've been doing and learning into some related career path—managing publishing operations at a corporation, writing, designing, or producing documentation for a software company, or working at a service bureau. As you would at any job, when you work for yourself, keep in mind an exit strategy.

Don't let a project flatten you

Nimbleness is a useful style, not only for the general conduct of your business, but also for individual projects and problems. It means you're always thinking of other ways to complete your current project, if:

- **Your hardware takes a walk.** These days, computers are hot property. Though your office should be protected and insured, make sure you keep copies of your client files and business data in a second off-site location.

- **You mistakenly erase a file.** Of course you should be backing up frequently, and you should have installed an unerase utility to recover deleted files (more on that in **6. Rescuing data**). The less frequently discussed but essential companion to frequent backup is a strategy to save documents in progress regularly under a sequence of names. That is, if you lose a document that was your eighth set of page proofs, which you called DOCPRFH, you'll have to start over unless you can backtrack to the seventh proof you worked on a few hours before, or yesterday, which you saved as DOCPRFG.

- **You mangle the data file you're working on.** If you have all the earlier versions, you're in pretty good shape. If you didn't take that precaution, you'll have to start over unless you own and know how to use one of those utilities that enable you to extract data from corrupted files. As a desperate last resort for word processor files, try importing the file into your page layout program and then exporting it back to its original format. Sometimes it helps.

- **The client decides to rip a design apart or make major editorial changes at a late stage of the job.** Often there's a way to set up the specifications for pages and type styles that makes later revisions relatively painless. Usually, it takes more planning at the start of the job. (We'll talk more about this in 7. **Create a structure, then build on it.**)

- **You discover the software you're using can't do what you intended after all.** If, for instance, you've mastered several graphics packages, you've already found that there's never only one way to do something. There may be one best answer—but there are always other good answers. As you work, always be thinking of alternate solutions, and be ready to switch to them when needed.

- **A job gets out of hand.** If a project is taking far longer than you expected, and you're trapped because you bid a flat fee, try to think differently about your misfortune. Maybe you're in a software package's unexplored territory. If so, perhaps you can accept the reality that you've turned off the meter. You might even lose money on this job. But you're learning skills that will help you bid and complete the next job.

- **Your client is unhappy with a design.** If it's a matter of money, offer alternatives that will take less of your time. If they just don't like the final result, pull out a couple of printouts or data files of approaches that occurred to you along the way, which you saved as intermediate versions for just such an occasion.

Help is at hand

Yes, there's lots to keep track of—especially for one person trying to run a business, do the work, and know everything about the computer.

Fortunately, reporters and technical writers are compiling most of the information you need—you just have to take the time to read the **magazines**. For starters, get *InfoWorld*, the leading microcomputer weekly, and *MacWeek* or *PC Week*, if you use either of these computer platforms. Also subscribe to two or three platform-specific monthly magazines and to the main DTP monthlies, *Publish* and *Personal Publishing*. Some of these are free to qualified users. But if your answers on the application form don't persuade them that you're a ripe enough target for their advertisers, and you still need the magazine, then pay for a subscription. Eventually, you may also get one or two specialized DTP newsletters. These cost from $50–$500 per year. Their publishers are smart about industry trends and well connected to industry rumor mills. (See **Appendix 2. Magazines** and **Specialized resources**.) We keep back issues of most magazines. Generally, we write lists of what we're interested in on the cover of the magazine. For the ones that are so glossy the ink won't take, we write our notes on the first inside page, or on a piece of paper stapled to the cover.

You can also sign up with an electronic **bulletin board** (BBS). CompuServe is the biggest one. When a company makes a product announcement, you can often get the full text of the press release from the BBS. Some companies maintain their own areas on one or more BBSs, so it's the most up-to-date way to see users' reports of problems, download software upgrades, and stay in the know. It's a handy source for free and near-free software, and you'll find sections, called areas, on Working From Home, International Entrepreneur's Network, and a DTP Forum, all dedicated to promoting information and exchanges.

The CompuServe DTP Forum has an active group of 10,000 members, some of whom get together for electronic conferences on Tuesday nights. They welcome newcomers with questions about DTP, and it's not limited to any type of hardware. The Forum also has more than a dozen library areas with demonstration versions of popular applications and utilities, transcripts of previous conferences, resource lists, and free templates, fonts, and clip art.

Of course, BBSs have been known to swallow people up entirely—there's so much information, and logging on can become addictive and expensive. Fortunately, you don't have to read everything on-screen. You can download it and print it out once you're off-line. With the right software you can automate the entire process. Set it up so that your computer calls the BBS in the middle of the night, when rates are cheapest, pulls in the latest information, and hangs up without your being there. CompuServe Navigator automates the process for Macintosh users; for PC users there's CompuServe Information Manager. Check to see if your modem, communications, or applications software came with a free CompuServe startup kit, or call (800) 848-8199 for a free trial run. MacNet, (800) 638-9636, is an even more user-friendly BBS for Macintosh users. GEnie, (800) 638-9636, also has a Design to Print Roundtable and a home-based business section. (All these phone numbers are for voice information, not for modem connections.)

Meet your tools' creators

You can also mingle with the people behind all those products that have absorbed so much of your attention and money. You can glimpse them at local product rollouts and demonstrations sponsored by area stores and training centers. But usually you won't get to talk to anyone but an area sales rep.

The best place to see the authors and experts is at trade shows. Now that you're a DTP pro, they're eager to meet you. All you need is a company name, registration badge and business card (corporate attire often helps, of course), and *presto*, you're an end-user, a prime representative of a market they need to understand and reach.

Industry professionals respect honest and direct feedback from DTPers. We've had productive talks with product managers and engineers about aspects we like and don't like, what we'd like to see, and our experiences getting products to work together. Once you've met one, you now know a person to call in the months after the show. We've liked these folks, and they seem delighted to meet with DTPers who are immersed in the products they created. The opportunity to meet these highly dedicated and creative individuals personally is unparalleled. When was the last time you met the people who designed your car or TV?

So if you can spare the time, try going to some of the major national trade shows. The largest one, COMDEX in Las Vegas, is too big, and designed more for manufacturers to meet with distributors and retailers. But the periodic PC Expo, MacWorld, Folio, Seybold, Type-X, and others are ideal expositions to go from booth to booth, buttonholing vendors and collecting shopping bags full of information. You can decide to register for the high-priced seminars and workshops, which may be useful, or just stick to the affordable (often free if you pre-register) exhibit hall. (See **Appendix 2. Trade shows and conferences.**) Take along a small stapler so you can attach exhibitors' business cards to their product material on the spot.

If you become deeply absorbed in computer culture, you'll hear about great parties and private demonstrations the vendors put on in hotel rooms near the show. If you can get access to these exclusive events, good for you. But even if you can't, you can accomplish three other useful goals at trade shows. First, if you keep an eye on the badges of fellow conventioneers, you may meet some people who share your interests and can be helpful to you. Wherever they come from, it can be very stimulating to meet fellow DTPers. You might even get some business.

Second, if you locate the key person at a booth, you may establish a more substantial relationship with a company. You can become a certified trainer for their product, which could mean they would refer clients or work to you, or a demonstrator for them, which would mean they would pay you part-time to show off their product.

Third and most intriguing is the possibility of becoming a test site for a hardware product or software upgrade. Companies developing products use their staffs for in-house tests of early prototypes, called alpha versions. When the product is moderately stable, they send it out to a network of beta-version testers to find as many bugs as they can while they use the product in their work.

Being a **beta-tester** can be fun and exciting. As you tell the programmers or engineers what you're finding, you become part of the design team. It can also be frustrating. You may spend many hours installing and working with a half-finished, often undocumented product. As you receive successive beta versions (sometimes weekly software revisions for months), you learn the product, so you're a step ahead when the final version is released. Incidentally, beta-testers sign a non-disclosure agreement swearing them to secrecy. If you honor it, until the product is released, you can't even boast to your friends about your privileged status.

Your best help: user groups

You can get help most conveniently through your local computer user group. They're usually structured around platforms: Amiga, Apple, Atari, DEC, PC, Macintosh, or NeXT. Sometimes they reside under a common umbrella, such as the huge Boston Computer Society. Usually the platform-specific user groups will have subgroups, called Special Interest Groups (SIGs). In New York City, for instance, DTPers rendezvous in the Big Apple Users Group; they congregate at the NYPC 's Publishing, Ventura, and WordPerfect SIGs, and they mingle in the Macintosh Users' Group's Graphics, Freelance, Multimedia and DTP SIGs. Call your computer manufacturer, a dealer, or an imagesetter service bureau to reach a nearby group. You could also consider as large user groups the CompuServe DTP Forum, mentioned above, and the National Association of Desktop Publishers. (See **Appendix 2. User Groups.**)

What happens at a user group meeting? Platform groups generally meet monthly. In large cities, in particular, they are often treated to talks by the CEOs of major computer and software companies, and to product demos by the authors of major programs. Often the best part of the meeting is the open forum, where anyone can ask for help and impart information, advice or warnings to the entire group.

The general group usually sends out a monthly publication with articles, news flashes, product reviews, ads, and classified announcements, plus listings of classes, public domain, and shareware disks. Some of these are good enough to be worth subscribing to, even if you live in another city. You can probably browse through exchange copies of other SIGs' publications at your local group's office or library.

The more focused SIGs generally meet monthly as well. Their agendas may include product demonstrations, go-around-the-room introductions, or a presentation or show-and-tell by a member. At general meetings and at SIGs, people find out they shop at the same computer store, trade stories about mail order miracles and horrors, compare systems, boast and complain, offer to work for each other on projects. They consult with each other on the spot.

In a community-oriented style, user groups are voluntary operations, except for management and support staff in some of the large groups. Members generously donate their time to program and run meetings and SIGs, write and produce newsletters, and offer quality new-user and applications classes. Everyone is so helpful. If it all weren't so normal, we might feel that we were part of a cult.

We've found no better source than our user group for someone to save our skins when we needed help at 10 p.m. on Friday night (or worse). Whether it's a simple question we feel almost too stupid to ask, or a crashed drive we've been wrestling with for hours, someone has an answer, or a suggestion for what to try next. Sometimes, like magic, just reviewing the situation with a sympathetic voice on the other end of the phone helps pinpoint the problem.

Fellow user group members are almost unfailingly generous with their time. But this doesn't mean their only rewards come in the afterlife. SIGs help computer people combat the frequent isolation of computer work. Many volunteers have gained new skills, achieved national visibility with vendors, gotten jobs with computer companies, started writing for computer publications, and gained the confidence to start their own consulting, programming, or production businesses. And we can't begin to list the number of people who met at user groups who've become business partners, or started working with, for, or around each other. We haven't heard of too many romantic matches made—but maybe we just weren't looking.

In our user group and DTP SIG, by concentrating on helping one another, telling everyone what we discover, and helping each other get out and stay out of trouble, we've acted as mutual backups, technical supporters, and cheerleaders—helping all of us to succeed. Though at times we may be competitors, we've treated each other as allies, and, in an expanding market for DTP services, it continues to work.

Connecting with other desktop publishers

Unless you live in a very small community, if you're starting out now, you're probably not the first DTPer in town. You might imagine your arrival would be greeted with suspicion and fear by people who see you as a competitor. Of course, you can't expect to be welcomed warmly if you act like you know it all, or hang out your shingle right next door to another DTPer and actively try to steal clients. But if you're helpful and respectful, you may well find other DTPers to be a great resource. And chances are, some time, you'll work for them and they'll work for you.

Today, only a small proportion of our society's typography is completed electronically. But computer and DTP technologies are contributing to a rapid expansion of the demand for graphics and typeset pages. Since it's now so easy to make printed materials look better, growing numbers of people figure, why not take the extra step? Business, government, arts, nonprofit, and community-based organizations are producing more and more electronically created memos, manuals, handouts, newsletters, books, slide shows, and animations.

For some time, we expect the growth in market demand will exceed the supply of talented and experienced DTPers. That's why DTPers often see each other as allies. Every satisfied customer of this fledgling technology will be a convert and therefore a source of referrals. As a novice, you're counting on other DTPers' success to help spread the word. And as you become successful, when you start to reach your own relatively limited capacity, those other professionals out there can help you get your work done. See **Appendix 2. User groups, trade shows, and professional organizations** for meeting places for DTPers.

Even DTPers who appear to be general practitioners are, in fact, specialists. You bring a unique mix of editorial, graphic, and business skills to DTP. You then buy different hardware, and become expert in particular software. And finally, you concentrate on different markets for your customers. Each DTPer has a different take on the business. And most are willing to help others out.

Some DTPers are entranced by the technology—they become encyclopedias of hardware recommendations and tips. What you dread as a troubleshooter's nightmare, someone else welcomes as a challenge. Some are the type who call you up to brag about discovering an undocumented software feature. Others love to produce graphic effects never seen before. Still others get their kicks finding ways to use DTP tools to replicate traditional graphic techniques. For all these types, the existence of other DTPers encourages excellence.

With all the information sharing among user groups and in weekly magazines and specialized publications, discoveries that start out as unique secrets soon become common knowledge. So you're not likely to find most DTPers acting like they know just where to find the buried treasure, but won't show you the map. We're increasingly seeing published compendia of tips and workarounds. The most impressive ones so far are *Real World PageMaker 4: Industrial Strength Techniques* (Bantam, 1990, $24.95), by Olav Kvern, an employee of Aldus Corporation who helped create the software, and Stephen Roth, a publishing journalist, and *Ventura Tips and Tricks* (Peachpit Press, Third Edition, 1990, $27.95), by Ted Nace and Daniel Will-Harris.

Your DTP colleagues may not reveal every secret they know—but they will most likely help you out. You'll hire each other and refer work back and forth. Your calls, visits, and joint projects will relieve your long solitary hours in front of the screen. You'll hobnob in user groups and trade associations, compare notes about trade shows and products, and share the latest gossip about the corporate takeovers, software releases, and industry personalities. Some colleagues will become friends, with whom you'll talk about families, politics, even movies.

5. ASSEMBLING YOUR TOOLBOX

You may want to start with a bang—go out and rent space, incorporate, buy everything you'll need, and start taking in work the minute you have production capability.

Or you may take a more gradual approach. Perhaps you'll build up your DTP skills while you're on someone else's payroll. Or you'll start by taking courses, then hire yourself out through a temporary agency or even apprentice yourself to an established DTPer.

If you're not sure you have the temperament and talent for this business, perhaps you'll want to learn one or two software packages before you buy much of anything.

However you start, eventually you'll need to buy your own rig. At that point, it helps to know where you're heading. We'll get more specific later in this chapter, but first we need to establish some principles and parameters for your choices.

High or low end?

You can't even put a price tag on your ideal hardware and software setup until you know what kind of work you'll be doing. You'll probably want to begin with the capacities found at a small typesetting shop:

- The ability to produce laser printer quality camera-ready mechanicals using a range of typefaces for single-color or simple spot-color work;
- The ability to accept a variety of floppy disk and word processor formats for text your clients send you;

- A relationship with an imagesetter service bureau for high-resolution type and pages larger than legal size;
- You can go one step up, yet stay within the low end, with the capacity to scan photos and art at low resolution, transmit data by modem, and the ability to produce drawings, illustrations, and special type or graphic effects and transformations.

If you buy all these basic tools, at late 1990 prices, you'll probably spend about $10,000, but the range may be from $5,000-$20,000.

In another league entirely are people who replicate what used to be the exclusive preserve of million-dollar facilities for **prepress** functions like continuous tone color separation, stripping, and color proofing. Most of the capabilities relate to the CMYK (cyan/magenta/yellow/black) model used for process color in printing. The software to manipulate and color separate these images, and some of the hardware to input and output them, have become increasingly affordable. You can now buy add-ons to popular page layout software so their completed files can be moved into traditional high-end magazine-quality systems from Hell Graphic Systems, Scitex America, and Du Pont Crosfield. High-resolution calibrated monitors capable of accurately displaying millions of discrete colors, scanners from Nikon and others that copy color slides and photographs, and full-color 300 dot per inch (dpi) printers are all available for under $10,000 per item. Other high-end capabilities such as OCR (optical character recognition or text scanning) are also migrating down to the desktop.

The high end is a part of what people call "the bleeding edge." The technology is in flux, universal formats don't yet exist, dominant vendors haven't yet emerged. Conventional methods for producing the results are often cheaper and better. Traditional prepress operators spend decades learning how to translate a designer's intentions to the printed page. DTP tools are starting to offer controls similar to those in conventional technology—but features don't guarantee results. Yet, solutions to many of these obstacles are within view.

Unless you're setting up a corporate department where you need to have everything at once, you're usually better off keeping things simple *to start*. For color in particular, begin by mastering some of the basics of spot color, with its trapping and knockouts. Even if you sell your backers on DTP's capabilities to accomplish everything in publishing, you'll waste lots of time and money if you invest in the high end before you know what you're doing. Color is coming, but if you wait even six months, you'll save money and probably buy something better than what you can get now.

Evaluating hardware and software

If you've been taking classes or working someplace where you've had a chance to try out DTP tools, you may have found a combination you love—or something you never want to go near again. In either case, you're in a good position to start shopping.

Next best is to find a DTPer you respect and trust. If you don't know any, hook up with a local user group, or talk with the manager of a laser printer or imagesetter service bureau. Be prepared to pay a systems consultant a few hundred dollars, if necessary, to get information faster, and, in the long run, save money by making better purchases. If you can't find someone within hailing distance, try the computer bulletin boards. (See **4. Help is at hand.**)

You can benefit from other people's recommendations and warnings. Keep in mind, of course, that most people need to justify their past courses of action. You're starting with a clean slate, so if you detect signs of intense brand loyalty, ask tough questions, and don't rely on only one recommendation.

As you start getting closer to a list of products to buy, immerse yourself in the consumer literature. At a minimum, look through the last year of the main DTP monthlies, and the one or two main monthlies and weeklies for the type of computer you're expecting to buy. You'll find ads, product reviews, and, every few months, face-offs between products vying for market dominance. (See **Appendix 2. Magazines and catalogs.**) Your public library is probably not the best place to find these back issues—a more likely source is the library of a college computer center or a DTP training center, or the bookshelves of a well-established DTPer.

One way or another, before you buy anything, get your hands on the tools. You'll be able to see and try out the latest equipment at a trade show, industry seminar, or perhaps your local computer store. (See **Appendix 2. Trade shows and conferences.**)

> Be especially cautious in picking a monitor sight unseen. Beauty and specifications are only part of the story. The morning after, your eyes may tell you that you object to something you didn't notice at first glance.
>
> *—Margaret Styne*

What to get first

Everyone always says, "Pick your software first; then buy the computer." Yet we've never met anyone who followed this advice. Of course, the hardware is more immediate and exciting—though that's only part of the story. Usually the hardware is a bigger decision in dollars. And if you aren't sure what software you'll use, you could do worse than going ahead and buying a computer with enough capacity to run *any* of the packages you're considering.

Of course, the software decision must come first if you've settled on a particular package that won't run on all types of hardware. (The lingo is "single- or multi-platform"—use it and you may get some more respect among those in the know.) Even then, check with the manufacturer and the journalistic rumor mills. The package you've set your heart on may be scheduled for release next month for other platforms.

What really makes the most sense is to think in terms of your entire system:

- The formats for the text and other data you will receive;
- Where your graphics will come from;
- The fonts, utilities, and automating aids you'll want to use;
- The kinds of output devices you'll use;
- The tools used by major potential clients;
- The tools used by DTPers and temporary agencies you might work for;
- The tools used by people you might hire or subcontract work to;
- Whether you'll be working as part of a network of computers all wired together.

When you know all this, then you can add to the equation:

- Your favorite software;
- Your favorite user **interface** (look and feel of the computer in use);
- The level of hardware performance (speed) you demand.

We try to keep current on all the product categories that interest us. We go through the magazine articles and ads, and fill in the postcards in the back of most computer magazines offering free information about the products mentioned inside. We take all the flyers and direct mail about the products that might interest us and put them in files we've organized in categories for hardware: • storage • memory • accelerators • monitors • input devices • output devices • portables • specialized cards • accessories/cables/furniture. We keep a folder with the flyers and specs for the hardware we own, and one called "hardware under active consideration" for material on products we're currently thinking of buying.

We also have categories for software: • page layout • word processing • database • financial (spreadsheet/statistical/charting) • project and business management and accounting • presentation and outlining • integrated (business) • graphics (draw/paint/3-D/animation/image manipulation) • scanning/optical character recognition • fonts • utilities • data security • games and novelties.

Your hardware starter kit

Don't be shortsighted. Get everything you need to be a going concern. You must be able to accept data from clients, then produce and deliver camera-ready mechanicals without depending on anyone else. That doesn't mean getting top-of-the-line equipment all at once. If you get a good and complete set of working tools, you can later upgrade them one by one.

> Besides the fact that things are going pretty well financially, I am incredibly happy when I get a gut feeling that I might need something and I can just follow through and buy it—without even writing one memo!
> —*Rich Metter, desktop publishing consultant, NYC*

Computer, keyboard, hard disk

The box may be an all-in-one unit including a **central processing unit** (CPU), keyboard, data storage devices, and screen. Or, as with audio, you may buy individual components.

Performance is the key. You really are better off buying a computer with the speed and capacity to accept enough internal working **random access memory** (RAM) to run any software you're even remotely considering. Memory is easy to add later, so don't worry too much about buying it all at once.

> Read the reviews or the blurbs on the cartons for the main software you're going to run, find out the recommended amount of memory, and double it. For the PC, you can't use more than 640K unless you're using special expanded or extended memory. If you're using Microsoft Windows 3, you'll need at least two megabytes. —*Margaret Styne*

By the way, if you ever had trouble trying to explain to someone the different kinds of computer memory, one of our profiled DTPers relies on metaphors from everyday life:

People know food. I tell them that computer random access memory is like your mouth. It can chew on so much information at a time. Hard drive memory is like your stomach. It's where information goes and is stored. And I tell them that using PageMaker without a mouse is like putting salt through the little holes in the shaker one grain at a time.

—Joel Landy

Get a **keyboard** that feels comfortable to you and has all the function keys you may need. For the PC, having those F1 to F10 function keys on the left allows you to use them with one hand in combination with the shift and other keys.

To store your applications and data, get a **hard disk** with at least 20 or 30 megabytes *to spare* after you've installed all your software. We're talking at least 100 megabytes for PCs or Macs. For the Macintosh in particular, we generally recommend external hard disks. You have a greater choice and often can get better performance:

- It doesn't contribute to heat build-up in your computer;
- You see the drive's reassuring blinking activity lights when it's working;
- You can take it with you on a job;
- If it goes down you have an easier time isolating the problem;
- It's easier to replace a freestanding model if the need arises;
- On the other hand, internal hard disks tend to be quieter and cheaper.

If you buy a slow computer (under about 16 mhz), you'll lose the productivity advantage and the pleasure of a computer that really zips along. To understand the need for a speedy processor, test **screen redraw** in your page layout software. Time how long a setup takes to go from one 100% view to another page, and how long it takes for text to reflow after revising or repositioning.

Get as powerful a computer, in speed and capacity, as you can afford. When you shop, look ahead six months. Assume that the next version of your software picks will require more horsepower to run well. Tempted to wait? You could postpone the decision repeatedly because of a price cut mirage.

There's no way to avoid the price depreciation of computers. Often, when a company introduces a new model, it reduces the prices on the existing ones, thus affecting the value of used equipment. As technology and manufacturing efficiencies improve, the cost of new equipment with a given level of performance halves roughly every two years.

You'll always wonder about that new machine in the works, that may ship on time and fulfill all its promises. But you need to weigh all those benefits against having a reliable machine working and earning for you sooner.

We suggest you buy one level below the top-of-the-line computer of the brand you're considering. It will be more affordable, it will be thoroughly debugged, it will perform well, and compared to bottom-of-the line, soon-to-be discontinued hardware, it will hold its value.

It's a good idea to buy an upgradable computer. That means an expandable one with **slots** (parking spaces inside where you can plug in specialized boards as needed). When it comes time to graduate to more size or speed, even if you decide to sell the hardware and buy a new model, you'll get a better price for your old equipment if it can be upgraded by the next owner.

As long-established DTPers, we tend to be the second kids on the block with the latest toy. So far, we've found that using top-end models for our main machine brings the best payback on our investment. Usually we wait until it's been on the streets a month or two, and if we encounter no bad reviews or recalls, we go ahead and send in our money. We try to buy computers and peripherals from manufacturers that have been in business at least three years.

Meanwhile, we start lining up a buyer for the old machine (unless it's turning into our new spare). Once the new one has been up and running for a month or so, we sell the old one. The longer we hold on to it, the less it will be worth. We try to remain unsentimental about the old jalopy. Sure, we have an emotional relationship with our equipment—sometimes we'll give a CPU or printer a name or paste a sticker on it—but we try to remember it's really just a commodity, and remain poised to sell or trade it in at the appropriate time.

Monitor

Get as large and sharp a video display terminal (VDT) as you can afford and make space for. You can't beat a screen that shows two facing letter-sized pages actual size—that's 21 inches diagonally. The bigger the screen you get, the more time you'll save by seeing more and rarely switching views. We recommend at least 19 inches; as a DTPer starting out, you can't make a more short-sighted decision than to buy a screen under 16 inches. Software can help, though:

> I'd like a larger monitor for my PC, but with my limited startup resources, I made the decision to save money on a monitor and invest in a good PostScript Printer, which I think is indispensable. I use Aristocad Soft Kicker for Ventura Publisher and Windows to put the entire screen in memory, so I can scroll around a small screen as if it's a window on a much larger screen.
> —*Rich Metter*

For the Mac, Berkeley Systems Stepping Out is a similar screen panning utility.

You probably don't need a large color screen. There's no major problem in completing simple spot-color jobs on a monochrome monitor. You just won't be able to turn your pull-down menus orange or your guidelines blue. When you do need color for illustration or process color, you can get a smaller auxiliary monitor. On the Macintosh, you can run both at the same time.

A large monochrome or gray-scale monitor is much cheaper than a color monitor. Moreover, because it doesn't have to align three color beams, it will show small size type more clearly than a color monitor. You owe it to yourself to be as easy on your eyes as possible.

Get a monitor with a vertical scanning or refresh rate over 65 hz, so the image doesn't flicker. The horizontal scanning rate, measured in megahertz, isn't a crucial measure for flicker.

Look for a picture element (**pixel**) density of 72 dpi. The further away from 72 dpi you get, the more discrepancy you'll get between the screen size and the actual size of a drawn object or a page on the screen. Ideally you'd like a one-to-one correspondence.

Laser printer

It may not be obvious that you'll need your own 300 dpi laser (or inkjet) printer. Unless you're literally sharing office space with someone who lets you remain continuously networked to the printer, you'll be wasting time and money saving up your jobs to print elsewhere.

But that's not the worst part. Despite all the hype about What You See Is What You Get (**WYSIWYG**, pronounced whizzywig) display technology, there's no replacing a hard copy proof. Until you're holding a black image on a white piece of paper that you can move around, fold, and hold next to another image, you remain in the realm of the *theoretically* acceptable page.

In DTP, you need to feel completely free to try out a dozen variations of a design, illustration, or layout while you're working. You want to learn how to do something on the spot, see how it looks immediately, and keep trying new effects. It's the equivalent of having a Polaroid for test shots when trying to learn the art of portrait lighting.

What's more, minutes or days later, you (or a client) might consider several alternatives and decide you prefer an early version after all. That's why you need unlimited access to a laser printer. Renting time at a laser printer service bureau doesn't work as well. We've never met anyone who can comfortably act like they have all the time in the world while the meter ticks.

Why are laser printers so expensive? Because they're not just laser-driven photocopiers. Three hundred dpi means nearly nine million dots on an 8½- by 11-inch page, each of which needs to be turned on or off by the computer that directs the printing engine of the laser printer. Usually, but not always, this computer is inside the laser printer. Some exceptions are QuickDraw printers that use the Macintosh's computer, NeXT printers that depend on the central processing unit, and LaserMaster printers for Macs and PCs which come with a card that goes into the computer. One reason high-resolution imagesetters are so expensive is the size of the job they have. An 8½- by 11-inch page at 1,270 dpi maps, or turns on and off, over 150 million dots.

If you already own a Hewlett-Packard LaserJet IIP or clone, or a LaserJet III which provides even sharper type at small sizes, you can use it for DTP. If some of your work goes to high-resolution imagesetting typesetters (Linotronics and similar machines), or if you're Macintosh-based, spend another $500 or so to get a printer with PostScript capability. This advanced page description language provides expanded capabilities for special graphics effects and access to the industry-standard Adobe Type 1 typefaces. PostScript appears to be in every DTPer's future.

QMS is a good source for PostScript printers. You can also get add-on cartridges from Adobe and other sources for well under $500 to turn the HP LaserJets into PostScript printers. This is particularly important for the II series, which won't print reverse text (white text in a black box) using some page layout software unless you get additional hardware. If you don't already own a HP, you might be better off buying a printer with PostScript built into the hardware, which is likely to run faster than a cartridge.

Whatever printer you get, make sure it has at least 1.5-2 megabytes of memory, so it can run complex pages without choking. If you plan to run envelopes or legal pages frequently, get the appropriately sized paper trays.

If you're inclined to get a PostScript clone printer, check the magazine reviews to make sure it runs as fast as true Adobe PostScript, which usually means it's a hardware solution, not a software add-on. And make sure it's fully compatible with the graphics applications and special effects you plan to use. If you're an exacting graphic artist, the arrival of the new and more complex Adobe PostScript Level 2, which provides better color halftones and other features, means the compatibility claims of existing clones must all be retested.

You can also check out printers that produce higher resolution (400-1,000 dpi) on plain paper. Some of these units run as fast as 300 dpi machines, and you may be able to justify spending thousands of dollars more by saving the $5-10 per page you've spent for output to 1,270 dpi imagesetters, which use glossy resin coated (**RC**) paper that's developed in tanks with chemicals. (We printed this book on a plain paper LaserMaster printer at an interpolated 1,000 dpi (the company calls it "1,000 Turbo-Res".)

The principle holds for larger format printers. If you're carving out a niche producing broadsides or tabloid newspapers, you may find it worth spending another $5,000 for a printer than runs 11- by 17-inch sheets.

Some laser printers come with hard disks for storing fonts, or can accept an external hard disk for this purpose. It's a nice feature, but it doesn't always result in the speed improvements you might expect. Check out magazine reviews and tests before getting too optimistic.

Scanner

This magical device is becoming an essential tool. Even if you never use it for advanced purposes—manipulating black and white or color images—it's very handy for dropping low-resolution representations of graphics into your page proofs.

Printers call these **FPO**s (For Position Only). Once they're on your page, you can crop and scale them at will, and never have to fool with one of those confusing round slide rule calculators to figure out enlargements and reductions. You can keep the FPOs on your pages until you produce your camera-ready pages. At that point, you send the printer a dummy set of the publication with FPOs included to give exact and uncontrovertible instructions about what the page should look like. For platemaking, the printer replaces the FPO with a high-quality screened velox or negative of the original image.

You can also use your scanner to copy line art (drawings, cartoons, and logos) for actual use on the camera-ready pages. If you intend to enlarge the images, first use an enlarging photocopier and scan the resulting larger image. Standard 300 dpi scans look okay when printed at original size or smaller, but when enlarged or printed on an imagesetter, they'll start to look rough. (See 7. **Some of our favorite shortcuts**.) For the best reproduction, especially on imagesetters, you can scan line art and then trace the images, manually or with automatic tracing software, to convert the graphics into more digitized art you can size and transform without limit.

Get at least a gray-scale scanner for $1,000-$2,000, or one of the color scanners that are now coming down in price to $2,000-$3,000.

Hand-held scanners that can handle a four-or five-inch wide image for $300-$800 are finally reaching an acceptable quality level, now that most come with software that enables you to stitch together segments of larger images.

What about optical character recognition (OCR), where your scanner could eliminate the need to have to type in text you receive from clients? The short answer is that the technology is not yet perfected. You may play around with it, but we don't recommend you buy a scanner exclusively for this purpose—yet. You'll need 99.5% or better accuracy. Think about it. Even 99% accuracy means one mistake every 100 characters. On this page, that would be over 20 errors—far too many to have to correct. When you read reviews about OCR products, make sure any software you're interested in makes primarily recognition errors (where it can't identify a character and flags it for you) rather than substitution errors (where it replaces the actual character with some other character, without realizing the mistake or informing you). OCR is improving. It gets the best results with original sheets, not photocopies, and it already works pretty well with tables of numbers. With some software and certain texts, you or an OCR service bureau can approach 99.9% accuracy.

A further problem with buying a scanner for OCR is that for optimum productivity, you'd need a sheet-fed scanner you can load up with 50 pages of text and leave to do its work during off-hours. You don't want to sit there and tie up your time and your computer feeding in pages. Yet for graphics scanning, you're better off with the flatbed scanner's better alignment.

So far, we think you're still better off going to a service bureau for OCR, at $0.50-$2.00 per page. But this technology is changing rapidly. High-end products like Calera and Xerox/Kurzweil are coming down to the desktop, and the low-end products are getting better very rapidly. One in particular, Caere Typist, for PCs and Macs, is a low-cost hand-held scanner that shows promise primarily as a smart scanner combined with software that elegantly and transparently brings text directly into the application you're using.

Test drives

Imagesetter and computer-by-the-hour service bureaus are excellent places to try out monitors, laser printers, and scanners before you buy.

Accessories, peripherals, and supplies

Necessities
- A multi-outlet **power strip** to manage your tangle of 115 volt cables, and simplify shutting down your entire system. This can be combined with a **surge suppressor** for spikes in your lines.
- An **uninterruptible power supply** if your voltage drops or goes out. (See **6. Protecting your tools.**)
- A **mouse** pointing tool to take advantage of the graphic interfaces that are coming to dominate most computers.
- Or perhaps the alternative, a **trackball**, similar to those you'll find in arcade games, for navigating quickly around a large screen. If you're an illustrator, you might check out Wacom's pressure-sensitive tablets.
- Extra **cables** with the right kind of plug at the end, so you have them when you need them. For printers, monitors, and external hard disks or modems, extra cables will also speed troubleshooting. Micro Computer Cable Co., (313) 941-6574, is the lowest cost vendor we've found. You can pay only by check or C.O.D.
- A **tablet** to use as a more precise drawing tool if you're doing much illustration.
- A box of 50 or 100 **floppy disks**, so you don't have to scrounge around, and you can treat them like candy bars. No reason for you to have to pester someone for forgetting to return your disk.
- Treat yourself to a few useful accessories, like a **speakerphone** with auto-dialing, so you can type and talk, and work while waiting on hold for technical support; a good **copy holder**; a quality magnifying glass or **loupe**; and a large polyurethane kitchen **cutting board** for pasteups.
- It's nice to have protective **mailers** for disks and for mechanicals. When you need to send camera-ready pages or photos to someone, and don't have cardboard handy, draw on your supply of rigid letter envelopes from Federal Express, Airborne, UPS, or the Postal Service. Don't feel guilty, especially if you're giving them business.
- Special **laser printer paper** for your final camera-ready pages. Hammermill Laser Plus is the most popular. Also look at Mohawk Poseidon Premium Laser Text, from any paper supplier, and Laser Edge, from CG Graphics Arts Supply, (212) 925-5332. Do a series of tests with different papers and different typefaces and sizes. (See **Fig. 8.1 Printer resolution test page.**) You'll find ads offering paper sampler assortments in the DTP magazines.

- **Printing paper samples**: Keep a stock of a few types of high-quality 25% and 100% rag (cotton) bond paper, in white, off-white, and gray, in flat and linen finishes, for emergencies, and to give clients a preview of finished publications from offset printers. Accumulate sample books from Mohawk, Hammermill, Warren, Strathmore, Nekoosa and others, so you can bid on printing jobs using standard industry papers, and so you can show clients samples.

And, because we can never find that table of equivalents for printing paper types when we need it, here it is. Use the last column to calculate mailing costs.

Bond	=	Text (Offset)	=	Cover	Weight of 1,000 sheets
20#	=	50#	=	27#	9.84 pounds
24#	=	60#	=	33#	11.80 pounds
28#	=	70#	=	38#	13.76 pounds
32#	=	80#	=	44#	15.74 pounds
47#	=	119#	=	65#	23.38 pounds

In addition to the obvious office supplies, you'll need a good **reference library**, including the *Chicago Manual of Style* (Chicago University Press, 1989, $37.50) or *The Chicago Guide to Preparing Electronic Manuscripts for Authors and Publishers* ($9.95); M. Skillin and R. Gay, *Words Into Type* (Prentice-Hall, 1986, $39.95); Kate L. Turabian's *A Manual for Writers of Term Papers, Theses and Dissertations* (University of Chicago Press, 1987, $7.95), for academic work; an up-to-date almanac; a one-volume encyclopedia; an unabridged dictionary; and a list of current postal rates, size, and mailing regulations. These will all come in handy to deal with clients' questions on the spot.

Options

You don't have to go overboard on first purchases. For some peripherals, *ready access* may work just fine, at the start or even for the long term.

- **Disk conversions**: If you won't need to read different size and format floppy disks frequently, you can use another DTPer's or service bureau's setup. (Though it is handy to be able to tell a client who drops off a disk, "Wait, let me make sure *while you're here* that I can read your data.") Otherwise, you could buy an external drive, from Dayna Corp. or others, that reads the disk formats you need. Mostly this is for Mac users who want to read 5¼-inch PC disks, since any Mac with the newer SuperDrive can read the 3½-inch PC disks.

- If you don't expect to telecommunicate immediately, you can live for a little while without a **modem** and the time it takes to master it—though you'll surely miss one the first time you're in a rush or a crisis that you could best handle with a five-minute electronic file transfer.

> Modems are one way to keep in touch with the world when I'm a prisoner in my studio and don't want to be isolated. I need my privacy. I need my concentration. That's the reason I'm stuck here, because the kind of work I do can't be done with a casual approach. I need to have my little enclave, but I also need to be in touch with the rest of the world. I have an assistant, and often we work at different locations and communicate by modem. For information, I can leave questions on a public forum and get the question answered in a reasonably short time. And of course, I use it for clients to send me their text. One client sends me virtually everything directly from an IBM to my Mac. The modem is one way of helping me reach out while I'm here.   —*Rick Barry*

- If you have easy access to a colleague's **scanner**, you may not need one of your own for a while. The same holds for a **photocopier** and **fax machine**—going to a copy shop or stationery store is cheap and convenient. Live without them until you feel the trouble outweighs the cost. On the other hand, it is true that you and your clients will appreciate the convenience of your having a photocopier. Don't forget that most faxes can make copies on thermal paper of single pages. And in a pinch, you can even enlist your scanner and laser printer to copy a page: It's not efficient, but it works.
- A **binding machine** is a useful item to have. (We give you some sources in **9. Help clients visualize the final piece.**)
- And though the price of **color printers** is falling rapidly, the quality is still low. Unless you're in the advertising business, you're probably better off using a service bureau for color proofs.

If you absolutely must have one of these peripherals, but the price tag fazes you, consider shared ownership. Think about buying any of these items, as well as a backup second computer system, with one or two other DTPers. Write an agreement with a mutual buyout clause in case you need a business divorce.

PC versus Macintosh

Until recently, people starting out in DTP would usually pick an Apple Macintosh unless they already owned an IBM PC or a PC clone, or were already at home in the world of MS-DOS. The Macintosh was built from the ground up as a graphics computer. In fact, the pixel or dot size for the original screens of the first nine-inch Macs was set at 72 dots per inch with typesetting point sizes in mind. From its start in 1984, the Mac was known for WYSIWYG. The Macintosh was the first successful commercialization of the microcomputer **graphic user interface** (GUI) where the user interacts with the computer by pointing, clicking, and dragging on **icons**—graphic representations of types of data and actions.

The Mac's simplicity in matching and linking input, display and output devices, and its consistent interface, where most applications can be operated and controlled in similar, intuitive, and familiar ways, have meant that people who were more interested in results than in computers could have an easier time learning software and producing work. With the Mac, you need to learn only once how to open, save, and print a file. That saves time and reduces anxiety. When polled, people who use Macs are familiar with and use many more software packages than their PC-based colleagues.

From the point of view of DTP software designers, the Mac has been the superior machine. With the exception of Ventura Software (formerly Xerox) Ventura Publisher, most of the important and innovative DTP software was developed first for the Mac. Some packages, such as Adobe Illustrator, Aldus PageMaker, Computer Associates Cricket Presents and Microsoft PowerPoint, have since been ported, or converted, into PC versions. And Aldus has sold more copies of the PC version of PageMaker than of its Mac version.

Yet the Macintosh has also always been a relatively more expensive machine. Even the Mac's lower cost Classic, LC, and IIsi, aimed more at business and school users than at DTPers, are price-competitive only with IBM and Compaq, not with other PC clones.

The Mac also tends to crash (inconveniently but not fatally) more frequently than PCs. Part of this instability has resulted from the demanding nature of graphic software, which puts much more of a strain on a computer's resources than most applications.

DTP and multimedia are virtually the only applications where the Mac has staked out a convincing position of superiority. But with the introduction of Microsoft Windows 3, a better case now exists for the PC as a competitive DTP platform. For the first time, the PC has a speedy and functional icon-based interface. It's a graphic environment superimposed successfully on top of MS-

DOS, which remains a character-based system. With Windows, you still need to understand the somewhat intimidating DOS file system, with its rules for naming files and setting up paths and hierarchies. And it breaks what is unified on the Macintosh into two distinct and inconsistent concepts: the Program Manager and the File Manager. Nevertheless, it is far ahead of the old C> prompt that used to greet PC users.

> There's a tremendous amount of Windows software development. This means more software sharing the same fonts and printer/screen drivers, more software with the potential for easier exchange of data and graphics between different packages, and more software with graphical interfaces that don't look much different from Macintosh software. However, now that I'm using Windows 3.0, a complicated environment that taps into more of the system's resources than older PC programs, I'm running into incompatibilities with my IBM-compatible computer, and the kinds of system crashes that people experience on the Macintosh. Mac software is often a step ahead, but given the difference in startup costs, being at the technical cutting edge may be less important than being able to afford the tools to do the work you've decided to do.   —*Rich Metter*

> As soon as Ventura for Windows comes out, I'm converting. I don't know if people will migrate from Mac to Windows, but the argument that people make about Macintosh and the icon-based graphic interface will disappear and won't be an issue anymore.   —*Susan Glinert Stevens*

Though the Mac's graphic capabilities are still superior, and keystroke compatibility for commands and interface among different packages is still largely an unrealized goal for PC software, the PC has taken the lead in some areas, especially database typesetting and printing speed. The PC buyer also has the reassuring advantage of being able to buy a central processing unit from any one of dozens of vendors. Yet the Mac remains ahead in the areas of color manipulation and output. For instance, **calibrated color monitors** are not yet available for the PC. Both Mac and PC now have some forms of **multitasking** (the ability to switch between applications very rapidly, and in some cases, run several applications simultaneously). Both Microsoft's Dynamic Data Exchange and Apple's Interapplication Communication allow applications to work together in sharing data and completing jobs. Both are being extended steadily to provide more capabilities.

On the horizon for the PC is OS/2 Presentation Manager, a more advanced operating system than Windows, with improved memory management and smoother multitasking. It's been introduced, but few applications run with it. There are still many incompatibilities and missing elements that will eventually ensure that monitors and printers all work well together. And it requires more powerful hardware to run well. Most PC users are sticking with Windows 3.

Quarterdeck Office Systems DESQview is a multi-tasking windowing environment that preceded Windows. Some PC-based DTPers have been using DESQview for quite a while, and now are running it along with Windows to achieve even more flexibility, particularly when they still heavily use applications not available in a Windows-compatible version.

Features and speed have become a game of leapfrog. Every few months, one of the players meets and beats its opponent's performance levels.

Though it's now more of a horse race, for general practice DTPers, if you can spend the extra money, we think the Mac retains its edge. It's easier to focus on the main issues—learning and using a wide variety of tools, and making money with them—with the Mac. Among graphic designers, graphic software developers, temporary employment agencies for graphics, and imagesetter service bureaus, the Mac predominates.

That said, if you have good reasons to pick the PC, your choice won't prevent you from succeeding in DTP. A survey of *Personal Publishing* readers found that 60% describe the PC as their main platform, 40% the Mac. As software becomes available on both platforms, some of the rationale for the Mac's superiority diminishes. Certainly the gap between the platforms is narrowing. A key issue is where innovative product developers choose to focus future efforts. It could be that over time, the tens of millions of PCs will by their sheer numbers eclipse the Mac, even in the graphic realm.

Other platforms

You can be a desktop publisher with **Atari's** technologically fine equipment, saving money on your hardware starter set. But you're limited to a few packages.

> My wife and I had an idea for a magazine we wanted to produce. We didn't start *The Prufrock Journal, The Journal of Secondary Gifted Education* for the money, but rather saw a real need for it in education. And it was something we could do together. However, we couldn't make a big investment in hardware and software. There was a limit to what we could get in loans and we didn't want to go scrounging. Our entire Atari system, minus the software, was $3,200. The DTP software was $299. We knew we wanted DTP technology because we were holding down two jobs and didn't have time for cutting and pasting.

The Atari's biggest drawback is its lack of compatibility with other platforms, but it's not as great a problem as one might imagine. Calamus, my DTP software, is able to import and export both Mac and IBM Encapsulated PostScript files and TIFF, GEM, and IMG graphic files. And, because WordPerfect files are completely transferable between the Mac, IBM, and the Atari version of WordPerfect, we have a great deal of text processing flexibility.

We are now using both the Mac and the Atari platforms extensively in our business. The Atari gave us a wonderfully inexpensive way to begin a successful business. We used some of the profits from that business to purchase and implement our Macintosh system. Both platforms offer advantages and we are able to reap the benefits from both. But we could never have started and built our journal without the extremely low startup costs the Atari offered.   *—Joel McIntosh*

Amiga is another technologically advanced and lower cost system whose primary attraction is for people interested in multimedia rather than DTP. However, some software is becoming available for this platform.

The **NeXT** machine shows promise as an advanced system with some excellent software. Currently, it's the only desktop platform to use the PostScript page description language to map the screen image as well as the printed page. This is advantageous but not essential. Major software publishers promise key products in 1991. The NeXT may succeed in becoming a competitor in the marketplace, but for now, as with the Atari, despite the technical excellence of the machine, if you choose NeXT, you'll be placing yourself outside the DTP mainstream, without gaining any significant capabilities.

Then come the **workstations**, like Sun Microsystems and Apollo, which began as engineers' tools, but are also used for highly-efficient large document production. They use the UNIX operating system and its variants, like OSF Motif and XWindows. FrameMaker, now available for the Macintosh and NeXT, and Interleaf Publisher, now available for the Macintosh and PC, both are available on many UNIX workstations. But unless you work as part of a team where this equipment is already in place, you'll have little reason to consider these platforms.

If you work with anything other than a PC or Macintosh, you won't benefit from help and support from the large community of established DTPers. You'll have a harder time finding freelance or subcontracting work or workers. And you may not be able to give back to your clients the files you create for them in a form they can use.

Your software starter kit

You can begin with a few essential pieces of software. The terminology here is **applications**—software designed to manipulate data. Think in terms of packages that will match the requirements for your system in **What to get first**, listed above, enabling you to:

- Create new text and graphics;
- Work with existing text and graphics;
- Provide a variety of output formats;
- Use the computer to help you run your business.

For the basic software packages, we list the leading applications most DTPers use for the PC and Mac. You won't go wrong with any of these, though you could find a good reason to supplement these packages or replace them with others. If you work with both PCs and Macs, you'll find it to your advantage to choose software available for both platforms. If you decide to standardize on Windows for the PC, you may decide to eliminate from consideration packages that aren't compatible with that operating system.

Word processor

On day one, get a high-end (feature-rich) word processor. You'll use it to enter data yourself and to clean up and transform text or word processor files that clients give you. Pick a package with typesetting capabilities: the ability to size type, specify fonts, and produce multiple columns.

Mastering these features is a fine way to become familiar with many DTP concepts and terminology. Sometimes you may complete entire DTP jobs using this software. It will come in handy as well when your clients start asking you questions and you can advise them about using their word processors to best advantage.

Mac: Microsoft Word; others are Ashton-Tate FullWrite Professional, WordPerfect Corporation WordPerfect, Paragon Concepts Nisus, TMaker WriteNow, and Claris MacWrite. Zedcor DeskWrite or Preferred Publishers Vantage desk accessory can make up for features lacking in Word, such as converting upper case text to upper and lower case.

PC: WordPerfect, Microsoft Word, and XyQuest XyWrite (pronounced zi-write) all are now or will soon be compatible with Windows. All have advanced typographical capabilities. Others are Ashton-Tate Multimate, Micropro Wordstar, and IBM Displaywrite. Some of the lower cost packages may not handle the **extended character sets** (technical letters, accent marks, and dingbat characters) that you'll need for DTP.

> You really have only three choices. Word is the most graphically oriented package. WordPerfect is the most popular, with the largest number of books and users to help you. XyWrite is hardest to learn, easiest to customize, and used widely in large installations.
> —*Luther Sperberg, publications specialist, Wheeler-Hawkins, NYC*

Graphics software

This doesn't have to be fancy. Even if you believe you lack artistic talent, you'll need to be able to create rudimentary solid and shaded figures, rotated type, tables, and graphs. On the other hand, if drawing or illustration is your strong point, get more than one package. You'll find far more differentiation in features and orientation among graphics than among word processor packages.

Mac: Adobe Illustrator or Aldus FreeHand. Supplementing these may be Claris MacDraw, Deneba Canvas, or Aldus/Silicon Beach SuperPaint, and Electronic Arts Studio/8 and Studio/32, or SuperMac PixelPaint for color painting. Utility applications like Broderbund TypeStyler, Adobe Smart Art and Adobe TypeAlign, and Zedcor DeskDraw are handy for creating quick special effects with type and graphics.

> FreeHand and Illustrator are both marvellous. FreeHand has layers, precise text control, and lets you work in preview mode. Illustrator automatically splits complex paths so they will print (*very* valuable), has the most natural feel—once you're used to it—and seems to me to output the smoothest, sexiest curves. Had Marilyn Monroe seen them, she would have been jealous. Both are shipping new versions any minute now so their relative strengths and weaknesses might change. Choose between them? Thank heavens, I don't have to.   —*Margaret Styne*

PC: CorelDRAW (which comes with a particularly good bonus collection of typefaces) or Micrografx Designer; also Computer Support Corporation Arts & Letters, Illustrator, and Digital Research Artline (using the GEM interface).

Page layout software

This is the key intersection of all your work. You'll import much of the material you create using your word processor and graphics software into files created with this package. This is usually where you'll finish most jobs.

> Page layout software is my design environment—where I assemble all the elements created by other tools.   —*Rick Barry*

Mac: Aldus PageMaker is the best-selling package. It's easy to learn and can handle practically any job. It's very stable, especially when it comes to using different fonts, exchanging files between computers, and printing to imagesetters. Quark Inc. QuarkXPress wins on the power and features tally, and is preferred by those who want to control every element of their page down to a thousandth of a point. Of course, PageMaker is catching up in features, and QuarkXPress in stability and ease of use. Other excellent packages are Xerox Ventura Software Ventura Publisher and Frame Technology FrameMaker, especially for long documents, and Letraset U.S.A. DesignStudio. Interleaf Company Interleaf Publisher, a major package, is comparatively weak on typographic controls and interface, but good for long documents. RagTime USA RagTime 3 combines a spreadsheet, word processor, and less powerful page layout module. Multi-Ad Services Multi-Ad Creator has very powerful and unusual features for single page layouts and display ads.

> I send corporate art directors to PageMaker, professional designers to Quark, and Ventura if they need to create tables.   —*Luther Sperberg*

PC: Ventura Publisher Gold Series (PS/2, Windows, or DOS GEM edition) is the best-selling package; PageMaker for the PC is popular especially for those who design single pages intensively, as compared to long documents, and for those who produce publications on both platforms. There are other packages, but none you could consider as your first, and perhaps only, page layout tool.

PageMaker has long been available for both Macs and PCs; Ventura Publisher has recently added a Macintosh version; Quark has announced its intention to release Windows and OS/2 versions of QuarkXPress in 1991.

> Most work can be done with PageMaker or Ventura, but I wouldn't recommend one over the other. It's best to let the type of document dictate which to use. Ventura is fast, powerful, rewards pre-planning and shines with long, consistent, multi-chapter documents. I respect it enormously but it's not much fun to use. PageMaker, on the other hand is a delight—it invites experimentation, encourages you to ask, "What if," and will do just about anything you ask it to. A four-fold flyer, a 200-page guide, a showcard, an inch-tall magazine to put in a doll's house— whatever you can think of. Design in PageMaker/execute in Ventura works well for some corporate templates, especially when lots of different people will be churning out pages. I'm looking forward to using Ventura on the Mac as well as the PC. I may learn QuarkXPress. Clients are beginning to ask about it.   —*Margaret Styne*

Some page layout software allows you to use add-ons for particular types of publications. In particular, to automate the conversion of database or other files, and to track versions of files for multi-user publishing, check out ElseWare DataShaper as well as EDCO Services ChangeRight and PM Designer for PageMaker; North Atlantic Publishing Systems CopyFlow, Em Software Xdata, and Managing Editor Software Page Director for QuarkXPress; and Letraset DesignScript Annex for DesignStudio. Oracle Software has announced but not yet shipped products linking PageMaker with Oracle's database products for mainframes, minicomputers, and microcomputers. For Ventura Publisher, look at Aristocad VP Data, Digital Composition Systems dbPublisher, SNA VPToolbox, and the package of utilities in Metroplex Digital Editor's Desk Set.

Most word processor and page layout software's style sheets are paragraph-oriented, which makes sense for most publications. Depending on the kind of work you do, you may want to look into software that enables you to use character-oriented style sheets. FrameMaker and DesignStudio have this capability.

Don't worry at this point about choosing the software you'll use forever. At the same time, don't be tempted to start with one of the modest low-end products, like Spinnaker Software Springboard Publisher, Timeworks Publish-It!, or PFS First Publisher, which, though getting better, won't give you the control and features you'll need for the range of jobs you'll be doing. Choose among the main competitors. Pick the one that appeals to you most, seems easiest to learn, or has features you're sure you can't live without.

Expect, in a few months, to spring for a second package if it turns out you chose wrong or are still hungry. You may be lucky enough to hit on a trade-in offer, where from time to time, also-rans or new contenders try to attract purchasers with special offers to registered owners of top packages. As in mastering foreign languages, you'll find it easier to learn the second package. And at that point, you'll have twice the marketable skills.

For one measure of the popularity of software used by DTPers, a survey of imagesetting service bureaus (reported in *Typeworld*'s second June 1990 issue) found that the original programs, PageMaker and Illustrator, accounted for 45% of all printout pages, while upstarts QuarkXPress and FreeHand accounted for 30%. Almost 75% of all service bureau work was Macintosh.

If you're plugged in with other DTPers, it's worth your while to pick packages that they use. You'll be able to work on jobs together. And it helps to be able to call on a colleague in a crisis, which invariably comes when the manufacturer's technical support is closed for the night or weekend.

Business software

You'll need one or more special packages if you intend to computerize the business side of your operation. Start by looking at integrated software that combines a database, spreadsheet, and word processor (and sometimes charting and telecommunications as well). You'll find the business parts of such an integrated program easier to learn, and the software will require less memory than high-end spreadsheets and databases.

You'll use this software to create mailing lists and budgets. And though many people do their invoices with a word processor, using a database or spreadsheet will bring many benefits. (See **12. Make a smart invoice**.) Make sure any integrated package you get can save or export data in formats read by leading stand-alone databases and spreadsheets. That way, if the individual components of this package turn out to be underpowered for your needs, you can upgrade painlessly. If you aren't sure about all this, ask for help from a knowledgeable database expert—or risk major troubles later. For both PC and Mac, Microsoft Works is a good integrated package.

If all you're doing is keeping your phone book or addresses on the computer, you may want to look at personal organizer software, including Portfolio Systems DynoDex for the Mac or PC, or Borland SideKick for the PC.

Operating system utilities

Get the most up-to-date software version matched to your hardware. If you use an old version, you're setting yourself up for incompatibilities with the latest versions of your applications software.

For the Macintosh, Systems 6.0.5 and 6.0.7 are stable and work with all applications. It's too early to tell with System 7. Essential system add-ons and utilities for System 6 include CE Software DiskTop and the shareware Boomerang or Now Software SuperBoomerang for file management. Add Symantec Utilities or Norton Utilities for multi-purpose file and disk management and protection.

For the PC, Windows 3 provides the graphic interface needed by DTPers, as does the more costly and more memory-demanding OS/2. Key utilities are XTree Company XTreePro Gold, Norton Commander for disk management, Fifth Generation Systems The Mace Utilities, Central Point Software PC Tools

Deluxe, and Norton Utilities Advanced Edition, for multi-purpose file and disk management. QEMM is for expanded memory management, Multisoft Super PC-Kwik for disk caching, and Laser Tools PrintCache to speed printing. You may not need all these add-ons if you use Windows, which has its own file management, print spooling, and caching utilities.

> With PostScript you need to be concerned about printing time, and PrintCache allows printing to take place in background mode.
>
> —*Lynn Walterick*

To bring together a group of Macintoshes, or a mixed group of Macs and PCs, Sitka Network Bundle (formerly TOPS) is the smoothest low-cost networking package.

Conversion utilities

You'll need these to exchange files with different formats. To convert files between PC and Macintosh formats, keeping intact as much of the information as possible, DataViz MacLink has the greatest number of translators, followed by MasterSoft Word for Word. MacLink translators are included as part of Sitka Network Bundle. But even with the best software, you'll still have work to do. (See **Fig. 7.3 Sequence for converting client files.**) On the Mac, Ventura is better than PageMaker in converting PC graphics.

On the Macintosh, most graphics applications software will convert some formats; Adobe Photoshop has the most translators.

For the PC, Systems Compatibility Corp. Software Bridge, and Word for Word Professional converts between different word processors. Inset Systems Hijaak or HSC Software The Graphics Link Plus convert and modify graphic formats. Ventura also works well as a file converter.

Protection

For details, see **6. Protecting It All.** Some functions are included in the operating system utilities listed above. In any case, you'll need:

- A **backup** system that's painless to use;
- A **utility** to find, sort, rename, and move files rapidly;
- An **un-deleter** to retrieve files you've accidentally removed (usually you've only deleted them from the directory, but they're still on the disk);
- A utility to **tune-up** your hard disk by consolidating files spread out in fragments;
- Rescue software to **diagnose** (and often retrieve and repair) damaged floppy disks and hard drives;

- A **screen saver** to keep from burning in your screen unevenly if you leave the monitor on and unchanging for long periods;
- Depending on your work environment, you may want a **security system** so anyone trying to copy or examine your data will need your password.

Fonts

Get a good selection beyond those built into the operating system, applications, and laser printer. Get at least one **serif** and one **sans serif** face in a large range of weights and widths, as well as a choice of attractive display faces for headlines. (Serifs are the little notches you see in the body type of this book; its headline type is sans serif without notches.) Even though Times and Helvetica, or their clone equivalents, come standard with most software and printers, you'll need the expanded family of condensed and expanded, light and black, in addition to the usual regular, bold, italic and bold italic for Helvetica in particular. When you shop for typefaces, make sure a vendor's price includes at least the standard family of four styles. (Some confusion remains because typographers traditionally called each type style and size a font, but that nomenclature has disappeared among DTPers.)

For the Mac, the industry standard is Adobe fonts. Make sure fonts from other vendors are in the Adobe Type 1 format that improves type reproduction at small sizes. For the PC, Bitstream fonts have been the industry standard for the HP LaserJet and its clones.

Adobe fonts are also gaining in popularity for PCs, and are the only typefaces you can be sure that every imagesetting service bureau will have available. If you use Monotype, Compugraphic, Treacy, or other fonts, you may have to supply the service bureau with copies of your fonts.

For Macs or PCs, Adobe Type Manager (ATM) significantly improves the representation of type on the screen, though it demands lots of memory and slows down your system. For the PC, Adobe typefaces, ATM, and a PostScript cartridge for a HP LaserJet printer is an excellent combination. Bitstream has announced FaceLift, a product similar to ATM for generation of accurate type on screen.

A competitor to PostScript in font and page imaging technology, sponsored by Microsoft as TrueImage and by Apple as TrueType, is just coming to the market, and has yet to demonstrate any significant advantages for DTPers over existing solutions.

> Adobe's faces are a little more regularized than those from other foundries, lighter and with less thick and thin variations. New users tend to prefer this and old hands to deplore it. It's like beer connoisseurs who prefer a beer with more taste, while the great mass of people find some beers *too* tasty.   —*Luther Sperberg*

Don't be seduced by cheap fonts: $100 for 100 typefaces you'll never use may be less valuable to you than one or two solid but higher-priced performers.

Some operating systems require utility software to facilitate storing, loading, and printing a wide variety of fonts. For the PC, look at ZSoft SoftType and Isogon FontSpace. For the Mac, you can use Fifth Generation Systems Suitcase or ALSoft MasterJuggler.

For the Mac, whatever typefaces you use, get a copy of the screen fonts your imagesetting service bureau uses. But avoid using Suitcase's Merge utility to combine variants of typefaces. It can create potential problems in identifying which face you're using when you move the file to another machine or send it to a service bureau. Adobe Type Reunion achieves the same end—reducing the number of type names on your menus—without complicating your font identity structures.

Options

You may want, but be able to live without, these additional items:

- Some software packages incorporate the ability to write **macros** (keyboard shortcuts for multi-step actions). For freestanding macro writing, use CE Software QuicKeys or Affinity Microsystems Tempo for the Mac, Alpha Software Keyworks or shareware NewKey for the PC.
- You may feel you need a more elaborate package for **business graphics**, such as pie and bar charts. For the Mac, DeltaPoint DeltaGraph, or Informix Wingz are good choices. You can do basic graphics with Microsoft Excel or Computer Associates CricketGraph. Adobe Illustrator's latest version for the Mac combines charting with advanced embellishments. Aldus Persuasion is available for the Mac and PC. For the PC, look at Software Publishing Harvard Graphics and Lotus Freelance Plus.
- For **presentation graphics**, overhead transparencies and slides, a drawing program may suffice at the start. Later, for the Mac, Aldus Persuasion, PowerPoint, Computer Associates Cricket Presents or Symantec MORE. For the PC, look at Microsoft PowerPoint, Micrografx Charisma, Cricket Presents, WordPerfect Corp. DrawPerfect, Xenographics Pixie, Freelance Plus, and Ashton-Tate Applause II.

- If you get a modem, you'll need **telecommunications software** (unless it's part of your integrated business package). For the Mac, Software Ventures Microphone combines simplicity with power. Datastorm Technologies ProComm and Microstuf CrossTalk are for the PC, and Smartcom is available for the Mac or the PC. (Novices tell us that mastering the ins and outs of modems is the hardest part of computer literacy.)
- Some people like **grammar checkers.** They are helpful if you type a lot and if your word processor's spell-checker doesn't pick up such mistakes as "the the" and unmatched open and closed parentheses.
- Unless it's part of your operating system, look into **spoolers** that quickly return control of your computer from printing tasks. If you get one, you may need more random access memory (RAM) for your computer.

Advanced and specialized software

Depending on your background and your estimate of potential business opportunities, you may want software for **animation, 3-D drafting, creating fonts,** or **multimedia** presentations. Don't rush into it. You have enough to learn at the start without further complicating your life. The same goes for any elaborate color software. Unless you know where you're heading, and are already comfortable with the basic DTP packages, wait until you need these capabilities, at which point you'll be a better shopper.

Your first specialized software may give you the ability to **manipulate scanned images.** For the Mac, take a look at Letraset ImageStudio or Silicon Beach Digital Darkroom for gray-scale manipulations, and Adobe Photoshop or Letraset ColorStudio for color manipulation. For the PC, gray-scale editors include Astral Development Picture Publisher, Image-In Inc. Image-In Plus, ZSoft PC Paintbrush, and Xerox Imaging Systems Gray F/X.

Compatibility

As you pick out your hardware and software, make sure everything works together. That doesn't mean getting reassurance from the salesperson at the store or on the other side of an 800 line. It means *seeing* particular pieces of hardware and software plugged in and talking to each other. The weakest links are usually output devices. If the video display and the printer both work with the central processor, you're probably in good shape.

Ideally, compatibility should go a step beyond the operating level. Some manufacturers specifically design, or as they say, **optimize**, their products for others. A page layout program can take advantage of particular features in a particular word processor. For instance, styling text and moving it back and forth between PageMaker and Word is very smooth.

Some packages contain modules to operate scanners within graphics software. Some packages establish **hot links** connecting data in different applications, so changes in one file are immediately reflected in the other. And you'll hear of third-party utility software that makes packages like XyWrite and Ventura Publisher even more compatible. As you read the reviews and talk to other DTPers, you'll be able to cluster logical choices into highly productive extended software families.

It's a major challenge to make good decisions as you assemble your tools. Once you're established, your goal is to have the most productive equipment possible within your budget. You'll find quality at the low end as well as at the high end. We look for advanced but proven tools. We try to buy products that enable us to do our work well, and, if possible, give us capabilities that distinguish us from other DTPers. The decisions aren't usually too difficult in shopping for the central processor. But storage media, printers, scanners, monitors and software come in many flavors.

You're confronted by too many options. To make shopping worse, vendors don't simply tout their existing capabilities. They tempt you with upgrades that promise to match the competition's features, remedy all shortcomings, and ship, in one of the computer world's favorite phrases, "real soon now."

You need to worry about future compatibility as well. It's always a challenge to find the conservatively innovative product. You try to pick the advanced tools that are predictors of the general direction of mainstream technology. The worst decision is to buy into a solution that turns out to be incompatible or irrelevant—a dead end because the standards evolve in another direction.

Ownership

Our basic principle: Get everything you need to become a reliable freestanding business.

For hardware, that doesn't necessarily mean buying it all outright or brand new. We've already mentioned the option of shared purchases. There's also no reason not to buy properly-functioning used hardware. If you buy it through a computer brokerage service, find out if they check out the equipment. If you buy it privately (on a physical or electronic bulletin board, through a user group, or from a newspaper ad), take along someone who can test the unit out, or bargain with the seller to split the cost of a store inspection or a service contract pre-qualification checkup. (See **Appendix 2. Resources for buying and selling used computers.**)

If you're short on cash and can't get a bank loan, sometimes a computer equipment manufacturer or store will open a charge account for you—usually, of course, at higher interest than a bank. Avoid using your everyday credit card, with the highest interest short of loan sharks, to finance your purchases. It may be a good idea to buy hardware with a credit card that extends the manufacturer's original warranty term (read the fine print to make sure it applies). But then pay it off with cheaper money from some other source.

If you're in a special tax situation or you can't afford a major expense at once, consider leasing. The IRS treats types of leases differently depending on the buyout provisions at the end of the lease. Rules on depreciation and expensing of costs vary, so consult your accountant. If you arrange for a lease directly from the manufacturer, you probably won't get discounted prices. Leasing, or leasing with a right to purchase at the end of the lease, can be expensive. But if your nest egg is small, you'll find dozens of deals out there, from manufacturers, stores, national and local leasing companies, and banks. Usually these arrangements will be cheaper than the monthly rental fees from national companies like General Electric and others. Figure out the pros and cons by consulting your accountant.

Software is another story. Compared to hardware, you'll find a greater variation in price within software categories. You'll find the heavy-duty industry leaders, with packages priced between $500 and $1,500. (Ironically, some costly items started out under $200, but their publishers found they didn't get credibility and attention as major players until they boosted their price tags to serious corporate levels.) Then you'll find the contenders, claiming to be easier to use, or to match the feature set of the best-selling packages, at prices from $100 to about $500.

You'll also find highly affordable applications and utility packages under $100. Some are **shareware** programs, available free from user groups or computer bulletin boards. Shareware usually flashes a screen upon startup, requesting a modest registration fee. As a reward for your honesty you may get notice of updates, better documentation, and occasionally even technical support. A few products have received enough user support to remain shareware. And some popular, low-priced packages began as public-domain **freeware** or shareware, then evolved into commercial but still low-priced products. Among the most famous for MS-DOS are PC-Write (word processor), Procomm (communications), PC-File and FileExpress (database), As Easy As (spreadsheet), and PKZip (file compression); for the Macintosh, Red Ryder (telecommunications—renamed White Knight as commercial software), StuffIt (file compression), Boomerang (file navigation) and Disinfectant (virus protection). A good source for PC and Mac shareware is the Public Software Library of Houston, (800) 242-4775. The Printer's Shareware Catalog, (214) 350-1902, lists mostly PC public domain and shareware software for DTPers. Or check your local user group.

Piracy

Then along comes a complication: a helpful DTP friend who offers to let you try out that snazzy package....

In the past, electronic or mechanical keys and copy-protection made nightmares of upgrades, hard disk management, and backup. Fortunately, the days of protected software are nearly over. As result, duplicating most software is a snap. For some of the most popular software from the early eighties, industry analysts estimate there are five to ten times more unregistered users than legal owners. Software companies believe that high sales figures for "how to use XYZ package" books reflect, in part, a large population of pirates using the software without access to the original manuals.

In computer publications, you'll find ads from software publishing associations, rightly pointing out, first, that software piracy is a crime punishable by law, and second, that the continued refinement of existing products and development of future products depends on income from software sales. You'll hear of software companies offering site licenses or deep discounts for multiple copies. That's proof that piracy extends from individual users to major corporations. And you'll read of lawsuits where publishers claim infringement on their original product by manufacturers of competing software.

In these same publications, from time to time you'll also find articles and letters presenting the users' viewpoint. Many find software overpriced. Some feel snared by high upgrade charges and poor or costly technical support. Still others complain of having to buy products sight unseen. DTPers bemoan in particular the cost of typefaces. Having bought everything else, now they feel they're constantly buying high-priced razor blades.

Of course, software takes lots of time and money to develop, and the creators and risk-takers deserve compensation and encouragement to continue putting money back into improved products. At the same time, some of the users' gripes are on the mark.

We'll stick to the practical issues from your perspective as you start a DTP business. We can't tell you to refuse righteously every friendly offer of a preview. It's great to be able to explore a package at your leisure in your office—testing it *before* deciding what to buy. (You have legal alternatives. Some software publishers sell demo disks, and major mail-order software sellers now offer 10-day to one-year money-back guarantees on many products.)

Whatever you do, as soon as you start using a package on actual jobs, we urge you to buy it. Software *is* expensive to design and sell. And if it helps you make money, you can't really justify remaining a pirate.

What's more, until you register a product, you're using it in the dark. Of course, your friend may not be around when the next upgrade comes out. The how-to books are intended to supplement the tutorials and manuals that come inside the shrink-wrap, and are not always available at the same time as the software is released, so you can't be sure to get the best use from the product without the original documentation. You'll want to be notified of minor maintenance upgrades, and be able to call the company when you're in trouble. If you in any way depend on a product, you have every reason to legally own it.

The principle holds for typefaces, and for those handy utilities like screen savers, games, and novelty items that are so easily passed around. If you use it all the time, pay for it. Especially if it's a shareware product distributed in good faith by some inspired programmer who is probably poorer than you. You'll feel better in the morning.

Retailers, VARs, and mail order

We assume you'll start with better than a minimum system, one that can handle the latest software for everything but the highest-end applications, and won't make you go out for coffee while you wait for the screen image to redraw. We figure you don't intend to squint into a small screen. And we know you want to pay street prices, which will be significantly lower than dealer list. Unless you're buying everything in one shot from a local store or consultant who's giving you a package deal and some credible promise of help, you're better off shopping around for each part of your system.

> Research everything carefully, and don't look for the cheapest program, the cheapest scanner. Just try to get the best deal on the best scanner, the best laser printer. —*Steven Gorney*

If you're not confident about your computer skills, it's a good idea to buy your basic system from a local dealer with a reputation for support and knowledgeable service technicians. You'll find it's worth the extra five percent or so. Alternatively, you may hook up with a **value added reseller** (VAR)—a company that gains the right to buy hardware at wholesale prices by bundling it for retail sale along with software, training, or some other product or service adding value to the original product.

Don't expect to get anything for nothing. Periodically (even in the high-class computer industry) companies advertise unbelievable deals. In 1987, a printing company called S.L. Graves, advertising in the major national Macintosh publications, sold copies of PageMaker and XPress to people who shelled out the $700 list price for these packages. In exchange, they were supposed to get not only the software, but $1,000 of free printing. The unlucky buyers at least received the software, but when they called the company to arrange for printing, they found the number had been disconnected.

In particular, for *software*, since none of your technical assistance will come from the retailer, there's little reason not to buy it from a reputable 800 number mail-order company, strictly by price and availability. You'll find the mail-order software at least 10% cheaper than the discounted retail dealer prices. Most mail-order companies don't charge for shipping, and don't add sales tax to out-of-state orders. We've heard raves and never a complaint about PC Connection, (800) 776-7777 and MacConnection, (800) 334-4444. Their prices are usually within a few dollars of the cheapest mail-order outfits, they offer far better service, some technical support, and they've replaced environmentally wasteful foam peanuts with old newspaper in their shipping boxes. Of course, your local dealer knows all about discounters' prices, and may meet their quotes.

When you're buying *hardware* mail order, deal with a company that's been in business for at least a few years. Make sure it has a 24-hour toll-free service and support number, on-site service, a money-back guarantee, and rapid deliveries. (See **Appendix 2. Discounts for new computers.**)

When shopping by phone, always pay with a credit card. It gives you much more leverage if you have a dispute. And laws prohibit companies from billing you for back-ordered items before they ship them.

> You have to view the purchase of computer hardware and software for DTP as a personal odyssey. The lack of profitability in the traditional computer distribution channel, storefront retailers, means they're often staffed by clerks with minimum qualifications. As a DTPer, you know more about your needs than most computer store clerks. You can learn more by attending user group meetings and reading back issues of computer magazines than talking to the typical sales clerk. (I'm always upset when the clerk asks: "Do you want fries with that?" when I ask for help choosing a software package at a typical store.)

> Most computer stores do DTPers a tremendous disservice by underselling. They rarely sell you what you need because they're afraid of losing a sale when high-performance prices escalate so rapidly. Years ago, I had an experience where a legitimate storefront retailer with an impressive location sold me what they thought I would be comfortable spending instead of telling me up front I had to spend twice as much to get the job done. I wasted months trying to run PageMaker with two floppy disks.

> For someone getting started, I recommend they look to independent VARs who specialize in DTP. You might pay a little more, but you'll end up with what you need, which might or might not be what you thought you'd need.

> Right now, I buy software from mail-order firms when I know what I want to buy. I buy hardware from a local independent consultant who operates out of his home, but comes to my office, sets up the equipment, and—most important—has proven his ability to respond quickly, that is, within the hour, when problems occur. You simply don't get that from most traditional computer stores.   —*Roger Parker*

How much will it all cost?

For the PC, we show mail-order prices; mail-order outlets for Mac hardware are not as numerous, so we show discounted retail prices. (See **Appendix 2. Discounts for new computers.**)

Typical MS-DOS (IBM PC-compatible) basic system (late 1990)

Computer (20 mhz or faster, 80386 processor;
4 megabytes RAM), mouse, keyboard,
100-megabyte internal hard disk . . . . $ 2,000
Removable cartridge drive or tape unit for backup 600
19-inch monochrome gray-scale monitor 1,500
PostScript laser printer 2,200
Word processor 400
Page layout software 500
Graphics software 400
Typefaces 800
Business management software 300
Utilities and Microsoft Windows 600
TOTAL $9,300

Typical Macintosh basic system (late 1990)

Computer (Mac IIci, 68030 processor at 25 mhz;
4 megabytes RAM), mouse, extended keyboard . . . . $ 3,800
100-megabyte external hard disk 800
Removable cartridge drive or tape unit for backup 600
19-inch monochrome gray-scale monitor 1,500
PostScript laser printer 2,200
Word processor 400
Page layout software 500
Graphics software 400
Typefaces 800
Business management software 300
Utilities 500
TOTAL $11,800

If you buy some equipment used, or get the minimum hardware system capable of running advanced software and use a smaller screen, you could easily bring the totals down several thousand dollars.

Adding a modem, scanner, image-processing software, and one other package to this list, will raise the total $2,500. Then add extra RAM, more fonts, a small color monitor, and additional graphics software, plus your office machines, equipment, and furniture—you're still well under $20,000.

> My recommendation would be to look for a used Macintosh II because the prices are very low and the money you save can be put into a big-screen monitor. It's an absolute, positive, unequivocal requirement that anyone involved in desktop publishing have a big-screen monitor. Big-screen monitors offer a geometric improvement in productivity over the Macintosh's standard nine-inch screen.
>
> In the PC world, I'd look for the least-expensive 386 machine I could find that came with a good, strong, local service back-up and put the money into a LaserMaster board. It offers a tremendous speed and quality improvement over the standard LaserJet printers. *—Roger Parker*

If you have no duplicate hardware setup to which you have reliable, rapid access when your system goes down, you'll be doing yourself a favor if you budget for a second computer (a slightly less powerful one is okay), hard disk, and perhaps a screen. If you buy a Mac IIsi, IIci or IIfx main system, get a used Mac II, or Classic, SE, or SE/30, with two megabytes of memory. If you buy a PC, get an 80286 or better as your second machine. For the additional $1,500-$2,000, you'll sleep better at night, and have peace of mind when you run into trouble. If you can't afford it, at least have a second hard disk you can take with you to some other complete system. Make sure your second system or hard disk has an exact duplicate of the system configuration, applications, fonts, and utilities on your everyday setup. That way you won't lose any time getting up and running.

For either platform, your second machine could be a laptop (Outbound along with a Macintosh SE, Toshiba for the PC), which would do double duty if you travel. But unless it can attach to your monitor, and run the latest system software, it's not a complete backup, but rather a word processing peripheral.

One final suggestion while we are talking about money. For a one-person business that will gross $50,000-$100,000 per year, saving perhaps $2,000 over two years is not as important as choosing the equipment you really want and need. So don't make your platform or hardware choices solely on price. The principle holds even more strongly with applications. You should essentially disregard price when comparing software packages. Far more important is your compatibility with the interface, your inclination to learn the program, and your sense of how well its features are implemented. The purchase price of a software package is only part of its cost. There's the time it takes to learn it, and how comfortable and productive it is when you work with it. If it falls down on any of these counts, you'll be out far more than the amount on the invoice.

Have a plan of what it is you want to do. That's the hardest part. Take enough time to do your homework. Don't go crazy, but once having made an appropriate effort, take the plunge. DTP is a moving, ever-changing world. To use an analogy: The water in a river is always moving; if you want to cross it, you've got to jump in and start swimming. By that I mean, if you wait for the next machine or the next piece of software to start DTP, you're never going to start. Get in there and do it.

—*Richard E. Luna*

6. PROTECTING IT ALL

Getting saved

What's a computer user's biggest fear? You've probably daydreamed about the moment that your biggest project or your most imaginative design vanished into a black hole. Then a voice like your scariest elementary school teacher or the Wicked Witch of the West in the *Wizard of Oz* cackles, "You didn't save, my pretty."

You need never experience this nightmare yourself to realize the necessity to avoid disaster. The more frequently you save, the less you'll have to reconstruct if you hit the wrong key or get in trouble through no fault of your own. When personal computers first came out, saving to floppy disks seemed fast, and felt like a luxury. Eventually, it became an unpleasant chore. We sat there while the drives chugged and groaned away for half a minute or longer. And we started running out of disk space. Now with gigantic, fast hard disks, and with some software capable of doing **incremental saves** and only occasionally requiring slower **complete saves**, the whole process is quiet and nearly instantaneous.

We've gradually trained ourselves to hit the save keys practically every time we pause to think, look around, or answer the phone. The happy result of this now unconscious good habit is that when our computer screen freezes on us, we relaunch the document and are usually pleased to discover we've lost far less than we feared.

Until the process becomes automatic for you, here's our rule: Save before you do anything that might upset or disorient the computer. That includes:

- Switching applications;
- Opening a desk accessory or system-resident application;
- Importing or exporting data;

- Cutting or moving any major chunk of data;
- Printing—think of Save/Print as one command.

Save every time you stop work to stretch, talk to someone, take a bathroom break or a walk. These are the exact times a voltage surge could zap the system, or a passerby could trip on a cable or tip over your hardware.

If you're about to save a giant file with many recent changes in it, and you think, perhaps based on experience, there's even a remote possibility you might run into trouble, stop. Rather than doing a simple save, over-writing the existing file, for extra insurance, save the file under another name, or even better, save it to another hard drive or floppy disk.

Be especially careful about global changes. An ill-defined search and replace through an entire document can mangle a file. Most people we know have tripped at least once on one of the most obvious ones: Searching to remove extra hard carriage returns at the end of text lines, and discovering that they've mashed together the last word on one line and the first word on the next.

Before making any drastic change, save the file. After completing the change, save the file under a new name. Then immediately look at the file very carefully to make sure you've achieved the intended result. If you erred, now is the time to go back to the previous version and do it right, or differently. (For more tips on global changes, see 7. **Think about workflow in making changes**.)

On the other hand, it sometimes makes sense to be conscious and selective in saving. Often you want to try something out and then discard the result in favor of some earlier version. Some graphics software supports multiple levels of **Undo**. But most page layout software usually allows undoing only the less complex actions. Some DTP software gives you another alternative, with a command to **revert** (to the previously saved version). To take best advantage of this feature, you need to be very aware of when you made that last save—and therefore refrain from that unconscious regular saving we just recommended. Making several copies of a small section of your work and experimenting on them, then deleting all but the preferred final version, is even faster and somewhat more secure than undoing or reverting.

What if you want to pursue several options affecting an entire document, such as different typefaces or sizes, and have them all accessible for further work? Just copy the entire file several times, and name them VersionA, VersionB, and VersionC. If you're trying several options while you're at an intermediate stage of the job and you'll be doing additional work after settling on one version, it makes sense to find typos and complete all the *other* changes you know about first, *before* splitting the file into all the possible options.

Sometimes clients will decide at a late stage that they prefer an earlier style for a document. As we discussed in **4. Don't let a project flatten you**, we generally save each successive proof, draft, or long document under a new sequential letter. Then, case by case, we can decide whether it's easier to start with an earlier version and incorporate all later revisions in it, or work to incorporate the preferred style into the document's current file. To avoid clutter, we'll consolidate these intermediate files and move them to a folder Felix calls Trash Soon, and Margaret Styne calls Garbage Maybe, which we empty weekly of the contents we know we won't need.

Saving variations and stages of files can become confusing unless you have a good system you use constantly. (See **7. Name your files with care**.) It also helps to have a large enough hard disk so you can save as often as you want while working on a project without worrying about running out of space. We think you should always have five to 20 unused megabytes on your main hard disk—another reason for getting extra capacity.

When we successfully relaunch a file after a crash, we're always wary of possible damage to the file. If we have any reason to suspect that it has been corrupted, we may print out the relaunched file as a reference, then go back to the previously saved version and incorporate all the new changes in it. We don't want to continue working on top of a ticking time bomb. In extreme cases, we may also reinstall the application from the original floppies to reassure us that the application file hasn't been corrupted.

We've never been fans of those utilities that save automatically for us at preset or user-determined intervals. In fact we usually disable the feature when it's built into applications software—especially word processors. (Even in databases, where for generally good reasons the feature is especially prevalent and often unstoppable, we've been sorry at times that we couldn't revert.) We don't like giving up that control, we don't want the computer to interrupt our work to start saving, and we want to be able to refrain from saving in special circumstances.

Take extreme precautions to avoid a mistake that can be easy to make: Copying your backup copies over your newer versions. Name your folders or directories in such a way that you'll notice if you're about to go in the wrong direction.

By the way, when you think you've screwed up very badly, make sure you really are sunk. More than once, we've been certain we had sent a file into oblivion, only to discover that we'd simply misplaced it. It's easy to misdirect a file. So after you react with horror when you discover it's not where it should be, first search through all the folders or subdirectories on your hard disk, in case all is not really lost. On the Mac, Apple's Find File utility is easy; DiskTop is much faster. Most PC file management packages come with find features to locate file names. ON Technology's On Location for the Mac, Microlytics GOfer for both PC and Mac, and Lotus Magellan for the PC find text within files. If nothing works, try to undelete it before giving up.

Backing up

You've heard how important it is. But backing up is a drag:

- It's unpleasant to think about why you're backing up. Imagining calamity is almost as unpleasant as writing a will.
- It requires foresight and logic to create an understandable, easy to use, and reliable system of organizing *all* your data.
- It demands a high level of precision and consistency just when you're usually eager to be out the door.
- It forces you to buy and maintain extra storage devices and supplies.

Three kinds of data are at risk. First is your operating system and applications, along with related utilities and typefaces. Second is your current data: projects you are working on, frequently used templates plus your billing and address data. Third is your archival data. Your clients expect you to retain *forever* final copies of publication files and graphics. And, of course, it's to your great advantage to do so. Also keep in your archive previous, no-longer-used versions of applications and operating systems, so you can deal with files created with old software with the least amount of trouble.

Here's the ideal: You need an up-to-date set of all your data available on a moment's notice, plus a second set far enough away to be safe from theft, flood, fire, or other natural disasters. The ideal is also to have a backup system that's simple and painless enough so you can update it every hour or so—or at least at the end of each day.

The less talk and the more action about backup, the better. No amount of preaching or advice from us to you, or from you to the next innocent Pollyanna, will have as much effect as one catastrophe. Despite our advice, it'll probably take at least one or two mishaps before you realize that hoping for the best, and being lucky so far, are poor safety principles. As a computer company's ad says, "It's not *if* you lose data—it's *when* you lose data."

At that point, you have to start thinking existentially. How much data are you willing to lose? If you're prepared to risk a day's work, back up everything every day. If it's an hour's work, back up every hour. If it's no work, save all the time, and find a way to back up all the time.

When you think about backing up, do you imagine sitting by the computer reading a magazine and feeding it floppy disks every few minutes? Forget it. These days, the only people who back up to floppies are uncomplaining office support staff whose bosses don't care if they're stuck using inefficient manual methods. Don't get us wrong. It works, and if you're on a shoestring budget and you have the discipline, a program like Fifth Generation Systems Fastback for the Mac or PC makes it as quick and painless as possible. But it's hard to keep track of the dozens of disks you'll need for a complete backup, not to mention multiplying those dozens three or four times if you want to ensure you have the intermediate, later discarded stages of your projects. Moreover, floppy disks tend to be a bit sensitive to heat, cold, and minor misalignments between disk drives of different computers.

Remember, we're talking about backing up everything. Not just every proof of the projects you're working on right now, but a mirror image of your currently installed operating system and applications, all the databases, spreadsheets, and correspondence you use to run your business, and final files for all the projects you've ever completed. And we're talking about finding a way to do it that is as easy as possible, so you stick to your resolutions about backing up often enough to feel secure.

> I have never had a major disaster. Disk crashes, yes; disasters, no. I always back up. And if my disk crashes—and it has—I manage to recover my data quickly enough before it actually gets destroyed completely. I use a tape backup for jobs I'm working on as soon as I'm done. I back up my database information—my clients list and billing—every time I use it. It doesn't matter if I'm just walking out the door for a couple of minutes, I'm going to back it up before I leave. About once every six months I clean off my hard drive and reformat it. Sometime the disk gets fragmented and the response time is very sluggish. After I do the cleanup, it usually performs better.   —*On Far Tse*

Backup strategies

You'll need to do three kinds of backup.

- Within a session, to save what you're working on to another place so you always have available the second-to-latest version. This protects you against small mistakes.
- At the end of every hour or every day, to protect you against equipment failure or accidental irreversible deletion of files.
- At the end of a project, to archive and easily retrieve old jobs any time you need them in the future.

I use a separate drive always connected to my computer. The removable **SyQuest** type drives, at $600-$1,000, combine safety, speed, and flexibility. (Manufacturers include Mass Micro, PLI, MicroNet, and Ehman Engineering. And they're available for both Macs and PCs.) The drive uses 44-megabyte cartridges called platters. Each platter sells for under $80, making creating and carrying around multiple backups simple and economical. At any time during a work session, I back up individual project folders. At the end of every session, I back up my whole Current Data folder. Or I use a utility to copy all files modified today. With my hardware setup, moving a megabyte of data onto a platter takes six seconds. So the problem is no longer the time to back up, it's just remembering to do it and taking the time to issue the commands.

In the past, I used a fixed hard disk in this same way, with the same advantages of having the drive on-line all the time. However, because the backup drive had a limited capacity, to fit all the data on the disk, I used backup software that kept track of all files changed since the date of the previous backup, and eliminated earlier versions of files.

Now, because the cartridge drive is so fast, and because I can exchange platters, I don't use backup software. I use a platter named Rotation A for two weeks; then move onto B, then C; and then erase and start over with Rotation A. This gives me a multiple insurance policy, and I can retrieve the intermediate versions of files produced within the past month.

One helpful technique, especially useful for hard disk drives larger than about 40 megabytes, is to use software provided by the drive manufacturer or a third party to **partition** or segment your drive, and then make complete copies of each. I enjoy the convenience of having everything handy, so I use a very fast 345-megabyte main drive, with partitions for Operating System • Fonts and Utilities • Applications • Current Data, plus usually unmounted partitions for Archival Data • Graphics • Miscellaneous and Previous Versions of Applications. I back up each partition onto a different platter.   *—Felix*

Removable hard disks are also handy if you're in a department with more than one person to a computer. Each person can have a SyQuest platter, and load current files onto the computer's main hard disk as needed. We also use them to take files for large projects or immense color documents to our service bureau. Imagesetting service bureaus are standardizing on the SyQuest format drives for transfer of large client files. We don't recommend these removable units for long-term everyday use as primary drives. Some people find the SyQuests to be unreliable and prone to failure because they aren't completely sealed from dust.

Bernoulli drives are another high-capacity removable disk type. Bernoullis, and similar drives made by Toshiba and resold by other companies, are sealed units whose heads float permanently on a cushion of air above the drive platter. Other promising removable disk technologies are on their way, including some 20-megabyte floppy disks.

The latest technology is **optical-magnetic removable hard disks**. These are available in two sizes: 128-megabytes on one side and 400- to 600-megabytes on two sides of a 3½- or 5¼-inch compact disk. At one time, these were real slowpokes. But the 30-millisecond access time of the newest systems, from Pinnacle, Maxtor, and other companies, is as fast as a medium speed hard disk. As optical storage descends in price from its current $3,000+ range, it will become a very reasonable alternative. You could store months of work, including intermediate stages, on one or two disks. This technology is more stable than SyQuest or even Bernoulli. Standard formats have so far been defined for the 5¼-inch but not yet for the 3½-inch opticals.

Tape is an entirely different alternative, very popular in the corporate environment, both because of its merits and because management information systems (MIS) people know it from mainframes. It's compact, efficient, economical, and fast. It's particularly well suited for unattended automatic backup of large drives at pre-scheduled intervals. Tapes come in capacities to accommodate any size hard disk. Systems using videotape or digital audio tape (DAT) can store gigabytes of data. Maggie's preferred backup method is once a week to tape.

Tape is actually more reliable than copying onto a working disk, because the tape is on-line only during the backup period. Its main drawback is that as a distinct storage medium, it's used only for backup. You can't put an operating system and applications on the tape and start up from it. And while it works well to copy or restore an entire drive, the quality of the accompanying software will determine whether it's convenient to copy or extract a few files using tape.

For what's called fault-tolerant storage, developers have come up with two ways to write data to two systems simultaneously. **Duplexing** is faster, **mirroring** is cheaper, and allows the computer to switch automatically to the second drive if the first one fails. Neither eliminates the need to back up off-site, or protects you from viruses and damaged disk directories. These methods are in favor particularly in corporations, for disk servers that are accessible to many users in large networks. Versions of these technologies are becoming available in low-priced formats as software utilities or hardware/software packages.

Finally, despite our slighting of the low-capacity floppy disk for backup, if you don't have a second hard disk on-line while you work, keeping a floppy in the machine at all times and copying files in progress onto it during a session is a great idea. And whatever methods people use for backing up their current and past files, many DTPers further reassure themselves by making one or more floppy disks for each client.

> For extra insurance I don't have to think about, I save the disk I get back from my imagesetter. For under one dollar I have an additional backup of what is unquestionably the final version of the file.   —*Margaret Styne*

> Backing up is very important, and relatively cheap compared with losing work. I use three backup methods: a second hard disk, removable SyQuest cartridges, and 1,500 floppies. Floppies are a good medium because they are easy to sort, easy to access, and very cheap when you buy in bulk. I'm very careful about backing up and have never lost more than one hour's work.   —*Ted Ostindien, DTP freelancer in NYC*

Before you back up your old client files, go through them to make sure their file names are understandable. Include the month and year of the project within the file name so it appears alphabetically in a printout: 0190 to 1290, for instance. (See 7. **Name your files with care** for more on file-naming conventions.) Eliminate all distracting extra files—then compress the files to save disk space. For the Mac, use Aladdin Software StuffIt Deluxe, Salient Disk Doubler or the shareware Compactor; for the PC, SoftLogic Cubit, System Enhancement Associates ARC, Central Point PC Tools Compress, or PKWare PKZip. To make locating files easier in the future, write the file name on the final paper printout proof of each publication.

Most compression utilities, particularly on the Mac, are not automatic or instantaneous. Thus they add to your housekeeping burdens. If you're the one doing the archiving, the solution of storing uncompressed files on a large hard disk or removable cartridges may be more efficient, cost-effective, and slightly more secure. On the other hand, having to make decisions about what to compress for archives forces you to tidy up your files.

Establishing and maintaining complete archive files can be critical to your success as a business. You never know when you'll need to update an old file, make a template for a new project for the same customer, or adapt a template or graphic for a new customer. For this reason, too, off-site storage of your archive file and your current files, as well as your accounting and address database, is vital. Keep a set at home. If your office is at home, stash a set somewhere else.

Rescuing data

Computers are quirky. Some particular sequence of commands may route a piece of data to an unexpected place, leading to an inexplicable freeze-up. If you've been saving often enough, you may be better off restarting than trying to figure out why. If the problem recurs, it will be worth investigating.

What happens when you delete a file by mistake, and you have no backup copy? Be aware that usually, you haven't actually removed the file—just the directory pointers to its location on the hard disk. If you realize your mistake right after you do it, immediately put to work an **Unerase** utility. The basic idea is to find the file as soon as possible. The more work you do after discarding the file, the greater the chances that new data will be written to the physical location of the needed old data (which the computer regards as vacant space). For the PC, Norton Utilities Advanced Edition, The Mace Utilities, and PC Tools all include an undelete. For the Macintosh, Norton Utilities or Symantec Utilities for Macintosh (SUM) will usually recover the file. The best documented and most complete software for the Mac is Microcom 911 Utilities, until recently called 1st Aid Kit.

To make sure your disk operates optimally, periodically consolidating data that's scattered all over the disk but belongs together, and to lock out bad sectors of the disk where data could get lost, use Gibson Research SpinRite for the PC, ALSoft DiskExpress for the Mac. Some of the general utilities listed above do this as part of their overall work, but often not as quickly or as well.

Hard disks lose track of a key byte or two from time to time. Even if you use one of these utilities, it's also a good idea to re-initialize the hard disk every three to six months—like using a sponge instead of an eraser on a chalkboard.

You also need **anti-viral software** to protect you from computer viruses that a few mean-spirited or thoughtless people among the generally well-intentioned hacker community unleash upon unsuspecting computer users. Some viruses are harmless. Some have a delayed reaction. All are a potential threat. You can get utilities to check every floppy disk as you put it in the disk drive, check all the files on your hard disk, and repair infected files. Sometimes, even after such a repair, you may have to go back to your original application floppy disks to re-install software. For the Macintosh, Microcom Virex and Symantec AntiVirus for the Macintosh (SAM) are the leading commercial packages; Vaccine and Disinfectant are fine shareware packages. For the PC, try Norton Utilities, or the shareware packages McAfee Associates SCAN, Interpath, or FluShot. Make sure you have the latest version of anti-viral software—or you'll fool yourself into thinking you're more protected than you really are.

What happens when (not if) your hard disk crashes? Often it will start right up again. But sometimes, your computer will think the drive vanished, or it may show up as present but you may be unable to get it to start up or to extract any of the data from it. Whatever you do, don't try to re-initialize or re-format the disk, which will usually erase your files. Check your manual, and call technical support. Most manufacturers include simple utilities for drive recovery. If these don't work, the commercial software mentioned above for file recovery is likely to succeed in bringing the drive back to life.

Failing that, one of these utilities may be able to recover the data, which you can then copy onto an empty hard disk. Or it may be able to extract part of the data, without directory or path information, leaving you to sort your way through hundreds or thousands of files named 0001, 0002, 0003, etc. If nothing works, the drive manufacturer may be willing to try to recover the data, or to recommend costly wizards specializing in heroic efforts to rescue data from dropped, flooded, and burned drives.

Your best strategy is to buy and understand one of these utility packages *before* you get in trouble. If you install it on your perfectly working hard disk, it will check the disk for potential problems, create alternative directory maps and other information on the drive, and leave you with a reserve savior floppy disk tailored to the characteristics of your hard drive. This will simplify and improve your chances for recovery of individual files or an entire crashed disk.

In case of a disk crash, immediately write down on a sheet of paper what you did before the crash. Then, as you attempt to recover the disk, keep writing down the steps you take and the messages that appear on your screen. It will help you avoid mistakes, reduce panic, and be coherent at a time of high anxiety when you call technical support or summon outside help.

Protecting your tools

Your DTP setup is vulnerable. You need to anticipate the worst, and be prepared so a disaster means a temporary interruption—not a business failure.

- **Insure your hardware.** If you're in a home office, your homeowner's or renter's policy will never fully cover your system, even if you can get a separate rider and a claim is allowed for equipment used in business. You need a separate policy. Safeware, (800) 848-3469, covers the replacement value or depreciated cost of your equipment. Computer Insurance Plus, (800) 722-0385, is not available in all states, but insures software as well. We can't vouch from experience with a claim for either company, though. Even if it is insured, don't be casual about making sure your office is safe, and your computers inside it are secure. If possible, bolt or chain your computer to furniture, making it harder for a burglar in a rush to walk off with your computer and hard disk. Secure-It, Inc., (800) 451-7592, makes special cables for under $50.

- **Pop the hood of your computer.** Especially if you bought it as a plug-and-play unit, find someone who will help you look inside, and perhaps install memory chips, controller cards, or disk drives. You'll reduce the mystery, you won't be as intimidated by the technical talk, and you can start to troubleshoot your next problem. (Felix has repeatedly confirmed a discovery of years ago, when his toaster broke down: Sometimes you can fix a gadget just by taking it apart and putting it back together.)

- **Get a service contract.** These days, service technicians don't fix equipment. They locate and then pull out the offending part. If you aren't under a warranty or service contract, they'll charge you for a new replacement, even though they may send out that broken component for repair. So it pays to buy contracts on your core equipment: the computer and printer, and perhaps the hard disk (if it's a separate external unit), and monitor. Annual costs for *on-site service* with a 48-hour response typically run from 5-10% of hardware's list price. For a premium, you can often get 24-hour or 4-hour response and a loaner if they can't get you back up quickly. You can also save money with *carry-in service* (not for laser printers, which you shouldn't move; and not practical for networked systems). You can get service contracts from computer stores or from national companies like General Electric and TRW. If you buy mail-order, don't get any hardware you can't get a good service contract for. If you're technically unconfident, you may be better off paying more, buying locally, and getting local repairs. On the other hand, contracts are costly; if you have several computers and are a technical whiz, you could get the service manuals and hope nothing comes up that you can't deal with. Larger installations and corporate locations may not need to take our advice about having a costly service contract on all their equipment. The more equipment you have, the less critical becomes any single component, and the closer you are to being able to, in effect, self-insure yourself.

- **Be like Tarzan.** Don't let go of the first vine until you're sure the new one will hold you. When you switch to new tools, keep the old hardware and software running until you know the replacements are capable and reliable. When accountants—some of the most cautious people around—start using electronic bookkeeping systems, they usually maintain a manual set of records for a full year, to make sure the numbers come out the same, and to be prepared for the worst. For DTPers, we'd say give it a month or so.

- **Secure your software.** Before using a new piece of software, make sure to **write-protect** (lock) it, by taping over the notch on a 5¼-inch floppy or sliding the little black button on 3½-inch disks. Make a copy immediately (for extra protection, make two, and keep one off-site). Now if a virus strikes or you otherwise damage your hard disk, you can always go back to a factory-fresh copy of the application. You can also write-protect removable SyQuest and optical disks.

- **Stay in power.** Keep electrical equipment off all lines with electric motors. Air conditioners and refrigerators, in particular, create power surges. Your laser printer and photocopier may also be power-hungry and could each require a separate line. Find out if the electric supply to your area is unreliable or if your home is underwired. Running a computer on low voltage can gradually destroy it. You could check with your utility company, or hook up a cheap volt-ohm-meter (a VOM goes for $15 at Radio Shack) to the power line to see what happens at different times of the day. If your power drops or is otherwise unreliable, consider using an **uninterruptible power supply** (UPS). If you dare, when you get your computer, and while you're under warranty, pull the plug while you're in the middle of a disk save. Plug it back in. If the computer starts up right away, you can feel somewhat secure from physical damage (though not from loss of data) even without a UPS. You'll need one with the amperage to run your computer, hard disk, and monitor. Devices from American Power Conversion, (800) 541-8896, are highly rated and reasonable in cost, and you can buy them discounted through MacConnection or PC Connection. Also check out ZeroSurge Surge Eliminators, (201) 766-4220. A **surge protector** is sufficient for the rest of your peripherals. Look for the ones in the $50-$100 range, with rapid response time, and lights to let you know if the protection circuitry has been damaged in any way. We like Panamax's products, (800) 472-5555.

- **Protect tools from the elements.** Cover all machines with movable parts: photocopiers, laser printers, and faxes. Keep them shielded from direct sunlight. Don't eat, drink, or use any spray can products over or near your tools. And we're not preaching, but you might try quitting smoking. Over time, smoke particles can clog up disk drives. At the very least, get a plastic cover for the drive openings, or puff in other directions.

- **Keep the cartons.** When you get a new piece of hardware, store the original box and packing material. There's no safer way to transport it, or return it for service. By the way, that cardboard will increase the equipment's resale value.

- **Don't lend your tools.** As you settle in to this business, your hardware configuration and your startup routines, macros, and key equivalents become unique and time-consuming to reconstruct. Resist desperate pleas for access to your desktop from nonprofessionals, even from friends. Do the work yourself or suggest places where a supplicant can rent time on machines by the hour. Otherwise, if you agree and then have problems, you'll never forgive the wretch—or yourself—for disturbing your setup, destroying a hard disk directory, changing settings, or deleting or moving files without even realizing it. If you feel an absolute prohibition on access is inhumane, you might permit some access to people who know *more than you* about what they are doing. If you're in a large office with no privacy, you can explore ways to secure your computer and data, including physical locks and muzzles, password access, file encryption software, and removable hard drives.

Should you turn off your system every night? The safe answer is check with the manufacturer. But in general, you can leave the computer (central processing unit) on. You won't use much power, and you'll reduce the chance of excessively straining your power supply. Hard disks are a bit iffy. Most are rated at over 50,000 hours **mean time between failure** (MTBF), so you'd have to leave it on for 20 years to reach the average moment of crisis. Turn off the monitor unless you're equipped with an automatic screen saver that kicks in after a few minutes to prevent burn-in of sections of the screen. Turn off your laser printer to save on your electric bill and, for models with the Canon SX engine, to avoid scratching or wearing down the cartridge through the automatic periodic rotation of the printer drum. Power off with your surge suppressor to save wear and tear on the on-off switches of your equipment.

When you first get a piece of equipment (especially one with a 90-day warranty, and especially if you're not taking out a service contract) keep it running all the time, on the off chance that you'll encourage an eventual failure to happen sooner rather than later. If you want to test what wear and tear does to the power supply, turn it on and off frequently during the warranty period.

Extinguish all computing tools when you go on vacation. And when the sky turns black and the forecaster predicts serious thunder and lightning, you'll feel better if you unplug everything from the wall (including disconnecting your modem and fax from the telephone lines).

Remember to protect your health

Your body is your most important tool. It's also irreplaceable. Though we all tend to be complacent about occupational safety, and some findings remain controversial, researchers are confirming hazards resulting from computer use. Evidence is piling up as increasing numbers of human beings spend most of their working days in front of keyboards and **video display terminals** (VDTs). Some studies have shown an increased risk of miscarriage, for reasons that remain unexplained, among pregnant women who spend hours in front of VDTs. Other dangers include:

- **Musculoskeletal disorders:** Back and neck pains and other repetitive strain injuries, including carpal tunnel syndrome (a disabling injury to a nerve in the wrist once thought to plague mainly factory workers, meatcutters, and similar occupations), now show up frequently in offices and newsrooms. Be alert to such early warning signs as tingling and finger pains. Explore the use of alternative keyboards. Using a mouse, trackball or other pointing tool may help by giving your hands breaks from steady typing. And take care to set up your desktop workstation according to ergonomic principles, taking into account your seated height, the tilt of your chair, and the position and slant of the keyboard. (See *Macworld*, January 1990, for a good treatment of the subject; see **Appendix 2. Ergonomic furniture** for some suppliers.)

- **Eye strain** and blurred vision are also turning up in reports. Studies on cataracts and permanent eye damage are inconclusive. But the weight of anecdotal evidence encourages you not to sit too close to your screen, reduce screen glare, and avoid placing the monitor in front of a window (where the contrast between the bright outdoors and the dim screen can cause problems). Choose a low-flicker monitor with a vertical scan rate over 65 hz. Frequent breaks and stretches every hour or two can reduce the likelihood of muscular and visual problems. If you wear corrective lenses, ask your eye doctor if you need a different prescription to focus at the monitor's viewing distance.

- **Radiation:** A report by the Federal Office of Technology Assessment, as well as investigations by author Paul Brodeur (who earlier spent 30 years tracking the dangers of asbestos), and others suggest that low-level electromagnetic fields surrounding video display terminals may have harmful long-term effects. Of course, people sit much closer to computer monitors than to TV screens, so any danger will be greater to the computer user. Recently, while not conceding any merit to the charges, Sigma and IBM have begun to offer monitors with lower radiation levels. Working on a portable computer using a liquid crystal or gas plasma display—the only way to avoid these emissions—is not realistic for most DTP work. (This option is chosen by some women who continue to work with computers while pregnant.) Radiation levels are highest behind the screen—so don't sit directly behind another workstation. And levels in front of the screen drop off significantly beyond about two feet. So sit back, at least at arm's length—though not so far back that you strain your eyes to see.

Computer magazines report on this subject from time to time. You'll find particularly good articles in the January 1990 and July 1990 *Macworld*. The most comprehensive and reliable information comes from *VDT News*, Box 1799 Grand Central Station, New York, NY 10163, (212) 517-2800. For a one-page fact sheet on VDTs and pregnancy, send $3.50 to 9 to 5, the National Association of Working Women, 614 Superior Avenue NW, Cleveland, OH 44113, (216) 566-9308. Contact the NY Committee for Occupational Safety and Health (NYCOSH), 275 Seventh Avenue, Eighth Floor, New York, NY 10001, (212) 627-3900, whose *VDT Book: A Computer User's Guide to Health and Safety* (1987, $5.70) turns out to be prescient and still very useful.

Try to find ways to avoid the inherent stress of working with a machine that keeps asking you for more, because it's always ready for you. (The answer isn't to buy a slower machine.) Just because the machine is willing to work around the clock, you don't have to agree.

- Get an alarm clock, to keep you from losing track entirely of the outside world. It's easy to let untold hours slip by. Sometimes, the longer you're plugged into the computer, the easier it gets to continue. For the Mac, you can get a utility that gives you automatic timed stretch reminders and related suggestions: Visionary Software, (503) 246-6200.
- No matter what your deadline pressures, take plenty of breaks. You could take the approach embodied in legislation recently proposed in a number of localities: Requiring employers to assign 15 minutes of a different kind of work after two hours of continuous VDT exposure.
- Stand up, shake your body out, and walk around every hour. Try the cherry picker stretch, reaching each hand over your head in a rhythmic, circular motion. See *Computer and Desk Stretches*, by athletes Bob and Jean Anderson, Stretching, Inc., PO Box 767, Palmer Lake, CO 80133.

Don't waste paper

Since DTPers are in the business of producing printed material, there's no way to avoid contributing to the more than 50 million tons (100 billion pounds) of paper thrown out in America each year. Currently, Americans recycle 26% of our waste paper, and only 6% of office and writing paper is made from recycled paper. A full 8% of all of our nation's solid waste is newsprint alone. We trail behind most other advanced industrial nations in recycling. But we can try to reduce our contribution to the problem.

For your own non-camera-ready laser printer output, you could switch to a recycled paper. Earth Care Paper, Box 1410, Madison WI 53714, (608) 277-2900, is a leading supplier of 50-70% and 100% recycled bond. It's sold like any copier paper in 500-sheet reams. The cost of $4 or more per ream is slightly higher than the cheapest paper you can get from discount suppliers, and you'll have to pay shipping on top of that. Earth Care also sells a $2.50 guide to office paper recycling. And you can write for a free report called *Using Recycled Paper: Facts for Business*, B&T Associates, 710 North Tioga St., Ithaca, NY 14850.

Some of the national office supply companies are starting to offer Hammermill 50% recycled paper at around the same price if you buy a case. They also sell envelopes and file folders, and they pay for shipping. (See **Appendix 2. Office and publishing supplies.**)

Recycled paper for your jobs will cost 10-30% more than virgin paper. But think of the social benefits. *Garbage* magazine says a ton of 100% recycled paper saves 17 trees, 4,100 kilowatt hours of electricity, 700 gallons of water, 60 pounds of air-polluting effluents, and three cubic yards of landfill.

Check with your printers to find out if they can get a stock of recycled paper. One major supplier to printers is Conservatree in San Francisco, (800) 522-9200. These days, to some eyes, there's not much difference between the fibrous off-white look of recycled paper and some other very classy and expensive blended color papers. Ask Ben & Jerry's, the socially conscious and highly profitable ice cream maker, for a copy of their annual report on recycled paper, P.O. Box 240, Waterbury, VT 05676, (802) 244-5641. You won't necessarily be able to ensure consistency among lots of recycled paper. On the other hand, it tends to be very opaque, making even light weights ideal for two-sided printing.

Particularly for covers, paper manufacturers take lots of trouble to make their sheets look white and uniform, using bleach processes. Most glossy cover stock made in the U.S. is bleached with chlorine, which when incinerated can produce dioxin. Some companies are starting to use safer, non-polluting oxygen-based processes. Ink and colored paper are also major polluters.

For information on recycled paper, contact *Greenpeace* Magazine, Paper Department, 1436 U Street NW, Washington, DC 20009. To get rid of all the paper you accumulate, if you don't know of any local program, you can get information from the Environmental Defense Fund, (800) CALL EDF, or from the U.S. Environmental Protection Agency, (800) 424-9346.

If you do use recycled paper for your own stationery, or for jobs you arrange with printers, add the recycled paper logo. In **Fig. 6.1** on the next page, you'll find it in several versions for you to scan.

**Fig. 6.1
Recycled
paper logo**

from Margaret Styne

While we're on the subject of the environment, recycle by refilling your laser printer toner cartridges. You'll save money and keep many pounds of plastic out of the dump. (See **8. Making friends with your vendors.**)

> We can get sucked up in the details of DTP and not see such bigger issues like how much paper we're wasting, and how much we're responsible for that pollution. The inks we use are poisoning rivers. As a person who is very much concerned about the environment, particularly as one who is contributing to environmental problems, it's becoming a major issue with me. I would hope that paper use starts to decrease in five years. Nothing would thrill me more. But something has to jump-start the trend—maybe multimedia or videodisks.   —*Michael J. Sullivan*

7. WORKING EFFICIENTLY

Take the average DTP project: Any DTPer can get it done. But how many can complete it successfully: meeting promised delivery dates, satisfying the client, and making money?

Successful DTP requires knowing what you're trying to create, deciding on the most appropriate tools, creating the most elegant, concise, and flexible structure, and following the letter and the spirit of the client's instructions. It means ending up with what you intended—or something better. And it means avoiding complications and surprises that eat up the profit in your bid.

You'll find loads of production tips in manuals and in DTP newsletters and magazines, mostly keyed to particular software. And you can buy great books about the major software packages. Chances are any of these books will give you useful ideas. But before you get to that stage, and whatever tools you choose, you'll need to think about general strategies and habits to improve your productivity and the quality of your jobs.

Tracking your time

To become good and fast, you need to know what's involved in doing the work, what takes large chunks of time, and what takes the most concentration. In **Fig. 7.1**, we've broken down the steps in a straightforward newsletter job.

It's important to start tracking your jobs. At the start of your career, watch them minute by minute. Start the clock the second you give your attention to the project. Some steps are nearly instantaneous; you'll take hours on others. Eventually, you'll be able to eyeball a project and mentally add up the time you'll need to get it done. As you become familiar with what takes time, you'll be in

THE STAGES OF DESKTOP PUBLISHING

Plan project
Determine scope (goal, audience, format, timetable)
Budget & schedule stages of job
Line up subcontractors & vendors
Assign deadlines & responsibilities
Get confirming job letter or contract modification, if necessary

Fig. 7.1
Steps in
preparing
a project

Prepare text
From client's typed or written copy
Add instructions for typist
Proofread & (optionally) copy edit text
From disk
Convert text from word processor, spreadsheet, database formats
Print out text if hard copy not supplied
Spell check, proofread, copy edit, or (optionally) send to professional copy editor
Combine into large files, clean up (see **Fig. 7.3**) & partially format & style text
Separate & partially format tables & specially styled material
Print word processor galleys
Editorial & revision cycles with client (or postpone to first page proofs)

Produce graphics
Original art
Create sketches
Create prototypes
Create individual illustrations & charts
Revision cycles with client
Material from other sources
For position only (FPO) scans
Line art & halftone scans for repro
Convert from other file formats
Gray-scale & color editing, image manipulation, color correction

Design pages
Create thumbnail sketches (pencil)
Produce prototype pages (becomes template)
Revision cycles with client

Create template
Define paper dimensions, printable area (check with printer)
Create master pages, columns, headers, footers, frames, guides
Define style sheets (part can be done earlier in word processor)
Build style hierarchies for body, headline, other type
Define paragraph specs: justification, spacing, indents, tabs, rules, hyphenation, widows & orphans
Choose type specs: size, leading, width, tracking, character & word spacing
Make standing elements: masthead, banner, coupon & placeholders
Print prototype pages (with dummy or Greek text if necessary)
Revision cycles with client

from Kramer Communications

Lay out pages

Break out text into story files
Import text & graphics
Format text in detail
Place copy overset on extra pages
Position, scale & crop art, add
graphic wraps & in-line graphics
Add rules, boxes, & tints
Specify spot color
Print, review, fiddle with page proof
Make design adjustments &
suggested copy changes (note on
client's original hard copy)
Send client first proof (taped or
bound, facing pages)

Successive page proofs

Send to professional copy editor
(optional)
Incorporate client's corrections
Check proofs against instructions
Overall fine-tuning: loose & tight
lines, kerning, hyphenation,
widows & orphans, baseline &
column alignments
Verify artwork
Confirm captions & credits
Balance on pages, photos
facing in and out
Verify transitions
Jumps (continued on/from),
reference continuity
Confirm first & last sentences
of each story
Revision cycles until client OKs
final proof

Create camera-ready pages

Laser printer output
Use best toner cartridge &
paper
Check pages for stray marks
Paste onto boards if necessary

Imagesetter
Prepare dummy showing
printer FPOs, spot color
(for composite mechanical),
pagination & folds (save a
reference copy)
Remove FPO graphics from
file, replace with holding
lines, rules or black boxes
(consult printer)
Fill out order form, delivery
& billing instructions
Confirm typefaces used,
include graphics files &
screen fonts on disk if
necessary, include printout
Check returned imagesetter
paper or film

Follow up with printer

Confirm schedule & instructions
on dummy
Review blueprints
Confirm completion & delivery

Review job

Analyze time & expenses
Send invoice (or wait until after
discussing job)
Compare dummy with printed
publication
Discuss job with client
Collect & log payment

Archive project

Place annotations on final proof
and/or in disk file
Clean out physical job folder
Discard intermediate computer files
& printouts
Save selected scans & graphic files
separately for future use
Compress & archive final version
Convert file to template (or wait
until starting next issue)

a position to assess your tools. Perhaps you need a faster computer, or software to automate some repetitive steps. And you'll be able to assess your own productivity. If you're able to compare notes with other DTPers, as you spot bottlenecks, you can see how others approach these time-consuming tasks.

> We know what the current project is by looking at the largest pile of paper on the floor. It's not scientific, but it works! We've run out of file space since our office (an extra bedroom) already has two desks with PCs, printers, books, and software. Because our projects are long-term, we work on only three or four at one time. We don't lose track of them and don't require sophisticated tracking systems. All materials for each job are kept in a folder with a cover sheet to track days, time, totals, and tasks. Since we bid our work up front, the tracking is for our records to see if we bid properly. It's mainly to help us refine estimates for future work. All in all, our estimates are pretty darn close.   —*Lynn Walterick*

For jobs that you're billing by the hour, obviously you need to log your time. And the first time a client questions your bill, you'll be happy to know the time you spent on each phase of the project. But don't let this external need be your driving motivation. You can't make good business decisions without knowing how long each stage of your work takes you.

If you're reluctant to take on this burden, check around—you'll discover that more white collar workers than you might imagine track their time. Lawyers and accountants routinely keep running time sheets, coded by client, and divided into 10- or 15-minute intervals. For monthly billing, these numbers go into time management software for analysis, a database module, or to a bookkeeper.

Here's the minimum you need:

Date	Start	Finish	Total time	Task & expense
Tues. 1/1/91	10:00	11:15	1. 25	Proof #1
Wed. 1/2/91	2:20	3:05	. 75	corrections, scans, talk to client

It doesn't have to be fancy. Felix keeps this information in columns down a page, with the client name and project name on top. When the job is done, he uses the blank parts of the page to summarize the information, document for himself the assumptions of the invoice (in relation to the original quote), and summarize the invoice. This way all the information stays in one place, the client folder, for easy reference. He uses green or blue copy paper for these tracking sheets, so he can easily pull them out of a crowded client file. Maggie uses a simple tracking form, showing dates, times, operators, tasks, and expenses, stapled inside the manila folder.

At a minimum, key the task column to proof version numbers. Keep every successive proof until you've been paid for the job and until you've completed any analysis you want to do of your time sheets. The more you break up the log, the more useful information you'll have. In the example above, you might have wanted to note that the center spread took 30 of the 75 total minutes needed for the first proof.

Don't be tempted to go high-tech on your tracking. Yes, there are programs to log the time you spend with an open document file. But they aren't smart enough to know when you're taking a short break, staring off into space, rummaging through printouts, or talking to someone about another job.

True, you can use a spreadsheet or word processor to keep track of your time. If you enter the amount of time you, employees, or subcontractors spend on each project every day, you can then extract the information you need by day, person, or project. But how often do you want to print out that page? Do you need to worry about another file to keep track of and back up? For convenience and safety, nothing beats a page next to your keyboard and a reliable mechanical thought processor (a pen or pencil).

> I keep a clipboard ruled with lines and I list each job as it comes in, assigning a job number in sequence. I put down the date, note the client, and add a brief description of the job and a cost estimate of what I either told the client or think the range the job should be. Two more columns show the billing date and the amount invoiced. I keep documentation for each job in a legal-sized file folder marked with the same job number as on the clipboard. Sometimes I make notes about special things. Normally I keep a listing of my time in Microsoft Word and keep that file with the job folder on the computer. I then make a printout of that.
>
> A lot of newcomers get tricked into thinking they need a complex job tracking system. When you begin hiring people, you really have to keep track of their time. Then you might have to go to something more sophisticated. For my small shop, I find my kind of cobbled-together system adequate. I can always check a job to find out when it was billed or what the number was simply by pulling my clipboard off the wall. And I can refer to a hard copy that's in the file jacket.   —*David Doty*

Since detailed records are essential for billing, taxes, and estimating, it's important to find a system you will actually use no matter how tired or rushed you are. Be realistic. Take a look at your personal life. How you bank, your bill-paying habits, the state of your closets—and tailor a

system to fit your strengths. I hate entering facts and figures into the machine at the end of a busy day so I use a diary method. Each morning I put a clean, dated page on top of the stack beside my phone. I write everything on it—transactions, dates, phone numbers, promises, problems, solutions, shortcuts, feelings, doodles, birthdays—anything that is or *might be* useful. I staple a week's worth of pages with a covering, quick-reference page and color-code them by month. The result is a source of information for my permanent files, a chronological record of events, and a storage system for all the day-to-day reference trivia one usually needs the day after it's been thrown away. The bonus is the actual diary. It's fun to read a year later.
                                                                        —*Margaret Styne*

When you work with subcontractors, ask them to log the same information. You must have their time sheets if you're paying them by the hour, not only to see how quickly they work, but also if you need to explain anything to the client. Even if they're charging you flat rates, looking at how long they spend on every step gives you both the opportunity to learn from each other.

If you get more ambitious, you can incorporate more information into your tracking sheet. Some of the items that could belong on this sheet are:

- Fonts, names of graphic files, and software versions used;
- Summary of styles used, printout of style sheet;
- Rates you charge client for your time, subcontractors, and faxes;
- Expenses (faxes, messengers, imagesetting);
- Subcontractor expenses and hours;
- Reminders to yourself to get all files and materials from subcontractors;
- Date invoice sent; date payment received;
- When, where, and under what names the final files were archived;
- Informal comments, like "This took 25% longer than usual because…."

Staple all this to the final proofs and clip the intermediate proofs to the package. Write the final file name and date on the final proofs, which should correspond to the date you last changed the file. Then when you're looking for the file to use for future revisions, everything will match up; you won't have to rummage around among your data files (or embarrass yourself by asking the client for guidance in identifying the final version). When you get copies of the final printed result, put one in the file. Together with the information you'll have on another page or on the outside of the client folder (contact names and phone numbers, word processor, printer, messenger, and other information about the client), plus your notes from the first and successive conversations with the client, you'll have all you need in one place.

I include information on my fax cover sheet to help me track jobs. I mark on this cover sheet time spent discussing the proof.

Before I archive a project, I capture a screen shot of the files in the project folder. I print it out and annotate it; I find the visual image is a helpful memory refresher. —*Margaret Styne*

Tracking and managing large jobs

Big jobs are not simply small jobs that take longer: they're very different. It's easy to lose track of where you are, what stages have been completed, and who has reviewed what. You'll have to manage many more data files and successive versions of files. Any time you spend setting up a special tracking sheet for the project will be more than saved over the course of the job.

For example, here are the column categories Felix used to track each new text file supplied on disk for the annual update of an almanac:

- Filename;
- Title;
- Page numbers of the previous version of this section in last year's book;
- Date received;
- Date converted and file size in kilobytes;
- Date formatted and styled;
- Date placed;
- Date first galleys sent to client;
- Date first galleys and layouts returned by client;
- Date first page proof sent to client;
- Date first proof returned by client … and on through second, third and final proofs and imagesetting.

For this job, tables and graphic files had slightly different sets of tracking categories to account for their evolution from spreadsheet to chart to art.

Newspapers and magazines tend to have these kinds of tracking systems set up on large wall boards or in proprietary computer software. Some project management software may be appropriate for you, or you may simply use a large piece of graph paper.

For a sample tracking form, see **Appendix Fig. A2 Job ticket.**

For a quick ID check of a document, hold a previous version of the document in front of a bright light, and lay the new version on top. This is a way to see if you have the correct version, and an easy way to spot layout problems. It's never a substitute for real proofreading.—*Lynn Yost*

Be an organized crackerjack

Some DTP jobs are constructed on the equivalent of a factory assembly line. For instance, you can lay out a novel practically without thinking. Once you set the chapter openings, the rest of the pages simply flow automatically, one after another. Depending on the software you use, you may need to check pages for widows and orphans and for hyphenated words carried over from page to page. The front pages will need individual attention, but otherwise it's strictly routine. It's hard to be anything other than very efficient on this kind of job.

On the other hand, many DTP projects involve much detail work—more like expensive handmade cabinetry. You'll have unique decisions to make on every page. And despite the immense power of the software you'll be using, if you plan poorly and then make a mistake, you might have to redo entire sections. Here's where a mindset that's constantly looking for the most efficient way to get a job done will help.

Efficiency is a combination of using your software well and doing the job in the right order with the right tools. We start big production jobs by making a list of the steps involved, usually on paper, with lots of crossouts and arrows. That slows us down enough so we really have to think about what we're going to do and why. Sometimes we realize we'd intended to do a step too early in the process, for the wrong reason—often eagerness or anxiety. We're better off when logic wins out.

> The key to productivity is simple: organization—keeping track of all the pieces of a project. And you must plan for and leave time for changes. Time gets wasted on computers by people having to go back and make changes that, if anticipated from the beginning, would not have been necessary.   —*Chick Foxgrover*

Make life easier for you and your client

- We help our clients keep costs down by showing them what they need to know to give us their data files in good shape. In **Figure** 7.2 (turn the page) you'll find the instruction sheet Felix hands out.

- For the most adept, we may train them to insert codes, similar to those used by conventional typesetters, for interpretation by our page layout software.
- We give clients a table showing how they can get special typographic characters either by using the Control/Alt/Shift keys on a PC, the Command/Option/Shift keys on the Macintosh, or by indicating ASCII codes for characters. For the Mac, this table will be universal; for the PC, you may have to give them one tailored to a particular software package or operating system.
- We go over tabular material very carefully with our clients. Most don't understand what we're talking about when we explain how they should format complex tables, so often we arrange to have the material typed ourselves.
- Know what your real deadline is. In determining a schedule with the client, we work backwards, starting by asking when the job needs to be delivered by the printer. Then we determine how much time the printer needs, and count backward from there. By the way, if they want us to do the job in two days, but they allow the printer two weeks, we may gently point out that we shouldn't absorb *all* the deadline pressure.

Think about workflow in making changes

Your goal is to do as much as possible in **batch** mode, where you have to perform an action only once rather than many times.

- If the text didn't come to you on disk, and you have to type it, concentrate first on getting all the words on the page before you do any formatting. Otherwise you'll slow yourself down significantly. If the client is sitting there watching you, explain this. Otherwise the client will keep interrupting you to ask for more space, emphasis, or different positions.
- Every application handles hyphenation and font metrics (character- and word-spacing) differently, so you can't depend on galleys from your word processor matching up with same-width columns from your page layout program, or even getting identical line endings from two different page layout programs. Don't confuse yourself or your client by making precise changes at the word processor stage.
- Create complicated templates for tables or grids on the master page, along with guidelines that will reflect on every page. If you do this on a real page,

YOU CAN USE YOUR COMPUTER
TO PREPARE COPY FOR OUR DESKTOP PUBLISHING SERVICES

The closer you follow these guidelines, the faster we'll turn around your job, and the less it will cost you. We're happy to clarify anything you don't fully understand or that seems counterintuitive.

Give Us Your Disk.
We accept MS-DOS (IBM-PC or clone), CP/M, Apple II and Macintosh disks, and can read most popular word processing formats. Check with us for our latest compatibility list. Or look in your word processor manual to see how to save files as "plain text only" (ASCII). Unfortunately these universally readable files lose all style formatting. (For ASCII files, if possible, use two carriage returns between each paragraph.)

Send along a **hard copy printout** of the file. Annotate layout and design instructions, and last minute instructions, on the printout. To avoid confusion, write corresponding filenames to be converted on the disk label. Delete unrelated files. And keep a backup of what you send!

File Away.
If possible, combine all your articles into a single large **Master File**, in the same order they will appear in the publication. If the result is larger than about 50K, make two or more smaller files. As the first line of text in each file, type the file name. Start each section with an all-caps "slug" identifying the text and its purpose or repeating its headline, and telling where the article is likely to go, eg. 1LEAD STORY, 2EDIT, 3MASTHEAD, 4CAPTION.

Type special instructions to us in ALL CAPS, on separate lines (e.g., CENTER NEXT 3 LINES) — or mark up the hard-copy printout. To identify standard formats, refer to your copy of our printout of typestyles used in the publication.

Include a **Memo File** listing the articles and any special treatment or style considerations. We can help you create an editorial style manual for your publication.

What To Format.
Is your document organized with chapter headings, bylines, A, B and C and level heads, subheads, body text, indents, pull quotes, and the like? If so, we can "tag" your text with custom style sheets that identify paragraphs. We assign specifications to each style for font, size, word and character spacing, justification (left, right, center, and full), bold/italic and indents. Our style sheets apply only to entire paragraphs, even when a paragraph is just one word. With style sheets, we can start work before you've concluded how the final pages should look; later, by changing the style specs, we automatically update the entire document.

To ensure consistency, **remove all formatting you've applied to entire paragraphs** for levels of headlines, etc. But use your word processor to format **individual words** within paragraphs of body text as bold or italic. If your word processor lacks italics, use underline and we'll substitute it (when you really want underline, alert us with a MESSAGE). *Note: italic, **unless also bold**, tends to de-emphasize text.*

With a typewriter, caps and underlines help emphasize important words. But all caps when typeset is hard to read and may look amateurish. Different layouts, bold and large type does a better job. So unless you're **positive** you want ALL CAPS, type everything upper and lower case. Later on, it's simple for us to make any text all caps. But we'll usually need to retype completely text you've given us in all caps to make it upper and lower case.

You can identify each headline by marking the hard copy, or by typing (A) or (B) immediately before the text. Or we can show you how to be an "advanced" formatter, tagging text in your word processor and further speeding your job.

Don't use tabs, spaces, or a word processor command to center text. If it's part of a headline style, don't worry about it at all; if it's a special case, just mark it on your printout, or type CTR FOLLOWING TEXT in the document file.

For characters not available on your keyboard, list in the Memo File the unique codes you use, such as: "replace my * with bullet (•), or change all e/ to é and /e to è." Specify codes for all accent marks, and for © and ®, ¶, ■ and □. Identify en dashes, used for dates, 1990–91, and times, 7–9 p.m.) For codes, use characters that don't otherwise appear in your document.

We automatically convert your three dots ... to an ellipsis that won't break at the end of a line…, and we change " to "curly" left and right quotes, and -- to —. Use one space after periods for better looking typeset copy (but don't worry, we can change this easily if you can't break old typewriter habits).

Whether or not you prefer a space before — and after — an em-dash—type it how you want it, and we'll leave it that way. Type the true 0 and 1, not lower case l and the letter 0 so you get 1990, not l99O.

Type footnotes in a separate paragraph immediately after the reference, if you want them to appear on that page. If you're not typing the footnote numbers yourself, but using the word processor's footnote function, give us a sample file as soon as possible so we can test it out.

Leave The Page Layout To Us.

If you tweak your document to look just right on your screen or printout, you'll create extra formatting we have to undo. **Don't ever hit the tab or space key twice in succession.** Leave text left-justified and single spaced. We can indent first lines of paragraphs with style sheets, but if you want to do it yourself, hit the tab key once.

Don't put lists or columnar items across the page. Type the whole first column, then the entire second column, down the page. For simple tables with one or two words in each column, type a single tab between each entry and a carriage return at the end of the line; for complex tables, consult us **before** keying data.

Typography uses proportional spacing, so each letter occupies a different width: mniii versus mniii. Until you see correctly sized type from us, you can't predict where lines will break. So don't try to force multiple indentations, hanging bullets or indented second lines. For bulleted or numbered lists, type the desired character or number (bold if you want it that way), followed by a tab, then the text. For forms, don't make "fill in the blank" underlines. Instead, tab to the next word or column, and we'll add the lines.

Finally, if something isn't clear, please ask. Don't try any formatting you're not sure about, especially if you're on deadline. It can only delay completion of your job.

from Kramer Communications

once you have your final style, you'll have to laboriously copy the guidelines to the master page.

- Plan the order of your work. Before you start making corrections, look through every page, to be sure the client didn't bury an important general instruction in the middle of the document.

- If you'll be cleaning up word processor files with a series of global search and replace commands, combine them into one big file (Felix calls it Combo), make the changes, then break them out again. By working only on copies, you'll be sure to have the original files if you make a mistake. You'll also be sure you're treating all files consistently, and you'll probably save time. (**Fig. 7.3** lists the steps involved in a typical conversion.)

- Complete all editorial corrections before changing any layouts. This may mean returning to a page twice, but it's the only way to be sure you don't overlook some of your client's changes.

- Start making changes from the end of the document, then work your way forward to the beginning. This approach won't make sense until you try it. Visualize a multi-page linked document in which you're incorporating text edits. If you start from the front, eventually you'll look for some text and find it's no longer on the same page as it was when you started. If you work backward, the reflows will affect only the already edited sections.

- Always be alert to alternative ways to make changes. For instance, if your client sends back heavily edited page proofs, and you did very little work to format the text, time permitting, consider asking the client to supply you with the revised text on disk. You'll be saving the client money by not having to pay high rates for typing. On the other hand, keep your eye out for the opposite situation. If the proofs look clean, but the client has edited many words in just a few paragraphs, don't start picking out the words to change. It'll be faster to retype the entire paragraph.

- If you're making changes yourself or hiring a typist, be aware that, as with any other production step, there are fast and there are inefficient ways of changing text. When two words with typos are separated by a correct word, it's best to select all three words (using a keyboard shortcut for extending word selections) and retype them. Productivity is a function of your typing speed and agility with your mouse or trackball. On the other hand, sometimes it's best to use keyboard commands or cursor controls. When two letters in a word are transposed, if your software doesn't include this function, you're better off writing a macro to switch them. If the author tends occasionally to put an extra space before a comma, you

CLEANING UP WORD PROCESSOR FILES

Some utilities and software packages can batch or semi-automate this process. Perform these steps on a copy of the client's file, retaining the original if you lose data, and printing out a hard copy reference before making changes.

Extra formatting

Convert or retype upper-case headlines to upper & lower case

Remove justification, bold & italic styled heads

Convert underlines to italics

Special characters

Convert double hyphens to em dashes, foot & inch marks to apostrophes & curly quotes. Add space before & after dashes and ellipses (optional)

Convert l to 1 and O to 0, as in l99O and 1990

Convert ligatures (fi to fi, fl to fl, ae to æ)

Convert hyphens to en-dashes where appropriate. (Semi-automate the search with wildcards to turn all 19??-?? into 19??–??, and ?? a.m.-?? p.m. into ?? a.m.–?? p.m.)

Convert accent marks, bullets, copyright & trademark signs, fractions, & other characters the client could not type. (Client can code for you with # for bullet, /e for é, e/ for è, etc.)

Remove bullets or numbers from paragraphs if page layout software automatically handles lists

Convert coding by savvy clients into style sheet tags

Extra characters

This order of the steps eliminates the need to repeat a step later on.

Remove carriage returns within paragraphs created by people with typewriter habits

Remove carriage returns & tabs used to create hanging indents;

Remove line feeds from ASCII text-only files

Remove spaces before punctuation marks including . , : ; ! ' ? "

Remove spaces before & after tabs

Remove tabs used to indent first lines of body text (optional)

Convert multiple spaces & tab stops to single tabs in tables

Replace double spaces with single spaces

Remove leading and trailing spaces in paragraphs

Remove multiple carriage returns

Uncleaning a file

To export a file from a page layout to a word processor or BBS, search for extended characters that the recipient equipment may not recognize, and could get hung up by. Replace them with their simpler representations:

Bullet becomes # or *

En- and em-dash becomes single & double hyphen

Curly left or right quote & apostrophe becomes inch & foot mark

Fixed space becomes space

Tab becomes five spaces

from Kramer Communications

Fig. 7.3 Sequence for converting client files

might perform a global search and replace to clean up all instances of the error. Remember whether your word processor or page layout program selects the space after the word as well as the word. Each one does that differently. If it selects the space, each time you change a word, make sure you retype the missing space.

- For global changes, sometimes it helps to take characters that are already correct, and hide them by changing them to a character that doesn't appear in the document, such as @ or ~. Then you can work on the document knowing you won't lose what's already right, and that those words won't interfere with what you're doing. At the end, change the @ back to what it was. For instance, while we wrote this book, the product name Xerox Ventura changed to Ventura Publisher. First we changed all instances of Xerox Ventura to ~. Then we searched for all the times we'd used the shorthand Ventura and changed that to ~. Finally we changed all the instances of ~ to Ventura Publisher. We didn't want to end up with Ventura Publisher Publisher or other awkward errors.

- And so on. There are more variants than we could ever cover. You just need to keep watching yourself and thinking about whether there's an easier way to do each step.

Automate your tasks

Customize your software and your template files. Enlist the computer's help. Keep trying to find ways to do things quicker the second time than the first.

- Except when it will be very time-consuming, make **macros** (small customized routines called up by a single keystroke) or style sheets for any step you do more than a few times. It's not easy to stop work to do it, even when you know it will save you time. But leave space in your production work schedule to create these macros. You'll find a very good demystification of macros for the Mac in Cynthia W. Harriman's *The Macintosh Small Business Companion.* (See **Appendix 2. Books on small business and working at home.**)

- Stay on top of all your keyboard equivalents for macros and other commands. As you assign the keys, leave yourself room to maneuver, to add new commands to logical keystroke combinations.

- Record all your shortcuts, macros, and style sheets in a special technical notebook you create for your work. (More on this later in this chapter in **Anticipate the worst case.**)

- Make the software work the way you want it. Don't take anything for granted. Always review the software's default choices before using them. For instance, unless you specify otherwise, leading may be set at an automatic value. **Invisibles**—markers for tabs, carriage returns, and spaces between words—may not show automatically, and new documents may always start on page 1. We don't like any of these factory settings, so we change them.

Don't let software delay you

Try to avoid any sequence that will result in your having to wait each time for the screen to refresh itself, which is still one of the main bottlenecks in DTP.

- Remember that screen refresh is often quicker in word processors, so don't wait until the page layout stage to execute steps that depend on scrolling around if you can do it earlier with the word processor. Execute your file cleanup wherever search and replace is quickest and wherever it's easier to automate the process using a batch utility or macros.
- Switching pages is slow, so don't leave a page or a spread until you've completed everything that needs changing on that page. The only exception is one we mentioned a few pages back: Make all your editorial changes before changing layouts.
- Carefully select the view at which you make the change, to minimize screen refresh time, simplify keeping track of what you've done, and speed your moving on to the next correction.
- With some page layout and graphic software, switching tools can slow you down, so do everything on a page with the text editor or a graphic tool, then start moving around the pieces.
- With some software, the computer takes less time to respond to an action that affects a part of the page not in view. You could select an area to work on, move it off screen, and then issue your commands. Or go to a high magnification and work on one small area at a time.
- If you're making many changes in a section of a document that's linked to other parts, copy the section; make the changes; then copy the changed paragraphs back so you'll have to wait for only one screen refresh.
- Many software packages will postpone refreshing the screen—if you issue a sequence of keystroke commands quickly enough—until after the entire series. Experiment.

My all-time favorite sequence in Microsoft Word for the Mac enables me, without having to wait for any of the intermediate stages, to cut a section out of my master Combo word processor file, open a new file, paste in the section, name, close, and save the new file so it's ready to import into my page layout. I do all this in one pass by selecting the text, holding the command key down and typing in rapid succession XNVW, then the <NEW FILENAME> and finally hitting a carriage return.   *—Felix*

Use the right tool for the job

Just because you've developed a trusty way of doing things doesn't mean you can't branch out.

- Use paper proofs for editing. Never edit exclusively on screen. It's less convenient, but you'll always catch more errors looking at hard copy. Editing on paper will also leave a paper trail of who changed what. That's important both for independent DTPers and people working in corporate DTP centers. Editing hard copy is also much easier on your eyes.
- Use different hardware when it makes sense. If you need a faster central processor, or some scanning or color capabilities better than those you have, get access to whatever will speed your work. Buy it, borrow it, rent it, or barter time with someone.
- Don't be dogmatic. If you're Macintosh-based, you'll eventually encounter a project that's more appropriately done with a PC, and vice versa. If you don't know the ins and outs of some hardware, this is a perfect time to subcontract the work, and look over your sub's shoulder if appropriate.
- Don't try to put a square document into round software. Some DTP projects should never leave a word processor. Sacrificing some of the more advanced formatting and layout capabilities may be a small price to pay for the word processor's flexibility in other areas. And some publications ought to remain in spreadsheets or databases rather than migrating to page layout software. In particular, for publications with frequent last-minute updates, explore spreadsheet, database, and presentation graphics packages with advanced formatting and layout capabilities. In general, for data coming to you from databases and spreadsheets, think ahead to future uses of the information before you forever lose much of the information and organizing principles for the data. If in any doubt, explore these questions with the client.

- Some specialized word processors (Nisus on the Mac, XyWrite on the PC) have very advanced capabilities. They can parse text, looking for patterns of characters. (Remember parsing sentence structures in grammar school?) This means that if, for example, you want to make all the lead-ins (introductory phrases) bold in a section, you can define a search for any number of words preceded by a carriage return and followed by a colon, and change the style. And they often have better built-in macro capabilities, to turn tedious repetitive work into automated menu choices. If you don't own one of these, you may be able to improvise. For instance, in Word, search for the colons and replace them with tabs; adjust the tab margins as needed to give you a clear space; then use Word's command to select a vertical column, and make all the text in the first column bold. Then replace the tabs with colons.
- Sometimes you can imaginatively use software as file format converters. For instance, if you get a file in a format you can't read directly with your word processor, perhaps your page layout software has a filter for that format. If so, you can import it to a page layout file, then export it to your word processor format. Similarly, some graphics and page layout software can take a PC .TIF file and convert it to a Mac TIFF file, and so on. PageMaker and Ventura Publisher both have a wide selection of filters.
- You can use your page layout or illustration software to design thumbnails with simple placeholder gray ovals, circles, and boxes, keeping the actual text and art out of the picture until you're happy with a layout.
- For some projects, when you're in the design stage, it pays to take the extra time to set up your pages and your type and graphic elements more carefully than you would for a traditional rough sketch. If the client likes your comp, you'll be closer to a working template.
- Use the tools right. For instance, PageMaker has such a straightforward interface that it's temptingly easy to just work by instinct, nudging blocks of type around until everything looks right. Don't succumb to this temptation. Learn the program's capabilities and shortcuts. Don't make something that looks right but will be hard to change if the words change.
- Be flexible about the rules you establish for yourself. Chances are you generally tag your type for styles in your word processor, because it's more efficient. Yet sometimes it may be more fun, and result in a better design, to wait and tag your type on the fly in the page layout program, where you really see your pages.

- Think of your time as a limited resource. For instance, it's almost always a good idea to pay for a delivery service, rather than run a package over yourself to a client or service bureau. You can turn the time you'll save into billable minutes. The only problem is that you might not get the exercise you need after sitting around all day.

Create a structure, then build on it

Don't reinvent the wheel. Instead:

- Build an electronic library of shapes for future use. For example, create X boxes for letter- and legal-sized pages, plus all standard photograph sizes (3 by 5, 3½ by 5, and 8 by 10, both vertical and horizontal) to serve as placeholders in layouts. If you create them with graphics software, it will be easier to retain their original aspect ratios when you resize them in your page layout program. Make quick-and-dirty crop marks using a graphics program. Keep any useful shapes you've developed for use as electronic whiteout—to cover parts of pages temporarily or permanently. Put the recycled paper logo in your library. (See **6. Don't waste paper**).

Fig. 7.4
X boxes

- Keep a library of standard text files. For instance, here are some commonly used **kerning pairs** (letters that tuck into each other for better visual appearance). You can use this list to test out the quality of the kerning pairs built into a typeface, as well as the type default settings and controls of a page layout program.

Fig. 7.5
Frequent kerning pairs

Av Aw Ay Ta Te To Tr Tu Tw Ty Ya Yo Wa We Wo we yo AC AT AV AW AY FA LT LV LW LY OA OV OW OY PA TA TO VA VO WA WO YA YA

- Keep a library of styles, for such elements as drop caps, rules above lines, or complex tabulated material, and store these styles in template documents. Most DTP software allows you to copy single, multiple, or all styles from one document to another, through a menu command or by selecting a block of type with the styles you want and pasting it into the next document.

- Store copies of library elements and graphics in one easy-to-find place—a folder or subdirectory for repeating resources. You could keep them in their original graphic file formats, using easy to find names like 8X10VERT, and perhaps store them inside consolidated page layout documents as well.

- Use blocks of text as placeholders for one- or two-time elements like mastheads and date lines that don't merit creating a unique style. When these elements change, just retype the text in place of the existing text.

- Create placeholder boxes or rectangles in page layout software sized correctly for pictures, if you aren't using scans, or if you are waiting for art to arrive. You can wrap text around the placeholders, write inside them what they'll be, or give the author a reminder. If your pictures are FPOs, you can take all your scanned images out after you print the final camera-ready laser output. That way when you save and archive the document, it will be more compact. When you take the file to the imagesetter, if you've wrapped text around a graphic you scanned for position only, you can usually replace the image with a white, outline, or black box while retaining the wrap, so you can retain your layout, reduce the file size, and speed imagesetting. A hairline or black box may be just what the printer needs to help place the graphic correctly.

- Copy what you've already done. Say you've just made a complicated headline with a kicker, lines, and a particular kind of spacing. The next time you need one of these thingamajigs, don't start over: Copy the first one to the new page and type over each line with new text. Sometimes you'll even copy entire pages of layouts and then paste in new contents to the page. Some software lets you copy the paragraph marker for a paragraph to some new text, thereby giving that new text the same attributes—or there's a copy format command.

- Make your own tools. If you've created an unusual layout and want to ensure that you continue to follow your own rules, make your own measuring implements. You can make rulers, overlapping graphic shapes or boxes to be sure you've left the same amount of white space between elements, within the page layout software or in a graphics program. If you want an easy way to get line counts on page proofs that are 30 lines deep, set up a block with numbers one through 30 running down the page, in the master page so they show up on every proof page.

- Take all those books about graphic design seriously. Learn about **grids**. If you fear they'll constrain your design, you'll find that, like the rigid structure of a Shakespearean sonnet or a Japanese haiku, the limits will release your creativity.
- Take work you've completed for one client and use it with someone else: an inventive grid, a set of styles, a return coupon, or a business-reply card. With modifications, each can serve again and again.
- Try to avoid designs that require changing elements on a page if you add an odd page, making succeeding *versos* (left pages) into *rectos* (right ones), and rectos into versos.

Become a style sheet whiz

DTPers need to be style sheet experts. If you forego tags or style sheets, you'll waste time, lose consistency, have great difficulty working well with sub-contractors, and you'll feel rusty every time you come back to the next issue of a publication you haven't looked at for a few weeks or months. Style sheets will also help you look like you know exactly what you're doing if you ever work with the client right beside you.

- Build your styles on top of each other. Felix starts with a BaseStyle. Then he creates two branches: BaseBodyText and BaseHead. If he wants to change everything in the document, he can alter BaseStyle. To change all the display type, he can modify BaseHead. If he has a series of tables in the document, he'll create a BaseTableStyle, and build TableHeads, TableNotes, etc. on this style. This way, even if every table ends up slightly different because of different column widths, tab, and spacing settings, they're still controllable from the style sheet.
- Create one story or text block showing a line of each type style and size used in the publication, to refresh your memory and to improve communication with the client. Having this block available also simplifies copying some or all of the styles to another publication file. **Fig.** 7.6 is a sample reference style list for *Desktop Publishing Success*.
- Create potentially invisible styles for annotations on proof pages to clients or dummy pages for printers. At the end of the job, by changing the color of the styles to paper or white, you can make them disappear from the final camera-ready pages.

STYLE SHEET FOR *DESKTOP PUBLISHING SUCCESS*

When we want to give a client a shorthand way to refer to the styles in a publication, we give them this kind of a printout.

Headlines: Adobe Futura family

Text: Adobe Garamond family

HEADER & FOLIO: Book 8 point with 1/2 point rules

CHAPTER TITLE: 24/26

Level 1 subhead: Bold 12/14

Level 2 subhead: Bold 10/14

Body text: 12/14 with 4 points of space after paragraphs

Quote: 11/12 with italic IDs, 2 pica indents left and right

Profile: 11/12, 9 point indent for biography

Figure text: 10.5/11 and 11/12

FIGURE TITLE: Bold 12/15

Figure Caption:
Heavy oblique (italic) 12/14 with 1 point rules

TABLE OF CONTENTS CHAPTER TITLE: Heavy 12/14

TOC chapter subhead: 11/11.5 with 10.5 italic references to figures

Appendix resources: 11/12 with 3 points of space after paragraphs

Index alphabet: Bold 10/10

Index entry: 10/10.5 with 2 points of space before first level entry

Fig. 7.6 Sample printout of style sheet for client

- Precede the name of styles that are rarely used, were created for one-time special sections in a publication, or are invisible, with a z or a bullet. This distinguishes them from the styles for everyday use—and puts them at the end of an alphabetical list of styles. That way you won't have to scroll through them in menus looking for the styles you need. To put styles at the top of an alphabetical list, for the Mac you can use a space or a period. (Don't use this tip for *file* names. It's not a good idea to use periods at the start or colons anywhere in file names on the Mac, because they interfere with the computer's file directory, and can crash the system if you try to copy the file. You can't do it on the PC, even if you try.)

Organize your pages for productivity

Don't feel compelled to follow the intended numerical order of a final publication, if it doesn't make sense for you.

- If your page layout software is limited in its flexibility to break a document into sections, or to provide many numbering options, don't fight it. When you're doing long reports or books, start the file with page 1, so the software gets the pagination right automatically. Then put all the introductory front matter pages either at the end of the file, or in a separate file, where you can manually adjust the pagination as needed.
- If the software can't mix tall and wide pages in one file, for a standard report with a couple of horizontal tables, make a separate file for those wide pages. Duplicate the header and footer from the main report (rotated into correct position) to eliminate the extra step of mechanically pasting up the tables into blank tall numbered pages.
- Just because your software can handle thousands of pages, don't be tempted to cram a huge document into one file. To reduce file sizes, ease tracking of revisions, and reduce the danger of losing all your work with one false move, break the document into logical parts—chapters or 50-page sections. Depending on the software you're using, you may have to manually adjust the starting page number of each file before you print your camera-ready pages, but that's not a heavy burden. (There's always an exception to every rule: To fine-tune the total length of this book, we placed it into one giant page layout file, almost two megabytes in size. And we adjusted some specs to see how it affected the number of pages, but we never used it as a working file.)

- Get accustomed to creating your own end-of-file pages as your primary location to store needed elements. Here's where you'll make **overset** pages for articles or stories that don't fit in the client's original layout. It's much easier, and more cost-effective, if you run out the overset galley-style. This way, before you do extra work, the client can decide between copy-editing, changing the layout, adding pages, or deleting articles. You can also store on these pages unused articles from the current issue of a newsletter that are candidates for inclusion next time.
- DTP software can show you left and right pages side-by-side, and that's how they show up on a two-page monitor. So it makes sense to set up the first and last page of newsletters as a **facing spread**. This way you'll reduce the amount of page switching you do, and also get a better sense of how the final publication will look. Ventura Publisher lets you start the first page as a left or right page. If your software package can't do this automatically, here's how to do it: For an eight-page newsletter, insert a blank page one, or start the document with page 2 (which the software package will interpret as a left page). After page 8 (the back cover), put the front cover on page 9. If you have a header, footer or page number for all the inside pages, cover it over on page 9. What if the newsletter's next issue runs 12 pages? If your software permits it, insert four pages somewhere in the middle of the document, to minimize disturbance to standing elements such as masthead, coupon, or departmental columns.
- Sometimes it may pay to take additional time to set your pages up specially to save money on imagesetting. If you have a booklet-sized publication (typically 8½ by 5½ inches for each page), putting two pages on each 8½- by 11-inch sheet will cut your imagesetting bill in half. Putting four pages on each 11- by 17-inch tabloid-size page may further reduce imagesetting costs. In either case, until page layout software packages get smarter, in the page proof stage you'll have to settle for one automatic folio (page number) on each sheet. When everything about the job is final, put the actual page numbers individually on each page. If you do it earlier, and the pages are reorganized, you'll have done extra work.
- For your own use, especially to keep track of changes in page or story order, print out the pages and make a stapled dummy copy of the book in progress. And at the end of the job, you'll make one for the printer. It may help you or the client to use the **thumbnails** feature of many software packages to print out 4-64 mini-representations of the pages of a book on one single page.

- You may be tempted to set your pages up for **imposition**—the way printers set up pages for their presses and binders. Typically, for a simple offset job like an eight-page newsletter, printers often like to receive camera-ready pages on boards as follows: 8-1,2-7,6-3,4-5. (It's easy to remember: The two page numbers always add up to one more than the number of pages in the publication.) You can set up each pair as a single page for imagesetting output. But you'll no longer see the reader's actual facing pages on your screen, and you'll spend time jumping around from page to page in your file. You're often better off with a simpler page setup.
- A few software packages are starting to offer the option to print pages in imposition order. This single capability is not likely to cause you to switch software packages. Until your software of choice offers it, you're better off leaving the entire problem of imposition to printers, or, if necessary, preparing mechanicals in printer spreads by cutting and pasting the repro. In any case, printers often make small adjustments to take into account the publication's thickness, so the feature may not be so important.

Name your files with care

You can easily lose track of where you are in a project. Consistent and carefully planned file naming conventions can help immeasurably.

The PC understands all file names as upper case, and doesn't allow blank spaces, so a readable Mac file name like MyGrtWrk will, after transfer, turn into MYGRTWRK. In any case, don't put blank spaces in your Mac FILENAME.

If you're using a Macintosh or Unix machine, or a PC utility that enables you to go beyond the PC's FILENAME.EXT format, you should stick to the eight characters plus extension, unless you're sure your files will never have to be transferred to a computer or a file list that can handle only those 11 characters.

You might, for instance, reserve the first two characters for the client or project name; the next two for the chapter or publication; the last four for the month and year. To avoid confusion, have the name refer to the *date of the issue*, not the date you completed the work. For example, call the invitation for an October 16 event INVT1090 even if you did the job in August.

You can use the three extension characters for the application file type (.WP/ .WS/.XYW/.DCA/.WRD/.DOC/.ASC/.TXT/.PCT/.GEM/.TIF/.EPS) or (for the Mac) lower case versions of these initials, or the file category

(.TXT/.CHP/.CAP/.PUQ/.STY/.SDB for text, chapter, caption, pull quote, style sheet, sidebar) or the proof number (G1/P2/Lino, etc.). Or you might use a/b/c/d to identify successive file versions. Remember that letters give you 26 distinct options for each character instead of 10. So this Chapter 7 of *Desktop Publishing Success* might start out in DSCombo.g (part of one large word processor file with the entire text); then become DS07.G1 (Chapter Seven's first galley file); then go into DS070890.A (first page proof); and end as DS071190.Fin (*Desktop Publishing Success* Chapter 7 November 90 final file). Be sure to use 01 for January, not just 1, so files sort correctly in lists.

You could develop a variant on this system, using different conventions for page layout files than for component files (word processing, graphic, spreadsheet, chart) that will be combined to make the final document. If you develop a system like this and always use it, you'll be able to use wildcard searches on your hard disk files to find all the files starting with the client name, or all files completed in a particular month or of a certain type. If you have a different formula, fine. Many systems will work as long as you're consistent, you don't inadvertently assign the same name to two different files, other people know about your abbreviations, and you're consistent about the folders or subdirectories in which you locate your files.

Be consistent

By definition, DTPers must be fastidious followers of precedents. Do it for yourself, for your clients, their readers, and for potential clients to whom you give samples. Observe yourself as you work. Do you find yourself trying to remember how you set up pages or tables, or flipping through back issues of publications to see how you spelled a word? Or do you just go ahead and do it again in the way that seems right to you now? Either way, you're making consistency a harder problem for you than it has to be. If you're a nit-picker, you'll find the computer to be an ideal work partner. The more you use the computer's power to standardize, define, and automate procedures, the better off you'll be. A few *non-electronic* practices will also help you.

- Start and end each session with your screen showing the master page or the header or footer, so you remember each time to change the galley or proof number before printing out.
- Always check to make sure you've run out every drop of text from a word processor into a page layout document. Check the first and last word of

the story and all jumps and transitions. While you're at it, make sure the continued on and continued from direction signs are correct, unless the software does that automatically.

- Stick to round numbers whenever possible. For instance, when creating tables, or other work that's time-consuming and requires you to place elements by eyeballing them, make your life simpler, and that of your successor working in the file, by choosing unit increments that are easy to remember and to calculate. Don't set tabs every 34 points if you can live with every 36 points (3 picas).

- Document what you do. In **Create a structure, then build on it**, above, we talked about making electronic measuring tools and placeholders. To increase the utility of these aids, find ways to annotate them. The idea is to leave yourself (or your successor or subcontractor) enough information to know what to do next, even when resuming a project after months of being away from it. Ideally, this information will exist in two forms: Printed out on a sheet in the client's physical file folder (and often in a general technical notebook) and in a logical spot inside the computer file. For instance, if you create a complex grid or series of nonprinting guidelines for elements on the page, print out a page and draw in the guidelines. And in the file, identify each guideline with a label however you can, such as on the pasteboard or in invisible type. Similarly, the style page you produce as a reference for your own use and to educate the client could also include, in both its electronic and printed forms, samples of standard graphic elements (rules, boxes, line widths, specially made measuring tools, and even colors) and descriptions of when each is used.

- When you're scanning a series of photographs, include in the scanned area an identifier for the picture: a photo number, or the person's name. When you put the photo on the page, you can crop out the ID—but it's always back there in case you lose track of who's who. You can do the same with art you create, by including on the graphic's edge a note showing the file name and any typefaces used in the graphic.

- For imagesetting, color jobs, and for jobs where you're printing small unnumbered pages on a printer, identify all pages with a line of text outside the crop marks. That way, you or the printer will be able to keep track of which pages are which, without guessing or having to worry about erasing some label you don't want to show on the printed page. Anchor the text block to a master page, or create one for individual pages. Depending on the software you use, to keep the text showing but beyond the crop marks, you may need to create a large text block, with carriage returns to force the text beyond the live page area.

- If all these elements seem to clutter up your computer file, you don't have to keep them there. You can instead create a template or master document. Whenever you make a change in the current issue of a publication or add or modify a style, you can add it to this source document, so it's always updated. It adds an extra step, but this method is essential for workgroups, since it removes all questions about where to find the most recent standard for formats, standing elements, and styles.

- It's also a good idea, in cooperation with each client, to develop an editorial style sheet. This is usually just a handwritten list of how to treat all those troublesome words, abbreviations, spellings, capitalizations, and other rules that are judgment calls. It's a big help to the client. Once you both have the list, even if they slip up in the copy they give you, they can hope you'll catch their mistakes. Chances are no single commercial style manual will do the job, especially for technical words like dot-matrix, so you're better off recording the decisions you and the client make on the fly. One good system divides a single sheet of paper into a tic-tac-toe grid to handwrite the choices for each element that might be treated in more than one way. For a longer publication with many more style choices, you might take 16 pages or so, recording all words and styles beginning with abc on the first page, xyz on the sixteenth. For an article with more detail on this subject, check out *Personal Publishing*, April 1987, page 69. **Fig.** 7.7, on the next page, is the tidied-up editorial style sheet for this book.

Anticipate the worst case

We're all subject to wishful thinking. But DTPers can't afford to hope that everything works out okay. It's much easier to plan a good defense, and be surprised when you don't need to draw on it.

- Every time you take out your mechanic's tools, assume you could end up with a brain-dead computer. Allow yourself time to get outside help or backup hardware. That means you shouldn't start adjusting your hardware (installing new memory, data storage, or circuit boards) or your software (updating your operating system) during working hours. Unless you're not fazed by the possibility of a crippled system while you're on deadline, save the upgrading for weekends. Try to line up a sympathetic

EDITORIAL STYLES FOR *DESKTOP PUBLISHING SUCCESS*

7.7 Sample editorial style sheet

AAs not AA's Adobe Photoshop Aldus FreeHand	End-user freelance gray-scale (adj) gray scale (noun)	Numbers: write out under 10 except page 9 NYC on-line	Three-dimensional troubleshooting, troubleshooter typeface type style
Back up (verb) backup (noun) based: PC-based beta-tester bold for terms and emphasis bullets: use semi- colon after bulleted items; use period after last item	Hard-copy (adj) high-end and low- end (adj); the high end (noun) high cost and low cost (adj) high-resolution type 65 hz for monitors 10-hour job	PageMaker page: one-page newsletter paper: 8 ½ by 11 not 8 ½ x 11 parentheses: remove where possible pasteup (noun) paste-up people PCs per hour not /hour or /hr	Unbillable not nonbillable (hours) up-to-date (adjec- tive before noun) user group, not user's or users' except in official name. NY Mac Users' Group
Colon is followed by upper case when a complete sentence colon and dash— remove where possible color: one-color work; single- color work copy-edit, copy editor	Inch: 17-inch in-house publish- ing; bring the project in house. inkjet kilobyte laser printer LaserJet (Hewlett- Packard) LaserWriter lay out (verb) low resolution type lower case and upper case	Percent: % for numbers over 10 pick up (verb) pickup (noun) PO Box: no periods PostScript prepress products: CompanyName ProductName the first time it's used (no apostrophes)	Ventura Publisher well-known worklife workflow workspace workstation
Dates: 1990s decision-maker, decision-making dot matrix dots per inch (dpi) not dots/inch; write out first time used in each chapter double check DTPers	Megabyte: 80- megabyte disks; 2 megabytes of RAM mhz mindset multimedia	Setup (noun) set up (verb) side: two-sided newsletter spot-color (adj) spot color (noun) startup (noun) start up (verb) style sheet SyQuest 44- megabyte removable cartridge drive	

standby guru you can reach by phone if things get hairy. And remember that if you make some drastic change before everything is working right, you may need to wait until Monday morning to reach a technical support number or get to an electronics or computer store.

- Try everything out before you're on deadline. Ideally, try it out even before you establish a deadline. For instance, make sure a client's files convert easily to your system. But don't delay seeing if global changes will give you the results you hope for, or finding out if a graphic effect will satisfy you and the customer, while not making more work for the printer. Your best *modus operandi* is to solve all the difficult issues at the start, then coast in to the deadline.
- Never assume you can save time by building on someone else's DTP work. If a client wants you to pick up production of a publication from someone else, bid the job and budget your time assuming you'll start from scratch. You certainly can't judge the quality of work simply from a printed page or final output. The template may be insufficiently documented, poorly constructed, or even damaged in some way. As soon as you get it, open up the file and select all elements on the page or spread to see how it's built. (See **8. Managing subcontractors**.)
- If you're designing a publication for a client, make sure your design accommodates the most complex example of each element. Find the most wordy titles and subheads in the text. In tables, find the longest headings or categories, or numbers in columns. Use them in the prototype, along with average and short examples, to give a sense of how they work together. Seeing the most extreme instances of text elements may prompt the client to rewrite or reorganize the material. And the earlier they do that the better.
- Compile your emergency information so you don't have to hunt it down when you're in trouble. Create a special notebook for your most needed technical information (the kinds of things you'd put up on a bulletin board with a pushpin if you had a big enough piece of cork). Among the things you should include: technical support phone numbers, software version numbers, and serial numbers; special macros and shortcuts you've assigned to your keyboard; special tricks you can almost remember but keep having to look up; and typefaces available in your system.

Some of our favorite shortcuts

- For proofing tabloid pages on standard 8 ½- by 11-inch pages, reducing the page size to 65% fits the entire page. And if your eyes are good, the text is still readable.
- If you output mechanicals at 300 or even 1,270 dpi, when the client wants the finest quality screens, make **keylines**. These are boxes made of hairline rules to indicate the position of a tint the printer will make.
- You can improve the coarse tints you get from your 300 dpi laser printer. Check your software manual or technical support. Usually you can specify a higher screen frequency on a software menu or customize a printer description file to improve your results compared to the default settings. (See **Fig. 8.2.**)
- If you have a logo you want to use directly without tracing it with software, first photocopy the logo at an enlarged setting, then scan the copy at 300 dpi as line art. If you can double the size of the original, you'll get an effective 600 dpi scan.
- If you get an eight-inch tall by 10-inch wide photo and your scanner can handle only an eight-inch width, scan it as if it were a tall photo. Print it out at 66% size, and then scan the smaller printout turned sideways. Unless your scanning software can quickly rotate an image, this is a fast way to get a size you can work with. The only faster solution is to use a reduction photocopier to bring the size within the range of your scanner. In either case, because the image will be copied twice, its quality will degrade—but it will be fine for an FPO.
- For business cards or other small items, create them actual size. Print them out at 200% or greater magnification for reduction by the printer, and you'll have 600 dpi or better without using an imagesetter. This is practical unless the printer wants, say, "eight-up"—eight cards on a page.
- Use non-computer tools when they make sense. For instance, if you can't get your photos to line up in a flatbed scanner, use Post-it Coverup tape, or paste them onto squared-off sheets of paper. Another example: Use artists' **matte fixative** (a noxious spray, so do it outside if possible) on laser printer output to punch up the black toner for presentations.
- Accumulate samples of designs you like; keep them in a file of other people's samples. Magazines like *HOW* and *PRINT*, the DTP monthlies' before and after departments, *Printed Media Outstanding Newsletter Designs*, and *The Page Makeover Book*, all have ideas that can inspire you. (See **Appendix 2. Magazines** and **Books on DTP and graphic design.**)

- Some documents simply refuse to print directly to the laser printer. We try printing them to disk as PostScript files, then downloading those files to the printer. Or we try one of the public domain utilities like Error Handler for Postscript printers that shows us where the output device choked up so we can locate the problem area on a page. (Get them from your imagesetter service bureau.) Often we're unable to locate where the problem is; we just have to live with it .

- Sometimes we can't figure out a mystery, so we stop trying, and work around it. For instance, we have a numbered list, and one line just won't fall into place. The spacing is off, and everything is typed correctly, with no extra tabs or thin spaces. Rather than waste time investigating where we went wrong, after we wrestle with it briefly, we'll copy a good line from another block of text, paste it in, and carefully retype over it. Most of the time, that clears up the problem. It doesn't make us more confident in computers, but it works.

8. SUBCONTRACTING AND VENDORS

Choosing employees and subcontractors

You may start off on your own. But sooner or later, you'll need full-time, part-time, one-time, or temporary help. You may have too much to handle yourself. Or you'll decide that part of what you do is drudgery. Or you'll need some expertise you lack.

You may decide to expand your business by hiring staff. You can often find them through your user group, from a pool of people with whom you've worked before, through newspaper want ads, temporary agencies, and college placement bureaus.

Get set for the headaches of any traditional employer. These include establishing employment policies and benefits, hiring, training, managing, and evaluating employees, remodeling or enlarging your space, and buying lots more furniture and equipment. You'll boost your fixed costs and take on the responsibility of finding work to keep your staff busy. As the boss, you'll spend less time in front of your computer, and more time managing your business and selling. If you intended all along to go this route, you probably already know what you're doing and appreciate the risks. Otherwise, unless you happen upon a few secure long-term retainer clients, and you have no other way to deliver work to them, we suggest you embark in this direction with great caution. (For some issues in hiring and managing staff, see **Appendix 1. Corporate Desktop Publishing**.)

You could go about hiring people in another way: subcontracting. Social and technological changes have produced a vast expansion of the part-time, freelance, and consultant workforce—particularly, it turns out, in computers, publishing, and related communications fields. Among this workforce you'll find people perfectly positioned to be your DTP subs.

Virtually all DTP veterans have their own computer systems, painstakingly individualized and configured to maximize their productivity and pleasure in working. At times they can be pried away from their screens and persuaded to work in someone else's office. Yet, unless it's a collaborative project, or a training job, or the client has much better equipment, many DTPers prefer to work in their own homes or offices. In fact, we think of DTP as an electronic version of the traditional cottage industry. Scattered through the cities, suburbs, hills, and valleys are hardworking artisans, each with their own toolboxes, linked by the technologies of phones, overnight mail, faxes, and modems. (See **4. Connecting with other desktop publishers.**)

Over time, we've established informal networks of these electronic craftspeople as subcontractors for our businesses. We're like a confederation: A flexible set of interlocking experts who can count on each other to produce quality work on deadline. We met mostly through our user group, and that's where many of us still meet new confederates. We treat each other as equals, though the hourly or daily rates we charge clients and each other may vary. Because we work on many jobs together, we trust each other and don't have to worry about complicated contracts. We establish our network before an emergency situation arises where we have to scramble to find the right person. We can confidently bid individually on major projects, knowing we can deliver if they come through. Though each of us has at times hired temporary or permanent, full-time, on-site staff, many of us prefer to stay solo.

Felix and Maggie have each tried training novices or bringing in eager apprentices. We've usually found enthusiasm doesn't translate into skill. Often recruits have been overconfident, reluctant to ask questions about instructions, and thus prone to misunderstandings and costly mistakes. Some never mastered the art of working quickly, consistently, and accurately. Others never became dedicated to producing high-quality work. Most required too much handholding. Maggie has found exceptions among computer science majors at local colleges, Felix among grads of college-level computer graphics programs.

Fortunately, there seems to be something about this technology that encourages imaginative and serious people to become entrepreneurial about their own vocations. We've been most successful hooking up with people after they've perfected key skills and gotten the bugs out of their own careers. At this point, incidentally, they are mature and able co-workers who are willing to act as trainees when necessary. If we need to make sure they do things in a particular way to meet our needs or a client's requirements, they'll be more understanding.

Managing subcontractors

Supervising the work of independent subcontractors is very different from walking around an office and looking over employees' shoulders. Since they won't be working on your premises, you'll need to build trust and rapport gradually. During your first jobs together, you'll evaluate each other to see how well you know what you're doing. From then on, good communication is the key. You're best off going over every detail and assumption of each job at the start. The less you leave up to interpretation, the more you'll retain control. Ideal subcontractors will make your life easier without your asking. They'll bring potential inconsistencies and problem areas to your attention, and, as you work together, they'll learn how much you as the contractor (and ultimately each end client) want them to use their best judgment.

Using subcontractors risks our reputation for good quality—something that's hard to rebuild once it's lost and word gets around. So we're careful to search out subs with good technical and communications skills.

> Make sure you emphasize to subcontractors never to ignore warning signals. I gave a subcontractor a catalog project to update. The subcontractor went ahead and made the changes. Only on returning the completed job did the sub mention that the version on the disk seemed to be different in minor respects. It turned out I had given out as a template the second-to-last proof of the previous issue. As a result, I made work for myself because I had to compare the printed version and the new proof to pick up the final changes that had been made last time. It was my error originally. But the sub should have stopped working and called to find out how to proceed immediately upon noticing the discrepancies.
>
> —*Felix*

In one sense, quality control in DTP subcontracting is easy. Except for complicated color work, the intermediate proofs and the final mechanicals either do or don't look right. Yet a DTP document, like anything that is built, can be well designed and rest on a sound foundation, or it may be a rickety hodgepodge. Usually, you can tell only by eyeballing the computer file:

- Check if the person has taken advantage of automated features like style sheets and master pages;
- See where blocks of type are broken up;
- See how the subcontractor used grids, rulers, and non-printing guides;
- Look for the electronic equivalent of last-minute patches stuck on top of the main structure.

The quality of workmanship is doubly important because this month's final project becomes the starting point for next month's revision. Often a good test of a well-built document is whether you can easily make major changes—such as new sizes and typefaces for both body text and headlines—without having to redo every page from scratch.

A good measure of a professional workstyle is the information the sub leaves for the unknown next person who will work on the file. Self-documentation is ideal. Clues to the use and order of such resources as style sheets, graphics, and files should appear in file and style names. The subcontractor should flag or explain anything not immediately understandable, both in a printed (hard-copy) memo and/or in a non-printing note somewhere within the document. Or the sub can create a separate text file, using the industry standard name README, with the necessary information. On the hard-copy material from the client or on the laser proofs, the sub should write messages and questions to you. If it's material that's going back to the client, and you don't want the client to see your internal dialogue, have the sub use Post-its.

For much of DTP, templates and style sheets are the key to high quality and consistent work, and to productivity savings that translate into profits. If you find subs who can design good templates and style sheets, consider yourself fortunate. Even then, make sure you are involved and approving every step. It's in your interest and that of your client to be sure to build in maximum flexibility and automation. (See 7. **Become a style sheet whiz.**)

If you can't find subs at this level, do the setup yourself, and have the subs work within the framework you create. Whatever you do, keep your disks out of the hands of people who don't know what they are doing, or who can't adjust to your way of working. Most of the times we've lost money or fallen behind schedule have come when we didn't ensure that documents were built right, then had to tear them apart when the client needed to make changes.

One good way we've found to try out subs, and convey to them our methods, is to transfer work in stages. For instance, when we've worked out the kinks in a periodical, and the work has become routine, we'll produce the first proof ourselves, then give the job to a subcontractor for corrections, layout changes, and subsequent page proofs. That gives the sub a chance to become familiar gradually with the overall structure without the burden and anxiety of mastering the entire working apparatus at the start of the job. If all goes well, next time the sub can handle the whole job.

Paying subcontractors

Knowing how much to pay subs isn't easy. Generally, you know how much a particular job costs when you do it, and what you can charge for it. Now you need to factor in another person, with different equipment and skills—and your mutual desire to establish a long-term satisfactory work relationship. It's easy to slip up and either lose money or pass along the extra costs and risk ending up with a client who feels overcharged. (See **10. Negotiating.**)

Since we bill most of our own production work by a combination of hourly and per-job rates, we tend to follow the same structure with subs. We establish hourly or daily rates for projects. Then we set estimates for the amount of time we think it should take, based on our understanding of the work involved, our past experience with the client, and, if it's a periodical or a revision, how much time previous issues have taken. At the start, we review these numbers with the sub. Depending on the job, the results of this analysis might boil down to, "I will pay you $500 to complete every phase of this job," or "There's no way these revisions should take you more than three hours. And adding in these graphics looks like two hours to me. Do you have a problem with that?"

Some of our subs happily agree to flat fees. That way, they don't have to worry about watching the clock. Some people work very quickly. Others have accepted that they work at a slower pace; many of these people would rather do the work and have us worry about how much time it takes.

Just as we do, subcontractors may vary their charges for different kinds of work. Maggie once hired a proofer for a large project who charged different rates for proofing text and for proofing format. But, to her annoyance, the sub didn't explain this policy until the project was underway.

We also establish a markup rate to the client for the subcontractor's hours, as well as our rate to the client for the time we spend on the project. As is the case with the time we spent marketing for the job, we don't consider our time orienting the subcontractor to be billable hours to the client.

As the job progresses, we get updates from the sub. Along the way, we deal with problems and answer the sub's questions. We don't charge the client for messengers, faxes, or our time spent on internal reviews of pages, unless our reviews turn into a major effort to redesign or edit the document.

At the end, the sub gives us a detailed record of the time spent on each phase of the job, including, if the changes from the client's side were much greater than expected, hard-copy documentation of those changes—what typesetters call

author's alterations or AAs. We may then negotiate with the subcontractor. If, for instance, the sub took much longer than we would have taken, we may want to reduce the hourly rate. And if the sub spent time doing things we wouldn't have done or hadn't authorized, especially if we're sure they should have called us and asked us what to do, we may disallow some of those hours.

At this point, before resolving everything with the sub, we'll usually check in with clients to be sure they are happy. We make a point of asking clients how they liked working and communicating with the subcontractor, and communicating this information back to the sub, along with a copy of the final printed publication if we can get extras. Our clients' experiences are crucial in determining our relationship with our subcontractors.

We make clear to our subs they'll be paid upon completion of the work, submission of copies of the finished files and documentation on disk, and complete time sheets and invoices. For large jobs, we sometimes arrange partial progress payments. We tell our subs they won't have to worry about any difficulties or delays we encounter being paid by the client, unless the quality of the sub's work is in question. Our firm policy of immediate payment doesn't help our cash flow, but it removes a large potential area of friction, and makes us more desirable employers.

When all goes well, we enjoy working with the subs and we learn some-thing from each other. The sub gets paid at a satisfactory rate for all the hours spent, and we're able to bill the client for a reasonable number of subcontractor's hours plus our time managing the project.

That's the ideal. In reality, many DTPers don't do as well financially on work they subcontract as on work they do themselves. They feel frustrated that they can never find people as capable and careful as they are. Then why do it? The benefits—accommodating our clients, building the potential to get other work, being able to handle jobs requiring specialties we don't have—usually outweigh the drawbacks. (See **10. Subcontracting and referring.**)

> We tried subcontracting twice on large projects—once for word processing, once for graphic design. As for vending out the page layout portion, we haven't found anyone available with the same level of quality and concern for the projects. The people I do trust are in the same boat— they're overloaded and can't help us out. When you subcontract, you begin to lose control of the project, and then you jeopardize the very quality level the client is paying for.   —*Lynn Walterick*

A final word on subcontractors: Tell the clients about them. You might not bother discussing your typist subcontractors with your clients unless you aren't particularly confident about their work. But don't hide the existence of specialty subs or DTP production people who are exercising some design or editorial judgment. You could, with some effort, make sure they never meet or talk; you could be the go-between for all instructions. You could even pretend you're doing all the work yourself. But what's in it for you? Probably just headaches and some awkward, embarrassing moments. So why not come clean? Your clients might wish you did nothing but their jobs, but they'll respect you for being busy and well scheduled, and for being a good manager.

We usually introduce clients and subcontractors as soon as we are reasonably sure all will go well. We assure clients they are still getting our attention. When it's true, we remind them that we will review all the work that comes from our shop. We tell them about the qualities of the subcontractor. And we ask them to tell us if they have any problem or difficulty. When applicable, we emphasize to clients the benefit to them in faster turnaround or lower charges. At times we may give the client the option to save money or time by taking on more quality control. (An example might be when we leave it up to the client to double-check our original data entry or later corrections to texts.)

Sometimes clients are happy with the results of subcontracted work. Sometimes they're dissatisfied and willing to try working with another of our subcontractors. Some say they want to work only with us. Here the customer is always right.

From time to time, clients ask our subcontractors if they can work directly with them. One of our subs suspected this was a client's way to motivate the sub to work harder. But the client may actually prefer working with the sub, or find some part of the arrangement more convenient. We establish ground rules that our subs will respond to any such feeler with the explanation that they have an arrangement with us, and that they are sure something can be worked out, if the client talks to us about it. A sub who is at all savvy about long-term relationships and basic morality will not consider stealing your clients. Still, the situation can get sticky.

Typists, proofreaders, and copy editors

Chances are most of your texts will come to you on disk, or are short pieces you'll type yourself as you produce the pages. Nevertheless, sometimes you'll need to subcontract work to a typist, or, as they say these days, a data entry person, who uses a word processor. Good ones aren't easy to find. You're looking for speed and accuracy. Even more important, you'll need a person with a flexible temperament who can follow the special directions you'll give, which will differ from the methods of hard copy typists. For instance, you'll want one space after sentences, and often you may want tables typed column by column rather than across the page. If you get a real winner, you may train the person to tag body text, bullets, and levels of heads for your style sheets, and format bold and italic within paragraphs.

No matter what their claims, we rarely find even 60-100 word-per-minute typists achieving effective speeds over 25-40 wpm. They have to stop to figure things out, perhaps spell-check, and take breaks. Felix prefers to pay typists effectively at piece rates, working out to about $1 to $2 per thousand keystrokes. That simplifies the relationship, because he doesn't have to worry about how much time the person takes.

Here's how the math works. A 30 wpm typist produces 1,800 words per hour or about 11,000 characters and spaces between words. (The word processor file's size in bytes is roughly the same as the number of keystrokes.) At $11 per hour, which would be high for many geographical areas, you've got $1 per thousand keystrokes. If the person is faster, or doing tagging and styling, or holds out for more per hour, you can adjust the rate.

For text you type and jobs where the client doesn't want to have to check your typing, you'll gain considerable relief from an ace proofreader. Sometimes you'll be amazed at the colored ink on pages you thought were ready to go. Reliable proofers are hard to find, so when you find a good one, thank your good fortune and hold on. Some will provide the additional service of incorporating their corrections in your word processor files.

Sometimes you may need a copy editor, who may combine proofing pages for typos with a more comprehensive review of the document for consistency and readability.

You may find typists, proofreaders, and copy editors among the ranks of the part-time workforce. They are perfect jobs for the parent at home with small children, or the retired office workers. They're not jobs for just anyone, but we know some DTPers who have put to work capable members of their extended families in these jobs.

> Copy editing and proofreading are even more important in DTP because the entire production process is often executed by only one person.
>
> —*Lynn Yost*

Making friends with your vendors

As we saw in **4. Meet your tools' creators**, as the end user you're the person every computer, software, and accessory manufacturer, and every seller of business services and supplies, seeks to reach and please. The vendors need to understand you, and to get your business. Nor can you live without them. Local vendors rank right behind customers and subcontractors in their importance to your business.

Shop around, and when you find good vendors, go all out to establish close relationships. Find ones small enough so your business is important to them. Make clear your high expectations for service and the special treatment that all customers theoretically deserve. Tell them that if you're satisfied, you'll recommend them to your colleagues and customers.

Imagesetter service bureau

This service business is your most critical vendor—one you will not abandon lightly. You'll send your files here for high-resolution RC paper output (1,270 to 3,300 dpi) from Linotronic, Varityper, AGFA Compugraphic, or other machines. A service bureau may also offer lower prices for 600 to 1,200 dpi plain paper laser output. Many now have color proofing printers, and some will soon have high-quality color dye sublimation printers. You may also get disk, slide, multimedia, or video conversions; monochrome or color scanning; and optical character recognition (OCR) scanning. If your service bureau also rents computers by the hour, you may find yourself using its hardware in a pinch. If it doubles as a traditional graphics shop, you'll use it for veloxes, complex pasteups, and advice about photographs. And if it's also a printer, sometimes you and your clients will use it as a one-stop shop.

If your chosen service bureau doesn't offer 24-hour seven days a week service, line up a backup outfit that does. If you don't live in a big city, you may have to find someone you can reach by modem, or you may have to find someone willing to open up for you after hours at a premium charge. You never know what kind of turnaround your clients will ask for.

The more work you send, the better your position to ask for routine discounts—and favors. Occasionally, when your disk was already on the way to the service bureau, with the offset printer standing by, we've asked our vendor to make a small change without charging the usual minimum price for working on files. In return, we've passed on referrals and swapped useful technical information that we hear first.

Once you've chosen a service bureau, keep in line with its versions of fonts, system, and applications software. That's the only way to guarantee consistent results in all your output.

Always include a laser proof when you send your file to the service bureau. Felix has established a smooth enough relationship with his service bureau, and ironed out enough incompatibilities, so that except for the most critical jobs, he has the imagesetter manager eyeball the output and send it directly to the client or printer. It eliminates two messenger runs and cuts off half a day or more from turnaround time. He's been tripped up only twice in three years.

> I'm not particularly enthusiastic about PostScript service bureaus—I consider them a necessary evil. There seems to be so much work available for them that—like computer stores in general—customer service suffers. A case in point: I went to one with a 400-page book, a job they could have made a lot of money on. They didn't have the typeface I was using and showed no interest in purchasing it. The book had numerous large screen dumps and, as a result, they had trouble printing the test pages. But, rather than telling me they were experiencing problems, they kept saying: "It will be ready tomorrow!" When I would call the next day, a different voice would answer the phone and give me another promise.
> Traditional typesetters were often difficult to deal with and capricious in their pricing. Many service bureaus seem to be following in the same tradition—partly because they're often run by the same people.
> —*Roger Parker*

Don't blithely offer to produce imagesetter film rather than paper for your clients. Yes, it saves one step at the printer and therefore logically should reduce client costs. But it requires you to have much more confidence in your imagesetter's product. Sloppy procedures, overused chemicals, a dusty workspace, or a machine out of alignment can give you poor or inconsistent quality film. Film adds higher costs for corrections that have to be stripped in. And, even though it results in better quality screens, it takes away some of the printer's ability to compensate by over- or underexposing the mechanical to fatten up light type or be sure that thin reverse type or graphics still print.

When working with imagesetters, especially if you're outputting film, make sure you know what you're doing before you send dozens of pages to the imagesetter at $5-$20 or more per page. At times you *must* use film. For instance, if you're producing very fine screens or thin lines, producing it at 2,540 dpi on RC paper will give your offset printer nightmares, while producing it on film makes your printer's life simpler. Yet film, while able to preserve more detail than RC paper, is also much less forgiving of small variations.

Ask if your service bureau uses the latest **raster image processor** (RIP) to produce its files. The Linotronic is up to RIP 4. You're much less likely to encounter files that won't run, or will cost you overtime, with the latest, fastest RIP. See if your service bureau is careful to check automatically for viruses and disinfect its disks—or when your disk comes back you may find yourself on the receiving end of the latest infection.

If you're doing precise work for imagesetting (for instance, film for color separations) make sure your imagesetter service bureau has the latest generation of accurately calibrated, small-increment paper or film transports. Ask to see samples of similar work produced for other customers. Make sure the bureau uses a densitometer daily or more frequently for consistent output.

If you're trying to match tints prepared conventionally, don't assume your 10% electronic screen from an imagesetter is the same as the one the printer made using Rubylith. Run a set of test screens before you finish the job. For a critical project, offset print a test page with the paper and ink used previously for the job.

For color work, if you haven't produced your separations and traps correctly, until the job is coming off the press, there's often no way to know if you or the imagesetter have done it right. See how much help and guidance you'll get from your imagesetter, and look carefully at any fine print disclaimer that appears on the imagesetter's order form.

Preparing your files for imagesetting requires a high level of knowledge from you, the DTPer. Some service bureaus and training centers offer half-day courses on the topic. You'll find articles covering the basic points in some of the DTP monthlies. (See **Appendix 2. Magazines and catalogs**). Some service bureaus go out of their way to educate their users. The *Linotype Survival Manual*, by Imageset Design, a bureau in Portland, Maine, (800) 272-4738, is a free and useful 100-page reference with tips and tables about screen frequencies, scanner resolutions, and other information that's hard to find in any single publication.

Printers

Find a conscientious and reliable local offset printer for everyday jobs. A significant portion of your work is likely to be straightforward offset printing on standard letter, legal, and tabloid (11- by 17-inch) size paper. After you've learned the basic vocabulary and mechanics of printing, you can call up your printer to ask more specific or advanced questions.

Find out your printer's maximum paper and image areas, house ink colors, papers always in stock, cutting, collating, folding, and binding capacities, and usual turnaround times. For comparison's sake, also get a price list from a local quick-copy, quick-print operation, which may provide cheaper and faster (but poorer quality) offset printing services. Then, when your clients ask you how much an entire job will cost—or when they ask you to handle the entire job— you'll be able to give them approximate terms. Also line up a printer able to handle a web press (for newsprint) and a high-end one for process color. And find at least one union shop: The prices may be nearly double, but some clients require a bug (the printer's union label) on their work.

If you regularly prepare traditional mechanicals for a printer, ask the printer if it's more convenient for you to work with their boards. That may improve their efficiency, at no cost to you. Many of our printers have told us they don't care if we don't give them boards at all—just individual pages out of our laser printer or from the imagesetter with crop marks. Eliminating the tedious step of making old-style mechanicals has been a real relief and timesaver for us.

> I don't make my own mechanicals. When I need real camera-ready boards, I hire paste-up people.   —*Rich Metter*

You and your favorite printers may be able to work out referral fees for sending clients to each other. If you do set up some such mutually beneficial arrangements, don't hide them from your clients. You may also want to develop a working relationship with a **printer broker**—someone who acts as an intermediary by being in touch with many printers, taking care of advising clients on the best way to print a job, and then bidding out and shepherding the job to completion. Printer brokers usually bill customers for printing, marking up the printers' invoices to include their services. Or they may get sales commissions from their printers. They can work for you or directly for your clients. They can protect you and your clients from unforeseen problems, and once you get to know them, on occasion, they can become a source of work for you.

Computer retailer

You need a local vendor. Though you may buy most software mail order, for hardware, you need some connection to a local store or a **value added reseller** (VAR). Local vendors can help you with serious hardware problems, or at least give you a peek at service manuals and bulletins. If you have a good service contract with some other company, this relationship is less important. But you need at least one local place to buy hardware. As you grow, your consulting may put you in the role of helping clients buy and set up systems. At this point, an association with a store or VAR may bring you commissions or other perks.

Toner cartridge vendor

Find a good local source for toner cartridges and toner refills, for laser printers and photocopiers that use removable cartridges. If you keep buying new cartridges and throwing out the empties, you're both polluting and wasting money. You can save up to 50% of the cost of the cartridge by establishing a relationship with a reputable refiller. Just make sure the vendor disassembles and reconditions the cartridge. Some still drill holes in the cartridge to refill it, without performing necessary maintenance. This can endanger your print quality and your health. Toner powder is toxic, so you don't want it floating around your equipment or office. That's a reason for not even considering learning how to refill it yourself.

Test the output quality carefully. We've made a test sheet showing waterfalls of type (and frequently used faces like Helvetica Light and Times) at all sizes from four points to 14 points. (See **Figs. 8.1** and **8.2** on the next page.) The page shows us how evenly and finely screens print, plus the printer's usable image area on the page. We use this file to check on toner cartridges, and to run printers, imagesetters and even faxes, through their paces. In the sheet shown, we've used the typefaces found in this book. But usually we use a combination of the faces resident in a printer (Times, Palatino) and downloadable fonts with very light weights and delicate strokes to test quality and measure printer processing time.

For camera-ready copy you produce in house, you want even, dark, and sharp pages to roll out of the machine. We often find that cartridges vary in quality. When we find one that seems willing to grace us with sharp and even type, we put it aside. Then, before we print camera-ready finals, we switch from our everyday proofer to our favorite toner cartridge.

Drum coatings and toner particle chemistry are evolving, and we try to find vendors who know what's going on. We've acted as test sites for toner suppliers, in exchange for discounted or free toner refills (the local equivalent of beta-testing described in **4. Help is at hand**). Many vendors will pick up and deliver for free. They can also be sources of client referrals, they may help you decide what kind of papers to use in your printer, and some offer service contracts on laser printers.

Test of 1270 dpi Linotronic by Kramer Communications

Test of 1270 dpi Linotronic by Kramer Communications

November 1990

Fig. 8.1 Printer resolution test page

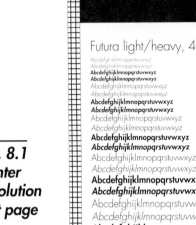

Futura light/heavy, 4-11 point text

Abcdefghijklmnopqrstuvwxyz
Abcdefghijklmnopqrstuvwxyz
Abcdefghijklmnopqrstuvwxyz
Abcdefghijklmnopqrstuvwxyz
Abcdefghijklmnopqrstuvwxyz
Abcdefghijklmnopqrstuvwxyz
Abcdefghijklmnopqrstuvwxyz
Abcdefghijklmnopqrstuvwxyz
Abcdefghijklmnopqrstuvwxyz
Abcdefghijklmnopqrstuvwxyz
Abcdefghijklmnopqrstuvwxyz
Abcdefghijklmnopqrstuvwxyz
Abcdefghijklmnopqrstuvwxyz
Abcdefghijklmnopqrstuvwxyz
Abcdefghijklmnopqrstuvwxyz
Abcdefghijklmnopqrstuvwxyz
Abcdefghijklmnopqrstuvwxyz
Abcdefghijklmnopqrstuvwxyz
Abcdefghijklmnopqrstuvwxyz
Abcdefghijklmnopqrstuvwxyz
Abcdefghijklmnopqrstuvwxyz
Abcdefghijklmnopqrstuvwxyz
Abcdefghijklmnopqrstuvwxyz
Abcdefghijklmnopqrstuvwxyz

Adobe Garamond, from 4-11 point text

Abcdefghijklmnopqrstuvwxyz
Abcdefghijklmnopqrstuvwxyz
Abcdefghijklmnopqrstuvwxyz
Abcdefghijklmnopqrstuvwxyz
Abcdefghijklmnopqrstuvwxyz
Abcdefghijklmnopqrstuvwxyz
Abcdefghijklmnopqrstuvwxyz
Abcdefghijklmnopqrstuvwxyz
Abcdefghijklmnopqrstuvwxyz
Abcdefghijklmnopqrstuvwxyz
Abcdefghijklmnopqrstuvwxyz
Abcdefghijklmnopqrstuvwxyz
Abcdefghijklmnopqrstuvwxyz
Abcdefghijklmnopqrstuvwxyz
Abcdefghijklmnopqrstuvwxyz
Abcdefghijklmnopqrstuvwxyz
Abcdefghijklmnopqrstuvwxyz
Abcdefghijklmnopqrstuvwxyz
Abcdefghijklmnopqrstuvwxyz
Abcdefghijklmnopqrstuvwxyz
Abcdefghijklmnopqrstuvwxyz
Abcdefghijklmnopqrstuvwxyz
Abcdefghijklmnopqrstuvwxyz
Abcdefghijklmnopqrstuvwxyz

hairline ———————————————   ——————————————— ½ pt.

10% screen	20% screen	30% screen
10% screen	*20% screen*	*30% screen*
	20% screen	30% screen
	20% screen	*30% screen*
40% screen	60% screen	80% screen
40% screen	*60% screen*	*80% screen*
40% screen	60% screen	80% screen
40% screen	*60% screen*	*80% screen*

Extend outside grid beyond paper size to test printer's usable print area.

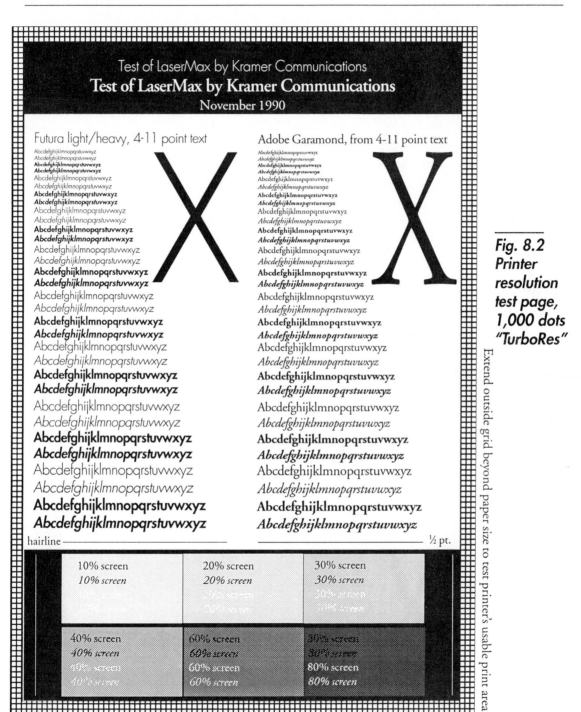

Test of LaserMax by Kramer Communications
Test of LaserMax by Kramer Communications
November 1990

Futura light/heavy, 4-11 point text

Adobe Garamond, from 4-11 point text

hairline ——————————— ——————————— ½ pt.

10% screen	20% screen	30% screen
10% screen	*20% screen*	*30% screen*
40% screen	60% screen	80% screen
40% screen	*60% screen*	*80% screen*
40% screen	60% screen	80% screen
40% screen	*60% screen*	*80% screen*

Fig. 8.2 Printer resolution test page, 1,000 dots "TurboRes"

Extend outside grid beyond paper size to test printer's usable print area.

Office supplies

Establish a local account for stationery, art, and office supplies. Usually, if you buy a minimum amount a month, you'll get 10-30% off the artificially high catalog list prices on your rush purchases. When it comes to buying cartons of paper, boxes of file folders, and small furniture, compare your local store's discounted prices to the major national companies (see **Appendix 2. Office and publishing supplies**). Chances are you'll save with mail order.

As with software, always compare the local vendor and the remote source for time, money, and convenience. But buy enough locally to keep your vendors happy and willing to do a favor for you when you need it.

Follow the Golden Rule with all your vendors. Treat them with respect. Give them us much advance notice as possible about your needs, and notify them immediately when you'll be late turning over scheduled work to them.

Make sure they never have to worry about being paid on time. And as soon as you have a good record with them, ask them if they mind being called when and if you need a credit reference.

9. TREATING YOUR CLIENTS RIGHT

Shopkeepers get sentimental about their first days in business and their first customers. They'll show you their framed first dollar bill, and tell you how they started their store in a hole in the wall. We're that way too. We remember fondly Maggie starting NYC's first DTP service bureau—Felix was her first customer. And we enjoy reminiscing about our phone calls and user group meetings as we figured out all the undocumented problems and intricacies of the first DTP tools, and turned technology into a business.

First customers are special. That is as it should be. Generally, first customers treat your failures with tolerance. And chances are you might feel a bit guilty for not telling them all the problems you had meeting your promised goals and deadlines.

After your first successes, some of the newness wears off. You may start to take your clients for granted—and court disaster. DTP is a service business; and satisfying your clients is the key to success.

You can get good clues about how to keep your clients happy by watching yourself. Notice how you react when you, as a customer, are treated well and when you're mistreated. It can have nothing to do with DTP. For instance, Felix's experience when he designed, contracted, and supervised a major renovation of his apartment helped him learn about what clients need, how communication should work, and how good intentions aren't always enough. So take advantage of every opportunity you have to get glimpses of what it's like to be on the other side of the service relationship.

Treat all your clients like they're most important

It's very simple. Until you decide you don't want them as clients anymore, treat all your clients as if they were your first, and as if you want them to stay forever. That means finding out what they need and giving it to them, anticipating their problems, and going out of your way to help and protect them.

Think about the saying, "The customer is always right." It reflects one important lesson: The customer pays you and therefore deserves every consideration and benefit of the doubt. It doesn't mean you need to kowtow.

Sometimes treating them right means telling them they're wrong. Particularly in DTP, where customers may know little about computer and printing technology—and may think they know more about language, type, and graphics than they actually do—the model of the always subservient vendor doesn't make sense.

Fortunately, some customers come to DTPers with different expectations than when they sent detailed specs to typesetters. They see you as a broadly trained and skilled collaborator who will help them shape their projects. And typically, they may be surprised, bewildered, and unhappy if you give them "exactly what they asked for."

"It's not *my* job to tell them that." As a DTPer, don't expect to think that way very often. Your job is to be their partner through the entire process. You know more than they about desktop publishing, and probably about publishing as well, including how much time each stage will take, and where pitfalls may lie. If they're about to start a project that you know won't work, tell them.

For instance, a client of Felix's once decided to produce a six-page newsletter (folded twice from an 11- by 25-inch sheet.) Felix knew from experience that the paper they used would crease badly when folded twice and then in thirds (down to a #10 envelope). He didn't know if their printer would alert them to the danger, so he did. Had he done nothing, and if the job had been ruined or required extra expense for scoring the paper, he would have shared in blame that really belonged to the printer. Instead, he ensured a successful outcome, and no one had to be blamed at all.

On the other hand, don't be stubborn. Do it the clients' way if they insist, after you share your recommendations and reasoning. They might know better, even if they don't communicate what they know. For instance, you may think a graphic design is inferior. Yet sometimes the customer doesn't want something to look too fancy. A nonprofit organization may be wary of having its contributors and supporters think it spends too much on a slick image. Or a newsletter publisher may want to give the impression that the contents are too serious and urgent to waste time on design. *The Kiplinger Letter*, a newsletter targeted at busy executives, is a good example. It's all typewriter type with the important words underscored. Some market researcher probably found that an arty look wouldn't sit well with the potential subscribers or readers; therefore the publisher consciously underdesigned the newsletter. So the customer may be right after all. If that prospect is too unpleasant for you, quit, or pass the client on to another DTPer.

Technical and production issues aside, as in any relationship you want to keep healthy, sometimes treating your clients right means standing up for yourself—letting them know if something they are saying, doing, or asking for might jeopardize your positive feelings about them. If telling them doesn't work out well, sooner or later you'll have a big problem, and you may be better off not working together.

Don't juggle in public

Customers know they're not your one and only, but they wish they were. And they at least want to feel that you take their project as seriously as they do. Give them your full attention when you're working with them.

Never begin a significant phone conversation with clients when you're on another call, preoccupied, on deadline, or you know they're likely to want information you don't have. You'll sound like you can't wait until they let you get off the phone—and they'll hear it. If a client calls you when you're tied up, tell them, "I want to give you my complete attention. Can I call you right back/can I call you at a particular time?"

Don't act as though you can't remember them by asking for their phone number if you already have it written down. We've taken to noting all of a client's vital statistics on the outside of their main file folder: names and phone numbers of principals, secretaries, messenger services, the word processor they use, the rates we've quoted, their standard typefaces, and the printer they use. Call back when you're ready, after you've pulled their folder and reviewed any work in progress or outstanding invoices they might be calling you about.

When you note the word processor software your clients use, make sure you know which version number they're using. Often clients will be one or two versions behind the current release. You want to avoid the inconvenience of one day exporting for their use text from your page layout, only to find that they can't read the file.

You might write each of your current clients' names and phone numbers on a three-inch Post-it note, and leave the notes in the client folders. When the client has a job in progress, you can stick the note, in large enough lettering to read from your chair, on a wall or bulletin board.

Don't rely exclusively on computerized Rolodexes. Keep a printout handy for those times when your computer is off or tied up.

If your clients come to your office, space your appointments so they don't bump into each other. Don't have another client's job spread out all over your office or on your screen. Clear it all out. Don't keep one client waiting while you finish a long call with another. Don't complain to one client about your problems with another.

Of course, if you feel like pushing back on an overly demanding client, the opposite approach makes sense. *If you can risk the relationship*, say you feel responsibilities to keep other customers happy too. If a client misses a deadline, explain that other work was scheduled just like this job, and now this one has to take its place in line. Sometimes a firm approach can turn a pesky client into a much more cooperative one.

Level with your clients

DTP is not a mystery to you, nor should it be to your clients. Some professionals (in the popular view, most notably physicians) are snobs—they enjoy the power that comes from a specialized language and secret knowledge. They don't notice or care that they're making their clients uncomfortable.

Yet clients you intimidate will never be enthusiastic about working with you. And you'll have trouble simultaneously withholding information from them and involving them as decision-makers in their projects, not to mention respecting or liking them.

You're better off beginning as early as possible by explaining the process of DTP to your clients. Inevitably, some day you'll need to divulge the details of their project. You may have choices to present, or you may need to explain why it's costing more, or taking more time than they expected. That moment is likely to be tense. It's not the ideal time to expect a defensive and pressured client to be intrigued by an introduction to computers, typesetting, or graphics.

We believe our clients *need* to know how we get from raw data to finished mechanical and printed piece. We especially try to clue in those who claim they're not even curious. These tend to be the very same people who call you up and ask, "Can you just run out a few pages for me?" Explaining the steps involved is the best way to counter the idea that DTP is automatic, simply a matter of pushing a few buttons. You can show them what you have to do to fix the material that's come to you, before you can begin to run out the pages. Tell them how many steps you take, and outline the choices you make before the job is done. (See **Fig. 7.1 Steps in preparing a project.**)

We also think our clients need to know when we're not going to do all the work ourselves. One of your big worries as a sole proprietor is that you won't have enough capacity when work starts coming at you from several directions at once. It's only natural to fear that if you ever say no to a job, you'll never get work again from that client. Of course you're better off saying yes, and getting it done somehow, by yourself or with help.

If you're swamped and can't find the right subcontractor, you could say no. Chances are the client came to you for a reason—one that doesn't disappear if they have to go somewhere else one time. We've found that many clients we've referred elsewhere in emergencies come back to us. And when we worry that a hot prospect or a past client may permanently switch to someone we're about to suggest, we call our friendly competitor and arrange for a referral fee.

Don't misrepresent your capabilities

At the start, try to avoid the temptation to make exaggerated claims for your abilities. As you gain experience, you'll find you can get jobs without creating mirages. Meanwhile, when a client asks if you can do something, level with them if you've never done it before. For "of course," substitute "I'm not sure, but I can find out and get back to you," or "that shouldn't be any trouble, but I won't know for sure until I try it."

> You get more respect, and more work, in the long run if you admit right off you can't do a particular job.
> —*Denis Shedd*

If it turns out you can't deliver some type of work, you need not say no. You can find someone who can handle it, get a bid from them, make them your subcontractor, and tell the client that's what you're doing. Or you can take the time to master the needed skills or software.

If you choose to learn on the job, tell the client you can't even attempt a dollar or time bid until you know what's involved. This is the worst time to succumb to the temptation to make a ballpark estimate. Trying to wing it is a risky idea. What happens if days later you discover you were mistaken and you can't meet a deadline or produce a particular effect?

If you try to learn at the client's expense, combining your learning time and production time, you'll have no idea how much to bill the client. You're best off finding what an expert would charge and making that number your bid, then taking as much time as you need to reach a level of proficiency—without worrying about how much you make on this first project.

> The big word I learned when I had my own business was *deliverables.* When you're consulting or doing a project, clients want to know what they're paying for. In other works, "Let's see what you are giving me." Basically, that's what being in business is all about: you've got to deliver your expertise!   —*Wendy Richmond*

Underpromise and overdeliver

Clients will *always* ask you how long their job will take. Even when they're in no rush, try to get them to set the timetable. If they bounce it back to you, try for twice the time you expect it to take. Then if you're even a day earlier than you promised, you'll still satisfy them.

For clients who don't know what's involved in your work, be careful about offering to turn a job around on the spot. Of course, that's what you do if the customer is watching you work, or is waiting in the next room for the job. But otherwise, you're taking a risk. Suppose you get a desperate phone call from another client, who's at the printer and needs last-minute changes? Or what if your equipment breaks down? Your brash promise could blow up in your face.

Besides, such a commitment is usually unnecessary. Often customers will appear on your doorstep or sound out of breath on the phone, saying "I'm in a real rush." Find out what they mean. Your key question is "When do you need it to get to the printer?"

If they answer "yesterday," try to determine how serious a jam they're in, what they're hoping for, whether they are prepared to pay rush charges, whether they have any alternative to giving you the job, and the consequences to them of further delay.

If the answer is "10 days," be glad you held your tongue. You were probably prepared to promise five. Just tell them their deadline is, as they say, no problem. You're in a great position to try to finish in six days, and still look good if you come through in eight.

If they ask for a rush job, and are accustomed to paying a premium for rapid turnaround, but you don't define their requirements as that much of a rush, you're then in a good position to decide how much of a surcharge to set.

If you've bid the schedule conservatively, you're also protecting the client. Maggie had once reached the final approval stage for a 300-page manual. She expected to finish the job with minor tweaking. Then someone new at the customer's office took a look at the proofs and added major editorial changes and reorganization. Though a one-day wrap-up turned into almost three long days, the job still came in before the original deadline.

You may be tempted to show off—especially as you learn your way around the software and become a whiz at the mouse. If you're good, your clients will come to expect a high level of performance from you. Remember, you can't always be a miracle worker. The best way to preserve your reputation and keep your work-life on a steady course is to *underpromise and overdeliver.*

Allow yourself a margin of error

Underpromising will give you some breathing space if you run into trouble. For instance, leave time to send your job to your imagesetter a day early. That way, if you're not satisfied with your high-resolution output, you can run all or part of it again. If you were at fault, there's no reason to tell the client what happened—but if you didn't leave time to recoup, your client will *have* to know.

If you inadvertently erase or corrupt your working file at a late stage of a large project, let's hope you have a little spare time. If you've taken our advice, you'll have previous versions of the job, and you'll be able to reconstruct your most recent changes in a few hours or less. Otherwise, you may have to start again, and you'll need all the time you can get. Again, you have no reason to burden your client with the problems you're having, unless you're out of time and you need to convince them you weren't out betting at the track, or worse, you haven't put their job behind another one.

When you don't know how long a job will take or how much it will cost, a trial run is good way to protect yourself. Once, Felix avoided a double ambush. Early on in a book project, he asked the client for a chapter file on disk, to make sure everything would work smoothly. Right off, he discovered that all the footnote numbers in the text were variables—mathematical references rather than actual typed numbers—which dropped out entirely when placed in the page layout file. Further testing showed that if he had the client retype the numbers as text superscripts (his first inclination), the files would still not convert correctly when placed. He then considered, and presented to the client, the pros and cons of producing the book entirely with word processing software. His final decision was to build into his bid the time and money necessary to type the footnotes directly in the page layout files. (By the way, since this 1988 project, software upgrades have largely solved this problem.)

We strongly advise you against making a firm bid or schedule for work based on material supplied by a client on a disk you haven't seen. If you must, build in enough margin to protect yourself. And qualify the bid—tell them that it's subject to your checking out the format and organization of the data.

Give away as much information as you can

Everyone likes a freebie, and experienced DTPers have many to hand out. Never miss an opportunity to give clients free information that will save them time or money. It may be a tip like suggesting they do an entire short-run job on your laser printer, rather than putting up with the delay or cost of photocopying or printing. It may mean suggesting they use a particular page size to save them money with a printer. Or it could mean steering them away from a paper size that could raise their costs. Few clients are aware, for example, that the cost of the 11- by 25-inch format for a six-page newsletter can vary enormously from printer to printer, depending on their printing, folding, collating, and cutting equipment.

Don't wait for your clients to come up with the important questions. It's better to face the hard problems and make the tough decisions at the start of a job. Help your clients get comparable bids. Explain why they should get new quotes for their routine printing work every year or two, unless they have a printer who provides unusual service or terms. Based on your understanding of their job, help them develop a standard set of specifications for content, materials, and production and delivery schedules.

Tell them what they ought to be asking you and every other vendor they're dealing with, including designer, writer, photographer, printer, and mailer. Chances are you're the only person who will protect them in this way.

We tell our clients we want them to pay us for what we do well—not for something they could do better in a different way. Nothing impresses a potential or existing client more than our *telling them they don't really need our services*. When we do this, we let them know we're intentionally giving them advice that might lose us a little money, but is in their best interest.

- For people having difficulty extricating themselves from a relationship with a conventional typesetter, we'll suggest they see if their typesetter will accept their data on disk. We explain how most modern typesetting systems can receive ASCII (pronounced askee, sometimes also called text only) files or common word processor files from PCs with relatively little effort, and suggest that a resistant typesetter is too far behind the times. This may mean we won't get this project, but we'll save them money, and we'll get the next job, or a referral.

- We educate our clients who don't know their options and want to do things the hard way. For instance, when someone wants us to make huge posters by pasting together individual pages, we'll give them a single laser or an imagesetter page that they can have enlarged photographically. Or we'll clue them in to the new service bureaus that create poster-sized color images from computer graphics files. (See **11. Finding a niche.**) Going the other direction, we'll show clients how to avoid imagesetting costs but still get sharp type by laser printing small ads at 200-400%, then having the printer shoot them down. (See **7. Some of our favorite shortcuts.**)

- If a client has a high-end word processor and a laser printer, and is tight on time or money, we'll tell them they may get good enough results with their in-house tools. We may suggest they pick up a good book on using their word processor for DTP. Sometimes they do that, appreciate our tip, and come back to us for their more elaborate jobs. Other times they stay with us because they need our speed, type library, or our design capabilities, or because they can't spare the time to master additional skills.

- When we're too busy for a job, or we feel someone else could do it better, and we don't want to be involved even in bidding it or managing a subcontract, we'll sent clients to our colleagues. Sometimes we'll get a referral fee, sometimes not.

We also enjoy telling clients *not to use our elaborate computer and DTP technology where the old way works better.* This approach will pay off in the long run, in other work from foregone clients, referrals, goodwill, or just your own feeling of being a straightforward and honorable person.

- We'll explain the relative pluses and minuses of using scanned graphics and photographs versus veloxes pasted on the mechanical or negatives stripped in by the printer. In general, unless the client wants a digitized, rough, or high-tech look, or wants to manipulate the image in some way (such as silhouetting speakers at a podium, or modifying an image's colors), we'll usually encourage them to accept scanned graphics as FPOs, to be replaced by conventionally produced halftones.
- Felix sometimes helps out low-budget nonprofit groups that have a talented, free designer and paste-up person on call. Rather than producing camera-ready copy, Felix quickly produces galleys and a page of headlines, which they cut and paste into traditional mechanicals.
- Or we may show clients how they can pre-print thousands of sheets of paper with color elements, to convert a job we might do as a complex and time-consuming two- or three-color project into two simpler, faster, lower cost jobs.

If a client offers to send you files by modem once in a while, try to beg off. Chances are they just want to use this capability, without sufficient reason. We're prejudiced against this method for communication with clients because we've found it's highly inefficient. If you've never communicated by modem with the client, plan on spending at least an hour the first time. Expect to tie up two phone lines (one for voice and one for modem), and don't count on succeeding. Modem hardware and software seem to be among the hardest computer areas for people to master. And even if you're very skilled, chances are the other party won't be. Phone lines can be plagued by static, leading to faulty or incomplete transmissions. You can try to explain to the client that they're better off spending $10 for overnight mail or a messenger across town than paying for an hour or more of two people's time.

You can also explain to the client why you'd prefer getting a printout or sketch along with the file. For the same reason, you're usually better off sending an imagesetter your files on disk, along with hard copy so the service bureau can check that what you asked for is what you got. Of course, if you want to be really high-tech, you could modem the file and fax the hard copy.

Modems are unsurpassed if you haven't got a second to spare, and you've already established settings and procedures that work between you and the other party. Sometimes there's no other way to get data from your client's highly incompatible computer. We've used the Kermit protocol, which is found within a number of popular microcomputer telecommunicating packages, to download information from minicomputers.

Help clients visualize the final piece

Sometimes clients will tell you that the results they got from the printer aren't what they had expected. Your job is to give the customer a close representation of the finished piece as early as possible in the production process. As the technology improves, DTP increasingly approaches this ideal.

Before you start production, try to find samples of work similar in design, ink, and paper color to the way the piece will look. If you can't, and you or the client worry that the client may not end up liking what you've agreed on, suggest making a prototype. Once you've created a template from an approved design, you can easily produce a mechanical with dummy text. To offset print 100 copies of a sample page, on high quality paper, with black plus one specified PMS color, a printer will charge $100-$200. That's money well spent, especially for a start-up publication. It will enable you and the client to spot troubles, and improve the client's sense of security and control about the job.

Use DTP's software features to make your proofs closely resemble the job. If you give the client galleys from a word processor, set the column width to be the same as in the final pages. But don't hyphenate the text, or your client may start correcting breaks that will be different when you go to page layout. In your page proofs, make X-boxed or shaded box placeholders for graphics that are to come. Even better, of course, scan, scale, and crop the photos and art to provide exact but low-quality FPO representations of the graphics.

If the client tells you the captions aren't written yet, put placeholder captions under the scans or boxes. If you're expecting a three-line caption identifying 10 people in a photo, insert a three-line placeholder to show what fits.

If the client tells you to leave room for a 350-word article on page 6, give them nonsense syllables in that place. Many companies provide a *lorem ipsum* file of Greek or nonsense syllables to pour into pages at the design stage. Aldus distributes a Copy Fit file of nonsense syllables with a word count number at

25 word intervals. You can convert one of the standard Greek files into a word count file yourself without much trouble.

In the body text, replace the TK (to come) used by veteran pre-computer writers and editors, or the question marks or other symbols used by people to indicate text to come, with placeholder characters that will stand out. It's hard to miss bullets. A phone number to come would look like this: (•••) •••-••••.

Here's an easy way to print copies of a document, using both sides of each piece of paper: For a 6-page document, print it once. Then put the pages back in the printer with the even-numbered pages before the odd ones, printed side face down, counting from bottom to top, 5,6,3,4,1,2. When the printer runs 1,2,3,4,5,6, you'll have two complete sets back-to-back. It seems confusing, but when you try it, you'll get the principle. Of course, it works on photocopiers as well as laser printers. Printing back-to-back copies is even easier if your software lets you print all even pages, then all odd pages.

For books, magazines, newspapers, and newsletters, emphasize to the client the importance of thinking in terms of facing left and right pages. But talking about it isn't good enough. At some point before the final proof (if possible, for every set of proofs) show your client proofs in **spreads**, or facing pages.

Assemble the page proofs into trimmed and folded sheets resembling the final printed result. That's *the most important step* you can take to help your client preview the job. For a brochure or a card, cut, paste, or tape your laser printout on both sides of the page, then fold the result appropriately. For a window envelope mailing, fold the letter down to right size and deliver it in an envelope. For a return coupon, give the client a complete and a torn off version.

If your client reviews proofs exclusively by fax, try to talk with them about each page in relation to its facing page, and make sure at some point to deliver at least one set of physical proofs. This is necessary not only to make sure your clients see facing pages, but also to give them a chance to spend some time with a sharper, cleaner version than the 200 line/inch fax copies.

For a four-page newsletter, use tape. Beyond that, invest in a binding machine. A VeloBind, (800) 824-6423, GBC, (800) 323-8362, or UniBind system, (800) 229-2463, will run you from $60-$750, depending on its features and capacity. A binder is a good piece of equipment to own—you can also rent time on it to other DTPers. In fact, it turns you into something closer to a traditional publisher. When Felix has produced a trade book, he has used his laser printer, a photocopier, and his binding machine to produce page proofs for distribution to dozens of reviewers and reporters.

If you do spot color work, get a color toner cartridge for your laser printer, and make the second color of the publication in another pass through the printer. Or use a highlight marker to note the colors on your black toner proofs. If your page layout software can make thumbnail mini-representations of the entire publication, you can mark the colors on the thumbnails.

If clients apologize for having second thoughts and making so many changes after seeing their material in galleys or proof, you can reassure them. Tell them, "That's what's supposed to happen. Words look different when they're typeset." By the way, often the most apologetic people are in fact only minor culprits.

Clients love pleasant surprises

Give your clients more than they expect to get. Nothing makes them feel better than when you take care of them without their asking—or give them something they didn't even know they needed, but are happy to have.

Offer to teach your clients about picas, points, and leading. One great way is with a gift. Unless you're sure they have one already, give each client one of those transparent rulers, showing pica measures, serif and sans-serif type from 4 to 72 points, leading options, and line widths. (Be sure to use ones that adopt the simplified standard of 72 points per inch that is used by DTP software, rather than the older and more exact typographers' 72.27 points per inch.) Show them how you use it, and why printers' pica measurements are so much easier to use than inches. You can buy the rulers by the dozen and attach a sticker with your company name, produced on mailing labels made for laser printers. Or you can photocopy the ruler, along with your business card, onto transparency sheets. Clients will appreciate the freebie. And you'll be demonstrating you respect them enough to let them in on your special language, making it easier for them to tell you what they want.

Even if they don't think to ask for it, give them a catalog of the typefaces you own. Get enough copies of the flyer from Adobe, Bitstream, or whatever company is your main source of typefaces, to be able to hand them out—or make your own catalog, including only the ones you have on hand.

When appropriate, aggressively advise your clients, as discussed earlier in this chapter in **Give away as much information as you can**. A few clients may be threatened or disoriented by your departure from their expectations. Of course, be prudent if you encounter a high-powered designer, a particularly knowledgeable client, or when you smell serious office politics. But if you get a positive response, move on to make suggestions about content, design, and the production process.

If the client asks to see two design alternatives for a page or a publication, and you think a third has merit, include it. If the pages seem too dense, show how they look with looser leading. You won't risk much time. If the client wants to try out many formats or typefaces, it will be easy if you've done a good job setting up style sheets. Once you have your template made and the client's text in place, you can produce and print out a half dozen rough versions of a four-page newsletter, showing alternative typefaces or formats, in less than an hour. Tape them up into dummies and send them to the client. Keep a set for your sample book to demonstrate one of DTP's fortes.

Clients hate unpleasant surprises

More than anything else, clients want you to solve all their problems for them. Unless you tell them otherwise, they'll assume you've encountered no glitches and are on schedule. And they'll assume you've accurately estimated the scope of work and costs. If you ever have bad news, share it as soon as possible.

We make rare exceptions. For instance, from time to time, we can't find a client's art or photo that we've scanned. Usually, before we panic and call the client, we keep looking in the hope that it's still in the scanner or buried under a pile of papers rather than out with last night's trash. Of course, this shouldn't happen. Lately we've gotten into the habit of keeping irreplaceable material packed up in large recycled envelopes.

If you make a mistake, and the client is important to you, tell the client immediately. Then offer to do whatever you must to make up for your error. Don't charge for the correction, pay for reprinting, or reduce your total for the cost of the job.

Ward off unpleasant surprises by making sure you and the client agree on what the job is about. If something doesn't seem clear, confirm it with a memo on the scope of work as you see it (it's less formal and adversarial than a contract). For instance, we think it makes sense to have your clients take final responsibility for typographical errors, even when we've done the typing. (Felix generally suggests skipping the stage of spell-checking documents, because he finds the spellers to be slow, and tripped up by too many correctly spelled words. Maggie generally finds spellers to be worth the effort.) We explicitly go over each of our assumptions with the client before starting the job.

Most clients want to hear from you frequently. From their perspective, if they're expecting an update and you don't call, they have plenty of reasons to start worrying. This is especially true if it's your first job for them. Chances are your non-communication will trigger some memory of a past disaster they didn't learn about until much too late. For many clients, no news is bad news.

So keep your clients informed. Until your work with them becomes routine, when you receive their material, check out the instructions, layout, and disk immediately. Then call to tell them it arrived, how it looks, and whether your original estimates still hold. If one aspect of the project looks iffy to you, don't plan to deal with it later. Work it out before you face a delivery deadline. If your work progresses much more slowly than you expected, tell the client as soon as you know. Explain why you won't make the original deadline, or why you'll be going over budget.

If you're ahead of schedule when you're halfway, avoid too quick a promise of early completion or revision of deadlines, unless that information is crucial to the client. You could still run into trouble and need all the time you projected. And if you do stay ahead, the news will have greater impact if it's delivered only once.

Don't assume you can read your customers' minds. If an instruction is at all unclear, call for clarification. Think back to **8. Managing subcontractors**, where you're the client. You don't want to pay your subs for hours spent misunderstanding your directions. Now your clients are in the same position. If their instructions are incomplete or illegible, you're better off spending time asking rather than second-guessing them.

In particular, for newsletters, insist that your clients give you a layout. We're not necessarily talking about a full-scale design—just an indication of priorities. There's no way you can know what they have in mind—what's the most important page-one story, and what's to be buried. If they leave that first cut of decisions to you, they may end up tearing apart your layout and feeling ripped off by what the changes cost them.

At the same time, we strongly urge you to take the initiative and incorporate many of your suggestions. You're taking the small risk of spending some time the client won't pay for because you overstepped your authority. By trial and error, you'll quickly see how far you can go without checking back.

When you do make *any* change to your clients' material, you *must* give them some easy way to see what you've done at the same time as they receive your proof. It's simplest to mark their original copy or drawing with your notes and comments. If this doesn't work, send a log—either a handwritten sheet or an additional page of printout—with notations like "edited page 3 para 2 to move widow subhead" or "made capitalizations uniform in invitation text."

Use colored pens for messages to clients. Felix favors green, since it stands out, clients don't use it, it has none of the negative associations of the teacher's red pen, and he likes its subliminal environmental message. We mark up the client-provided printout. If they give us a disk only, before we clean it up at all, we print it out immediately so we can write on it and refer to it. If we want to suggest further or more drastic changes in layout or text, beyond those we've ventured to do without approval, we highlight or annotate our ideas on page proofs. To keep our messages from being overlooked, we usually style them bold all caps. If we spot a typo after we've printed a proof for the client, and we don't want to reprint the page, we correct it in the file and mark the proof so the client knows we've already spotted and taken care of it.

These methods get more complicated when you're faxing material back and forth, because you won't routinely send back the client's marked-up pages along with your new proof. We've found the best solution is for us to mark the fax we receive with our questions, as we incorporate the indicated changes. Then we transfer notes about our questions to the new pages we've printed out, before we fax them back to the client. Alternatively, you could fax longer jobs and send the client's original proofs back by messenger or mail.

Don't lose steam

Clients often arrive on your doorstep, disk and layout in hand, frustrated by what it took to extract stories from unresponsive people, exhausted by their deadlines, and worried about the schedule. They've had it. They've given the project their best shot.

This is your time to be their savior. As you take over, they'll see you cast a fresh eye on the project, and they'll hear you estimate when the job can go to the printer. They'll be relieved to give up primary responsibility. The more you help them, the more they'll appreciate you—and the more they'll revive and help out.

> I've been called in to major banks and brokerage houses for last-minute changes to executive presentations at the end of a long day. The clients are always waiting for last-minute data. And I've had to keep my good humor—sometimes as the hours went from double to single digits. As long as I have enough to eat, I can keep going. —*Maggie*

Keeping up your enthusiasm, creativity, and resilience until the job is wrapped up will tap your storehouse of focus, concentration, and tenacity. At a certain point, of course, you too may be tired, wishing the job were done, and eager to get on to something new. You, like they, may be tempted to slack off at the end. Yet if you ease up, you'll probably regret it. You could ruin all the work done until that point. It's like when you paint a house: The initial taping, priming, and undercoats are time-consuming and crucial preconditions for a quality job, but the last coat of paint is the only one you see.

Stay open-minded to the very end. When our copy editor for this book proposed changing some type specifications for the Profiles, at first we dismissed the suggestion. But we ran out a proof page, found we agreed with her, and decided it was worth the extra effort and a slight delay.

Avoid last-minute shortcuts that could hurt you or your client. At a late stage in a job, when a client sends you a few final changes, you're likely to be rushing, and less careful than usual. Don't try to save a few minutes by assuming you've done everything just right. Take the time to print out the pages one more time, and check them against the client's requested corrections.

We can't count the number of times we've noticed a typo or other flaw as we were delivering a job to the printer. Usually we'll go back and fix it, regardless of whose fault it is. If time is at a premium, and we feel reasonably sure the defect won't overshadow the publication's positive qualities, we may let it go. If we can't judge the importance of a wrong address or a missing photo credit, we'll ask the client if they want to delay the job further to fix it.

Don't lose track of clients after the job

Stay in touch when you've completed and delivered the job. Call to find out if everything went well with the printer. Ask clients how they liked working with you and your subcontractors. Remind them to send you the agreed-upon number of sample copies of the publication. Get on the customer's mailing list, so if they forget to send you copies, you'll know when it's done and sent out.

If you've worked with different people on a project, make sure the person with the authority to contract for additional work knows that the staff is pleased with the job you did.

When we first started out, receiving final copies felt a little like getting birthday gifts in the mail. Since then it's become more routine. But the printed version is the whole point of the DTP process—so make sure you take the time to look it over. Check the printer's work. See if the pages have consistent gutters and top and bottom margins. Compare them with your final proofs to see how closely the printer followed your instructions for artwork. Look for uneven inking, usually a printer's problem for which DTPers can be wrongly blamed. Of course, your toner cartridge could be uneven, and some typefaces just don't hold ink well when they're reversed out of a solid box, or when they're run in small sizes at imagesetter resolution. Those aren't printers' errors. They might be yours, but they might be something you couldn't have foreseen, and will simply have to fix for the next time.

Look for your errors. No matter how experienced we become, we sometimes see something we hadn't been able to visualize. Flip through and record what you would do differently. When you're done, and after you've congratulated yourself for your overall workmanship, call the client and compare notes.

If we or the client spot a mistake after the job is printed, and we need to commiserate, we'll emphasize to our client that we've *never* produced a sizeable publication that was perfect in every way. And if you notice as many typos and extra spaces between words as we do, both in magazines about DTP and in national consumer publications, you can feel reassured that the big guys aren't perfect either. (We'll try to accept all the flaws in this book we discover after it's too late.)

How to let go of a client

Clients' personalities can be one of the things you like best about DTP. If you work alone, their appearance can be a pleasant interlude. But clients can be a source of pressure and stress, and sometimes you just don't get along. Some insist on calling you at all hours, or take it personally when you can't accommodate tight deadlines, or ask you to schedule time for their jobs and then consistently fail to deliver their material on time, or hate your suggestions, or treat you as if you are inferior in some way. Perhaps you dislike their graphic designs, their resistance to your suggestions, or the subject matter of their publications. Maybe you have trouble getting them to pay what they owe you.

Before giving up, try to talk a problem through. You may have each been looking at a problem in different ways, and you may find a solution. If not, ideally, at this point, you can afford to lose their business. Even if you can't, try to work out some other arrangement. First try to hook them up directly with a subcontractor. If that doesn't work, raise your rates to the point where you would grit your teeth and continue working with them. Or send them to another DTPer, with whom you can work out a referral fee. Explain to that person the difficulties you encountered and give them the opportunity to see if the chemistry is better for them.

10. PRICING AND BIDDING

Of course you'd like your work life to be intellectually, emotionally, and socially satisfying. But the bottom line—making a good living—is the bottom line. Ideally, you'll figure out a way to price your work well, so potential customers decide to hire you, you feel good about doing the jobs, and your clients feel they're getting their money's worth. Think of these as objectives. You'll increasingly approach them as you improve your marketing, pricing, managing, and production skills. If you succeed, you'll be able to pick and choose your clients and jobs.

You'll be tempted to start by looking around at everyone else and worrying about what other DTPers are charging. Don't pay attention to this premature impulse, which belongs most properly at the end, not at the beginning, of your calculations and deliberations. You're not yet in a position to judge even who your competition is. You don't know who else (if anyone) your potential customers will be talking to. And if you pursue particular market niches, or present your skills as unique, your services may *never* be directly comparable to anyone else's.

Our estimated hourly and daily rates are generally based on coastal metropolitan areas: San Francisco Bay Area, Los Angeles, New York, Boston, Philadelphia, Washington. That's where many large service and media corporations make their homes, where the cost of living is highest, where traditional publishing and printing is a big industry, and where you'll find the most people already doing DTP. For smaller cities and towns, you may be able to scale down some of our overhead and price estimates.

The numbers that follow are not intended to substitute for the usual financial planning steps you'll take in preparing a business plan or setting up your books once you are in business. These will include estimates for start-up expenses and continuing expenses, income and cash flow projections, break-even timetable, and profit and loss statements. They'll also include figuring out your monthly **nut**: The amount you must make every month to cover your basic expenses. Your nut will be much lower if you work at home.

How much can you make?

The answer to that question gives you your starting point. Set targets for your net *pre-tax annual income*. That's an all-important number: the crucial assumption upon which you can build a pricing structure. Let's start with very modest goals, reasonable assumptions, and easily divisible numbers, and see where it takes us. (Don't worry, it gets better!)

Allocated startup (fixed) costs	$10,000
Office operating costs	7,500
Expenses and supplies	7,500
Desired net pre-tax income	$25,000
Total billings needed	$50,000

The main purpose of this exercise is to short-circuit the typical thought process of a full-time employee. If you're making $40,000 (pre-tax) now, you might figure that your $800 per week for 40 hours, or average of $20 per hour means you'll do much better as a freelancer if you earn even $30 or $40 per hour.

In fact, our highly simplified summary tells us that to meet the goal of netting even $25,000 a year, you'll need:

Net pre-tax income: 1,000 hours per year at $50 per hour . . . $50,000

Here are our assumptions:

Allocated startup costs
We figure you're going to shell out $10,000 to $20,000 for hardware, software, and office equipment. It might be in one shot, or you might get it in stages. For your purposes (not the IRS's, which looks at depreciation differently—talk to your accountant), we think a reasonable assumption is to spread this cost over two years, so we've put $10,000 into year one. Of course, if you already own a computer, furniture and equipment, or you rent or buy used hardware, your numbers will be much lower.

Office operating costs

We're figuring on $500 per month for rent, and another $125 per month for utilities, cleaning, and property insurance.

Expenses and supplies

We're shoehorning in $1,500 per year for phones, postage, and delivery services, $1,000-$1,500 for service contracts and repairs, $1,500 for consumable office and computer supplies, $500 for promotion (printing, mailing, and perhaps advertising), $500 for publications, memberships, and conferences, $1,000 for professional services (legal and accounting, not including the cost of incorporating), and $1,000 for contingencies.

Missing items

We haven't budgeted anything for technical consultants or training. You might have room for it in the startup costs category. We haven't accounted for $1,000–$2,000 per year for health insurance (not to mention contributions to an IRA or Keogh). That's all coming out of your pre-tax net income. You could also add benefits as a business expense to the list. If you're fortunate enough to have a working spouse with a health plan that covers you, you may not have to worry about health insurance.

Revenues

We're giving you weekends, holidays, and two weeks off, and assuming that you'll be able to churn out your clients' jobs for a very conservative 20 hours per week. This doesn't include all the time you'll spend marketing, bidding, managing, and billing the work, plus all the time buying, installing, trouble-shooting, learning, upgrading, and cursing and blessing your tools (for more details see **1. Staying on top takes time**).

This isn't such an encouraging picture—especially if you aren't confident you can bill at an average of $50 per hour in your part of the world. And if your business expenses are as substantial as we show, even though your Schedule C tax form may show you don't owe the government much in taxes, you could come to rue the day you went off on your own.

Here's an independent way to confirm these ballpark numbers. If you're currently employed full-time in some field related to DTP and you want to figure how much you'll need to charge to match your current salary, people in dozens of service businesses have developed a standard formula. They use a magic 2.5 multiplier to get the hourly fee they need to charge to cover overhead, fringes, administration, marketing, and other unbillable time. Take your annual salary; divide it by 52 weeks, and by 40 hours to get your hourly salary. For $50,000, that comes to $24 per hour. Multiplying $24 by 2.5 tells you that you'll need to charge $60 an hour to do as well in your own business as on salary. That's not far from our number. And if you used a 2.1 multiplier because your office overhead and capital investment are likely to be lower than in many service businesses, you're back to our $50.

First year strategy

What does our $50 per hour figure tell you? It's your target rate: An average of what you'd like to be getting once you're up and running smoothly, with enough clients coming through to keep you busy all the time. Knowing this number will help you avoid succumbing to the temptation to lure potential clients with bargain rates because you're just starting out.

Often manufacturers who bring a new product to market knowing they'll sell only 1,000 in the first year still price their products from launch assuming they'll eventually move 5,000 a year—with the resulting economies of scale. The same strategy holds true for you: Price your work *today* based on where you *want to be*. If you think you're not yet worth $50 per hour to clients, don't apologize for your inexperience and announce a low hourly rate. Instead, look at the job and figure to yourself how many hours it should take you to complete it six months from now. Based on the $50 per hour rate, if it's a 10-hour job, ask $500. And if it takes you 30 hours to complete it the first time, 18 hours two months later, and 10 hours in six months, congratulate yourself for a great bid. How do you tell if it's a 10-hour job? Consult other DTPers, and see **Hours and dollars for typical jobs** later in this chapter.

Obviously, you won't gross one-twelfth of $50,000 the first month you're open. Remember, *startups are supposed to lose money.* You're launching a business with relatively low initial cash outlays. But your initial revenues will be low because:

- You'll be spending untold extra hours learning the ropes;
- You won't have enough clients;
- Every one of your billable hours could represent two or three actual hours that you can't expect your clients to pay for.

Worst case, during your first six months, figure you'll make $50 per hour for 10 hours per week, or $12,500. If you're fortunate enough to reach cruising speed within this time, and you make your targets for the second six months, you'll end up with $37,500 for the first year—and a net income of $12,500.

What if you can't afford to make so little in your first year? If you hold the billable hours and the rate constant, the only way to make these numbers look much better at the start is to buy used equipment, reduce your operating expenses with a home office, and work as many hours as you need to get the full 1,000 billable hours at $50:

Allocated startup (fixed) costs	$ 8,000
Office operating costs	1,000
Expenses and supplies	7,500
Revised desired net pre-tax income	$33,500
Total billings needed	$50,000

Second year strategy

What would you have to do in your second or third year to double your desired net pre-tax income (assuming by then you are renting office space, and will still be buying hardware and software)?

Allocated or continuing fixed costs	$ 5,000
Office operating costs	7,500
Expenses & supplies	7,500
Desired net pre-tax income	$50,000
Total billings needed	$70,000

You'd have to find a way to increase your average billing rate, and you could probably squeeze in at least three more billable hours a week: 1,166 hours per year at $60 per hour = $70,000.

Some DTPers make much more

If our starting point were the whole story, you wouldn't be seeing too many people in the DTP business. In fact, some people find ways to significantly increase their billable hours, particularly if they specialize, and if they spend fewer than 20-25 hours per week keeping up with the technology plus managing the business.

Quite a few charge more than the $50 per hour rate we chose for our examples. Some are able to skew their work to consulting and training, which commands higher hourly rates. Some are able to pick up a few thousand dollars a year by marking up their reimbursed expenses such as messengers, faxes, service bureau output, and printing. And some hire other people, turning into managers or marketers rather than production people. For these and other strategies, see **11. Expanding Revenues.**

> The greatest problem DTPers have is pricing. Too often they are working too cheaply, and they go out of business in a flash. But there always seems to be another beginning DTPer to take that one's place. Lots of DTPers work under the assumption that DTP is cheap (which isn't really true) and that, therefore, they must charge cheaply.   —*Denis Shedd*

How do most people charge?

Elliot Epstein, with a couple of decades' experience in type and graphics (he's one of our profiled DTPers) describes at least six possible ways to charge:

Per hour
Best suited for work done on the client's premises. It's a good way to begin a project, getting a sense of its scope and of the client's needs. Some clients won't be willing to embark on an open-ended commitment, so it helps them if you can put a cap or limit on at least the initial phase of the job.

Per day
Also good for on-site work. Many corporations prefer to pay in full- or half-day chunks. In figuring your daily rate, assume a seven- or eight-hour day, with a premium for overtime. Elliot reminds you to build in preparation time researching technical issues or preparing for workshops and demonstrations.

Per head
For training or presentations, this can be attractive for companies or professional groups. It can be very lucrative for you, but even if you build in a minimum charge, you run the risk of unexpected low attendance and therefore a low fee.

Per project
This is the favored option for most DTPers. It offers you the advantage of your being the only one who knows how you figure your charges. It forces you to track your work carefully so you perfect the art of estimating future jobs. It also gives your customers set figures, so they don't have to worry about how much

time you're taking. It gives you both the opportunity to tailor the job to fit a budget. Typically, you might say to a client, "I'll give you the biggest bang for your buck. You have $1,000 to spend. Here's what I can do for you for $1,000." For new and unknown clients, and for people who are clearly amateurs, Elliot doubles his time estimates to account for time wasted by the client, unexpected changes, handholding and consultations, client delays that throw off his schedule for other work, and work that doesn't match its description.

Flat rate

If you're providing the same services regularly—for instance doing a monthly publication—after you've done it once or twice on a per-project basis, you can set a fixed figure. Nothing always takes the same amount of time; but more often than not the longer and the shorter cycles will average out.

Retainer fee

Most people would rather have retainer fees than any other arrangement. They combine the advantage of steady income with the freedom of self-employment. On the other hand, the sense of security you get from one major client can be dangerous if it leads you to reduce efforts to diversify your client base.

You can enter into a retainer agreement once you've gotten to know a client, working on a project or per-day basis until you can set a fair rate for a long-term association. You'll need a clear agreement, entitling the client, say, to 10 hours of your time a month. You'll need to decide if hours can be carried over from month to month.

> I have standard per diem and half-day rates I charge everyone. If I'm on retainer, I'll lower that rate by about 15%, depending on what perks may be included, such as access to high-end hardware. —*Steven Gorney*

> When clients need my services more than just occasionally, I try to sign them up for a systems consulting contract. For example, my normal consulting rate is $100 per hour. If a client calls me for eight to 10 hours a month, it could run up a big bill. I offer them a technical support contract giving them the benefit of my time for a fixed number of hours at a reduced rate. I'll bill them $75 per hour, if they guarantee at least eight to 10 hours. If the time exceeds the specified number of hours, I hold to the $75 rate. I guarantee they'll receive a return phone call within four hours, and I'll be on premises within 24 hours. Sometimes a special project will come up, such as a move, which means a total rewiring of the network. Then I'll bill that separately, but still give them a break so I'll be more cost-effective than a competitor. I don't want anyone else in my client's office. —*On Far Tse*

So how much should you charge?

In real life, you'll be keeping your target income in mind, and trying to exceed it any way you can. If you feel comfortable doing it, you might charge some well-heeled clients far more than your usual rates, to help move up your average billing rate. Often you'll charge by the job, not by the hour—though in your internal accounting and analysis, to come up with bids, you'll always need to start with your hourly target.

Each type of service you provide is worth a different amount to you—and to your clients. The only way to determine your market's price-sensitivity is to experiment. To your clients, if your services are unique or in short supply, they are worth more. For yourself, you can try to get more of the work you most enjoy by slightly undercharging for it, and conversely, you can raise your rates slightly for work you're less happy doing.

In every case, the quality of your efforts and your reliability in delivering promised services have an unquantifiable but high inherent value. In the examples that follow, we're again assuming the typical rates for the large metropolitan areas listed at the start of this chapter.

Production

The value of your production work is determined by your experience and skills—including raw speed and ability to turn jobs around quickly. The greater your investment in fast, efficient hardware, the more your services are worth *per hour*. You can deliver more in a given time period.

Because we're not talking about your capabilities here, just your efficiency, your capital investment doesn't affect your value *per job*. However, the more you invest your money in software and your time in becoming an expert, the more your services are worth *per hour and per job*.

It makes sense to have a standard bread-and-butter production rate. For starters, it can be that target rate ($50 or whatever you come up with when you adjust the calculations to meet your own circumstances). For a particular client, you may choose to increase or decrease that rate. What if, for instance, you get a last-minute new story to add to a newsletter, in typewritten form, not on disk? If time doesn't permit you to arrange for typing at, say $7-$20 per hour, you're entirely justified in telling the client you'll be charging $50 per hour for your time, whatever your agility on the keyboard. If copy comes to you in hard-to-decipher scrawls, you may want to charge extra for your suffering, or stick to your hourly rate.

You should establish a minimum rate to keep time-consuming small jobs from clogging up your day. For changes to jobs, a quarter- or a half-hour minimum allows you to take into account phone conversations, stopping other projects, completing, and delivering the work. For new jobs, a one- or two-hour minimum, perhaps depending on the affluence of the customer, is entirely reasonable. If you charge in quarter-hour increments, you'll need to decide what to do about those two- or five-minute phone calls. For production, you might decide not to count them, but for consulting, if the client is calling you frequently with urgent problems and questions, you could count each as a separate quarter-hour. Again for small jobs, you may want to charge for supplies that you probably won't worry about with larger jobs.

For work you bid by the job, you'll need to specify:

- The number of galleys and page proofs included in the set fee;
- The number of copies of each set of galleys or proofs;
- Costs for additional copies;
- Hourly and/or per page charges for author's alterations beyond an agreed upon maximum;
- Hourly and per-page charges for changes to camera-ready output or mechanicals;
- Overtime and weekend rush charges.

When you're starting out, you may not be able to ask for surcharges for rush, night-time, or weekend work. Mentioning them to clients as a possibility, then adding them as you get busier, is easier than raising your standard rate.

For large jobs, charge for output from your laser printer, including the life cycle cost for the equipment, service contracts, toner, and paper. This could come to perhaps $.05 per page, so the dollars can mount up.

Don't forget that practically any project you do will involve not only production, but also conversations, trips, and meetings, as well as passing materials, information, and advice back and forth between you and writers, editors, designers, paper vendors, printers, shippers and warehousers. You should bill the time you spend running around higher than your production rate. (See **Managing Projects**, below.)

Designing and illustrating

The value of your illustrations or graphic designs derives from expertise you've developed over your *lifetime* in art, graphics, typography, and communications.

It begins with a creative fee that has little relation to the amount of time you actually spend at work putting designs on paper. Before you sit down to solve a problem for a client, you've already been working. Chances are you ruminate on design problems in the shower, in the car, on the bus. Every time you look at a publication or an advertisement, you're checking it out and learning from it. Only you can decide what this preparation time is worth.

Your final bill will include the initial design fee plus charges for each additional modification or redesign request, and finally for incorporating the final design into a publication. For instance, for a newsletter, you may charge $1,000 for the initial design plus one revision, $250 per additional revision, and then $750 for the first issue, based on $50 per hour for 15 hours.

Graphic designers talk about **comps**—comprehensives, or visualizations for the client of how a finished page or illustration will look. They talk about tight or loose comps, referring to the amount of detail and accuracy in a sketch. Elliot Epstein breaks his design work into pencil thumbnail sketches, comps done on the computer, and comps that are near-finished as complete layouts or color proofs. His bids specify the number of designs or comps included in a price, the price per extra comp, and a rejection or kill fee, enough to cover his costs if the client decides not to use the work. Elliot also reminds you to include time for research, to find samples or material necessary to produce editorial or technical illustrations, graphs, charts, and maps. The more you establish these ground rules, the more you let clients know you're serious, and the less likely clients are to take advantage of your good nature.

Don't feel you need to show the client the first proof in 20 different typefaces, just because it's not too hard for you to do it. Do it if you've built the time into your bid, and if the client asks for it.

Some clients will think that just because they gave you a rough sketch, you didn't have to do any design. Yet sometimes implementing such a comp, though much less dramatic, involves more work and creativity than creating a new design. It's also more work than following complete design specifications. Some clients may imagine that because they were sitting beside you while you completed the project, they were the designers. But you still need to charge them for your design work. After all, solving problems on the fly, under their eye, can be the most difficult and stressful circumstances for you as a designer.

A few clients will appreciate and respect you for your design efforts. Remember to remind them that many of the most memorable logos and graphic designs appear to be simple and obvious when complete—yet they are often the most difficult to create.

Some clients expect DTPers to throw in graphic design as part of their services, charging no more for design than for production. We can't advise you whether to go along with this financially disadvantageous approach. In some cases, such a request may reflect a disrespect for the design process. In others, it may simply result from fiscal realities. Felix often encounters nonprofit organizations that can't stretch their budgets to pay for a separate professional designer. When they are creating a new publication, he usually attempts to include some charges for design in the start-up costs for creating the template. If he can't persuade them to pay such a fee, then he decides whether he still wants to do the job.

Software training

Your value as an instructor may change from stage to stage. If you're helping to get someone started using a computer, some of your most useful advice will come at the start of the training schedule. On the other hand, if you're training a person who has already read the software manuals for a particular application, though you may provide some valuable hints and shortcuts at the start, your best nuggets may come as you demonstrate advanced techniques. If you meet a potential customer who wants to work with you on an open-ended basis, it probably makes sense to establish an inverse pyramid fee schedule. You might bid $400 for the first half day, $275 for successive half days.

If you're in a position to sell the client a training package by the week, you don't have to worry about where the most useful information is found. Felix often encounters clients who are familiar with computers but not with publishing, or those who know editorial proofreading marks, typography, and graphic design but are computer novices. He may offer a training package to fill in the gaps, which may include organizing the hard disk, demonstrating needed software utilities, and introducing typesetting and design concepts (one to two days). This can then be followed by training in word processing and page layout software, which will often leave the client with a finished camera-ready publication, largely produced by Felix (two to five days). This can then be followed some time later by the client producing a document under Felix's supervision (one day), and later by the client working alone, with telephone consultations. Following the above half-day rates, you might bid such a training program at a minimum of five days at $2,750 with additional days at around $550.

You might bid on introducing a knowledgeable computer user to a graphics package at three mornings at $300 per half day—encouraging the client to spend each afternoon trying out the techniques learned in the morning. You could offer follow-up in-person or telephone consulting at $80 per hour.

You can always charge more to train more than one person at a time. But you need to make sure your intentions match the client's expectations. For instance, if you contract to train one person, and two people show up, renegotiate, or make clear that the second person is an observer who is expected to refrain from interrupting the first person's training by asking questions.

> I charge only by the hour for training, never by the day or half day, because there are differing opinions of what a half day means. I have a minimum of four hours. I keep the clock running when the client is interrupted or called away. I don't charge more for training additional people, but I'm careful to point out that the training will become more general in character when there's a larger audience. However, one of my most effective group training sessions was a two-hour lunch seminar where I gave a general overview of DTP. People with overlapping responsibilities were able to understand the collaborative effort required by DTP.
> —*K.C. Genzmer, DTP trainer and consultant,*
> *teacher at Pratt Institute, and chair of NY Mac Users' Group Freelance SIG*

Many trainers recommend allowing a one-to-two ratio for training time and practice time for students learning new DTP software. If you find a system that works, stick to it. Don't agree to train people in less time than you think it will take. You're probably right about your estimates—and if the clients get their way, they'll probably end up needing more help, and feeling resentful about it.

> Most of the first waves of users were familiar with at least some aspects of design, publishing, and production. Increasingly, new users of DTP know next to nothing about these matters. At the same time, the software is becoming more complex, so new users have more to learn at the start. I suggest a five-day, eight hour per day training program for new users, breaking down DTP into digestible parts: the basic concepts of DTP, structured documents, details of using the software, and practical tips. At the end of this period, the user should have enough background to be ready to read the software manual and be ready to learn. Alternatively, a combination of time spent studying written materials and one-on-one instruction with an experienced user can be a most productive training regimen.
> —*C.J. Weigand, editor of* The Weigand Report, Essential Information
> for Communicators, Desktop Publishers and Small Business Users

When you are training, keep your antennae out for the way office politics and gender relationships affect training. Make sure to give your attention to the people who most need to be trained, even if they're low on the totem pole and seem intimidated by their superiors.

Consulting, including systems consulting

As in designing, the value of your advice may also have little relation to the amount of time it takes you to communicate it. If you're asked to help a client specify, purchase, or install hardware and software, or establish a DTP production facility, your experience may enable you to have extremely valuable advice on the tip of your tongue. Or you may know exactly where to find the ideal vendor with one phone call, or one flip through an article you read months ago. And you may be able to zero in on an intractable technical problem because you encountered a similar case last year. Literally, your 10 minutes could be worth hundreds of dollars, because it could save your client thousands.

Even more than with training, the inverted pyramid bid makes sense. If you're intending to charge $100 per hour for systems consulting, consider charging $1,000 for the first day, $700 for successive days, or $600 for the first half day, $500 for the second, and $350 for successive half days.

The inverted pyramid pricing will help you get used to restraining yourself during the selling phase. You need not tell clients who are interviewing you how you would solve problems. You could refer to the options available, or provide some intriguing references to parts of the solution. Your only goal at this point is to prove your expertise, and persuade clients that they need your help.

Many consultants live in fear of telling the client too much, and working themselves out of a job quicker than they wish. Computer programmers are sometimes suspected of protecting their livelihoods by writing software that calls for a programmer's intervention whenever a change is needed.

But once hired, we think you should tell the client everything you know. (See **9. Give away as much information as you can.**) You should price your services at a point where you feel good about spilling all the beans. Of course, if you think the client is making a mistake in attempting to do everything without help, you can say so. Sometimes we'll tell clients we think they should stick to what they know best, and leave the most complex and difficult DTP or illustration projects to specialists who do them all the time. But this is a decision the client must make.

Managing projects

The client may ask you to take charge of some or all facets of a publishing operation: Keyboarding or optical scanning of text (OCR), locating or commissioning graphic or photographic materials, choosing paper and ink, bidding and hiring a printer and a fulfillment (mailing) company, and even handling all messengers and deliveries. For the larger items on the list, in particular printing, we recommend being very careful about taking on a direct financial responsibility for the project. In general, have the printer bill the client directly, or someday you might get stuck in the middle of a fight that could cost you as much as you make in months. (For the pros and cons, see **11. Bidding on printing.**)

Traditionally, especially for advertising agencies, graphic designers tacked on a 25-100% surcharge to all the ancillary services they bought for clients, including messengers, typesetting, and photostats. Our somewhat less profitable approach, for clients who pay us promptly, is to add a 10-15% surcharge to bills we pay (including imagesetting), plus an hourly rate for the time we spend arranging for these services. Even if your subcontractors lay out some of this money, you don't have to share this surcharge with them, because they bill you for the time they spend preparing and delivering the materials, because you're the one who got the client and is assuming any risks on the job, and because you're reimbursing them when they bill you.

How much to charge for managing projects? Presumably the client asked you to take over because of your experience and your contacts. Accordingly, it seems reasonable that you charge your training rate or slightly higher.

Subcontracting and referring

If you would have charged the client our usual hypothetical $50 per hour for production work, and you hire someone to do it at a hypothetical $25 per hour, how much should you charge the client? With the exception of highly skilled work, your subcontracted work should cost the client somewhat less, while still returning a profit to you as compensation for the risks and headaches involved. To make money with subs, you need have enough *margin* to charge the client the money you pay the sub, plus:

- Compensation to you for the orientation time you spend talking to or meeting with the sub;
- The time you spend checking the sub's work;
- At least 15-25% in profit on the sub's work.

Otherwise, hiring other people simply won't be worthwhile for you. (See also **8. Managing subcontractors**.)

Ideally, you'll have some benchmarks for judging the sub's productivity. For instance, you may know that because the sub has less experience or uses slower equipment, you could have done in two hours ($100 to the client) what took the sub three hours, costing you $75. Sounds good. If you have enough maneuvering room, in the client's bill, you can include a modest amount of time (say $20 for 20 minutes) to cover your management of the sub, plus $100 for the work and profit. But now the client is spending $120 for work you could do at $100. If that's a problem, this experience is a *strong message* to you to pay the sub less per hour, find a more efficient sub, or sub only larger jobs requiring a smaller percentage of management time. On the other hand, if the client doesn't squawk about $120, you could stick to this sub, or net more by doing the work yourself and charging $60 per hour!

In some situations—if you don't see a way you can happily make money on a job, if you're eager to stop working with an existing client, if you're too busy, or if a client would prefer to work directly with your sub—you could hand over the work to your subcontractor or to another DTPer. If it's an inconsequential job, or a troublesome client whom you feel guilty inflicting on any other DTPer, you may simply refer the job. But if you see the work as potentially profitable, you can negotiate a **finder's fee** with your replacement.

Among architects, lawyers, and other professionals, such fees (often for work costing many thousands of dollars) range from 5-15%. If it appears to be a large one-time job, we'll be quite satisfied with 10-20% of the final invoice. If we're sending someone a source of regular work (particularly if they're a longstanding client), we may arrange a smaller (5-15%) continuing or a declining percentage of the billings for the first six months or year. This protects the person we refer the work to, since they pay only as long as they keep the client. Whatever the terms we negotiate, unless we are simply relieved at the prospect of never talking to the client again, we usually assure them that they can come back to us, or at least call for advice, if they have any problems.

You can be reasonably sure to collect your finder's fee from a subcontractor you work with frequently, or you met through a user group. But if you think you might refer the job and never hear from the person again, put the arrangement in writing, and ask for a periodic accounting, plus, if you're really being careful, photocopies of the client's payment checks.

What can your client afford?

You can start sizing up your client by determining the end use of the published material. Always find out how it will be produced: paper quality, number of colors, type of press, how many copies will be printed, and how and to whom it will be distributed. Obviously, the larger the print run or the more important the product, the more the client can afford, and the more inconsequential your bill for services will be as a percentage of the total publication cost.

The client's perspective on price may not always be clear. Potential customers are often less concerned about costs than about quality work, a smooth and pleasant relationship, and timely turnaround of their jobs. Of course, many nonprofit organizations are chronically underfunded, and people in some companies are under very tight budget pressures. Those clients who are most concerned about price are also the most likely to give you a hard time, to jeopardize your margins, and to be reluctant payers. All of which argues for trying to sell yourself before you sell your prices.

Here's where it helps to try to find out whether you're competing against traditional typesetting, other DTPers, or in-house production facilities. In some cases, a potential client is just beginning to explore options, and is talking to you to find out what's involved. Take our earlier advice about selling: Ask direct questions to determine what you're up against, and whether the decision-maker is ready to close the deal if the terms are okay. (See **3. Selling fundamentals.**)

For potential clients who are considering DTP as an alternative to traditional typesetting, you may have an easy time. When they ask how much their job will cost, ask them straight out: "How much are you spending now?" or "Do you have a budget for this?" They often answer! If they don't, maybe you can come up with a more subtle or tactful way to ask it. Or you may be able get them to tell you by offering to undercut their last invoice, or match it while providing more services. If you find out the numbers are too low, you can, if necessary, back out on the deal, or refer the work.

If you can't find out, remember that typographers traditionally charge whatever the traffic can bear. Ad agencies have been accustomed to paying $75 to order one line of type, and lawyers and financiers have paid stratospheric prices for fast turnaround of stock and real estate prospectuses and reports. Purchasers of design and type for corporate annual reports have expected to spend in the tens of thousands of dollars. Small-scale typesetters often charge $100 per page or more for typesetting and pasteup. Typesetters that read customers' word processor disks with embedded format codes charge $1-$2 per thousand keystrokes to produce galleys.

One source of baseline prices for design in particular is the *Handbook of Pricing and Ethical Guidelines* of the Graphic Artists Guild. (See **Appendix 2. Books on the business and graphics and DTP.**) This reference work gives design and production costs for a range of project types and budgets, for clients in large metropolitan areas. Of course it assumes the bidder is a professionally trained graphic artist. If you're not, you can use their numbers as a yardstick, adjusting them based on your estimate of your own informally acquired design expertise and your ideas for the particular job. You don't have to pretend you studied personally with Herb Lubalin or Jan White.

If you're able to find out their budget, you'll be able to see how your estimates compare. If not, in general, you can still go ahead and say, with some confidence, that you can complete their job "somewhat faster and somewhat cheaper" than their current vendor. At the same time, you need to emphasize that you can't say how much cheaper until you know more.

To start, you can emphasize the savings in time and money when the client gives you text on disk. You can then explain or demonstrate the benefits of creating a template for a publication to simplify the process of making revisions and expedite production of new issues of periodicals. Clients usually understand when we explain that the bulk of the savings will come in second and subsequent production cycles.

It also pays to emphasize the other benefits of DTP. You can describe or show how proofs with type and graphics in place provide a close representation of the final product at an early stage of production, and how computers automate and facilitate global changes to text and type styles.

What about the client attracted to DTP who hasn't used a typesetter? Typically, a company wants to upgrade its typewritten materials. (See **3. Finding your first customers.**) Or a small business or nonprofit group wants to produce a new newsletter or promotional material. You'll often be faced with unrealistic expectations. You'll have to explain how creating practically any page for the first time will take more than an hour, and how virtually any newsletter will take at least five to 15 hours.

Inexperienced clients will need a higher level of service. In many cases, they will completely rewrite your first proofs. If you've explained to them the stages of

DTP, and how much time each step takes, they won't be surprised later, and you won't have disappointed clients.

What about the small nonprofit groups that are always short on funds, and tell you they had hoped DTP would be even more affordable? If you don't have one labor of love, we suggest you pick one. Volunteering to help out a cause you care about is especially appropriate if you have many clients you charge high hourly rates. You're far better off volunteering your services than offering bargain basement prices. Your relationship with the group will be better, you'll get more respect, and you'll probably pick up additional clients through the exposure you gain, including a credit printed in the publication.

Negotiating

Entire books have been written on the subject—lately emphasizing how both sides can come out winners. Here are a few elementary principles—obvious, but so important we need to say them. They apply to your financial negotiations for services or for buying or selling equipment, to contractual negotiations with subcontractors, and to reaching an agreement on scopes of work and deadlines.

- Always ask the other party to make the first offer or set the asking price. You might get better terms than you ever expected.
- Decide what you want before you start. Know where you'd like to end up, what you'd settle for, and whether you're willing to risk losing the deal if you hold out for your terms.
- If the negotiation is a complicated one, offer to write up a preliminary agreement. That allows you to define the terms according to your needs. A written agreement helps ensure that all parties agree on what is involved. If a lawyer's help is needed, your outline could save time and money.

Making the bid

When a potential customer asks you for a bid, you're in an excellent position. Usually the customer has come to you hoping that you'll say the right words, and you'll have a deal. Unless the electric company is about to turn off your lights, you have no reason to feel desperate, hurried, or under fire. Here's your chance to do yourself justice.

The initial contacts are critical. That's when you specify price and turnaround time. Later, as soon as possible during the job, clarify production and delivery, so there are no surprises later on when you send your bill. It's the repeat customers that build a business. The communication process is at least as important as the work itself, perhaps even more so.   —*Richard E. Luna*

On the next page, we've included a worksheet, **Fig. 10.1**, which you can use in conjunction with **Fig. 7.1 Steps in preparing a project.** The sheet may be helpful in figuring out what's involved in a job. Another way to use it is to fill it out after you complete a job, to get a better idea how to bid the next one.

Never bid blind

Get all the information available: printed copies of existing publications, designer's specifications, originals of text and artwork. If text is on a disk, look at the printout and word processor files. If nothing is available yet, keep asking questions. We often get callers who ask, "How much will a simple newsletter or brochure cost?" We ask whether the publication includes a complete, tentative, or no design; has one or many stories; many levels of heads and subheads; tables, charts, or graphics; and whether all the columns need to line up at the bottom. The way clients answer these questions, and how willing they are to help us evaluate the job, usually tells us how much time, energy—and hope—we should invest in making the bid.

For the casual prospect who has called you about what they describe as a simple job, we suggest you take our **Fig. 7.1** or your equivalent and tack it up on the wall or a bulletin board near the phone, to jog your memory when you explain to clients how DTP isn't ever routine.

Many longtime professionals advise: Never bid on the spot. When you're on a sales call, they suggest taking the materials back to the office, double checking all assumptions, and phoning back the next day. Why? It's too easy to overlook something under the pressure of the client's attention. What's more, an immediate response appears unprofessional and overly eager.

Though these points have merit, we don't always take this advice. If we feel very confident about the job and suspect the bid is a formality, we may go ahead. Usually we protect ourselves with a conservative bid that takes into account all the worst-case possibilities—and we explain how the fee will be lower if the job runs smoothly. We caution the client that we're giving a preliminary estimate,

CLIENT & PROJECT	CONTACT NAME	PHONE

AMOUNT	QUOTED TO	DATE

**Fig. 10.1
Bid worksheet**

Task	Work Time	Travel Time	Rate	$ Outlay	Total
Meet with customer to explore job					
Write & receive contract					
Conceive design or format					
Negotiate & plan with designer					
Produce comps					
Review design with customer					
Other: _____					
Meet to plan job & schedule					
Instruct client on data preparation					
Early editorial advice, consultation					
Get copy or enter text					
Hire typist; proofread; copy edit					
Transmit files and convert disks					
Clean up files					
Print out & review files					
Talk to client					
Other: _____					
Design style sheets					
Partially format text					
Propose copy changes					
Print out galleys for client					
Insert corrections, (# free + AAs)					
Create or obtain graphics					
Other: _____					
Set up page layout templates					
Place text & complete formatting					
Make rules, boxes, tints					
Modify design					
Add end of story dingbats/graphics					
Fix and fiddle with pages					
Prepare original & alternatives					
Print & deliver first page proofs					
Other: _____					
Insert corrections (# free + AAs)					
Major client revisions, relocations					
Fine-tune & adjust pages					
Print & deliver second proof					
Make final changes					
Print third proof					
Per additional proof					
Produce repro or disk for imagesetter					
Liaison with imagesetter & printer					
Prepare & deliver mechanicals					
Billing and archiving					
Other: _____					
Totals					

from Kramer Communications

and we'll give a final bid when we've actually seen the material. The important principles here are to protect yourself and to appear serious.

Of course, you don't always have to play it safe. If you really want the job because you're just starting out, or it seems like a challenge, or you want to get your foot in the client's door for other work, or having a prestigious client on your list will help you get other work, take as much risk as you want. If that means bidding aggressively, chancing losing money on the job, or working days, nights and weekends for a while, none of these are life-threatening activities. It's up to you.

Take your time with bids

Anything you say can be used against you. Keep careful notes about your methods of calculating time and costs, and exactly what you say. Don't hesitate to take a few notes while you're talking, if you spell out some assumption or if the client asks you to bid the job in a particular way that you want to get right.

If it seems appropriate, begin by explaining the process and your assumptions about what the job involves. That's the only way to make sure you're talking about the same job.

If you've never worked with a potential client before, be extra careful. You have no way of knowing how you'll work together. If you're dealing with a completely open-ended situation, such as the creation of original artwork, protect yourself by completely avoiding a fixed fee. Give a minimum quote for initial design plus additional hours. If you don't get the job, you can probably assume you're better off without the headaches and risks.

Start with quality, not cost

Explain to the client how you'll do the job. If you know you're up against other bidders, don't criticize them either specifically or in general. If you're bidding to replace an old-style typesetter or another DTPer, and you want to draw the client's attention to shortcomings in the existing publication, do it casually, emphasizing how you would improve it. If you know you can deliver faster, mention that without sounding too smug. If you know you're coming in cheaper, don't make a big point of it. Sometimes you might even risk announcing that you're 25% more expensive than most—and then explaining what the client will get for those extra dollars.

> It's not a good idea, when you're selling yourself, to say, "Don't hire that slob, hire this slob."
> —*Rick Barry, at an early 1987 meeting of the NY Macintosh DTP SIG*

If you've promised to get back to the potential customer, even if they've asked for it in writing, first run your bid by them by phone. It's easier and faster. And more than once we've encountered a friendly spirit who wanted us to get the job and helped us out by advising us to present an issue differently or to be sure to mention something we hadn't planned to include.

When you need to put it in writing, prepare your first bid with the idea that you're creating a word processor template for future bids. Gradually you'll refine your presentation.

Hours and dollars for typical jobs

It's hard to give typical numbers. The following are *roughly* based on Felix's production times, in cases where the client accurately describes the scope and complexity of the project, and where the client doesn't make major design changes or text rewrites during the job. Because so few jobs meet these criteria, and because of what's not included, potential *buyers* of DTP services shouldn't use the dollar figures to evaluate bids.

For simplicity's sake, we're continuing our assumption that you'll bill the work at $50 per hour. But if you're an expert, you might very well charge $60–$75, depending on your skills, equipment, market, and financial goals.

And if the resulting times seem too quick and the costs too cheap, remember that *design fees aren't included* (you could add $200-$1,000 easily for design), and that these are best case situations:

- Unless you work very quickly, know your software in depth, use every available shortcut, and have the fastest equipment, you'll take longer than the times listed;
- In making bids you must protect yourself from the unforeseen;
- To each bid, you could add $50 per hour for the second and successive series of AAs;
- If you bid with much higher assumptions of time or hourly fees, you'll still get some of these jobs.

The first two are one-time jobs, assuming that design and specs are provided by client, or you use relatively standard setups. The others *do not include initial set-up time* for templates; they are for second and successive issues. All but the first assume that text is provided on disk. Unless noted, they don't include imagesetting costs or time preparing traditional mechanicals on boards.

Simple one-page flyer

Scan logo or line art illustration; type text; set up styles for a standard design (one column of type inside a border around the page; type in about 10 lines of "who/what/when/where" headlines centered, with one long justified paragraph toward the bottom of the page). Without a template, you should be able to complete a first proof in under an hour, and complete any moderate revisions or redesigns in 15 minutes per proof. You're talking about $75.

Two-sided brochure

Convert and clean up text from disk; scan logo or line art illustration; define and apply styles (A head, B head, subhead, body text, bullet text); place text in six panels (some of which may be linked) for a brochure that folds to a #10 envelope. Without a template, assuming the text fits, this is a two-hour job for the first proof. The job could come in under $200.

Four-page newsletter

Convert and clean up text from disk; apply existing styles; open previous issue, remove old text and art; place new text roughly in position, leaving white space for short stories, running overset copy onto a fifth page. Getting to a first proof should take one to two hours. For scans, pull quotes, and many short stories and filler items, add another hour or hour and a half. With few revisions, the entire job could be done in less than six hours, for $300.

Eight-page newsletter

For second and successive issues, we find these take five to 10 hours for three proofs, or under $500.

Sixteen-page newsletter

For second and successive issues, these will routinely take eight to 15 hours, or under $750.

Eight-page tabloid newspaper

For second and successive issues, figure around 15-20 hours. You have the same amount of type as a 16-page newsletter. You'll have more complex layouts and spend more time scrolling around pages that don't fit on a two-page display. Your computer may slow down. When you proof the pages, you'll spend time putting together tiled sections of pages for the client. Unless you're using an imagesetter or large-format laser printer for final output, you'll be assembling tiles for the mechanical as well. This could cost up to $1,000, plus $5-$15 per page for recommended 600 dpi plain or coated paper output.

Forty-page report

Assuming the text is well structured, count about 10 minutes per text page and 30 to 60 minutes for each large and complex table, especially when you have to reorganize text for columns. The first proofs of a typical 50-page report or manual might take eight hours for narrative, plus four hours for half a dozen tabular pages. Including revisions, say $1,000 for the job.

Books

For a typical 400-page trade book, with 10 or 15 chapters, some subheads, a few styles for indented quotes, a few footnotes, and the bottoms of pages lined up, you could expect to complete first proofs in under 25 hours. At $50 per hour, that's $1,250, or about $3 per page. Add 50¢ per page plus an hourly charge for AAs and additional proofs. Add $4-$5 for imagesetting at 1,270 dpi on repro paper (or $1-$2 for 1,000 dpi on laser paper) and you can compare your work to traditional typesetters' charges to book publishers (not including copy editing) of $15-$20 per page for camera-ready pages on simple books.

> Newsletters are easy to do and profitable for me. The first couple of issues are hard, but after that you know what to expect. Designing annual reports is least profitable. I've designed annual reports in the past with a shop of four or five people, but it's tough for one person to do. I can only handle one or two annual reports a year. —*Gan Young Wong*

> Newsletters and books are my most profitable business. For example, when I first started a newsletter it took me 10 hours, then eight, now I have it down to two and a half hours. When I can do a six-page newsletter, get it all working and make it come out looking good in two and a half hours, with two cycles of revisions, send for output to a service bureau for $80 including delivery, and I can turn around and charge $600-700 bucks, that's fine. With three or four newsletters, I can stay at home and work. With a book, I can take advantage of programs and automate a lot of the process of formatting. If I have 10 ads to do, every one of them is different. There's no way I can automate that process, but I can with a 500-page book.

> I've made the least money doing system design and installation. It's happened to me a number of times. I don't charge for the first meeting. Then I do a demo and apparently I do a terrific sell because they love it and now they're involved with the Macintosh but they do everything themselves. I get nothing out of it. I've learned to become a little bit more self-protective and much more circumspect. —*Richard E. Luna*

Some pricing methods

Felix has developed a method of bidding that's worked very well for him. You could summarize this method as bidding based on hours spent on a project, up to a fixed price maximum, after which any additional compensation must be negotiated.

Simply put, he assigns an hourly rate to each part of the job using a sliding scale based on his targets, the resources available to the company or organization, the print run and production budget, and whether he'll be using subcontractors for part or all of the job. He then estimates the maximum conceivable number of hours for completion of the job, assuming first proof, corrections, second proof, minor corrections, final third proofs, and camera-ready copy. He bids the dollar figure for that number of hours. He presents this number to the client as a *guaranteed maximum*. He makes clear the guarantee excludes a major reorganization, redesign, or re-edit at a late stage of the process.

At the same time, he explains to the client that the actual charge will be the maximum bid or lower, based on the actual hours involved. He presents a second number: the expected price, if the job goes smoothly, with no surprises. And, for periodicals and other repeating publications, he presents a third number: the lowest the price is likely to go after the technical and communications bugs are worked out and the job has become routine.

Typically, for production of an informal 16-page newsletter with 5 or 10 major stories and a few pages of short items, scanned art, and photos for position only, let's say the hourly rates range from $40 to $80. The maximum hours may be 20 to 25, the expected hours may be 10 to 15, and the ideal hours may be eight. So the bid might sound like this: "I guarantee I'll do the job for no more than $1,550, but if all goes well, I'll charge you under $900, and next time, with no hitches at all, we hope to bring it in under $600."

From Felix's point of view, the benefits of this bid method are:

- A more relaxed mood for clients who know they're protected with a maximum guarantee;
- A more enjoyable work relationship, resulting from a greater sense of mutual self-interest between him and the client, each trying to make the project go as smoothly as possible;
- A better work process, because it's in the client's interest to keep the hours down, rather than get as much as possible for their money, so they pay

more attention to delivering clean copy and accurate dummies at the start of the job, thereby making Felix's work more enjoyable;

- A satisfied feeling of being able to size up clients and work to make accurate estimates. Jobs that exceed the guaranteed maximum because of faulty judgment have been rare.

The shortcomings of the method are:

- The occasional jobs that slip away because someone else has underbid Felix's maximum. In our example, a customer might hear only the top number, and think $100 per page—and then go with someone else who bid a firm $1,200 or $75 per page.
- The loss of the opportunity to cash in when a job that was bid very high turns out to be much cheaper to complete.

Similar methods are widely used in the construction trades (where the term is an "upset" bid), and though his clients (particularly nonprofit groups) welcome the arrangement, most DTPers seem to prefer open-ended hourly or fixed project bids.

The method does limit the amount of money that Felix can make. In some cases, where he suspects that the amount of money a client expects to spend on DTP services is of little importance, Felix may not use this approach, or he may modify it by bidding the maximum without an absolute promise to charge actual hours. He is then free at billing time to charge any intermediate figure between his actual hours times the rate, and the maximum.

Here's another perspective on pricing:

> When I worked in traditional design offices, project billing had two rates. Senior designers would bill at high fees for their expertise in client contact, concept, and design development. Junior designers and board people would bill lower rates to execute the design by spec'ing and ordering type, preparing mechanicals, and supervising outside suppliers.
>
> As I established my own design firm and came to embrace the world of DTP at the same time, I realized the dividing line between design time and production time had become impossible to distinguish. Preparing a design presentation on desktop means reviewing color alternatives, exploring different type styles, working up possible layouts and scanning in candidate photos to provide the client with comps for review. By the time the client chooses the design direction, much of what used to be production has already been completed—often leaving only simple cleanups before final output. The process is much more seamless than traditional design, and as a result, we've adjusted our rates to reflect the

changed process. We now bill at one rate for all our work—a rate roughly in between our previous design and production fees.

—Ken Godat, partner in Godat/Jonczyk of NYC and Tucson, Arizona

What if you don't get the job

After you've given a bid for production services, ask the potential client to let you know whether you have the project. Ask for a date by which you'll be notified so you can schedule the time to do the work. That way, if you don't hear—and many people hate to call people they're rejecting—you have a good reason to call the client, and find out what they decided and why.

For consulting and training services, you might not hear back from a potential client for months, even though from the initial discussions you had the impression you'd be getting started immediately. Often many levels of politics and decision-making are involved before the client is ready to move forward. Because there's usually so much you don't know, you can write many proposals, even occasionally spend money up front, and not get the work.

Many of your bids won't come through. If you don't get one you wanted, don't give up immediately. First try to find out why you lost it. This way you'll at least know if there's something you shouldn't say or do next time. At most you may lay the groundwork for bidding on another project with the same client, or having the job bounce back to you if it doesn't work out.

If the potential customer punted—didn't pick another DTPer, but just decided to postpone a decision or stick with their current typographer for production services—you can continue your pursuit. Try to reduce the risk and uncertainty for the client. One way is to suggest that you try working together on a small project—even a one-pager. If it goes well, you may end up exactly where you'd hoped to be.

Mid-course corrections on bids

As soon as you have your first clients, start recording how long each job takes you. (See **7. Tracking your time.**) Also note the amount of time you spent working up proposals for consulting and training. At the end of jobs, compare your invoices to the original bids and your working assumptions. The goal is neither to congratulate nor berate yourself, but to extract all the useful information from your initial experiences. If you have a list of all your expenses, and a record of all your time, you should be able to calculate your effective hourly rate, as well as your billable and unbillable hours per week. You should start to see where your bids have been overly optimistic or conservative. The more you look at these numbers, the more ideas you'll have on what to feel satisfied about, and what to do differently.

As the months go by, you'll begin to get a picture of who your clients are, and what kind of work goes smoothly. If you enter your invoices and receipts into a database (see **12. Getting paid**), you'll even be able to see who pays promptly, where your best margins show up, and where you should concentrate additional marketing efforts.

11. EXPANDING REVENUES

You don't have to be restricted to the model we've outlined for a DTP career, that is, starting a production service in your home or in a one-person office. You may conclude that your particular temperament or circumstances (especially prevailing hourly rates or the level of established competitors in your vicinity) will make it hard for you to make a decent living by following this path. Or you may want to cautiously launch a less permanent, more flexibly structured business.

Reducing your overhead

Some alternatives involve working directly for other people. If you're mostly working on your clients' premises, you can lower your overhead by not establishing a full-fledged office. You'll also probably improve your tax-saving opportunities, though commuting costs may replace some of the money you save from not establishing a complete home office.

You can keep your home computer system simple and under $2,000: A Macintosh Classic or a used Plus, or SE, or a PC-AT, with a 40-megabyte hard disk and a dot-matrix or inkjet printer, may be all you'll need to produce invoices, manage your database, and try out some software from time to time. You can forget the on-site service contract, the laser printer, and redundant hardware. You'll still be wise to be the legally registered owner of your working DTP software, but you won't have to own all the extra applications and the range of typefaces. You'll also still need to subscribe to all the publications, so if those thick magazines won't fit in your mail slot, get yourself a post office box and arrange for some neighbor who's home all the time to accept deliveries for you.

Becoming a freelancer

This is the simplest variant. Make yourself available for production work at clients' offices, during or after their regular business hours, with hourly, daily, or per-job rates. If you are able to work steadily, finding clients by word of mouth, you could do pretty well: for instance,

Annual expenses	$5,000
Desired net pre-tax income	47,500
Revenues needed: 35 hours at $30 per hour for 50 weeks	$52,500

In this example, assumptions about prevailing rates are the same as those we outlined at the start of the previous chapter. If you are able to improve on the rate, you may do even better. Or you might not work as many hours, so you could work 30 hours at $35 per hour. But don't count on stretching the hours beyond the already high 35. Though your time spent on business management and billing is near zero, you'll still need to market yourself, and you'll still spend five or more hours a week to stay on top of the technology. And chances are you'll be spending time lining up jobs and travelling between more than one job site.

Try to have more than one customer at all times, because you have no idea when the work will dry up, and because it may help you on April 15.

The objective distinction between freelancers and independent consultants who are sole proprietors may be very subtle, at times non-existent. It often comes down to how you describe yourself and whether you have a company name, business card, client list, and flyer about your services, or just a résumé. But the distinction in customers' eyes is great. It all involves control. If you're a DTP business, the customer contracts with you for services. If you're a freelancer, the customer becomes your employer, buying your time.

As a freelancer, you lose much of your autonomy, especially as far as working and payment schedules. And as just another proletarian, you may also lose much of your ability to make decisions or recommend improvements in computer systems and in the design and content of projects. We've seen several confident, knowledgeable consultants, intimidated by their new role and by their employer's expectation, turn into passive, compliant freelancers, afraid to point out ways their part-time employers could get better, faster or cheaper results.

Becoming a temp

What most people generally call temp agencies are not employment agencies that help people find permanent jobs. Rather they are personnel service bureaus that employ freelancers and send them to their clients on a per shift basis. All the major national agencies have been scrambling to add DTP to their list of supported services, or to establish DTP subsidiaries.

> Temporary services are responding to the trend for companies that have converted substantial portions of their word processing departments to DTP, especially for documents such as sales proposals and reports which now often include graphics.
> —*Pat Stella, co-owner of Custom Word Processing, a NYC temp agency*

As a temp, your worries may be over. You work when you want to and, if you're good, as much as you want to. If you work a substantial number of hours for one agency, you can even accumulate vacation time and be eligible for health benefits.

> Many DTPers are thankful to have the recourse of temping. They like the experience. It can be easier, avoiding the wear-and-tear of having to market services and worry about cash flow.   —*K.C. Genzmer*

Still, we see working as a temp as branch of freelancing. You do it when you are not yet able, or no longer willing, to find work on your own. You do it because you enjoy seeing the insides of different offices every few days, or you take pleasure in feeling superior as you clean up the mess the permanent workforce leaves behind when they're sick or on vacation.

Taking a look at temping in NYC—one of the higher-paying markets—here's what the Personnel Express agency charged *clients* in mid-1990:

- $25-$28 per hour for a word processor;
- $27-$35 for an administrative assistant with some abilities to use spreadsheet, word processing, and page layout software;
- $34-$43 for a production professional who can create templates and stylesheets and recommend appropriate software;
- $42-$48 for an artist, art director, or studio manager;
- $47-$70 for a production consultant, specialist, trouble-shooter or trainer.

Agencies have surcharge policies. They differentiate between overtime (greater than 40 hours per week or greater than eight hours per day, for which they may charge 50% more), second shift work (for which they charge 15% more) and third shift and weekend work (for which they charge 30% more).

The dollars above are not what you make, of course. The worst part of temping is that you don't see about one-third of what the agency bills the employer. We've seen the numbers. With a 10-15% gross operating margin, the temp agencies deserve their cut. They have expenses in overhead, marketing, training, and quality control before they make a profit. Still the result is that you will make $15-$30 per hour for work that could net you $25-$40 on your own, if you can find the work yourself.

Good reasons to temp, other than an emergency need for income or a family situation that requires you to work irregular hours, are to deepen your experience, find employers who will pay you to learn on their time, or gain entry to unusual work environments. You might find a specialized temp agency that can place you into high-level training and consulting work that you can't find on your own. You could collect $40-$50 per hour from such an agency.

As a temp, you might connect with an employer who will buy you away from the temp agency and convert you into a full-time employee. Don't be tempted to circumvent the agency's policy for a finder's fee paid by the employer. You never know when you'll want to work through the agency again.

Making special deals

In business, everything is negotiable. If you have something that someone else needs, you can create a solution that's in everyone's interest. If you're just starting out and you don't know what you're doing yet, you can be an aggressive networker and impressive at interviews. Then you may be able to find a company that wants to bring its publishing in house and is willing to turn you loose to learn on the equipment they buy. At the start, you can come to an understanding with them that you'll give them a stated number of hours a week of work for an agreed-upon period of time, or eventually turn into a full- or part-time employee.

We know printers, public relations firms, market researchers, and ad agencies that have made deals with experienced DTPers. Some have gone ahead and bought hardware, then looked around for someone who knew how to run it. Typically, the printer wants to trade access to equipment (sometimes including high-resolution imagesetters) for time and/or expertise. They'll be open to sending their printing customers to you for DTP, and you'll be able to direct your customers to them for bids on printing.

As in any such arms-length arrangement, make sure you know your partner. Check out their reputation among their vendors and clients. Make sure you both have the same understanding about what you are giving each other, at the start and down the road. If you have different needs or expectations, any such arrangement could end up being more trouble than it's worth for either party.

Confederating with other DTPers

You can be on the other side of the arrangements described in **8. Choosing employees and subcontractors** and **Managing subcontractors**. Find one or more DTPers you like and respect, and work for or with them. If they're willing, arrange to use some of their equipment when they're out, move into a corner of their office and be there when they have too much to handle, or find someone to take you in as a junior associate and hope you'll eventually move up to partner. An affiliation may not only reduce your overhead, it may also increase your number of billable hours by eliminating some of the time you spend finding clients.

Don't overlook imagesetting service bureaus and laser printer rental companies as likely venues for you to park your business for a while. Any office that has equipment idle for a substantial amount of the day or night may welcome your proposal. You just need to persuade them they can trust you with their keys and tools.

Working harder

If you can increase your billable hours to 30 or 35, while still managing your business and keeping up with the technology, you'll *vastly* improve your bottom line. Looking at the second year budget from **10. Second year strategy**, if you can squeeze in 35 billable hours per week at $50 per hour, you can gross $87,500, spend $20,000 on fixed costs and operating expenses, and take home $67,500 before taxes. But unless you reduce the unbillable hours, you'll be working 12-hour days. How long can you keep that up?

Raising your rates

In theory, you should be able to make more money doing the same kind of work. As time goes by, tools become more efficient and faster, enabling you to produce more work in each billable hour. Unfortunately, these gains don't always materialize. Some of the profit is absorbed by expenses for new equipment and software, and some gets eaten up as you take advantage of new capabilities to produce more complex or better looking work. If you bill by the page or by the job, you will benefit. A job that used to take you eight hours may now take you five or six.

If your hourly rate has always been a purely internal calculation, even when you increase your hourly dollar rate by 10-25%, if you have at the same time been getting more efficient, your clients may still receive invoices for the same or lower amounts.

But if your *billing* is based on hourly rates, you'll have to raise them. Most clients will understand when you ascribe some of your increase to general economic inflation resulting in higher costs of doing business. It may take some explaining on your part for them to understand that you're also charging more per hour to reflect your higher productivity through improved skills and increased capital investment. They'll appreciate your informing them that they too are benefiting by receiving more during each hour you work for them. You'll explain it all and they'll know in principle they're getting more for their money and you're earning more because you deserve it. Still, they would rather hear that you're holding your rates steady.

Since you're probably not going to charge every client the same amount for each job, another way to raise your average hourly rate is to **change your client or job mix.** This is simply a matter of finding customers with greater resources or higher circulation publications, or ones that seem never to care what you charge them. Some of these jobs will be fun, as you experiment with bigger budget productions. Some will be the driest of all. Of course, it's hard to generalize, but you may find your most challenging jobs pay less—the ones from the entrepreneurial startup company or the underfunded nonprofit group with an important message to convey on a tight budget. So you may find a trade-off as you move to blue-chip corporate clients to increase your revenues.

> Some projects are boring, but bring in good money. Business graphics is my least favorite thing to do. But when you're on your own, your standards have to be realistic. Not lowered, just realistic, particularly when there are little birdies back in the nest chirping for their worms.
> —*Steven Gorney*

Bidding on printing

Many DTPers will strongly suggest you never include printing services in your bids. It's responsible advice, but we don't always take it. Felix has bundled printing costs and he's never gotten burned, but has come close. Maggie has never included printing. We're presenting both sides of the issue.

Some customers want to deal with only one vendor. They don't want to have to worry about coordinating typographers and printers. Sometimes they ask us to bid against others who are providing a complete package. Moreover, chances are you'll already be involved to some extent with the printer. So why not manage the entire job? This will allow you not only to charge for your time and expertise in printer liaison, but also to add a markup on the printing bill. For a typical newsletter, you might be charging the client $1,000 for your DTP services. Yet the cost of printing could come to many thousands of dollars. If you manage the job, adding 10-25% to the printer's bill could easily bring you more income than all your production work on the job.

Moreover, chances are you'll know how to locate vendors who can do the job for less than the customer's existing or intended printer. In some cases, your greater involvement could save the customer money. In fact, occasionally the idea that we handle everything comes from us, as part of our routine suggestions to our established customers to rebid their printing work periodically.

If you do bid printing, make sure your printer isn't jobbing it out, which they'll do if it's too large or complex a job for their shop. At that point, you or the customer will be paying their markup, and you might as well bid the job directly to printers with the capabilities you need.

Of course, the reason for the original advice to stay away from printing is the risk. If there's a mistake or a dispute, and the customer demands a reprinting, much is at stake. You didn't go into DTP to become a speculator, investing 10 or 20 hours of your time to risk the loss of thousands of dollars.

For this reason, we'd modify the absolute prohibition:

- If it's your first job with a client, don't include printing unless it's a short run, and the risk is small.
- If bidding on mechanicals and printing is the only way you can get an important and large job, try for some compromise. Felix has at times managed the job, but arranged for the customer to send the printer a purchase order and pay the printer directly. He's gotten sales commissions from printers, and management fees from the client.
- If the job involves anything more complex than spot color, don't risk it.
- For established customers, always work with a printer you trust, who will help you stay out of trouble.
- Evaluate the risks on a case by case basis. If you've never handled a job similar to the proposed project, don't take the chance.

Finding a niche

If you can find specialty work, you'll be able to charge more than the everyday DTPer. And if you can develop a niche where you don't have to spend time marketing, you'll be able to bill more hours. Here are some possibilities:

- **Slidemaking** commands a premium because it's relatively new. Presentation graphics software is very easy for DTPers to learn, since it usually integrates drawing, outlining, and charting functions you've already mastered. Customers have been accustomed to paying $75-$100 for each slide produced using traditional means. If each slide takes you 15-45 minutes to make, with slidemaking service bureaus charging well under $10 for moderately high-resolution slides, you can charge up to $100 per hour for slide presentations and still meet or undercut traditional pricing. You can use presentation software packages to speed the process of producing templates for series of similar slides. You can also use any of the general drawing, illustration, and DTP software. (See 5. **Your software starter set.**)

- If you can find a major consumer of **business forms**, you can develop a profitable specialty creating these time-consuming pages. Automated tools enable you to create with a few keystrokes multiple check boxes, coupons, and what they call a number comb (ruled or boxed fill-ins for 10-digit Social Security numbers and the like). More advanced software enables you to design smart forms that allow on-screen data entry and work as the front end for databases. Software for the Mac includes Claris Smartform, Softview if:x Forms Designer, Adobe TrueForm, and Antic Software FlexForm Business Templates. Software for the PC includes Delrina Technology PerFORM, Ventura Systems FormBase and FormWorx FormPublisher.

- **Signmaking** can be a lucrative occupation. The printing technology for large color presentations and posters has improved recently. Two service bureaus, Colossal Graphics, (415) 328-2264, and National Reprographics, (212) 366-7073, will reproduce your Encapsulated PostScript documents for banners, displays, signs, and other full-color work in very attractive full-color sheets, up to 42 inches by 12 continuous feet. S.H. Pierce PosterWorks is an application for the Macintosh that includes sophisticated color controls and tiling capabilities to print up to 100-foot posters. A subcategory of signs might be small labels, presentation folders, and similar work. You can prepare camera-ready copy and job out the printing of glossy or foil adhesive labels. Short Run Labels, (800) 522-3583 in California, and (800) 522-3549 in Maryland, will produce 1,000 self-adhesive labels for $19.50. For other sources, see the ads in *Quick Printing* (**Appendix 2. Magazines**).

- Apple and other companies have been trying to get **desktop mapmaking** off the ground as a hot area. They haven't succeeded very well, but the tools are available to produce attractive maps. Mapping Information Systems Corporation MapInfo, (800) FAST MAP, is able to present data graphically from a geographically oriented relational database.

- You can be a **personalizer**, tapping into an unexplored market, such as letterhead for children complete with pictures. You may be able to carve out a lucrative field until the competition arrives. We've seen outfits at street fairs, running their personal computers on gasoline generators, charging $25 to print 50 sheets plus envelopes, standardizing the process with two or three layouts and type styles, further boosting revenues by selling colorful paper by the dozen sheets.

Chances are some other opportunities will come along next year, as new software applications develop. For some other general and speculative avenues, see **14. A few alternative directions for your worklife**.

A double-edged advantage of finding a specialty niche is that you can concentrate on raking in the money while you command the market, and keep less careful track of the rest of DTP technology. You may be able to increase your billable hours, but don't get too caught up in focusing exclusively on one area. Within a short time, you'll have competitors knocking on your customers' doors, and clients will want to pay much less for these services. If you latch on to what's hot, you always need to keep looking for the next opportunity.

You can also, of course, branch out into related fields. For instance, if your contacts among potential customers and subcontractors are very good, without becoming a full-fledged temporary agency, you can operate a sideline business sending work to friends and colleagues and getting referral fees, or recruiting them for full-time positions. Do check with a lawyer before you determine how you can collect placement fees.

Becoming a consultant or trainer

If you know lots more than most people about anything, you can turn your knowledge into money.

Most people who own and use computers learn only what they need to know. When they want to rearrange or expand their work environment, they need an expert. That's where **systems consultants** come in. If you're a computer wizard, you can help set up a local area network, make different types of computers talk to each other, add new scanning, modem, or printing capabilities, and upgrade central processing units and monitors. Most people who buy from computer stores are dissatisfied with the support they get; and everyone who buys mail order expects either to do the installations themselves or get help. Your knowledge can save them hours or days of frustration, failure, or uncertainty.

Most people hate learning new software from the officially supplied manuals and tutorials, so they call in **trainers**. Some people go to training centers, work with video- or audiocassette tutorials, or learn from books. But a very substantial number of computer users prefer one- or two-on-one training. If you understand the processes of DTP, know software inside out, enjoy teaching it, and are sensitive and sympathetic to the plight of the unenlightened pupil, you can become a good trainer.

In computers, the old saying, "those who can't do, teach" does *not* apply. The technology changes so quickly, and the tricks and tips are so intricate and so often undocumented that you won't make a good trainer unless you frequently use the tools you teach all the time. Being a real-world user will also help you stay fresh and enthusiastic about giving information to others.

How do you dispense your information as a systems consultant or trainer? You'll find no set rules. Everything depends on what you know and what the client needs and is prepared to pay. The goal is to get the customer up and running—not to impress them with how much you know or how reluctant you are to share all of your expertise with them. For some guidelines, see **10. So how much should you charge?**

What about teaching? We distinguish it from training—you'll be employed full- or part-time by an institution that will recruit and register your students. Every graphic arts college, many community and technical colleges, and lots of training centers need people to teach DTP and graphics. Don't go into it for the money. The pay is low, the preparation time is high. Do it for the satisfaction, as a break from your other work, and in some cases, the prestige or contacts.

Becoming a specialist

If you can do something unique, you can throw out all the rules. No one cares much about the prestige or, within some bounds, even the physical presentability of the artistic or computer genius who can solve their problems. When you have the reputation as a specialist, you can charge any fee within reason to the client who needs what you have to give. So keep looking for a specialist's niche. At the moment:

- **Database virtuosos** who can write utilities to turn information from databases into published documents are in some demand, especially until the features of database typesetting software catches up with the need.
- **PostScript gurus** will remain in the pantheon for the foreseeable future. Though illustration software is becoming more sophisticated, some procedures work better by being written out in programming code. And some files won't run on imagesetters or on PostScript clone laser printers until they are massaged in PostScript.
- **Color mavens** who can navigate confidently through RGB, CMYK, PMS, CIE, PhotoYCC, hue, gamma, undercolor, color keys, and all the high-end hardware can name their price. There's a vast audience of DTP users eager to approach the quality of traditional color separations using new and affordable tools, and anyone who can bring color from the desktop to the printed page with accuracy is in high demand.
- **Package designers** are just starting to realize how DTP tools can make their lives easier. A number of software products are just beginning to come out, as well as Cornerstone, a hardware-software combination by Scitex.
- **Typeface masters**, who can create new or customize existing fonts, may find fertile fields in the next few years. This is a job opportunity for very creative and disciplined people.
- **Customizers** who can take advantage of the trend to design publishing and graphic software as open systems. Just as central processing units have slots for circuit boards, some programs can now accept plug-in utilities to enhance or modify the software's existing functions. In general, people with the ability to modify or extend open software, or write utilities or filters for off-the-shelf software, will find a ready market for their services.

Expanding your business

Leverage is the age-old secret to increasing revenues. Even if you become a specialist or find a high-paying niche, you can stretch your working time by no more than 10 or 15 hours, and you can raise your rates only so far.

You may be able to create or latch onto something to sell, such as a package of templates customized for a page layout, graphics, or word processing program. Or, you may come up with some unique ideas for using software and turn them into an advisory or tip sheet newsletter. In either case, you're actually selling consultant services in volume. If you meet a real need, you can do well.

The only way to further increase your billings is to employ other people. If you go the subcontractor route, you reduce your risk, since you're not giving yourself a payroll to meet. If you hire people, you'll trade those risks for increased ability to define, supervise, and profit from your employees' work. In either case, success depends on your being careful, astute, and lucky enough to find workers who share your enthusiastic, meticulous approach to work, and are reliable, charge you low rates, and produce jobs you don't have to fully review and redo.

Felix has found that the down side of hiring others to do the work is that the more he farms out, the less he gets to do the production and design work he still enjoys, and the more he becomes a salesperson, a boss, and an accountant. He doesn't want to be like a classic small businessperson who worries in the middle of the night about contracts, finding more business, quality control, and keeping all the balls up in the air. His solution generally has been to do as much of the work as he can himself, drawing on other DTPers for special jobs and overflow.

A few years ago, you might have been able to put together a grand scheme for increasing your revenues by creating a major training center or a first-rate imagesetting service bureau, or by selling companies DTP hardware and software plus training. But these fields are pretty crowded by now, and startup costs are much higher than for establishing a small DTP production company. So unless you have a brand-new idea, or an exceptional reputation plus an exclusive or very fertile territory, you'll have a hard time in these areas.

One exception may be international work. DTP is just getting started in many parts of the world. You could box up your hardware (modified to run on local current), and become DTP CEO in Shangri-La. But stay away from the tropical rain forests: the humidity is hell on toner cartridges.

In capitalist society, the only way to get really rich, as opposed to earning a good living, is to buy and sell. You could even say that Microsoft's Croesus, William Gates, built his fortune largely this way. At the right moment, he spent $50,000 to acquire from its authors, Seattle Computer, the operating system which he modified and sold to IBM, and licensed to everyone else, as MS-DOS. Since we're not talking about inventing and marketing a hot new software package, since it's hard to corner any markets in DTP, and since most computer retailers are not doing particularly well these days, you're probably not going to get rich in DTP. But you can prosper.

It's a real challenge to manage any service business. For DTP you must retain an affordable, enthusiastic, and conscientious staff, ensure a consistently high quality of work on unstandardized products, and even out the flow of large and small projects. If you manage and sell your hours of services well, you can look forward to steady growth, satisfying work, and enjoyable relationships with clients, colleagues, and employees.

12. GETTING PAID

Work for clients who pay their bills

Your clients don't just pick you; you pick your clients. Be selective. If you're just starting out and you think you can't afford to turn down *any* work, ask yourself if you can afford to do work for which you won't be paid.

Trust your instincts, especially when you smell a problem customer. Protect yourself if a prospective customer:

- Can't stop complaining about a previous typesetter or DTPer;
- Doesn't want to talk about anything except what it will cost;
- Shows no interest in your ideas or suggestions about improving the job or saving time or money;
- Shows no evidence of understanding the scope of the job or its possible snags.

In all these cases, your only alternative to walking away from the job is to write a contract.

When to write a contract

When you start your business, it's a good idea to develop and refine a typical contract. That way you're prepared for any eventuality, and you can gain control of more aspects of each job. Your first contract may take the form of a proposal letter, with a space for the client to agree and sign at the end. But on the assumption that you'll be starting with small and relatively predictable jobs, we don't think you need a contract for every job.

When should you plan on writing a contract?

- **When you're worried** about the job or about getting paid. If the customer takes offense at your caution, interprets it as evidence of your mistrust, and walks away, examine your behavior carefully. Unless you can figure out something you did wrong, count yourself lucky for having avoided trouble before you invested time and money.
- **When you expect the job will take more than a month** to complete. Extended jobs have a way of taking on a life of their own. By the time they are done, memories may differ as to what was included.
- **When you'll be advancing substantial sums** for the job, such as for data entry, optical character recognition, design or illustration, imagesetting, or printing. Certainly, if you are purchasing hardware or software for eventual delivery to the customer, you need to establish your assignment in writing. If you're spending more than you're willing to risk losing, take this additional step to protect yourself.
- **When the customer is a cog in a large corporation**, and you're worried that your contact may leave the company and disappear before the job is done. Or when you're a sub and have had no dealings with the original client and you get a funny feeling that no one has really authorized your work. In such a case, at a minimum, ask for a purchase order (P.O.)—a short standard contract the customer provides and fills in.
- **When you're part of the way through a job and it changes character.** If your original bid called for a simple three-proof cycle, and you start getting major revisions late in the game, protect yourself with a contract, a memo, or a letter that has the same effect and can be countersigned by the customer. Don't spring this on the customer. Talk about it on the phone, reassuringly but firmly. Send it over initially in draft if necessary, but get it signed. Don't postpone your discussion to the moment you're ready to prepare your final bill. You're better off resolving any misunderstandings while the customer still needs you to produce the final material. If you haven't been fully documenting the work you've been doing, tracking the time and steps, you'll have an easier time establishing that paper trail now. You'll also still have the intermediate stage proofs for the job. Again, you're better off finding out about customer resistance as soon as possible, before you invest more hours in the job, as well as charges for subcontractors, deliveries, and imagesetting.

I never start work without a purchase order. It's that simple. If you do a job without one, even if you're friends with the client, you're in a very vulnerable position.   —*Steven Gorney*

How complex should your contract be?

By all means, write a plain language contract. It will protect you just as well as legalese, and you and your clients will be able to understand it. If you write the first draft of an uncluttered contract, a lawyer will be able to tighten it up and resolve ambiguities without making it unreadable.

Many contracts routinely invoke procedures for arbitration of disputes by the American Arbitration Association. For jobs over $10,000, such a process is preferable to expensive and time-consuming court proceedings but it's not without expenses and delays. Here's the boilerplate to put in a contract so you can call an official arbitrator. Don't put the clause in if you're not prepared to pursue the process and abide by the results.

> *Any controversy or claim arising out of or relating to this contract, or the breach thereof, shall be settled by arbitration in accordance with the commercial arbitration rules of the American Arbitration Association, and judgment on the award rendered by the arbitrator may be entered in any court having jurisdiction thereof.*

You'll find model contracts in *The Desktop Publisher's Legal Handbook, Business and Legal Forms for Graphic Designers*, and the *Handbook of Pricing and Ethical Guidelines* of the Graphic Artists Guild. (See **Appendix 2. Books on the business of graphics and DTP.**)

Ultimate recourses

If you have any problems or misunderstandings, even an uncountersigned memo you sent the client may help establish the rights and wrongs. But a contract is your best protection. In the few occasions in which it actually comes to a confrontation, simply reminding the customer of the existence of the contract is often sufficient.

Felix had to file a Small Claims Court action once, against a customer who clearly understood the amount owed, but was overextended and attempting to avoid paying a charge. He filed for the amount owed, plus compensation for his time attempting to collect the amount owed, plus interest on the amount owed, through the date of filing. With a contract in hand, plus memoranda from the client, copies of intermediate proofs, and photocopies of checks for progress payments, Felix was confident of prevailing. Even better, the day before the scheduled hearing, he called the client, who finally believed he was serious about going to court, and was told to pick up a check in full payment.

In most states, an individual (not a corporation) may file a Small Claims Court action for up to several thousand dollars, and you don't have to hire a lawyer for the procedure. The filing fee is usually under $10.

Aside from saving time, settling any dispute without going to court is by far preferable, not just because you'll save time going to court and avoid the uncertainty of a judge's decision. Even if you win a Small Claims action or a judgment in some other court, you don't automatically collect the amount owed. It's one thing if your client genuinely disagreed with you and abides by the court's ruling. But if you're facing a deadbeat, collecting can be much harder than winning the judgment. You may have to pay a court officer or sheriff to collect. You may have to file additional papers and pay additional fees (most of which can ultimately be collected from the defendant).

To be prepared for the eventuality of a collection effort, always photocopy the first payment you receive from a new customer. The check establishes for a court that you were, in fact, reimbursed for services performed for the client in the past. And the account information on the check will simplify locating and attaching bank funds if it becomes necessary.

Many retail businesses and some service industries use credit cards so they don't have to worry about bouncing checks, and because they expect that accepting the card will bring them more business. We don't think either consideration applies directly to the DTP business. You're not likely to get bounced checks. If you do, and you need to threaten court action, there's no better evidence of the client's acknowledgment of the debt. We doubt credit cards will help you attract customers, and they'll cost you at least three percentage points of income right off the top.

And in case you never looked into it, collection agencies can help you, but they take a large percentage of what they collect.

> Dun & Bradstreet has a credit division that will go after a deadbeat for a percentage of your fee. A friend who hadn't been paid for three months got the check by messenger 48 hours after getting notice from D&B. You have to protect yourself. You may be sitting at home, feeling cozy curled up in front of your computer, but business is business. —*Steven Gorney*

If you sell your old hardware privately, ask for a certified check unless you know the person very well. Felix has occasionally sold equipment in installments, because that's the only way he could get his asking price, or because he was helping someone get started. To avoid aggravation and wasted time making sure the monthly checks came in, he arranged to get an entire set of postdated checks from the purchaser for every installment. If that's not possible, at least include a penalty clause for late payment in the contract. **Fig. 12.1** is a sample contract for equipment purchase.

AGREEMENT FOR PRIVATE INSTALLMENT SALE

In consideration of the receipt of one (name) computer (serial number •••) with ••• floppy disk drives, ••• megabytes RAM, ••• video card, and (name) monitor (serial number •••), all of which shall be in good working order, I,

buyer name,

residing at (address/phone), employed at (company/address/phone), promise to pay

seller name

the sum of $•,•••.••, as follows: $•,••• cash or certified check upon receipt of the above equipment, and •• equal monthly payments of $•••.••. The first monthly payment shall be made on month 1, 199•, and each $•••.•• amount shall be made on the first day of each succeeding month up to and including month 1, 199•, at which time the entire debt shall be paid in full.

Payment shall be made at:

seller address

or whatever other address I am directed (by certified mail, return receipt requested) to pay.

In the event of default in the payment of any of the installments required on this note, if such default continues for a period of seven calendar days, after written notification of such default by certi-

fied mail return receipt requested has been received, the holder of this note may without notice or demand declare the entire sum then unpaid immediately due and payable. In such event I shall, within 30 days thereafter, pay to the holder of the note the entire outstanding balance on this promissory note, or, upon the consent of the holder of the note, deliver to the holder the aforementioned equipment in good working order.

The failure by the holder of the note to assert the right of demanding the payment of the entire unpaid balance upon a default shall not be deemed a waiver thereof.

In the event that this note is not paid when due, I agree to pay the reasonable costs, expenses, attorneys' and other fees paid or incurred by the holder of this note in collecting the amount due. I specifically agree to pay a reasonable collection charge if collection be referred to a collection agency.

I hereby waive presentment, demand, protest, notice of dishonor and/or protest and notice of non-payment.

buyer & seller's signatures
notarization
date

from Kramer Communications

Fig. 12.1 Contract for sale of equipment

Invoices

Think of your invoices as part of your work product, not an incidental afterthought. Don't begrudge yourself the time and effort to produce a high-quality invoice. We're not really talking about appearance here, though an attractive invoice, clearly and cleanly presenting all the information the payer needs to have enhances your image of professionalism. We're talking mainly about content. Giving clients the information they need may speed your receipt of payment. Your invoices should include:

- Client's company name
- Name of authorizing person or contact;
- Time period during which services were provided;
- Simple name for the job;
- Simple description of the job (length, scope of work);
- Itemization of work done (optional, see below);
- Itemization of partial payments received;
- Grand total for job;
- Balance due (highlighted);
- Statement of when payment is due;
- Name and address for endorsing and sending the check;
- Your company tax number or Social Security number;
- Your identifying or invoice number code;
- Date the invoice was sent.

Among the descriptive details you may wish to itemize in your invoices are:

- Meetings and telephone reviews;
- Training and consulting, related and unrelated to the job;
- Editorial development and research, interviews, writing, and rewriting;
- Data entry or keyboarding, and disk conversions;
- Graphic research and design, prototypes, and templates;
- Subcontractors' work;
- Galleys, page proofs #1, 2, and so on;
- Consulting and coordinating with artists, writers, printers, and mailing houses;
- Preparation of mechanicals and material for imagesetter;
- Service bureau and other production charges;
- Messengers, overnight services, faxes, and other expenses;
- Taxes and rush charges.

Make a smart invoice

Use some kind of software to generate invoices—not just a word processor. The most useful part of any accounting software is the reports it generates. If, as is likely, you're not using an accounting program, set up your invoices in a database which has the graphic capabilities to produce an attractive invoice. Claris FileMaker on the Macintosh, Symantec Q&A on the PC are typical choices. Make each invoice a new record, linked to a record with the client's name and address.

This client record could be part of your house list database of current and potential customers. (See **3. Finding your first customers**.) Set up this database with maximum flexibility. For instance, keep the first and last names in different fields, and make fields for categories like nicknames, fax number, sample materials sent, bid description, computer and word processor type.

If you take the time to set up your invoices as manipulable data, you can track and learn from the information you enter. For instance, you can find out:

- Total monthly billings or annual billings, or comparative annual billings for one or all clients;
- Ranking of clients in volume of business;
- How long clients take to pay.

If you are more ambitious, you can add all available information about your time and money costs on each job to your database. At that point, you can analyze:

- Which services you offer are most profitable;
- Comparative performance of subcontractors;
- How much you make on each job;
- Comparative profitability of clients or types of work.

Don't condemn yourself if you can't seem to get around to creating a working invoicing or accounts receivable system from an off-the-shelf accounting or database package. This isn't your specialty. Rather than postpone this difficult but important task, get help. Ask a database maven to help you create your database or invoicing system. It's much easier to understand how to use one of these files than to set one up.

Most DTPers don't use software to keep tabs on their hours. (See **7. Tracking your time**.) However, one possible tool is Colleague 2, a graphic studio management software package for the Mac that combines a calendar, a client/

prospect database, job tracking, accounting, and billing, $395 from Colleague Business Systems, (512) 345-9964.

Whether or not you use the computer to do it, set up some kind of start-to-finish billing system. Otherwise it's too easy to overlook unpaid invoices.

> For billing I do an invoice on the computer in Microsoft Word. I don't have an invoicing program. Some invoicing programs have so many features that they turn into a kind of "Swiss army knife." They get pretty complex and hog disk space. —*David Doty*

Don't spring your bill on the client

Our "no surprises" rule from **9. Treating Your Clients Right** holds for invoices. If you've been keeping your clients informed, they should have a pretty good idea what's coming at them. For big jobs, you're better off submitting partial invoices along the way. You'll get paid sooner and your cash flow will improve if you've been laying out money for materials or subcontractors long before the job will be completed. Vendors in any number of service industries routinely ask for one-third at the start of a job, one-third in the middle, and one-third upon delivery. Some clients may suggest a variation: 30/30/30 with a 10% holdout until some later point when the job is truly done.

Partial invoices help clients digest the final totals for jobs. So even if you don't send partial invoices, try to mention to the client along the way what the accumulated charges to date are, or how close you are to your original estimate.

How much detail should your invoice contain? As much as the client needs. If you've bid the job at a flat rate, you may simply list the total. If you've explained to the client in detail how you arrived at your estimate or if they tell you that they have to analyze and justify your invoice to someone, you may need to break it out, using some or all of the categories itemized above in **Invoices**.

When to send your invoice

We're each of two minds on this one. If the finished job goes to the client, not the printer, you could include the invoice with the mechanical. A satisfied client may immediately okay the invoice for payment. If the client has a question about the bill, this is the easiest time to explain what was involved in the job.

On the negative side, some people find it unseemly, as if a dignified practitioner like a DTPer needed to allow an interval before chasing after the bucks. Yet in these days when many physicians' receptionists practically bar you from leaving until you've settled the charges, it's hard to talk about professional manners.

A better reason to delay sending the bill is that about a quarter of the time the job isn't over when we think it's over. A proofreader calls in some new errors, a top executive finally gets around to reading it for the first time, an unexpected development means stopping the presses for a new final version, or the client asks you to revise a page for another purpose. Generally the client would rather have the entire job on one invoice.

On balance, then, if you can afford to delay the invoice, you might as well, unless you're worried about getting paid.

For walk-in customers, if you have any hesitation, ask for a 50% deposit up front. Give a bill with your last proof, and collect when you deliver the final output.

Precautions for invoicing

Whatever you do, prepare a draft invoice when the job is fresh in your mind. If you wait, you're likely to forget to include something, or you may not even be able to reconstruct your intentions from your records of time and expenses.

Whenever you send the invoice, keep all your proofs and notes, along with your time and expense records. Be prepared at any time for a phone call asking you to document any or all of your work. It's time to clean out the file after you receive payment.

If the job involves handing over the files to the client, you can arrange to give the camera-ready copy, but keep the disks until you get paid. For first-time customers especially, if possible keep the disks. This is tricky, but when you let go of the files, you lose much of your bargaining power.

Collections

You should specify payment terms in a contract. If you didn't write a contract, write "Net 10 days" on your invoice. That's a sign to the corporate check-writer on the other side that you won't be happy with the standard 30-day period for paying bills. You may not have the power to enforce your policy, but it never hurts to ask, and you do increase your chances of getting paid immediately.

If you want to be hard-nosed about payment terms, you can write a contract specifying Net 10 or Net 30 and specify monthly interest charges for late payments. Or you can write these terms on the invoice, and see what happens.

Address the invoice to the person who must approve it. Sometimes this may be a different person than the one you sold the project to. All the more reason to find out at the start of a job who holds the checkbook. In particular, when the scope of a job changes midstream, approval may have to go one level higher in the company.

When we work with an intermediary (for instance, a freelance editor or writer who produces a newsletter for a company) and the intermediary was involved in negotiating the job, we send the invoice to both parties. This way we're not waiting for the editor to forward the approved invoice to the checkwriting client.

You're bound to have some clients who always pay eventually, but are chronically late. You're not in the money lending business, and pestering clients is unnecessarily wearing on your psyche. For those whose cash flow is poor, Felix has at times insisted on payment upon delivery, and he reminds them of this policy as the production cycle comes to an end. For those who are always late, merely because their accounting and bill-paying procedures are inefficient, he has generally raised their rates slightly to account for the 1-2% interest they would ordinarily owe. Then he doesn't bug them about their late payment.

Sometimes the money won't come in because you haven't had much work. Many service businesses slow down early in the new year, in August, and perhaps during one other two- to four-week period during the year. Ask fellow local DTPers if they're aware of any such cycles.

If you're prepared, you'll be able to relax and even plan to take some time off yourself when you'll least be missed. If you can't bring yourself to take a vacation, at least you may be able to take whole chunks of days to learn software without feeling desperate.

13. INCORPORATING AND ACCOUNTING

No matter how much you know about graphics, type, or computers, you need advice to succeed in your business. You have decisions to make about how to acquire your tools (buy, lease/purchase, rent), your space, how to protect yourself and your tools (insurance, contracts), and how to come to terms with employers and employees (contracts and invoices). Your choices can have unanticipated consequences for the stability, viability, taxability, and profitability of your enterprise. So assume nothing, and, as in production work, try to foresee the worst-case developments and prepare for them.

Don't hesitate to ask for help from business advisors, lawyers, and accountants.

Do you need to incorporate?

Probably not. Here are your choices.

Sole proprietorship is simplest: You keep complete control and have the least complicated bookkeeping and tax records. Your business income counts as personal income on your personal IRS Schedule C form. You're responsible for any losses and liabilities. To get started, you can register your business name with local authorities, and get a business phone and bank account. The business does not survive you. If you die its assets are distributed according to your wishes in your will.

Partnership is similar to sole proprietorship, except that you share all responsibilities, gains and losses, and liabilities with one or more partners. You're each responsible for the other's actions. The partnership ends when any partner dies, resigns, or sells out. Partnerships call for people with complementary skills and resources, as well as a very carefully written agreement that attempts to anticipate (and usually does not) all the problems that could result from differing opinions, wishes, or needs among the partners.

Limited partnership is probably irrelevant unless you have an investor to whom you want to grant some ownership, but no decision-making powers.

A corporation is established under state law as an separate entity from its owners. Even if you're the sole owner, it survives your existence, and protects you from corporate losses and liabilities (though not from prosecution for illegal business acts). If you're worried about the house and kids or your nest egg, the entirely separate status of the corporation will preserve these assets from risk and bill collectors. It may be easier to borrow money, or sell off a part of a corporation. You may have more options in establishing a retirement plan. Profits may be doubly taxed—once to the corporation, once to you when you receive them as dividends. You'll have increased startup costs, and lots of papers and forms to fill out several times a year.

A Subchapter S corporation is designed for small businesses. It gives you most of the advantages of a corporation without the double taxation. Revenues go directly to shareholders. Business losses can also be deducted from personal income. Even if you don't make a profit, you may have to pay several hundred dollars in minimum corporate taxes each year. Some states don't recognize the status of Sub-S corporations.

A sole proprietorship is all most individual DTPers are likely to need. Talk to other DTPers who've made this decision, to find out if they still feel they made the right choice.

Business credit

Whatever the form of your business, immediately start establishing your personal creditworthiness in case you ever need to take out a business loan. Establish accounts with your vendors of imagesetting services, office supplies, and computer equipment. If you think you'll ever need it, contact Dun & Bradstreet for a business rating, (800) 234-3867.

Legal issues

Don't assume you can get all the advice you need from any book. When it comes to your business launch, professional liabilities, employment status, and tax matters, a book is a lowest common denominator opinion, and that opinion won't help you if you need to protect yourself. The law on many issues will vary from state to state and city to city as well. For instance, some localities will require you to get a permit, even if you run your business from your home. You might otherwise be violating zoning regulations.

We suggest you start by reading up on legal issues for small service businesses and talking to other DTPers in your state. Try to find a helpful, friendly owner of a printing, imagesetting service bureau, or typesetting shop to learn about any special wrinkles for our industry. (For instance, in New York State, the printing industry falls under its own set of rules for treatment of sales tax.) We recommend you look at *The Desktop Publisher's Legal Handbook: A Comprehensive Guide to Computer Publishing Law* for a review of issues about ownership of rights, permissions, libel, and other issues. (See **Appendix 2. Books on the business of graphics and DTP.**)

After you've done this research and developed some invoice and contract forms, you'll be in a good position to spend some time reviewing your assumptions and procedures with a lawyer. Prepare as much in advance as possible to keep the hourly costs down. And don't be surprised if your lawyer brings up issues that would never occur to you. (If you haven't yet picked your counsel, ask if they charge a minimum increment for a one- to five-minute phone call. It can make a big difference in your costs.)

We don't think DTP is a particularly lawyer-prone business. If you respect the confidentiality of your clients' work and act fairly to employees, subcontractors, and vendors, you aren't likely to be sued. And if you write good contracts, scrutinize your clients, and deliver good work, you're not likely to have to go after anybody else.

Who owns what you produce?

Most DTPers expect to retain ownership of all their disk-based work, giving only camera-ready mechanicals to their clients. Preparing specifications, templates, and style sheets for publications is challenging and complex work. The results, if well executed, are worth considerable sums. If the client decides to switch DTPers or go in house, access to your formats could save your successor money. If you, the customer's first DTPer, haven't charged fully for the effort involved in creating them—expecting to recoup through fees for preparing many issues of a publication—ownership of these files is your only form of protection. Unquestioned ownership of the templates also frees you from any hesitation about modifying them for use in projects for other clients.

That's why you should establish whether the client expects to receive and control rights to the disk upon completion of the first project, and if so, charge accordingly. If there's any question, resolve the issue at the start of a job, at least verbally, in writing if necessary.

> Even though you may think ownership is settled, if you send the disk to the client's imagesetting service bureau, not your own, you may be giving the client physical possession of the files.   —*Margaret Styne*

Many DTPers prefer not to even raise the ownership issue. It's a risky but often successful tactic. Clients not alerted to the issue may assume they have no rights to the original source disks. In fact, legally, the ownership is determined by what they are paying you for. Thus, if a client buys a design from you for a new publication, even if you never hand over the disk, you're on shaky ground if you incorporate essentially the same look in a publication for another client.

Recent Federal court rulings have limited the right of customers to purchase **work-for-hire**, a principle under which buyers purchased all rights to literary and artistic works unless contracts limited their ownership. Now, the tables are turned. If you're an independent contractor, and not an employee of the purchaser, you own the rights to your work, except to the extent that your contract explicitly gives those rights to the purchaser. This means that you're in now in an improved position when you leave ownership unstated.

Purchasers of graphic services are more accustomed to these issues, and are more likely to raise them at the start of a job. If you're preparing an illustration for a client, you should always establish whether you're free to incorporate it in other work. The client will purchase rights for one-time use, exclusive or non-exclusive U.S. rights, world rights, or some variation of these categories.

Who owns what you copy?

What material are you allowed to incorporate in your publications? What do you have to credit? What used to be simply unclear has become even more murky. Just as rap musicians are confounding the recording industry and its royalty procedures by incorporating chunks of other people's music into their songs (often modified beyond recognition) so have our tools for digital manipulation of graphic images exceeded the ability of existing law to make hard-and-fast rules. But there are a few basic principles:

- Works created before 1978 have a maximum copyright life of 75 years, so any image over 75 years old is no longer protected and, therefore, in the public domain. You can scan any such image for use in publications. Some images created in the past 75 years may not have had copyrights renewed and may also be in the public domain. Works created since 1978 are protected under copyright for 50 years beyond their creator's life. Government publications are generally not copyrighted.

- The **fair use** principle says if you use a small portion of someone else's text or graphics for illustrative purposes, and do not thereby diminish the economic value of the original material, you're probably safe from prosecution.

- Use any recognizable contemporary photograph or other image with great caution. You're liable to get an attorney's letter if you incorporate a corporation's logo in a widely distributed publication, if it comes to their attention and is deemed unfriendly or inappropriate.

- DTPers often use product names, when they say, for instance, a publication was produced with Aldus PageMaker or Ventura Publisher. Respect trademarks by using the TM and ® symbols, or at least with an acknowledgment in the front of a publication that the product names are trademarked.

- Read the fine print on the disk envelope for any electronic clip art you buy. Most illustrations give unlimited permission for use in non-consumer publications, but some outline the circumstances in which they want to receive a credit. Some of the higher-priced photographic archives that are available on CD-ROM disk (such as Comstock) offer images for examination only, and expect to receive additional payment for each use of their material in mass circulation publications. Take a look at the Dover series of published clip art books, each selling for a few dollars, for beautiful art and initial letters in the public domain which you can scan.

For more information, start with the article, "Copyrights & Wrongs," in the April 1990 *Publish* magazine, by attorney Brad Bunnin, author of *The Writer's Legal Companion* (Addison-Wesley, 1988). Also read COPYCO.TXT, the transcript of a conference on trademarks and copyright from the CompuServe DTP Forum. (See **4. Help is at hand** for information on CompuServe.)

Keeping the books

Set up a reliable and efficient record-keeping system at the start. Work with an accountant to design your chart of accounts (income, expense, and other categories). To keep track of your expenses and keep the IRS happy, set up a separate checking account for your business. It doesn't absolutely have to be a business account (often fees are higher and interest rates lower on business accounts). Apply for an additional credit card (again, a personal account may work fine) so you can buy from 800 number vendors and at trade shows without messing up your personal books.

Since you're working with computers, you may want to keep your books electronically. Double-entry accounting software and packages that can handle multiple bank or credit card accounts will give you a good picture of what's happening with your business. Chances are the personal accounting packages, Monogram Dollars and Sense, MECA Managing Your Money, Intuit Quicken, DAC Easy may be able to handle both your personal and your business income and expenses. Cynthia W. Harriman's *Macintosh Small Business Companion* discusses many of these programs. (See **Appendix 2. Books on small businesses and working at home**.)

If you intend to computerize your invoices using an all-purpose database, you might not bother with one of these packages—or you could look for a modest accounting package with an invoicing module. (See **12. Make a smart invoice**.) Maggie uses FileMaker, which allows her to print reports by company, time period, size of client, and to add sales tax and other calculated information.

If the volume of transactions justifies it or you hate doing it yourself, you may want to hire a bookkeeper to come in for a few hours once a week or once a month to keep everything up to date on paper or on computer. They charge about $25 per hour, so you can save money by paying someone else and spending that time on billable work.

No matter what system you use, you'll still need a professional accountant to be sure you're following the current regulations and taking advantage of every possible deduction.

Tax issues

As a self-employed consultant in a sole proprietorship or as a member of a partnership filing an IRS Schedule C return, you're entitled to many tax benefits. You can choose the length of time over which to write off your equipment. You can depreciate your professional library, and make claims for business expenses such as conferences, travel and entertainment, and subscriptions. You can sometimes charge off portions of your rent and utilities for a home office. You can hire family members. However, all these are subject to limitations. For instance, you must show a profit three out of every five years, and you are subject to strict requirements for documentation. For instance, if you regularly freelance for one client and work most or all the time on the client's premises using their equipment, the IRS may consider you an employee, and you may not be eligible. Thus, you might decide to diversify your clientele, and do more work in your own home or office for tax reasons.

If you have a spouse who is salaried, with careful planning, you may be able to take full advantage of Schedule C filing. Your tax filings will get more complicated, though, if you are married to another self-employed person.

On the negative side, you're now responsible for paying quarterly estimated taxes. And the home office is notorious as an item that increases your chance for an IRS audit. You must be able to show that the office space is used exclusively and regularly for business (see IRS Publication 587, *Business Use of the Home*). Furthermore, as a self-employed person, you pay both the employer and the employee portion of Social Security (FICA). The 1990 figure is 15.3% of a ceiling income of $51,300, meaning you could pay $7,000. (The numbers change every year and part is deductible from other taxes you owe.)

As a self-employed person, you have access to Keogh and more comprehensive Individual Retirement Accounts than do salaried employees of large companies. If you incorporate, you can eventually use your accrued pension funds as a source of financing for your business—lending money to your company.

Sales tax is yet another thorny issue. Registering with the state for a resale number introduces you to a time-consuming requirement for quarterly filings of your own sales tax collections. It frees you from having to pay sales tax when you buy goods or services you are reselling to the final purchaser. You charge the client the tax, and remit it to the state tax department. States have different rules as to whether you (as a consultant charging your time, but also producing physical objects) are delivering a product or a service, and therefore when and whether you are required to collect sales tax for your work. And, though some DTPers don't bother to get resale numbers or collect sales tax, they could end up in trouble sometime in the future.

You're also required, if you aren't incorporated, to provide your customers with your Social Security number so they can issue 1099s to you for your total services for the year. Similarly, you must file 1099s for anyone to whom you subcontract more than $600 per year of work.

As with legal issues, we recommend that you research the important tax issues by talking with other DTPers, checking with state authorities, and concluding with a conference with an accountant specializing in small businesses, sole proprietors, and consultants.

Selling your business

You're probably not thinking about it now, but you might someday want to move or change your life. If you have an accountant or you use a software program that produces a report on assets and liabilities, you might as well figure out what your business is worth. To start, make an inventory of all your equipment, listing the model and serial number, the address, phone number and warranty terms of the manufacturer, plus a photocopy of the original invoice. It's a good idea to store a copy of this information off premises in case you ever need it for insurance purposes.

That's the easily quantifiable part. The rest of the value of your business comes from your revenue base. If anyone ever wants to buy you out and you continue to work for the company, the buyer can expect your clients to stick with you. If you're leaving, a potential buyer will be looking for any long-term production contracts or other assurances of guaranteed future income from your existing clients. Other intangibles may have value, including your database of potential clients, your company name, and your business reputation.

If you ask accountants or financial analysts with some expertise in appraising service businesses (or some laid-off Wall Street leveraged buyout whiz), you can probably get some rough measure of the value of your business. It's often a multiple of gross revenues or net income, modified by your assets and intangibles.

14. LOOKING TO THE FUTURE

Two or three years from now you could be a DTP expert—on your own, in a small business, or in a corporate department. But in five years or more—who knows? Everything changes so rapidly in technology-based work that you must assume your job will be very different in the future.

Where will DTPers end up?

If you enjoy DTP and are willing to evolve along with it, you'll certainly still be working some of the time with toner and ink on **paper**. Don't let the hype throw you off. Although fax, videotext, hypermedia, and other methods now permit paperless communications, in real life almost everyone prefers to read, transport, and work with actual physical documents, then clip and save them in overflowing file cabinets and shelves. Each electronic advance has, despite many predictions, brought more paper into our lives.

Don't expect to trade in your **words** entirely for illustrations and **infographics** (the stuff you see in *USA Today* using icons or art to build charts or convey information—sometimes just for fun, but ideally to increase comprehension). They'll never come close to supplanting the communication of logically presented ideas and inspiring word pictures. Every non-verbal and electronic medium has its flashy rise, but people keep talking and writing all around them.

Will these increasingly sophisticated tools ever automate you out of your job? Judging by current trends, the more powerful the technology gets, the more it requires artistry and judgment. The people with these vital **skills** are those who gain experience using the tools, and manage their use by other people.

Many national magazines and major daily newspapers are now making the transition to DTP technology. That will mean more employment opportunities for consultants and for part- and full-time people familiar with these tools. If you keep getting better at what you do and expanding your expertise, the more the tools evolve, the more in demand you'll be.

The underlying economic trends of the 1990s are also likely to be favorable to the growth of DTP and the demand for skilled people. Institutions are adjusting to periods of recession, to corporate restructuring, and takeover-sponsored downsizing. The watchwords productivity and cost-consciousness are likely to be reflected in an increasing attention to the potential economic benefits of DTP. Institutions that successfully make the switch will also appreciate the careful planning and implementation, and the quality of work necessary to achieve those benefits.

We also see another development. Some corporations establish DTP departments, then decide it's all too much trouble and too expensive to support a staff and equipment. Sometimes they return to contracting out their work with an outside DTP service. This way, they hope to gain some of the savings and flexibility of DTP, yet avoid the headaches and overruns they experienced from in-house operations. If this development turns into a trend, independent DTPers will benefit.

Of course, everything will continue to speed up. More and more features of the software will be automated. From fax communications to optical character recognition, everything will move faster. Clients will expect you to turn their jobs around immediately.

A few alternative directions for your worklife

Stay a generalist, churning out those DTP publications, expanding your client list (the better the technology, the more clients you can handle), periodically upgrading your tools, and raising your rates as you become more expert. Keep your eyes peeled for new capabilities in software. Once in a while experiment, without risk, to see if any specialty tempts you. But if you like your clients and you enjoy production, there's no reason you can't prosper by sticking to basics. If (or by the time) you tire of the production process, you'll be well positioned to add training and consulting to your repertoire.

Become a specialist in one of the many emerging technologies that have begun as offshoots of DTP:

- **Database typesetting** is still getting started on the desktop. Thus far, the phrase "database publishing" is being reserved for the actual production and distribution of directories. As the software arrives to automate layouts and incorporate graphic libraries, we're likely to see more demand for people who can produce directories of all kinds. You'll need to know the language and enjoy the logic of database programming.
- **Image processing** is an exploding field. It uses software that allows you to manipulate and combine art from photographs or other sources with graphics created on the desktop. You'll need lots of computer memory.
- **Color** is a complex field. Don't be surprised when you hear that experts in color separation and related techniques spend years, even decades, learning the nuances of getting ink and paper to work together. So if you start now to specialize in color DTP, you might end up in just the right place in a year or three. You'll need vast computer data storage capacity.
- **Multimedia** goes beyond slidemaking and presentation graphics to include sounds, voices, and animation in presentations, created on the desktop and played back there, or transferred to videotape. Think of yourself as a one-person film production crew, creating and then assembling virtually any type of communicable information. Your hardware and software outlays will run several times the cost of a basic DTP setup.

Become an actual publisher with the technology you've been using. These days, publishing a book or starting a magazine, or writing and distributing a one-shot publication, are no longer such daunting prospects. Many new magazines and newsletters, and many special reports would never have gotten off the ground without DTP's convenience, speed, and cost savings. People have started small newspapers out of their homes. The National Newspaper Association estimates that over half of its small-town weekly publishers have converted to DTP, saving $25,000 or more per year on production costs. (Of course, some don't make it. An efficient production process is a necessary but not sufficient precondition of success.) Once you've found a subject and a market, you're in the best position to estimate schedules and costs. Just be sure you have help on the editorial side, if that's not your forte, and on the distribution side, no matter what. For ideas and resources, contact The Newsletter Clearinghouse. (See **Appendix 2. Books on the business of graphics and DTP.**)

You may want to consider **demand publishing**. That's a system to store documents, then laser print, collate, and bind publications, with frequent small or large print runs matched to the volume of orders. Variants on this approach are starting to show up. Kinko's Service Corporation has established Professor Publishing in over 200 college towns to electrocopy individualized textbook anthologies that professors design for their courses. Traditional publishers are starting to go the same route, producing customized or updatable versions of textbooks. One good source for information on the technology of personal computer demand printing is Don Lancaster, a microcomputer pioneer who has demand-published dozens of small booklets using PostScript commands. (Synergetics, P.O. Box 809, Thatcher, AZ 85552, (602) 428-4073.)

Future publishing software

You can trace the origins of DTP tools to other kinds of software: word processors that incorporated proportional spacing and columns, and drawing programs that combined text and graphics on complete pages. DTP borrowed its vocabulary from traditional typesetting, and absorbed the metaphor of the layout person's pasteboard as the assembly point for all the pieces that go on the page. Increasingly, the categories that once separated many different types of software and technologies are starting to blur.

Convergence of DTP and word processing

Most third- and fourth-generation DTP packages have incorporated full-featured word processors, including spell-checking and sometimes even thesauruses. At the same time, many word processors now allow users to create boxes, import graphics, and control spacing of type. The result has been a boon to casual users who want to try out some features of DTP while not committing much in the way of time and resources. However, in some cases, it has also tended to clutter up software menus with features most users don't need. Despite the overlaps, most DTPers still start preparing their texts in word processors, and most people using word processors leave complex publications to DTP software. Similarly, though we are seeing a few software packages that integrate page layout with word processors and spreadsheets, the combined programs never offer the complete feature set and versatility of the standalone software. Although boundaries between applications are increasingly indistinct, each type of package has such different purposes that they will never fully merge. Users will continue to match the appropriate tool to the task.

Convergence of DTP software

Many DTP packages are starting to look more alike. And in the medium-range future, we can hope that documents created with one page layout software package will be able to be modified by another—as is already the case with many word processing and graphics packages. Of course, the differences in the way pages are put together are far greater for the layout software. Nevertheless, software publishers are starting to see this as a goal. Efforts are under way to create a document interchange standard, and a PostScript-based page standard to define the geometry of pages and layouts, so they can be shared and edited across platforms and applications. Still, we're not likely to be able to exchange different format documents while preserving the links between different frames or stories spanning pages for some time. At the same time, with the support of many hardware and software companies, Kodak has taken the lead in proposing a universal standard for defining the digital representation of color. The new standard, called PhotoYCC, will some day allow color data to be defined, imported, scanned, displayed, and reproduced consistently across platforms.

Convergence of platforms

Where there was once a great distinction between DTPers who used Macintoshes and those who used PCs, those differences are lessening. The operating systems and graphic user interfaces are starting to look more like each other. Leading software packages like PageMaker and Ventura Publisher are now available on either system, with QuarkXPress and others on the way. It's increasingly possible to transfer projects in progress between the two platforms without losing much time or most attributes of a document. The convergence is now extending beyond the Macintosh and PC, as sophisticated Unix-based systems like FrameMaker, formerly used mainly on Sun workstations, are now becoming available for desktop computers. One of the great selling points for PostScript, the dominant page description language, is its platform-independence for creating and outputting graphics. Other page description languages, including DDL and Interpress, are largely falling by the wayside. Despite PostScript's relative slowness (somewhat improved in PostScript Level 2), it has emerged as the most flexible, reliable, and universal language.

Convergence of DTP and high-end graphics

The most advanced DTP software packages are now encroaching on the territory of the six-figure software and hardware combinations long in use in newspapers, four-color publishing, and broadcasting. We've seen the arrival on the desktop of Adobe Photoshop, color software that begins to challenge the Quantel Paintbox. Pixar Renderman is a 3-D program that migrated down from mid-sized workstations. Scitex Visionary, Crosfield StudioLink, Hell ScriptMaster and other packages are gateways to the large systems that produce consumer magazines. Many packages capture, manipulate, and convert video and color images between different input and output systems. Color scanners are becoming affordable. Nikon's slide scanner, Canon's smart color printer with optional PostScript, and Kodak's dye sublimation printers are paving the way to low-cost, high-quality color printout.

Convergence of DTP and typesetting

These days, it's hard to find traditional typesetters who haven't begun to incorporate DTP capabilities into their services. They have no choice. Many now accept customer's text files on disk. Some have purchased pricey packages to allow their Compugraphic and other typesetting machines to accept data from DTP software, as well as software to convert typesetting files to DTP files. At the same time, DTPers, some of whom began by feeling superior to typesetters, have gained respect for the high productivity and quality of traditional systems. They've learned what fine type really looks like. And software developers have incorporated into their products variants of the traditional coding systems and tags used by typesetters for specifying and styling type. A decade from now, DTP and typesetting may be virtually indistinguishable. The distinctions will be made in terms of power, speed, and quality, rather than technology or tools. DTP and printing will also converge. Two early signs of that trend are Printware's 1,200 dpi computer-to-plate imagesetter to produce direct paper plate masters without complicated chemistry, and Xerox's DocuTech Production Publisher, an all-in-one unit combining a two-sided PostScript printer, a scanner, and a binder.

A world of supermicrocomputers

Looking ahead a decade, soothsayers expect computers to work very differently than they do today. It's reasonable to project the continuation of current trends, with raw computer speed practically doubling every year, continuing price declines for chips, 50-fold increases in data compression, and quantum improvements in storage and display technologies.

Sometime in the next few years, we'll be getting that piece of equipment we've long been expecting: a combination scanner/copier/printer/fax machine. It will be able to input, transmit, or print out anything that comes to it. (Our editor also hopes it will be able to make coffee and massage her neck.)

Not long after, that box will be hooked up to a digital wireless telephone network. Like the cellular telephone, it will monitor broadcast signals to capture all messages that are directed to its identification number, and look in particular places at predetermined intervals to monitor specified information. That will enable any subscriber to become an on-line subscriber to continually updated publications, and to publications tailored to the customer's interests.

We already have previews of this approach. Many industry newsletters are created with DTP technology and sent daily to subscribers by fax. One company produces an instant newspaper from wire service copy, updated hourly, for distribution to passengers on a NYC–Washington air shuttle.

Another company has just started offering a service to allow users to transmit files anywhere in the world by commercial satellite. With transmissions at speeds of 400 kilobytes a minute, users can send a one-megabyte file to 10 locations overnight for $50—faster and at one-third the cost of overnight delivery services. Corporations and publications can transmit documents, then modify and print simultaneous, but not identical, editions in many locations.

Notice that all these technologies, though created and transmitted electronically, remain print- and page-oriented. That's not just wishful thinking on our part. The page remains one of our most useful modular communications and storage concepts. In a two decades, it might start to look like an artifact, but not sooner.

What about multimedia and color? Multimedia is still years away from being a mainstream product, as easy to use as a word processor. But sometime in the next decade, color will truly arrive. A near unlimited range of hues will be available to display, manipulate, and print. The monitor technology will probably be high-resolution color flat panels (active matrix liquid-crystal diodes, where an individual transistor controls each cell of the display). At the same time, software and hardware image compression will have evolved so the vast amount of data contained in moving color images can be stored, modified, and transmitted with no perceptible delay.

At some point, there will be a convergence between computer and television technology, with computers putting more control of images in the hands of users. People will routinely take all-digital data from television and incorporate it into work they do on with their computers.

We think getting into DTP is a good way to get a foot in the door for these new communication technologies, even if the form they finally take differs from the scenario we've outlined.

Impact on institutions

DTP's capabilities—chiefly its economy, speed, and flexibility—have led to major changes in the way businesses, nonprofit groups and the public sector produce their printed materials. We all benefit, certainly, from the general upgrade in the quality of communications we encounter. But there have been some other consequences.

Often we've seen real disruptions within hierarchies. In terms of content, many more people at different levels within institutions now have the opportunity—though not always the authority—to affect the words and looks of publications. Some institutions have been able to take advantage of DTP technology by decentralizing their communications production and turning out much more timely publications. Others have lost control of what was once a slower but predictable and consistent process.

Another result has been a major confusion about job roles. Some companies are trying to call versatile, literate, and knowledgeable DTPers "operators," a term that minimizes their autonomy and value. Who does what? Does the layout artist, the designer, or the editor get trained in the new technology, or do we hire someone else? Does the writer who is now asked to set type get paid more? What about the all-union publication? Is a union bug (the printed identifying label somewhere on the final publication) from the printer sufficient if the company brings the typesetting in house? These remain unresolved and problematic issues.

> At one printing company where I worked, 125 journeymen 10 years ago in the composition department have now been replaced by six experts. But many of those laid-off typesetters have started their own DTP businesses to survive.   —*Ann Raszmann Brown*

The changing art of communications

DTP is changing everything about print. Remember Marshall McLuhan's "the medium is the message" from the 1960s? For the printed word, it took 25 more years for it to be true. In the 90s, as Jonathan Seybold has said, "Increasingly, people are going to think of themselves as information communicators and they're going to think in terms of using digital technology to do this." (*MacWeek*, March 6, 1990)

In our experience, DTP has already changed how we communicate. For both writers and artists, an interactive, continuous connection to the about-to-be-printed page means our thought processes can become more focused and more creative. Writers so inclined can now start off by visualizing the look of their final published words. At the same time, artists can work to connect their graphics more closely to the content of the text, using a vast range of tools they probably couldn't afford or use in the old days.

For anyone with a message, whether it's text, graphics, or both, the ability to try alternatives and see how they work on a page can validate and enhance seemingly risky or experimental approaches. It's also immensely reassuring to know that our tentative ideas can be slightly tweaked or thoroughly overhauled anytime, before or after the world sees them. So along with DTP's prosaic but crucial savings of time and money, the messages we produce can have greater creativity, immediacy, and impact.

Impact on society

As a DTPer or a potential one, you're benefiting from the new job and business opportunities this technology has opened up. Congratulations on your career.

But you're also part of something more: the democratization of communications. As Computer Professionals for Social Responsibility put it, in its 1989 Annual Report, "The technologies we create shape democracy in many ways that we cannot anticipate. Technology is not simply a collection of machines that help make things easier to accomplish. Technology is also bound up with the distribution of power in society—an issue that lies at the very center of the concept of democracy."

Crusading journalist A.J. Liebling said it best: "Freedom of the press belongs to those who own one." Until the arrival of DTP, the price for independence used to be in the high five figures. Now the cost to get started is a few thousand dollars. Those who can't come up with even that amount, but know the tools, can rent equipment and produce their publications for $10 or $15 per hour, then run it over to the copy shop. That's a real change.

Anyone who is motivated to learn the ways of desktop publishing has the ability to produce affordable, readable, and revisable documents. From the unofficial, formerly underground, publishers in Eastern Europe, South Africa, and other repressive societies throughout the globe to the urban block association newsletter to the new business starting on the kitchen table, anyone whose fingers can tickle the keyboard can publish their messages.

There are no more secrets. We welcome this expanded universe of publishers. It will provide a hospitable environment for every desktop publisher, and hopefully, for everyone with something to communicate.

15. PROFILES OF DESKTOP PUBLISHERS

We present a range of successful people to show you the temperaments and character types of those who've been DTPers for years—what they do and how they do it. Many came to DTP as their third or fourth careers. If you're just starting out, and want to get some inspiration from people who've succeeded after entering the field more recently, check out your local user group.

You'll find quotes from many of our subjects sprinkled throughout the book.

Rick Barry

For 25 years, Rick has honed his design and illustration skills. His field is advertising, promotion, corporate publishing, and packaging. In 1984 Rick started using desktop technology; now his Desktop Studio is in Manhattan's Flatiron district, home of many of the city's publishers and ad agencies. He has worked both as an independent and within design firms. He teaches Advanced Electronic Prepress in the Computer Graphics Department of Pratt Institute and is a hands-on trainer for the Dynamic Graphics Education Foundation. Rick is a past president of the Graphic Artists Guild of NYC.

On starting a career as a DTPer: Treat desktop publishing like any other profession for which you have respect. Don't treat it like a push-button job, because there ain't no such thing! The more respect you bring to the profession, the more respect you'll get out of it. Because you assign a value to it, you'll be in a better position to realize you need to learn how to do it well. And the only way to do the job right is to have respect for it.

On computers and designers: Computers made a major change in the way I do things. Actually, I still do the same things I've been doing for years; I simply use this new tool. As an illustrator, designer, or creative professional, I'm accustomed to working in unknown areas, trying new things and not always succeeding, running into frustration and, hopefully, solving problems and learning from them. This experience has helped me deal with the learning process in computers.

On success: Aside from skills, you need a certain attitude and mindset. If you're hoping to persevere, be persevering. The biggest mistake of all is when people actually believe the simplistic notion that there's a point-and-click solution to a professional need. It's ridiculous! You also need a sense of humor. Because, on a regular basis, the absurd, not just the unexpected, will happen.

On productivity: Being a professional means having discipline. You must know when it's time to stop the creative process and focus on production. Imagine you literally have hats: your designer's hat, your production manager's hat, your editor's hat. Use your judgment to decide when it's time to take one off and put on another. Sometimes I need to kick myself to keep on a productive path. Do whatever is necessary to make sure you're doing only what you should be doing now—not something else. In this brave new digital world, it's so easy to go off exploring uncharted courses.

Toolbox: Mac IIcx with 8 megabytes RAM, color monitor, 44-megabyte removable drive, modem, LaserWriter IINTX, gray-scale scanner, PageMaker, FreeHand, Illustrator, ImageStudio, Photoshop, TypeStyler.

Lynn Walterick

Since November, 1988, Lynn's company, Genesis Publications, has been offering DTP services. Lynn and her husband, Michael Copeland, who joined the company in March, 1989, work from their home in San Jose, California. Previously she was a corporate publications coordinator and copy editor. Lynn also serves as the editor for *Ventura Professional!* magazine (see **Appendix 2. Specialized resources**).

On success: Initiative makes up about 80% of success. We provide tech support for people who don't take the time to read the manuals. They run across a problem, but don't try to solve it themselves. Many people, especially in corporations, feel it's enough to learn only the page layout program and then work at it from nine to five. To be a DTPer, you need the personality to become proficient in several programs. It's really self-motivation. You have to want to learn more. Perseverance goes hand-in-hand with initiative. The common view is that you need to have a design background, or that a traditional typesetter will have greater success. With enough initiative and perseverance, I think any-one, regardless of background, can be a success in DTP.

On the most rewarding aspects of working for yourself: *Flexibility,* espe-cially in the hours we work. We often work until two a.m. and then get up at nine or 10 a.m. We're gradually work-ing our way around the clock! We choose the hours and days. We also have flexibility in choosing jobs. We can take any direction we want—edit-ing, copy editing, a little writing, graphics, as well as page setting. If we want to do something like editing, then we offer that service along with a layout job, or offer it separately.

Satisfaction. In the corporate world you can work for months hoping for a little praise from the boss, and get little feedback on performance. But when I did my first Ventura project, I got im-mediate feedback. DTP is project-ori-ented, so you get both personal satis-faction and feedback when it's complete.

Enrichment is probably the greatest re-ward. We're constantly challenged to keep up with technology and new software, and always refining our pro-duction methods to be more efficient. It's never boring.

Would I ever go back to a corporate environment? Never—God willing. The rewards of working for yourself are tremendous, and the nature of DTP makes it a portable industry. With fax-es, modems, and Fed Ex we can work anywhere in the country. In fact, we're planning on moving to the Midwest next year. We hope to take our client base with us. That frees us from having to worry about the state of the local

economy, and lets us get out of the rat race (and the 120-hour weeks) to where we can really start enjoying life.

On the most frustrating aspects of working for yourself: When you're self-employed, it's difficult to take time for a vacation. When we got married last year, we were in the middle of a large project. The client suggested, only half in fun, we postpone our honeymoon. Since we were taking only two and a-half days, not three weeks, the request seemed a little unreasonable.

A frustration of working at home is that people know they can call after 5 p.m. and reach us. Clients have called us at midnight about nothing serious. Just casual conversation—at midnight!

In publishing, clients often have a hard time keeping to a schedule. We may think in three months we'll have a pocket of time before the next project. Then the copy arrives late, which in-fringes on that time. In a corporation, associates know you're going on vaca-tion and can fill in when you're gone. Not when you're on your own.

Toolbox: 33 mhz 386 PC, 4 megabytes RAM, Ventura 3.0 (GEM and Win-dows), Corel Draw, WordPerfect, Wyse monitor, PostScript printer.

Stephanie Hill

Stephanie is director of Graphics and Publications Development for the New York City Transit Authority. She's a trained graphic designer and knowledgeable in typography and computers.

Her department produces marketing and promotional graphics, as well as bus and subway maps. She manages six graphic artists and a typesetter, plus freelancers. In addition to overseeing the DTP operation, Stephanie is responsible for the group's printing operation in Jamaica, Queens.

On the transition: The TA graphics department works with information-intensive documents. We produce graphics for 240 bus routes, 100 bus maps, 500 transfer tickets, and subway schedules for 466 stations.

When I first came to the TA, the graphics had no consistent look. The format and typeface depended on which artist did it. As a whole, the department was not organized and therefore, couldn't get out timely information.

In 1986, when I was at the Operations Planning Graphics department, I put together a proposal to acquire Macs. I ran into a lot of resistance from the Information Services Division. They didn't think desktop computers had enough power. Nor did they understand our output needs. They were going to produce schedules with pen plotters.

For two years I dragged the MIS people from vendor to vendor, until I wore them down. It was a convincing act, and it was begging. As soon as DTP came in, everyone realized it was the right decision. It took one year to recover our $200,000 cost.

And that didn't include all the applications we hadn't planned for, but were ultimately produced with DTP. For example, we had vended out composition and printing of the bus transfers. They were frequently out of date and incorrect. We were able to bring the composition part of transfers in house. Within six months, we had transfers for each bus route, for each direction on the route. Now the Operations Planning Graphics department has 12 Macs, a scanner, and a Linotronic L300.

On staffing: Job functions have changed, and the city has acknowledged the changes by introducing new job titles like Computer and Graphic Designers. They have more skills and extra training, but no additional salary. I find my freelancers from agencies under contract with the city that formerly supplied traditional board people. Now they send me "computer-literate" or "Mac-literate" people.

On hardware and software purchases: I conduct research by talking to people, seeing demos, and reading. Although I'm always extremely conscious of price, my hardware and software decisions are based more on support and information from the vendor. I want to know about other users and be able to contact them.

On systems support: We're not supported by the TA systems people because we fall outside the megasystems (like Wang VS) they support. But we're not system administrators, we're designers and production people. The idea of networking, file servers, and systems administration is new to us. For now, David Jenkins, our manager, has taken responsibility for our systems administration. But it's stressful for him. I think he's overworked.

I've complained about not having systems support. Everyone likes the graphics applications, but they don't realize what it takes to pull systems together. We're good at cabling, but systems crash or files can't be found. It's a burden. And the technology is always changing too. You don't want to get left behind. If you stop looking for six months, you've had it.

On the greatest thing about DTP: I love it! We can do magic quickly and professionally. People can't tell the difference between typeset documents and ones generated on the Mac.

Our DTP systems make things possible. In an environment where we're limited in what we can get, we are able to turn out high quality, professional-looking graphics that weren't possible before. For example, trains break down. We need to get information about service diversion to the passengers quickly. Now we can produce high-quality, consistent looking output and add graphics easily. We can do things differently—and that's really great!

Toolbox: Eight Mac IIcis, Varityper 600W 600 dpi printer, gray-scale scanner, Compugraphic 9800, Intergraph CAD system, PageMaker, XPress, Illustrator, FreeHand, and Sitka TOPS network.

Gan Young Wong

Born in Canton, China and raised in Hong Kong and the U.S., Gan attended Newark School of Fine and Industrial Arts, and the School of Visual Arts. Nurtured for 14 years in the corporate environment of a major insurance company, Gan foresaw the need for independent DTPers to service corporations. He founded his home-based Hoboken, New Jersey design business in 1986.

On hardware: I'm a speed freak—the faster, the better! I've been upgrading my CPU quite a bit in the last six months. Because I'm a developer, I buy my CPUs for about half price. When I sell them, I sell for the same price I paid. It's a good deal for the purchaser and for me. I just keep trading up.

On working for myself: I worked for corporations for 14 years; that's why I went independent. With a partner, I would have to go back to the nine to five or six routine. I'm lazy; I want to control my time. Sometimes I like to go off fly-fishing for a couple of days. As an independent I can control my time better and work when I want to.

I've been lucky. Two big clients give me business all year round. That's all you need: Two large clients who keep you busy, and you have all the work you can handle. As a result, I haven't marketed myself in the last four years.

On blending ability with technology: I adapted to the technology from the beginning. I like to tinker and was never afraid of technology. Some of my designer friends didn't want to get into DTP technology because they were afraid of it and never adapted. One designer I know tried the Mac for two or three years and still couldn't work with it. I think it's a matter of personalities. Some people adapt fast; some don't. But this doesn't mean that a particular person can't design; he's probably a damn good designer but can't work with the newer technology.

On my rates: My clients force me into bidding on a project basis. You can put in a lot of hours for rewrites and redesigns, and maybe not get paid for it because you're locked into a project price. My consulting business is growing, so now my income is two-thirds from design and production and one-third from consulting. I enjoy consulting and like the idea that for every hour I put in, I get paid. I would like to get into more consulting and train people on the hardware and software. I find it less frustrating than design. I would market myself as a specialist in training other graphic designers; someone who understands the design field, printing, and color—the works!

On starting a DTP career: Go ahead and try it. Why not? But a little luck helps a lot.

Toolbox: Mac IIfx, with 8 megabytes RAM, 105-megabyte hard disk and 44-megabyte removable drive, color monitor, LaserWriter IINTX, color scanner, PageMaker, XPress, Illustrator, FreeHand, ImageStudio, ColorStudio, Word, and Excel.

John McWade

John has a background of 20 years in publication design. He was a magazine art director for six years before becoming an original beta-test site for Aldus PageMaker. John founded PageLab in Sacramento, California, one of the world's first desktop publishing businesses, in March, 1985. His clients have included Aldus (consulting, graphic design, two books, several magazine articles), Adobe (drawing screen fonts, beta-testing Illustrator) and Apple (writing and graphic design). His design work has appeared in ads in *Time*, *Fortune*, *Newsweek*, and *Business Week*. He has written for *Publish* magazine. John has lectured across the U.S., most notably for the first three Seybold desktop publishing conferences, Apple University and MacWorld Expo, and the Pratt Electronic Publishing Conference. He is the publisher of *Before & After* (see **Appendix 2. Specialized resources**).

On starting out: In March, 1985, I started my business. But the first day I had an odd experience. I didn't have any clients. So I got out a phone book and started making phone calls. I called up people, told them who I was and what I was doing. I would tell them, "I think you'll be interested in seeing my work" and "I'd be happy to show it to you."

I was always selling design and production. I told them I can design your publication well, get it printed, and do it for less and faster than anyone else. Clients don't really care whether you are using a computer or a chisel and stone as long as they get the job done.

The strategy worked: PageLab became viable. The tools gave me a flexibility no one else had. For one year, I had no competition. I could pick up work easily in those days and I didn't have to underprice by very much. If I could do a job using a computer in 10 hours that took a competitor working by hand 40, I could estimate it at 35 hours, win the bid, and keep an extremely high profit. It was win-win for the clients and me: They got superior jobs for a low price, and I made a lot of money. This scenario, played out many times in the early days of DTP, accelerated the market's move to computers. But I always sold design as well as production.

On setting up a DTP system: Choose

hardware and software together. For DTP and related graphics, Macintosh is the best. Why? It was planned and built as a picture-driven computer; drawing routines are part of its internal toolbox.

On what I like most about DTP: I can spend my time creating and designing rather than slogging through production. And I have a nearly unlimited range of graphics options at my fingertips. What don't I like? I can't think of a thing! The industry was created—and is run—by extremely bright people and has been handled very, very well.

On why I started *Before & After*: There's a rapidly growing market of people who find themselves with a computer, few or no design skills, and the desire to turn out presentably designed material. There's a secondary market of designers who have few or no computer skills and a professional need to learn quickly and well. *Before & After* was created to answer the needs of both. It's primarily about design and secondarily about handling the software, and the magazine is created totally with the tools and techniques it teaches. As of October, 1990, we have 7,000 paid subscribers; we are gaining about 700 per month. How many are in the market? I think about a million.

Toolbox: Two Mac IIs (plain old ones) with 8 megabytes RAM, one Mac SE, color monitor, 100-megabyte Rodime hard disk, 44-megabyte MicroNet removable drive, QMS PS800 printer (300 dpi), Agfa P3400PS (400 dpi), Agfa Focus 2 scanner (800 dpi), QMS Colorscript 100 (color proofing), PageMaker, FreeHand, FileMaker.

David Doty

A trained graphic designer with experience as an art director, Dave has been working on his own since 1970. His clients include a number of large textbook publishers and national associations. Dave is a strong proponent of design in DTP. For the past four years, he has been owner and editor of *The Page,* a monthly newsletter and tip sheet (see **Appendix 2. Specialized resources**). He also writes for *Personal Publishing.* Dave is founder and past president of the Association for Development of Electronic Publishing Techniques (ADEPT, see **Appendix 2. User groups**).

On local user groups: About four years ago, a friend and I became very aware that a support group would be necessary to help understand desktop publishing. We started ADEPT, a volunteer user group with 600 members from the Chicago area and as far afield as Denmark and Puerto Rico. We have monthly meetings and a workshop series where we talk about principles of design, issues of programs and hardware, how to charge for services, and so on. We have a newsletter about our members and a more robust quarterly

journal. The reason ADEPT has been successful, and will become more so, is because it's interested in supporting people who need a personal network. Our directory of members lists the computer software and hardware each uses. So members can call others if they run into problems.

On corporate DTP centers: Corporate environments offer a great potential for intermixing ideas and knowledge—a synthesis. But often the people who need that cross-fertilization are scattered around the company. They must look outside the organization for support. User groups, and sometimes dealers, can be of help. In the future, user groups, either formal or informal, will become much more important for individuals working in corporations who lack adequate support from the MIS department.

On the future of DTP: More of the same. It will continue to replace the conventional method of producing publications. More people will need to know the fundamentals of printed communication. They'll become more aware of the visual presentation of the material and of the need to make a conscious decision about how something looks. This is a struggle for many people.

Toolbox: Mac IIcx with 8 megabytes RAM, 105-megabyte internal hard disk, 80-megabyte external hard disk, color monitor, Mac SE, Mac Plus, Laser-Writer IINTX, PageMaker, Word, XPress, FreeHand, FileMaker.

Michael J. Sullivan

Michael founded Imprimatur Design Systems, a Cambridge, Massachusetts design and DTP firm, in 1986. He recently contributed to *The Verbum Book of Electronic Page Design* and *Desktop Publishing by Design—Ventura Edition* (see **Appendix 2. Books on DTP and graphic design**). Michael has a degree in computer science, and is a professional photographer.

On starting out: As a businessperson, I recommend filling a vacuum. If the need is at the low end, then fill that low-end void. If you're an artist, though, you'll tend to use the computer as a means of expression. Therefore, you'll need a more powerful desktop system that can connect to high-end equipment. You can never be complacent—not if you're going to fill a need people are willing to pay for. People in DTP should be talented individuals, not necessarily artistic, but at least knowledgeable in terms of the how-to of communications.

On information design: DTP is moving information around on an electronic page. How you communicate on multiple levels is really a question of dealing with psychology and information design: How two people communicate with each other via the printed medium. Ten percent of the population has the potential to be superb DTPers, using visual and cognitive skills in an abstract medium to communicate.

On multiple skills: I'm a network administrator, office manager, senior art director, and in charge of sales. I'm prepared to do spreadsheets, time sheets, and bill clients. It's a full range of skills.

On workgroup publishing: Once you get beyond four people interacting in DTP, you need to maintain efficiency. The situation demands a server environment. We have a staff of eight and 12 computers. At this level, passing files back and forth on a distributive network doesn't work. We're buying a Macintosh IIfx to act as a server. Many people may groan and say, "Why waste a IIfx on a server?" Because of its impressive throughput—that's the key.

On backing up: My biggest disaster was a 140-megabyte hard disk crash. The result was several thousand dollars in lost time. The Mac gives a false confidence of security, but it's just a machine and it can crash. You lose all your work if you don't back it up. We have a rule in the office: Each person is responsible for their main hard disk. We have several 44-megabyte removable disks for each person to use. They just say "back up" and go to lunch. The next person who doesn't back up or has a hard disk crash and hasn't backed it up gets fired.

Toolbox: Nine Macs and three 386 PCs, LaserWriter IINTXs, internal and removable hard disks, Word, WordPerfect, PageMaker, XPress, Ventura, Interleaf, Illustrator, FreeHand, ColorStudio, Photoshop, video digitizers, and gray-scale scanners.

On Far Tse

On Far took a computer course in his senior year in high school and was hooked. He worked in a Chinese restaurant to earn money for his first computer, an Apple IIe. He found it interesting to cheat at computer games by figuring out the programming. After high school he worked for several years in a print shop, doing pasteups and running the photocopiers and presses. This experience helps him visualize a DTP project from start to finish. He left the print shop to work with Maggie at SOS, the first DTP service bureau in NYC. He helped clients and did production work and system support. In September, 1987, On Far joined Acanthus Associates, Maggie's DTP consulting and production firm, as system support specialist and production worker. For the last year, he's been on his own, offering consulting, system support, and production services. He still works closely with Maggie at Acanthus and Fintec.

On skills needed for DTP: Anybody can create documents, but to create good-looking pages you definitely need a design background. It's also essential to know how to use an operating system.

Many times I've seen clients quit a program just to close the document. They don't know how to use the close box. People need to know about copying and backing up files, transferring files to diskettes, preparing work for service bureaus, and recovering lost files.

Most of my experience about systems comes from trying it out myself. New utilities are always being introduced. You just have to try them out to see if they're effective for you. I use about 150 utilities.

On quality control: Sometimes people get overwhelmed or bored with their job and do the work in sloppy ways. The look of the final product is not always the most important thing. It's actually how you create it. Particularly in group situations, if someone is not following procedures, someone else will have a hard time working on a document. The manager needs to check up on people's work and see if the job is being done right. That manager also has to keep up-to-date with the technology, more than everyone else.

I have a client with 42 devices on a network: computers, printers, and a server. I have a contract to do all their troubleshooting and some repair. No one at the company knows basic troubleshooting. A lot of times when they call me, it's nothing major. For example, they have an external hard drive that often gets moved around in their office. Whoever is backing up will grab a drive from one machine and bring it to the next one without checking the SCSI ID number. After they plug in the drives, they have problems in getting the system up because there's a conflict in ID numbers.

On free advice: Sometimes, I'm called in just to supervise the installation, but the client keeps calling for information after the work is done. I'll give free information, up to a point. Then I offer them a technical contract. It's a good way to determine if they are serious about doing business or just freeloading.

Toolbox: Mac II with 8 megabytes RAM, CDC 150-megabyte internal hard disk, CDC 170 and two Quantum 105-megabyte external hard drives, 600-megabyte magneto-optical drive, color monitor, Microteck 300Z color scanner, LaserWriter IINTX, PageMaker, XPress, Word, Illustrator, FreeHand, MacDraw, PixelPaint, ImageStudio, ColorStudio, Photoshop, Excel, Font Studio, Fontographer, and Microphone.

Roger Parker

Roger is the author of several DTP bestsellers, *Looking Good in Print: A Guide to Basic Design for Desktop Publishing* and *The Makeover Book: 101 Design Solutions for Desktop Publishing* (see **Appendix 2. Books on DTP and graphic design**). He also wrote *Newsletters for the Desktop: Creating Effective Publications with Your Computer; Using Aldus PageMaker; Desktop Publishing with WordPerfect 5.0 and 5.1; Mastering the Power of Aldus Persuasion 2.0; PowerPoint Presentations by Design;* and *From Writer to Designer.*

From his Dover, New Hampshire base at The Write Word, he conducts desktop publishing design seminars throughout the U.S., Europe, and Australia.

On hardware and software: For better or worse, I currently own and actively use four computers. I'm trapped into this excess of computers because my work is equally divided between Macintosh-based publishing/presentation programs and WordPerfect/Windows 3.0 programs. Also, I'm a very distrusting soul. Hard disks do crash, often when you can least afford it. By having separate but equal computers, I can use one machine to back up the work of another.

My favorite word processing program is WordPerfect 5.0, due mainly to habit and features such as its excellent spell-checker, thesaurus, and automatic timed backup. My favorite page layout program remains PageMaker. In the future I hope to put together some sort of networking scheme to simplify machine-to-machine backups and file transfers. I prefer writing on Compaqs with WordPerfect and use the Mac for page layout and preparing overheads, although this is partly because I have a larger choice of typefaces on the Mac.

On success as a DTPer: You need to be a print junkie and have an intense love of the print medium. You have to get a real thrill from the appearance of a well-designed advertisement or page. You have to be a compulsive perfectionist, to love tweaking things so they're perfect. You also have to be a word person, to really love words, enjoy games and challenges, and solving puzzles. DTP is a continuing challenge, it's really a game.

Your challenge is to take a series of unrelated parts—words, visuals, and white space—and arrange them together so everything both fits and looks right.

On profitability: My most pleasurable and profitable relationships involve combining my marketing background with DTP. Helping entrepreneurs prepare ads, brochures and newsletters is extremely satisfying. It provides the human contact I miss when I'm locked in a closet writing. The rewards are both tangible—immediate pay—and intangible—watching a store fill up with customers carrying the newspaper ad or direct-mail insert you prepared the previous week.

My most frustrating and least profitable clients are those who don't know what they want. Often, advertising is used as a BandAid to replace a sound business plan or market position. Client relationships are very intuitive: I can't do good work for a client I dislike or distrust. I find it worthwhile to turn down relationships I feel uneasy about—and often hear later that the person who undertook the assignment found it a nightmare. I also find it useless to deal with clients who ask for my opinion but have no intention of acting on it.

On profit-per-minute invested, my desktop design seminars are the most profitable. I enjoy preparing them, I enjoy delivering them, and I enjoy the audience feedback. The only problem is having to *be there*. Airlines and hotels do their best to make logistics into a nightmare. Once I was discussing design principles while in the next room, separated by a movable partition, a police chief's convention was showing a movie on satanic rituals and cult murders.

Cumulatively, books are very profitable, but they don't provide any sort of day-to-day cash flow. It's either feast or famine. At royalty time, I think I'm doing really well, but by the time I pay off bills and taxes—and buy a new typeface or printer—I'm back to zero.

On corporate DTP: Often the wrong people attend my DTP design seminars. Most DTPers have more talent than they—or their bosses—appreciate or allow them to exercise. Employers need to recognize that editing is an essential part of the design process. And I hear too many cases of "Everything has to be done in Korinna or Souvenir because my boss likes those typefaces!"

Employers need to give DTPers the tools they need to succeed without forcing them to beg or plead. Employers should recognize that big-screen monitors and printer enhancements like the LaserMaster boards aren't luxuries, but ways to speed productivity. Fonts should not be deducted from a DTPer's paycheck.

DTPers need more authority to establish reasonable schedules. Too often, employers expect the impossible. They set up impossible deadlines, don't provide information or copy until the last minute, and then blame the DTPer when the job doesn't turn out right.

The moral is obvious: Don't over-direct creative people. If you hire someone, give them the authority to do their best without interference. David Ogilvy once said, "Don't hire a dog if you want to bark yourself. "

Toolbox: Two Mac IIs, each with external hard disks, and two 20 mhz 386 Compaqs. Two Hewlett-Packard LaserJets, one with an 800 dpi LaserMaster board, a Hewlett-Packard PaintJet for color comps and overhead transparencies, plus first-generation Apple and QMS PostScript printers.

Wendy Richmond

Wendy ran her own firm in Cambridge, Massachusetts, developing workshops and helping designers learn about computers. She now works at public TV station WGBH in Boston in the Design Lab, an interactive multimedia and design studio. She's the author of *Design & Technology, Erasing the Boundaries*, a book on issues of design and computer technology, and a columnist for *Communication Arts* magazine.

On running a business: There are so many things to think about: business plans, financial management, insurance, and rent, as well as employees and whether they're happy. While I was running my business, I belonged to a small group that included companies with up to 80 people on staff. We were all in business for ourselves, but doing wildly different things like selling popcorn or running a trucking firm. At each meeting, one of us would talk about our business problems. Though we were in totally different worlds, we were in sync in terms of problems. I knew computers and design; no one else did. But when I told the group, "I seem to be getting jobs but I'm not making enough money," everyone agreed they had the same problem.

I was spending at least half of every day with issues that had nothing to do with computers and design. And frankly, I wanted to spend more time on the content of my work, computers and design. So I decided to apply what I'd learned in business to a new venture within an organization, and we formed the Design Lab at WGBH. Now I have support and expertise all around me.

On the Design Lab: WGBH's charter is to inform, educate, and entertain. That's a wonderful way of thinking of multimedia. Paul Souza, a designer at WGBH for more than 13 years, and I started the Design Lab to concentrate on the visual design of interactive media. This new area requires a more evolved set of design guidelines and principles. In DTP print, you look at a single medium and there are design principles. But in multimedia and interactive media, suddenly there are many more design issues because now you combine animation and sound with user interaction.

To develop and demonstrate new visual guidelines for computer-based multimedia, we need real projects and real clients. We're in this for the long haul because the field is young, and so much work needs to be done. And you can't write about guidelines until you've made a bunch of mistakes—or at least until you've made things. So we're busy making things.

We devote a lot of time and attention to user interface design. For example, we produce interactive exhibits where both good design and good navigational aids are required, including clear typography and dynamic graphics.

We'd love to do more research, but frankly, we're organized as a business within a business. We're responsible for finding clients and making a profit.

Paul and I have lofty goals. We're hoping to contribute to the way the use of technology evolves. Multimedia and interactive media can add a powerful form of visual communication to what we now have. But whenever things start to get a little too intellectual, a little *too* lofty, I always think back to my experiences in my own business. It's smart to be thinking of the bottom line.

Toolbox: Mac IIfx, IIci, Mac Plus, color monitor, LaserWriter IINTX, Director, Swivel 3-D Professional, PageMaker, FreeHand, Photoshop, Adobe and Bitstream fonts, HyperCard, and tons of storage.

Chick Foxgrover

A fine arts major who studied painting, Chick has developed a career as a DTP and multimedia freelancer in NYC. Having spent four years in multimedia and audio-visual production, he was quick to spot the potential of the Macintosh for designing and producing speech-support slides. He began using the Mac in 1985, and now works out of his home in Brooklyn, New York.

On success: My years of production experience have helped me sell myself. I know what it means to work under a deadline, to organize a job, and to plan for problems. And with that experience, I always approach my DTP projects asking myself, "How am I going to accomplish my job, what kind of problems do I have to account for with the software, and how am I going to make sure I meet my deadline?"

On client relations: I won't delude my clients about the capabilities of the DTP system. I point out the system's strengths and weaknesses. Many of the industry's problems come when people say a system is capable of doing things it is only marginally capable of handling.

On pricing: It's very important to keep developing your skills to stay competitive. I ask myself what kind of work I want to do. If I want to do work that further develops my skills, a client may only pay so much. It may mean I have to lower my rates. I've done that in the past—take the job, learn something, get a good sample, then use a new technology in a production situation. It's worked well.

On versatility: One key has been my ability not only to produce camera-ready artwork, but also to always be a generalist. I can set up a modem, interface with the Linotronic bureau, or troubleshoot systems. For situations beyond a generalist's knowledge, I call on consultants who specialize in an area like networking. A product may sound great, but I want to know how it really works. One thing I've discovered: Nobody has the whole answer. It's important to get second and third opinions.

On equipment purchases: I'm conservative in purchases, but when I have a clear need for a significant productivity gain, I spend for the best available solution. For R & D, I usually calculate what I can afford as a percentage of three months' cash flow.

On the best and worst of DTP: The computer is a tool to help me make the best use of my talents. But the equipment and software is never as fast or capable as I hope!

Toolbox: Mac II with 8 megabytes RAM, Mac Plus, 150-megabyte hard drive, 44-megabyte removable drive, color monitor, LaserWriter IINTX, modem, fax, Kensington Turbo Mouse, MacRecorder, XPress, Illustrator, Free-Hand, Word, Excel, Director, and Photoshop.

Denis Shedd

Denis began his career at age 13 working for a newspaper, and has been in typesetting, photography, and printing ever since. He and his wife, Marissa, founded Quad Right in 1977, and expanded into a full-service graphic design center in a storefront on Manhattan's Upper West Side. Quad Right incorporated DTP tools as soon as they became available. He's on the board of the Typographer's Association of New York and the New York Professional PostScript Users Group (see **Appendix 2. User groups, trade groups, and professional organizations**).

On my business: Quad Right is different from most NYC typographers. They traditionally receive the bulk of their work at the end of the day and work all night to have galleys and pages at their customers' doorsteps when they open in the morning. I never really broke into that. My client base became less selective. We service a broad range of customers, from small jobs to large corporate projects. I'm fortunate to have developed such a wide base. Many of the large typographers have suffered by losing one or two major corporate clients to desktop technology.

On imagesetting output as a service: If Linotronic were all I did, I'd be bankrupt. It's not the money-maker people think it must be. When I first put it in, I thought I'd have people breaking down the door. But it didn't work out that way. It took me a year and a half to develop a clientele, not making a penny while the rest of my shop supported the startup. I did it by spending hours on $10 pages (and still do). Because I'm willing to put in that time, I've developed a faithful clientele.

It's a fickle business. I've spent 10 to 50 hours with a customer, tutoring and setting them up at no charge so their files would run flawlessly, and they've left me for a dollar a page cheaper. So be it. Shops that are selling cheap pages always have little hooks in there for this extra or that: minimum prices, extra for crop marks, exorbitant overtime fees. People have left my service to save money, and I don't know if I can blame them. If I were very good at what I did and weren't worried when I sent my files out for repro, maybe I'd go to the cheaper shop. But many have learned the hard way. Murphy's Law is never so evident as on DTP's output side.

We show a lot of concern for our customers. I treat their type as if it were my own. If I see errors, or it isn't printing correctly, I don't print it. I call them up immediately and say, "I stopped your job. It doesn't look right to me. What should we do about it?" I'm concerned with every file. And that can be a lot of work, because imagesetting is very hard to do. Files don't always print right. It's much easier to get a file to print than it is to get it to print right.

On getting into the output service business: Be prepared to do everything, and I mean *everything!* Be ready to spend a lot of time and money purchasing, learning, and upgrading hardware and software. For example, I can output huge negatives. If I couldn't do this, I would completely lose a customer's 200-page Lino job just because I couldn't handle that one and only gigantic negative per year.

On using DTP and traditional technology: We consider ourselves fortunate that we can pick and choose from different technologies. Conventional typography is production-oriented and very efficient. We have thousands of kerning pairs at our fingertips that can be stored easily and quickly. Conventional typography is much more sophisticated than what is available on the Mac at this time. As a production tool the Mac is not yet as efficient as it could be, but that doesn't worry me. Nor should it worry any DTPer. There's no doubt in my mind that DTP is going to take over as a traditional typesetting tool, and fairly soon. After all, DTP *is* typesetting.

Toolbox: Linotronic L300 Imagesetter with RIP4, L530 Linotronic Imagesetter with RIP 30, QMS ColorScript 100 Model 30 11- x 17-inch dpi printer, LaserWriter IINTX, gray-scale scanner, complete Adobe PostScript Type Library, four Macs and four PCs networked to printers, and about $25,000 worth of software.

Elliot Epstein

Elliot carved out a career for himself as a book art director, then became a textbook and freelance designer. Since 1987, Elliot and Ann Meng, his associate in Riverside Graphics, have provided direct mail, publishing, and general graphic design services from a brownstone on the Upper West Side of Manhattan.

On primary interests: We're interested in producing professional-looking designs using the Mac as a tool. I have learned that esoteric programs that promise everything don't work. I prefer to stick to the basic layout and drawing programs and embellish them with my own creativity.

It's almost impossible to stay abreast of the latest technology. I subscribe to many magazines and I'm inundated with information. I try to sift out the small percentage of information directly related to my needs, productivity being of prime importance.

On profitability: As a small business owner, I try to select areas I can profitably exploit without undue risk. I prefer to work from initial design through composition, layouts, and mechanicals, up to the point of printing. Though there's money to be made in brokering printing, I feel it's not worth the risk. You can lose thousands of dollars on a job that goes sour. I prefer that my clients choose their own printers and invest their own money.

On productivity: It's the shortest, most profitable way to do the job a client asked you to do. How do you find that way? Sometimes by chance (puttering around), sometimes from other people's experience, sometimes from magazine tips. My associate and I share our short-cuts. I have a red folder where I save quick notes on my own and other people's discoveries.

On the 90s: In book publishing, people are slicing the same pie into smaller and smaller portions, reflecting their tighter budgets. Publishers don't care as much about type and design as they once did. The bottom line today is to bring in the job within the budget to make a little bit of profit. The same thing is true of DTP. Quality and esthetics don't count as much as they once did. Today, price is of the utmost importance. It's a reflection of our recessive economy.

DTP is extremely competitive, and becoming more so each year. Today, most of the major ad agencies and publishers have their own in-house Mac groups. This situation is forcing me to think about yet another career, or at least a variation on my present one. It seems the demand for slide presentations and computer illustrations is greater than the supply. I hope to become proficient in this field to stay one step ahead of the game for another year or so, until the next oversupply.

In my father's generation, it was one career for life. Today's it's ever-constant change—a geometric progression from 20 years to 10 years to five years. I've had three careers, going on four. I feel sorry for my son, who might have to go through six, seven, or eight careers in his lifetime.

Toolbox: Mac II, 19-inch gray-scale monitor, 14-inch color monitor, Laser Writer IINTX, 105-megabyte hard drive, 44-megabyte removable drive, Dest scanner with OmniPage, PageMaker, XPress, FreeHand, and Illustrator.

Joel Landy

While in college, Joel overcame a fear of computers and earned a Masters in Telecommunications from New York University. He developed and managed a graphics and DTP center at a NYC ad agency whose major account was IBM. In 1988, he started Big Apple Publishing, offering production services, consulting, and training for both PC and Mac platforms. Joel is the current chairperson of the DTP Special Interest Group for the NYPC user group.

On saying no: You know you're getting somewhere in your business when you turn down a client because you think working with them will be too much of a headache. They remind you of your Aunt Muriel who looks over your shoulder and complains all the time. You figure you don't need this in your life, and you're right.

I find myself trusting my intuition more and more these days. I trust what feels good about people, workload, and yes, even pricing.

On unexpected bottlenecks: When working on-site, beware of network bottlenecks. Once I quoted a rough price for a project done on-site. I was to be paid by the hour. The printer was tied to a network of Macs, which continually printed out other work, jamming up my output. It took forever to print out slight changes. The hours added up. When I presented my invoice for $1,250, the person who hired me took me into his room and screamed, "I thought you knew the program!" He appealed to my professional pride to feel ashamed of myself. Though I had a signed contract in my hands, I figured I would cut my losses and leave. I told him if he gave me $900 right now, I would never darken his doorway again. So he paid me. Footnote: A year later someone else at the firm hired me for a $4,000 job.

On job roles: At an ad agency where I worked, low-level copywriters didn't want to learn DTP. One told me, "It'll be just one more thing for me to do. And once everyone knows I can do it I'll be stuck with the job." I find it interesting that this "creative" person dismissed the task, yet many underutilized secretaries would love to improve their skills and income by learning DTP and graphics.

On IBM and Mac: So much software is available on both platforms. And Windows 3.0 should make it easy for DOS-hating Mac lovers to be productive on the other side of the computing fence. IBM people generally love the Mac. Mac people generally dislike DOS machines. People who know both have a distinct financial advantage.

On staying interested in DTP: I get to

be creative and be my own boss, choosing the work I'm paid for and the people I work with. I enjoy the role of the hired hero, someone who ventures into a situation with knowledge and skill and produces positive results. DTP gives me this opportunity. It also gives me the chance to empower organizations and individuals. As a teacher/trainer/consultant I help clients organize thoughts and communicate more effectively.

As more and more is expected from creative computer professionals with every passing nanosecond, the game gets ever more intense. The challenge to be my best is always in front of me. I know I haven't yet produced my best work.

Toolbox: Mac II with 8 megabytes RAM, 40-megabyte internal hard disk, 44-megabyte external disk, color monitor; 20 mhz 386 PC with 5 megabytes RAM, 30-megabyte internal drive, 286 PC-AT, PostScript printer, modem, PageMaker for Mac and PC, Ventura, XPress, PowerPoint, Persuasion, SuperPaint, Illustrator, Harvard Graphics.

Susan Glinert Stevens

Susan is a senior editor with BUSINESS ONE IRWIN (formerly Dow Jones-Irwin), specializing in microcomputer software and hardware with an emphasis on desktop publishing technology. Living in Baltimore, Maryland, she is the co-author of *Xerox Ventura Publisher, From the Screen to the Page.* Susan is a former technical editor of *PC Tech Journal.*

On success: First, have a solid understanding of the publishing process. When copy comes in, it has to be worked over by a competent copy editor. Then it has to be formatted using a design that projects the information in an attractive, easy-to-read manner. The next step is to understand what to do with the finished pages. If you're working with books, you need to know about paper, print, binding, and often color.

Second, have a good eye for design. Unfortunately, many people who are getting into DTP aren't graphic designers. Although it's not necessary to be a graphic designer to do DTP, you've got to be able to work with a graphic designer—or fake it. I fake it.

Third, master the complex hardware and software. This stuff is *not* easy. Learning how to make printers talk to computers, how to manipulate fonts, and how to work with software like Ventura and PageMaker is challenging.

Finally, you need to keep current.

On the future of DTP: We're going to see color prepress for real, something we don't have yet. We're going to see the elimination of type service bureaus because cheap high-resolution printers will be flooding the market. Why send type out to a house to do it at $1-$5 a page when there's a 1,200 dpi printer sitting next to your desk? We're also going to see DTP showing up in other ways—in compact discs, books online, and possibly multimedia in-house videos such as training films. In a few years, we'll see different ways of presenting information, called publishing, that are probably unimaginable right now.

Toolbox: 25 mhz 386 PC, PostScript printer, Ventura, Word for Windows, Micrografx Designer, HiJack, Publisher's Paintbrush, and a scanner won at PC Expo.

Ron Lockhart

Ron is general manager of NYC's Wheeler-Hawkins (formerly Electronic Directions), a company involved in DTP research, consulting, and training. Ron spent 15 years as a producer for Columbia Records. For ten years he wrote jingles, and says he stopped because he had nothing more to say about banks and hamburgers. Until last year, he ran his own DTP consulting, production, and training firm.

On publicity: I'm good at publicity. I learned from a brilliant PR person in the music industry that everyone likes people who are colorful. And if you just market yourself that way, the publicity follows. I always show up at SIGs and offer to write articles for local computer groups. There's a lot to be said, if you know what you're talking about, for going to a meeting and making yourself known and heard. I write articles for industry magazines. No single meeting or article does it, but visibility is cumulative.

When you think about publicity, first know yourself and know your strong points. For example, I'm enthusiastic about things. I'm also candid. Lots of people in the computer press are always looking for a colorful story. I started mining that. If I ran into them at parties, I'd tell them what I did. Sure enough, I got several articles written about me. You can construct yourself to be a little eccentric. I want them to say he's the guy with the ponytail, or the beard, or whatever. I want them to recognize Ron Lockhart.

On knowledge: I've made a conscious effort to learn those things I thought would be helpful to my career. I put myself in situations where I would learn about them. When you learn to sail, one of the quickest ways is to offer to crew on a boat in exchange for getting some tips. People love it. I'd say, "How about my set of hands and my knowledge of computers in exchange for giving me some insight into local area networks?"

Be careful not to get in over your head. I'd limit jobs to something I could do. I wouldn't take on a job I didn't think I could handle and I'd make a conscious effort to learn what I didn't know. The size of the job was less important. I went after installations where I knew what to do. I could have subcontracted the work, but that meant I would be subcontracting out something I couldn't supervise. I'd be tap dancing my way through the job. I'm not going to bill clients for experimentation; I'd rather turn down the work.

On limitations: Money versus technology is the biggest problem in the DTP business. You constantly have to keep expanding your equipment to meet the technology. When is it time to upgrade to a new piece of equipment and when is it not yet time? I prioritize equipment based on demand. The easiest way to know demand is to talk to your clients. Find out if they require the technology for hardware you'll need a bank loan to buy.

I firmly believe in keeping software 100% up to date—that's an expense, but usually a minor one. The hidden expense is the time it takes to install and debug the software. Whenever you install a new piece of software you expect it to be up and running right away, but it never is. It's never a question of just taking off the shrinkwrap. So you have to factor in that hidden expense.

Time is a limitation. There are a finite number of hours per day. To overcome that, I just work harder.

Toolbox: 33 mhz 386 PC, Mac IIfx with 8 megabytes RAM, 150-megabyte hard disk, Agfa 3400 printer, HP LaserJet III printer with PostScript cartridge and 3 megabytes RAM, Ventura, PageMaker, Illustrator, FreeHand, and Corel DRAW.

Richard E. Luna

Richard is in his third career in communications. He was a medical and technical editor/writer for 12 years. Next, he was in book, magazine, and advertising typesetting, first as a proofreader, later as a type shop manager. In 1985, he bought a Mac Plus, and in 1988 he produced the largest project done in Quark XPress 1.0 in the U.S.—a 474-page history of *The Unitarian Church of Brooklyn.* He then worked as Macintosh applications manager for a large prepress house. Now from his home in Bronxville, NY, he runs a DTP consulting and training company called Luna-Graphics Associates, working with magazines, ad agencies, and design firms.

On success: You need enthusiasm, a love of communications, and no fear of change. You've got to take a risk and be out there. I use the expression: Bold italic is a wonderful face. It leans into the future. You've got to be out there, just like bold italic.

I've worked for years in typesetting, writing, and editing. Now I'm a Mac expert. I've spent hundreds of hours working with the programs, but what I can do best is communicate my enthusiasm for desktop publishing.

The Mac is a subversive machine because it revolutionizes. It upsets current working relationships by putting power in the hands of the end-user. My enthusiasm for that is what I can communicate to people.

On keeping current: I read all the time: *MacUser, Macworld, Step by Step Electronic Design, Personal Publishing, Scientific American, Business Week,* and almost anything else I can pick up. I'm a member of the NY Macintosh Users' Group, the National Association of Desktop Publishers, and the Apple Consultant Group—and I'm on the board of the NY Professional PostScript Users Group. They all bring me into continuous contact with other people in the field.

On working for a company: I run my business from my home, but for a while I decided to work days for a company. I was motivated by salary, security, and the chance to gather contacts. The downside is the corporate culture you must deal with.

When you're completely on your own, there doesn't seem to be enough time in the day to keep up with everything, do the work and promote yourself. Nevertheless, I am now solo again.

Toolbox: Mac IIx with 8 megabytes RAM, 573-megabyte internal hard disk, 80- and 172-megabyte external drives, color monitor, LaserWriter IINTX with 70-megabyte drive, PC-AT clone with 20 megabyte hard disk, color monitor, NEC CD-ROM drive, gray-scale scanner, XPress, Illustrator, FreeHand, Photoshop, and MacLink Plus.

Sandy Mayer

Sandy is co-founder and director of corporate training for the Berkeley Corporation in Bala Cynwyd, Pennsylvania. It's a technical and management consulting firm that specializes in integrating people and technology in the workplace. The company consults in systems design and installation, software design, programming, documentation, technical training, and management and organizational development. Sandy's focus is to maximize return on investment through directed learning, communications, and operations management in high tech, production, and professional environments. She's a contributing editor for *The Desktop Publisher* (see **Appendix 2. Specialized resources**).

On defining a DTPer: There is no clear definition of what a DTPer should be. I perceive one to be an electronic page layout specialist. In my view, a DTPer doesn't need to be an excellent designer, typographer, or computer weenie. However, you need an understanding of, and exposure to, all these areas. You need to know about typography and prepress, have a good eye for design, or have the design principles memorized.

On changes in corporations from DTP: When DTP is introduced into companies, it can have a strong organizational impact. I see a lot of conflict. Individuals have sought to enhance their skills beyond graphic design or typesetting. If they're challenged, they'll save their company money by doing things cheaper and quicker. Their combination of skills now demands a higher salary. But employers—and as an employer I understand this—want to keep pay scales the same.

There are principles in every field. DTP is a new field and needs principles. I know what they are, our faculty knows, and some individual people know through trial and error. But how do you convey them to management in a short amount of time? Management knows what a typesetter, designer, or a creative director does. Those titles have been around for years. A certification process starts to solve the problem. By creating guidelines or expectations, schools will pick it up.

The issue can be handled through trade associations or unions. Trade associations can help individuals unite and communicate needs and grievances as a group. They're an excellent source for

education. Through education, companies and individuals can more easily assimilate or deal with the changes brought on by DTP.

I'm also thinking about strippers' unions and the Printing Industry of America. Strippers' unions can be powerful forces, but they could be at risk. Some members who shift from manual to electronic stripping may lose their union status. A company may try to say stripping electronically is not a union job anymore. My feeling is that somebody is doing it—whether on a table or on a computer. And if the union has anything to do about it it will be a union person.

I don't want to be perceived as pro- or anti-union. I work for management and get paid by them so I'm sensitive to their issues. But I have a strong loyalty to people who are making it possible to get work done. Unions can have a positive impact. People like me can only go so far in helping the industry. A union's livelihood and existence depends on its membership. Its members can leverage their presence and build some guidelines.

Toolbox: Day to day, a Mac Plus with a 40-megabyte hard disk, LaserWriter, Word, and PageMaker. For special projects, Mac IIx with a color monitor in the training facility.

Joel McIntosh

From 1986 to May, 1990, Joel taught high school English in Copperas Cove, Texas. Now he's an educational consultant for 38 Texas school districts, helping them develop programs in gifted and talented education. He's also working on a graduate degree in gifted education and he's a graduate assistant. With his wife, Stephanie, a graphic designer and managing editor of *Employee Assistance* magazine, Joel founded *The Prufrock Journal, The Journal of Secondary Gifted Education.*

On starting out: We moved from an idea to running a successful business and a second income. What carried me, especially in the early stages, was doing the research. I sat down and put hours into learning the basic page layout concepts, and I spent tremendous amounts of time learning how to market our product.

Everything you do is qualitative support for the creativity you put forth in your publication. It reflects you. So you want to put your best effort into it.

Don't be in a hurry to pay cash for everything. You can trade services with another company and get a better value. For example, I often let a company

place a full-page ad in *Prufrock* if they'll pass out my flyers at education conventions they attend. It's not cost effective for us to attend these shows, so this trade is valuable for us.

On marketing a DTP business: People just starting out need to realize lots of people are out there willing to help fledglings. One of our advertisers has offered to start packing a flyer for *Prufrock* with every order they send out. That amounts to about 24,000 flyers mailed each year. All we have to do is send them our flyers. Similarly, be willing to help others when you can. It's an excellent way to establish bonds with other companies that may pay off in the future. I've developed a number of advertisers for *Prufrock* by simply being helpful when I was needed.

There's a lot of good free advice out there. On several occasions, I've had experts offer advice that improved my sales. Get your name out there, make contacts, and ask a lot of questions.

On the newsletter business: One thing is seldom discussed in books on starting newsletters. If you're targeting a customer base that's unable or unwilling to pay more than $20 or so for a subscription, consider doubling the newsletter size and taking ads. That's what I did. Because I can pay for my printing and mailing costs with my advertising, I can use the magazine itself as my marketing tool. Each issue reaches 5,000 individuals, and it costs me absolutely nothing. Any subscription I receive from mailing (usually a 3%-4% return rate) represents pure profit.

On hand-held scanners: With the Atari, we use Migraph's scanner and Touch-

Up software. This combination allows us to scan in photos for position and proofing purposes. The quality of the scans isn't good enough for final pages. The setup offers a tremendous amount of flexibility while I lay out the journal. I can try any number of combinations of text and graphics, and never get up from the computer.

Toolbox: Atari Mega 4, 30-megabyte hard drive, monochrome monitor, Atari SLM804 laser printer, Calamus DTP software, Mac SE/30 with 40-megabyte hard drive, and FileMaker.

Paul Constantine

Since 1987, Paul has managed digital production for the Corporate Planning and Development Division of John Wiley & Sons, Inc. He and his staff have produced books and supplements on microcomputers since before the advent of DTP. Paul was previously involved in CD-ROM planning and software production management at Wiley and McGraw-Hill Book Company. He is the program director of the NY Macintosh Users' Group and co-chair of the New Technology Committee of the Association of American Publishers.

On our department: We have a staff using DTP to produce books in house. We also provide consulting services to other divisions and groups within the company who are thinking of getting DTP, and we offer consultation to authors on preparing their manuscripts. The key for us is transportability of the author's data.

On platforms: The Macintosh is our standard because we have much more flexibility on a Mac than on a PC. Our authors write math and chemical equations. When an author does an equation in WordPerfect on a DOS machine, we can't save those keystrokes. On the Mac, if the author does an equation in MathType, for example, it's a graphic file. It can then move into any other program or translate into text.

On sampling systems: Three or four years ago we bought a couple of Macs and a laser printer, put them in a room, and called it MacCentral. We left it as an open room for employees to use the equipment. The theory was that anyone could try to work on the computer. We thought this would give them an easy way to help justify the expense of buying their own computer. In its first year, MacCentral produced the equivalent of $70,000 worth of work. Considering that the original investment was about $5,000, that's a pretty good return. A number of departments within the company don't use the room anymore because they've gotten their own equipment, which was the intent right from the beginning. But the room is always in operation.

Toolbox: Mac IIs, IIxs, Mac Pluses, 80-megabyte Quantum internal hard disks, 320-megabyte WREN Runner internal hard disks, external Photon and Dataframe hard drives, Bernoulli 20-megabyte 8-inch removable drives, SyQuest 44-megabyte removable drives, Apple CD-ROM Drive, LaserWriter Plus, LaserWriter IINTXs, color and monochrome monitors, Hayes 2400 baud modems, DaynaFILEs for PC floppies, PageMaker, XPress, Word, MathType, Excel, FreeHand, Illustrator, Photoshop, ImageStudio, TypeAlign, LetraStudio, Fontographer, Metamorphosis, Art Importer, MacDraw II, Canvas, Dreams, PixelPaint Pro, MacDraft, MacLink, Smartcom, StuffIt, Suitcase, QuicKeys, QuickMail, and Alarming Events.

Lynn Yost

Lynn spent 10 years as a freelance graphic designer and copywriter for book and magazine publishers, advertising agencies, printers, and art studios before the Mac came along and changed everything. After editing *The Mac Street Journal* for the New York Mac Users' Group in the days before the Mac Plus, she consulted for a Wall Street law firm on special typesetting applications for Unix mainframes with Macintosh front ends. For the past few years, she's been writing and designing in the all-Mac Marketing Department of BankLink, Inc., an electronic banking service company in NYC.

On educating management: People get into a reactive mode in corporate situations because they don't know what's involved in setting up a publishing unit. It's not just the hardware and software and its learning curve. DTP is a publishing operation, and people who don't know about printing and publishing are poor candidates for corporate DTP. It helps to be able to know enough to offer management suggestions and options.

On tracking jobs: We have a standard log book with job sheets for requests and print orders for work to be sent to the printer. I also have a book divided into four sections: current jobs, completed jobs, jobs on hold, and jobs at the printer. I take my book to staff meetings so I'm prepared for questions. This system also accounts for jobs that sneak into the system. At first you think: "I'll just change this little thing." Suddenly it has to go through approval cycles, and then there are three revisions and design changes.

I need to keep track of time because we have a heavy production schedule and I actually do more work than I officially have. It's better to quantify time, if you can, because it helps you stay closer to reality. I want to have a realistic idea of how long jobs take. Charts and forms, for example, can take wildly different amounts of time.

On design: Design can get out of hand almost instantly, depending on who is running things, how much work there is, and how visible or important the piece is. Without coordination, you get crisis design. Particularly in the hands of part-time users, design gets watered down. If no one is coordinating design, it shows and will reflect poorly on your company.

On organization: Standardize, standardize, standardize! Coordinate, coordinate, coordinate! Somebody needs to be on top of things. DTP is labor-intensive, and when you are very focused on the job you are doing, you can't keep tabs on everything else. You're immersed in your work. You're like the pearl fisher under water picking up pearls. You surface and find that the boat has moved!

As in any publishing or design business, you need someone who coordinates everything. If you expect one person to do everything, there will be a serious overload. It's too much to do.

Toolbox: Four Mac IIs with 4 megabytes RAM and 40-megabyte internal hard disks, Mac SE, Mac Plus, LaserWriter IINTX, Montage film recorder, gray-scale scanner, DaynaFILE, Summagraphics tablet, modem, Word, MacWrite, FreeHand, Canvas, Illustrator 88, Image Studio, PageMaker, Persuasion, PowerPoint, OmniPage, MacPaint and Sitka network.

Lawrence Kaplan

Lawrence studied painting at Massachusetts College of Art. After working as a magazine illustrator and doing paste up and mechanicals in a design firm, he spent several years at a NYC slide production house producing multi-projector slide shows. He got hooked on the Genigraphics system and bought a computer to do storyboards. After a stint managing a DTP production center, he returned to freelancing. He now has his own firm, Hot-Tech Multimedia in Manhattan's SoHo district.

On multimedia: While I'd been working in print, the Mac was gaining speed and getting more powerful, so I could create complete slide shows. And the final presentation could be played back on the computer at trade shows, projected in board rooms, or transferred to video.

By the summer of 1989, desktop media and multimedia had become buzzwords. I felt excitement in the air. Faster computers and new programs combined video and sound. I began consulting as creative director for Electronic Directions. We had a contract with Apple to set up a lab and introduce art directors and advertising agencies to multimedia. The community of people using these tools was expanding right in front of me.

1990 was a breakthrough year, for multimedia as technology, and for its marketing. My clients read a stream of articles in *The Wall Street Journal* and trade publications. They used to be afraid to replace traditional methods of presentations, thinking they might put their jobs at risk if they used new technology. Now they know they need to be conversant in the new technologies to be effective.

I see many parallels between DTP and multimedia. Much of the software is the same. Often I create the presentations I assemble and animate in Director using DTP tools like Illustrator, Photoshop, ColorStudio, Studio 8, DeltaGraph and Swivel 3-D. And the essence of successful multimedia, as in DTP, is good design.

On starting a business: After 12 years of freelancing, I started my own company. Now I hire freelancers. Hot-Tech Multimedia creates new product introductions, corporate presentations, and interactive animations for Fortune 500 companies. We also train agencies and advertisers in Director and Illustrator.

When you freelance, there are limits to your involvement in a company or the projects you work on. As a small business owner, I'm involved in all aspects of the business, from selling to creating a concept, as well as production and management. Since my background is primarily in the creative fields, I took entrepreneurial courses at NYU to strengthen my business and manage-

ment skills. I learned the four ingredients to running a successful business: 1. management, 2. management, 3. management, 4. product.

On the future: We're the first generation to use desktop computer tools. There are new opportunities for all of us. I told a friend that as long as the technology gets better, so do I. Well, the technology just keeps getting better.

Tools: Macintosh IIfx with 8 megabytes RAM, 330-megabyte hard disk, color monitor, NuVista board, Pioneer laser disk, two 44-megabyte removable drives, Microtek color scanner, PostScript printer, Mac Plus with 20-megabyte external hard disk, Sony High 8 camera, digitizing tablet, PageMaker, other software listed at left, and MacRecorder.

photo: Beryl Goldberg

Margaret Styne

Margaret runs her company, Electric Page Unlimited, from her home on Manhattan's Upper East Side. With her DTP business, the British-born mother, former gemologist, model, painter, and dollhouse maker combines her talent in design and art with her love of computer technology.

On working in DTP: Since the Apple II, I'd been looking for a way to turn my passionate love for computers into something constructive. It's not enough to love computers. They're tools—you've got to find something to do with them. DTP is perfect because I can use a computer, I can work at home, create beautiful communications, and feel challenged. It's exciting—so many breakthroughs occurring so swiftly. Of course, it's work, very hard sometimes, but seldom monotonous. And I love finding ways to solve problems and share discoveries.

On reliability and speed: How fast? Faster. Provided your system doesn't bomb, freeze, or mangle your data, faster is always better. Too slow and you find yourself avoiding applications that run slowly, avoiding certain editing routines, fonts, graphic types, sticking with the safe and dull. That's why I'm against big screens. Gorgeous but slow, very heavy, very hot and demanding lots of desk space.

On success: Most important by far is knowing what's possible, what's practical, and how to actually accomplish it. Apart from formal training, you need to refuse to admit defeat, the ability to see the forest *and* the trees, top-level expertise in two or three core programs, and a critical eye for making those subtle adjustments that turn merely okay into first-rate. If people look at a document and say, "Oh, that's desktop published," something's wrong. They see the production, not the content. That's not good. Except other DTPers. They're allowed to notice.

On upgrading: I prefer to trade up fairly frequently, so I buy with an eye to reselling. Machines with standard configurations made by respected, name-brand manufacturers sell best. I stay away from the powerful but obscure—I don't need an expensive doorstop.

Selling through a broker is convenient and hassle-free. They find a buyer, pack up the equipment, and take it away. It's best not to sell to friends, unless they're technically sophisticated. I make sure I have backup equipment available—a friend, service bureau, or second machine. Oh, and I keep all the stuff that comes with any hardware. Packing, papers, disks, everything.

On productivity: For me, it's loving my work. It's easy to work hard when you're enjoying yourself. For years my toast has been, "May you love your work." I do. I'm definitely a lucky person.

Toolbox: Mac IIfx, 20 mhz 386 Compaq, Mass Micro 44-megabyte removable drive, Pinnacle REO-650 magneto-optical drive, color monitors, LaserWriter IINTX, gray-scale scanner, Apple CD-ROM drive, modem. PageMaker (on Mac and PC), Ventura, Illustrator, FreeHand, Word, WordPerfect, Photoshop, Digital Darkroom, FileMaker, OmniPage, MicroPhone, MacLink, 911 Utilities, Virex, and Sitka network.

Bob Mc Dowell

Bob began as a freelancer in DTP and databases using the Macintosh. In April 1987, with two friends, he founded NovaWorks, an Apple value added reseller (VAR). The firm services the greater NYC area offering a range of customized software for the Mac: NovaWorks project management software for individuals; NovaWorks productivity software for time and schedules or working groups; NovaWorks Production Manager, for small working groups for jobs, clients, deadlines, and projects. Sales of DTP hardware and software account for 60% of revenues.

On starting a DTP business: I tried to start a DTP company in 1985 with a 512K Mac and a LaserWriter. It just didn't work. It fell apart. The idea was not sufficiently focused, and we had no target clients. The four partners considered public relations work and design. We all had different skills and wanted to use them with this organization as a vehicle. I learned from that experience that having a solid concept for a business is crucial for success.

You have to pay attention to the business. It's not like playing a video game and having someone else put in the quarters. In getting started, don't overlook that you're running a real business with all the rights and responsibilities, opportunities, and threats.

One difficulty is money—making a lot of it. You could be a DTP freelancer in NYC, taking home $1,500 per week and your husband/wife/boyfriend/girlfriend is doing the same. Now you're talking about some real money. Now you have no free time, but a lot of cash. How do you turn that into a business? How do you stop freelancing and start being a company? Where do you want to end up—as a production house or design shop?

DTP is entrepreneurial; it's 90s stuff. There's a lot of opportunity out there. I can't think of anyone who's put out a shingle and done well because of a magic smile and a firm handshake. People I know have done well because they talk to other people, they care about the work they are doing, and they work hard at it. They pay attention to details. They have the ability to talk to someone to figure out what's needed and what's not. And they're not afraid of failure.

On having fun: *The most fun:* It had been very busy and I was leaving one night around 7 p.m. and was totally tired. I got a call from a client at a major bank. Help! She had a presentation for her boss's boss the next day and her hard disk wouldn't mount. I filled up a couple of sacks full of hardware, software, tools, and chips. I walked over to the bank and fixed it. I made it work. It was such pleasure.

The least fun: When other people don't

play by the rules and behave in a less than efficient way. For example, I order something and it arrives a day late. It doesn't seem a big deal, yet sometimes it's a big problem. I try not to behave that way. I know things can happen and I make allowances, but the supplier should call. There's too many people not paying attention to these matters.

On our business: Building a company over a few years is possible for anyone willing to give and take, and work at it. We had a crisp idea of what we wanted to do. The founders at NovaWorks are each very different, but we've accepted a common perspective on behavior. And we hold a common philosophy: To help people select and acquire tools, and support this process effectively and efficiently. We're unique because we have more support people (technicians, trainers, and telephone support) than sales people.

On the future: What's going to happen to electronic publishing, what's going to happen to Apple and Macintosh?

And how is NovaWorks going to grow, prosper, and have a good time?

Color will become more commonplace, easier to deal with, and much more important. As for Apple, people really like the company. Despite management problems and some weird products, they're in good shape in terms of sales, cash, and karma. Apple's strength has always been its ROM and its proprietary way of doing things. If Apple does well, we do well. In terms of how we behave, if we pay attention to why we started the company—to care about people, to make sense in a confusing marketplace—we'll do well too. Nova-Works won't be the biggest "anything" in the world, but that's not important to us. What's important is doing a good job and having fun.

Toolbox: Mac II, monochrome monitor, LaserWriter IINTX, ShivaNet modem, Apple Share Network, Microsoft Mail, Excel, and Accountant Inc. Professional.

AUTHORS' PROFILES

Felix Kramer: a career in DTP services

photo: Beryl Goldberg

I got into computers and DTP through writing. I've spent my whole working life editing newsletters, magazines, and newspapers, and writing reports, articles, business plans, and foundation grants. I've also managed staffs, run special events, and been a Congressional speechwriter. One way or another, I've always been in communications.

With DTP I can combine all my interests—working with people on subjects and issues I care about, improving my verbal and graphic skills, using the most innovative and exciting tools, and earning a good living in an agreeable environment.

I started typesetting in the 1960s, when I took a year off from college to help run a regional anti-Vietnam War communications and organizing center in Ithaca, New York. I improvised with chipped PressType headlines, IBM Selectric Composers laced with Kor-Rec-Type, and hand-drawn boxes. I got mimeograph ink all over me, and even learned to prepare and run a Multi 1250 offset printer.

Here I first experienced the pleasure of participating in every phase of a communications project—from deciding on an audience and message, through writing, editing, designing, typesetting, pasting up, photographing, stripping, platemaking, printing, and finally, even collating and distributing the result.

In the 70s, I spent lots of time *not enjoying* buying type from conventional typesetters: counting words, estimating story lengths, taking blind stabs at picture spreads, standing behind web press operators pointing out over-inking on photographs. I spent too much money to remake pages, and never felt I could get just what I wanted.

In the late 1970s, I backed into vocational counseling by writing a book for a state agency investigating commercial trade schools and community college programs that trained computer workers. There, my first computer typesetter was an IBM MTST. I struggled to produce typeset questionnaires on a machine with no permanent memory.

In the early 80s, I ran a non-profit energy conservation organization with a $20,000 monthly payroll and never more than a few thousand dollars in the bank. I tried to establish a sideline word processing income for the group with an Intertec SuperBrain, Magic Wand and Wordstar word processors, and Xerox Diablo printers. I discovered I needed to know much more than I expected about the technology to succeed in the business.

In 1982, I bought a Kaypro, and started consulting about setting up office word processing operations. As soon as MagicPrint gave Wordstar proportional spacing, I began producing newsletters with daisy wheel printers. I saw Apple's Lisa, and drooled at a $10,000 computer that showed white type on a gray page. I couldn't see buying a brain-

dead 128K Macintosh, but I sprang for a 512K Fat Mac. Since then I've owned and traded in successively more powerful Macs.

My DTP career started when I saw Apple MacDraw and the miracle of the first accurate, onscreen representation of sized and styled typefaces. But there was still no good way to get it all from the screen onto the paper. When the Apple LaserWriter came out, I was so excited I called California to get the press kit with its samples.

In early 1985, Maggie stood up at a NY Macintosh Users' Group (NYMUG) meeting to announce that her company was the first in NY to offer rental time on a LaserWriter. I showed up the next day. A week later, using Manhattan Graphics (later Letraset) ReadySet-Go 1.0 and Microsoft Chart, I produced a flyer headlined, "Spend Less, Look BETTER!" I proclaimed that "Every type point size is available, in Helvetica, Times, Courier, Symbol in a huge variety of styles: italic, bold, outline, shadow, and much more!" My guarantee: "Your cost will be less than you would spend on conventional type & design." Of course, despite my optimism, stable software did not yet exist, and the typeface range was too limited. It would be a year before I or anyone would be truly equipped to run a DTP business.

In early 1986, as one of NYC's first DTPers, I became a beta-tester of successive versions of ReadySetGo, one of the first page layout software programs. And Maggie and I organized the first meetings of the NYMUG Desktop Publishing Special Interest Group. (She was the founding chair; I'm the current co-chair.) I started accumulating my first DTP samples through donated work in January 1986, and landed my first paying customer in April 1986.

That summer, I began experimenting with a Linotronic imagesetter. In September, I produced my first 16-page tabloid newspaper; the job took me 80 hours. A few years later, it took well under 20. With the help of expert and adventuresome technicians at Boston's Advanced Computer Graphics, one of the first imagesetting service bureaus (later the birthplace of the National Association of Desktop Publishers), we were able to get the memory-short imagesetters to print those Aldus Page-Maker 1.2 pages.

I've been a well-established DTPer since the spring of 1987. I've had over 75 institutional customers, about half of whom remain clients. Most, but not all, are nonprofit groups—national organizations like American Playhouse, the American Civil Liberties Union, the Africa Fund, the Ms. Foundation, Educators for Social Responsibility, as well as Cornell University, the NYC Department for the Aging, and small local environmental, arts, and social justice groups.

I enjoy working for causes I believe in. Though sometimes I make less money, I get the satisfaction of helping causes I care about. I donate services to at least one environmental or disarmament group at any time. I've also worked for corporate clients, including International Data Corporation's LINK Resources and TIME Inc, as well as investment research firms, recording studios,

and other businesses. I enjoy remaining a one-person operation, with over a half dozen subcontractors as needed.

My most difficult decisions came in 1987 when buying my first 20-megabyte hard disk drive, then my first laser printer. The barriers were psychological, not economic or technical. Until I decided to get the basic tools I needed, I wasn't really investing in myself—or taking my business goals seriously. Since then, I've been able to make choices about hardware based on more pragmatic considerations.

I got pretty far for quite a while with a basic system, first a Mac Plus and then with a 60-megabyte hard disk and 17-inch screen. In fact, with that now seemingly primitive setup, I did my biggest projects—24-page tabloid newspapers and a 350-page professional almanac, with lots of tables, for Facts On File.

I love not having to make excuses about getting the latest hardware. Ever since that first thrill of saving a file on a floppy disk back in 1981, I've been impatient. I buy new, faster computers soon after they arrive on the marketplace, and then sell the old model privately. The three I now have are my fifth, ninth, and eleventh models. My still-distant goal is instant screen refresh, no matter what changes I make.

If my current setup sounds intimidating, remember that I began earning money as a DTPer with one small-screen computer. I now use an 8-megabyte Macintosh IIfx with an external Storage Dimensions MacinStor 345-megabyte hard disk, an E-Machines

QuickView 21-inch gray-scale monitor and a Sony 13-inch color monitor. My backup system is a Macintosh SE/30 with an 80-megabyte internal drive plus a SyQuest-type 45-megabyte removable cartridge hard drive.

I also have a Sharp PC-7000 computer (used mainly to read 5¼-inch PC disks); a NEC CD-ROM player; an Apple Scanner; an Apple LaserWriter IINTX; an American Power Conversions uninterruptible power supply; a modem; a Ricoh Fax (that transmits all but one-eighth inch of a page); a small Canon photocopier, and two phone lines. Most of my equipment is piled on a convenient and versatile Ergotron workstation, and I sit on one of those strange-looking Balans chairs that keeps me sitting straight and using my back muscles.

Until this year, I worked out of a 125-square foot office in my apartment on Manhattan's Upper West Side. I enjoyed working at home and had little trouble keeping the personal and work sides of my life separate. The lack of a 24-hour doorman was my major problem. I improvised with a post office box, friendly neighbors, my wife's mid-town office, and a fax machine. In February, to make room for a new baby, I moved my office to a same-sized Riverside Drive studio, right around the corner.

I find the work continues to engage my interest. Before I feel stale, some new hardware or software shows up to liven things up. Consulting, training, and activity in the users' group keeps things popping. I've been giving workshops on DTP technology since 1986, including one in June 1987 to the NYPC user group called "So You Want To Be a Desktop Publisher," and I've written about DTP from time to time. Back in 1988, I wrote a two-page article, "Warm Hearts/Cold Type," that contained the kernel of this book.

Like most people, I'm always feeling behind on something—usually a combination of reading, invoicing, and upgrading. And as a writer turned DTPer, I sometimes feel the limitations of being a self-taught designer. I often dream of taking time off to get professional training in graphic design. And I keep looking at my bookshelf and wishing I could stop everything else until I knew three more software packages inside out.

photo: Beryl Goldberg

Maggie Lovaas: a career in DTP management

I've spent the last nine years involved in some way with the technology surrounding desktop publishing. Along the way, I've been a systems analyst, production person, marketer, consultant, and a staff and team manager. Through it all, what keeps me interested is how the applications evolve, and how evolving technology changes the way people can do their work and communicate ideas.

My interest in DTP technology started during a 10-year career at Xerox Corporation. After a stint with the copier division, I moved to the Printing Systems Division where the Xerox 9700 was doing revolutionary things. It was a very large, high-speed printer (two pages per second) with 300 dpi resolution, capable of changing fonts, and adding graphic elements. Up to 16 fonts could be printed on a single page! (This was back in 1981.) The 9700 printers were able to access mainframe data directly.

Prior to the 9700s, that output had gone to line printers with monospaced type and no flexibility for adding rules or digitized graphics.

During my tenure at Xerox, we introduced an electronic publishing software package, Xerox Integrated Composition System, that could create documents with features like headers and footers, as well as such sophisticated capabilities as multiple imposition so the pages could be bound easily. Eventually the capabilities of the 9700 migrated to a smaller printer, the 3700 product, thus fulfilling the need for distributed departmental printing.

Around that time I moved from being printing systems analyst to national systems manager for the team servicing AT&T. I handled the evolving requirements for applications from demanding end-users at places like Bell Labs. It was quite a challenge, compared to the traditional requirements of DP managers. For example, simple tabular reports were no longer sufficient. And the scientists at Bell Labs wouldn't take "it can't be done" for an answer.

With Apple's introduction of the Laser-Writer and DTP software in 1985, I recognized that this was a system that would not only do what Xerox could, but had the added benefit of PostScript as a page description language. With PostScript came greater flexibility in the handling of type and graphics, and a virtual end to the insufficient font memory problems that had plagued earlier implementations. Today we rarely reflect on what a breakthrough it was to be able to place text and graphics easily on a single page. It seemed revolutionary at the time.

In March 1985, I co-founded NYC's first DTP service bureau, Software Output Services. (Felix was my first customer.) We started with a 512K Mac and the first LaserWriter shipped to NYC, renting time on the computer for output to the LaserWriter. Eventually we added DTP production work, slides, disk conversion and MS-DOS equipment.

I recruited staff from graphic designers and computer science university students. I took the management route and drifted away from the actual hands-on work. The business grew to two locations, with a staff of 10 full- and part-time people. Those were the days of early versions of DTP software, with limited fonts and features. How slow the system was! I sometimes thought I could take a vacation and the last pages would just be emerging from the printer when I returned.

As the business grew, I realized I was being pulled further and further from the corporate market I enjoyed most. So in September, 1987, I founded Acanthus Associates, a DTP consulting and production firm. With one full-time systems consultant plus freelancers, I set out my shingle in NYC's NoHo neighborhood.

I targeted my business to corporate clients, helping them set up and maintain DTP centers. Back at the office we undertook production of large-scale books, technical and how-to manuals for firms like John Wiley & Sons, Macmillan and W.H. Freeman.

Mostly, I did consulting plus sales and management. I was always very careful to pay my subcontractors weekly. That attracted and kept the best people NYC had to offer, but it was painful on the cash flow.

My 2,500 square feet was more than I needed, so I sublet part of my space to two very talented graphic designers, Ken Godat and Jeff Jonczyk. The relationship with their firm, Godat/Jonczyk, proved a great success. They gave us design expertise, while still maintaining their own client base. Our collaborations produced the most successful and best-looking projects from Acanthus Associates. Ken and Jeff currently maintain offices in both NYC and Tucson, but we still work together via phone, fax, modem, and overnight deliveries.

In my continuing work with corporate facilities, I increasingly came to see DTP as part of a corporate information strategy for electronic distribution, networking, and information flows. DTP became less a "nice to have" capability and more a key way to meet the business needs of corporations.

My changing outlook led to my affiliation with Fintec Corporation, an information management consulting and system design firm serving corporate clients. Fintec, founded in 1983, has offices in Mt. Kisco, NY, in NYC, Oakland, CA, and has 29 bright, energetic people on staff. We now share adjacent office space and a view of DTP as yet another way of managing information.

In addition to understanding the ins and outs of DTP, we offer corporate DTP centers software for job tracking, cost accounting and charge-back systems to bill work back to departments.

I manage projects through subcontracting to individuals who have been with me for years: On Far Tse (profiled in this book) for systems, Peng Olaguera for production expertise, Steven Gorney for graphic design and illustration and training, and K.C. Genzmer for training. We expand with others when there's a need. I consider myself lucky to be surrounded by their talent and enthusiasm.

APPENDIX 1.
CORPORATE DESKTOP PUBLISHING

Someone will soon write an entire book on the subject of corporate DTP departments. Until then, here's a look at your particular concerns, as distinct from those faced by DTPers starting their own businesses.

Your senior management has read about DTP and is inspired to consolidate your company's publishing operations and reduce outside expenditures for typesetting.

The project falls in your lap. It's your job to make it all work.

Or maybe you're the ambitious employee who wants to introduce DTP technology to management, or make a pitch for integrating the diverse capabilities scattered around in the company. Perhaps you'd like to run the corporate publishing center that results. When you're done, your company's publishing schedule, communications, and output will be improved—and we hope your costs will be lower. But it's a challenging job for you, and it may not make your boss's life simpler, either.

You'll be working with more PCs, more printers and networks, and more people. You'll face increased complexities and a bigger job coordinating how projects get done.

Why companies make the switch

Setting up a corporate installation can be as simple as buying and hooking up one computer and one laser printer as a seed unit. But it usually involves much more. Typically, a medium-size corporation will bring in 10-15 systems to establish a corporate publishing center. A newspaper could use twice that many units, and they may span wide distances. Maggie has helped coordinate the creation of a complex nationwide DTP operation so 14 bases scattered around the country could work together and produce consistent sales proposals.

Whatever the size or the nature of a corporate DTP center, people create, maintain and enlarge one to:

- Control creation of documents by bringing the process in house;
- Ensure a consistent style and look for the company's internal and external publications;
- Create a better public image for their company through better looking publications;
- Improve internal communications through higher quality and more frequent publications;
- Gain the ability to create, update, and turn around files 24 hours a day, seven days a week;
- Reduce time and money spent sending out for type;
- Cut operating costs by centralizing publishing functions previously spread out among subsidiaries or departments;
- Gain a competitive edge in the marketplace through improved publications and capabilities to generate personalized documents;
- Leverage existing investments in equipment, supplies, and people;
- Upgrade jobs of existing personnel, giving them more interesting and satisfying work;
- Take advantage of the in-house tools in ways they can't yet foresee. Maggie finds that potential clients never think of their internal phone directory as a publishing candidate, but invariably make it an early DTP project.

In the 1990s, everyone wants to save money. But when some people talk about the benefits of DTP, they don't emphasize cost savings. Rather, they concentrate on improvement in product quality and control over deadlines. Yet that first item is often another way of saying that they are able to produce much more work within their budget, which isn't very different than cost savings after all.

If you're looking for ways to document and illustrate corporate DTP's benefits and savings, *The Hammermill Guide to Desktop Publishing in Business* includes an section that outlines the benefits of in-house DTP systems using a corporate vocabulary, giving lots of specific numbers, and including flow-charts, bar charts, and other illustrations that you can present. (See **Appendix 2. Books on DTP and graphic design**.) You'll also find case studies and profiles that describe cost savings in practically every issue of the DTP monthlies.

Planning the change

Creating a DTP center or making a transition to a group publishing process will transform the way many things are done in a company. Change can be tricky, especially if it's done without planning or when office politics take over. A decision may have been made to set up a DTP center or enlarge the existing center without a clear picture of the justification.

First comes the motivation for the change. Then do your research. You'll need to tell management the answers to a few simple questions:

- Where are we today?
- Where do we want to be?
- What will it take to get from here to there?

These topics are often handled informally—in a hallway, at the tail end of a meeting called to discuss another problem, or over a cup of coffee in the lunch room. Maggie has found that this treatment of these topics can lead to miscommunication and problems down the road. *Don't be casual.*

Before putting pen to paper, talk with others in the company and consider forming a taskforce. Of course, a taskforce evokes images of needless meetings, pompous memos, and inconclusive results. But if you're charged with developing or expanding a DTP center, you need to bring in everyone who will be involved or affected. If you overlook or avoid anyone, that neglect will come back to haunt you. You may get pretty far with one-on-one discussions, but you'll probably need meetings.

Who should you to include in your investigation? Talk with the owner of the problem, if it's not you. That's the person with ultimate responsibility for what you are trying to achieve through DTP. It could be your manager or the vice president of marketing. Get a handle on that person's problems and expectations. From the start, see if you can get a sense of how much money and personnel the company is willing to commit to the center. If nobody gives you an answer, feel free to take as your starting point what you think the company needs.

If your company is large enough to have its own management information systems (MIS) department, get the big picture from them. How is your firm's network and information flow handled? How will DTP fit in? What kind of support you can expect?

When DTP first filtered into corporations, MIS people often reacted with mistrust or open hostility to requests for equipment and software. Frequently, the MIS manager was unfamiliar with the tools for graphics and type, or the requests challenged company standards, especially when someone in an all-IBM installation asked for a Macintosh. The trend now is toward a more flexible attitude as DTP's benefit to corporations becomes more apparent.

Talk with your finance people to see if anyone has a handle on what the entire company now spends on publishing. See if you can break out typography, graphics, design, photocopying, audio-visual, and printing costs. You may want to look at departmental photocopying policies and expenses to separate the cost of reproducing correspondence from the cost of producing manuals and similar multiple-copy jobs. See if you can find out existing company purchasing and bidding procedures.

Explore with the personnel or human resources manager what will happen as job titles change, along with job levels and career paths. With DTP, job boundaries can blur. Editors may be doing layouts. Designers may be rewriting. Secretaries may be modifying standard documents on templates. Should they be paid more for their redefined jobs? If they feel they're working harder without better pay, you're in for trouble. Certainly, we feel that people with new responsibilities and skills should be paid more. This is a hot issue and it needs to appear in the budget of your feasibility study or plan.

Establish who the new center's client is. Will the work come from throughout the company? Will some work continue to go outside? Chances are, you won't be starting off with any responsibility for your firm's annual report, consumer advertising, logos, or product packaging. But maybe the manager who gave you the assignment has this in mind in the long run.

Speak to all users and potential users of the center. You'll have to keep them all happy to flourish, and their needs will influence the tools you buy and the people you hire.

You need to include offset printing in your analysis, if the DTP center wasn't expected to include printing. The amount of printing may differ as documents go from typewritten to typeset, and with the new center, more or less use may be made of in-house photocopiers. If the company already has in-house offset printing capabilities, perhaps it should get out of that business and send that work out. If it doesn't, maybe it should acquire them, as well as binding capabilities. All this needs to be included as part of your analysis of a DTP center's functions and potential benefits.

Preparing your report

Now you're ready to develop a report to management. Your report can be a few pages or it might run several chapters.

Where we are. Determine how documents are currently being created by using our checklist for the major topics. Copy the list in **Fig. A1. Where we are** on the following page, adding to, or deleting from it to tailor it for your company needs. It's meant to guide you, but you may need to add your own firm's unique issues. For each item on the list, describe your current operation and list your current costs. Take time with this checklist, because it will become the backbone of your study.

Where we want to be. State explicitly the reasons why you're proposing to establish or expand your company's DTP capability. It could for an entirely different reason than those we listed above. It might reflect your corporation's overall strategic plan: Where is the company headed? Or it might reflect a tactical plan: How will the company implement its policies?

You'll need to justify your recommendations with a cost-benefit analysis. Management will be most interested in these concepts, not in the pros and cons of buying hardware or where the center will be located.

What it will take to get there. Now comes the fun part. You have the opportunity to be resourceful in seeking out information and to be creative in your problem solving.

Start with lots of research. Read, read, read DTP magazines articles and reviews. (See **Appendix 2.**) To be aware of trends in DTP and its impact in your particular industry, read industry and general business periodicals. Contact vendors for product specifications. If you have the muscle, get a list from vendors of corporate sites using their products and managers who will talk to you. Ask them why they chose products, find out about unresolved problems, service, installation, reliability, and software support. Seeing tools in use and talking to their users is far more valuable than reading reviews or watching demonstrations.

Check out your local user group. Look at demos in stores. Attend trade shows and seminars. The Seybold seminars are excellent for corporate users, but they're expensive. If your corporation picks up the fee, not only will you get the latest information, you'll be surrounded by other corporate DTP types so you can learn from them while you find out about the latest trends.

WHERE WE ARE

type of work

- [ ] reports
- [ ] technical documentation
- [ ] financial reports
- [ ] sales proposals
- [ ] marketing materials
- [ ] advertising materials
- [ ] catalogs
- [ ] forms
- [ ] direct mail
- [ ] brochures
- [ ] newsletters
- [ ] books
- [ ] magazines
- [ ] other

present equipment

- [ ] hardware
- [ ] software
- [ ] network
- [ ] backup
- [ ] modem
- [ ] copier
- [ ] fax

production

- [ ] length
- [ ] frequency
- [ ] resolution requirement
- [ ] content
  - [ ] text
  - [ ] graphics
  - [ ] business charts
  - [ ] scanned images
    - [ ] for position only
    - [ ] final
  - [ ] illustrations
  - [ ] photographs
  - [ ] page layout
    - [ ] simple
    - [ ] complex
- [ ] color requirements
  - [ ] spot
  - [ ] process
- [ ] reproduction & binding
  - [ ] copying
  - [ ] printing
- [ ] distribution

procedures

- [ ] job tracking
- [ ] archiving

*Fig. A1
Checklist for
a corporate
DTP center*

departmental structure

- ☐ job titles
- ☐ job levels

personnel skills

- ☐ data entry
- ☐ copy editing
- ☐ proofreading
- ☐ writing
- ☐ design
- ☐ illustration & graphics
- ☐ page layout
- ☐ pasteup
- ☐ management
- ☐ support services

workflow — schedule

- ☐ input
- ☐ design
- ☐ composition
- ☐ revision cycles
- ☐ final approval
- ☐ reproduction
- ☐ distribution

company-wide MIS structure

- ☐ standard platform
- ☐ standard software
- ☐ telecommunications
- ☐ network

corporate graphics standards

- ☐ design
- ☐ paper type/color

current costs for doing work

- ☐ salaries and benefits
- ☐ hardware/software
- ☐ telephones
- ☐ training
- ☐ outside vendors & consultants
- ☐ service agreements
- ☐ wiring & cabling
- ☐ supplies
- ☐ space costs

money issues

- ☐ source of budget allocation
- ☐ signing authority

from Acanthus Associates

If the scope of the job or the technical requirements exceed your expertise, bring in an outside DTP consultant. If you're unsure about areas like networking and training, don't punt.

Cost and profit centers

Corporate publishing is big time. Interconsult, a Cambridge, Massachusetts firm, estimates that U.S. companies spend 6-10% of their gross revenues on printing and publishing. Thus the dollars in corporate DTP are a major motivating factor and concern.

As an in-house DTP center, you'll operate in one of two modes: **cost center** or **profit center**. In a cost center, management understands that the DTP center will be an expense. As a profit center, they will look upon it as a business within a business.

As a cost center, your managers are saying they're looking to some of the less quantifiable benefits of a DTP center, rather than explicitly to reduce its expenditures. For instance, they value the convenience of having an in-house, central facility for producing documents. Or they believe the DTP center will enhance the company's sales, through more timely distribution of key information that's been slow in getting out to salespeople or customers.

As a profit center, management expects you to charge other departments for your services and to be charged by other departments for their services to you. If clients don't like the service, quality, or costs you provide, they can go outside, unless they're constrained by an edict from top management. This can motivate the DTP center to provide quality work. Management expects the center to turn a profit within a reasonable period of time, and in some cases, even start taking in work from outside the company.

Tracking, allocating, and controlling costs will be an issue in both cases. But the future of the profit center will be directly linked to its profitability. In this case, the methods and assumptions of cost analysis need to become explicit, and a part of your initial proposal. Both will scrutinize costs. But the profit center will either survive or not, depending on its profit.

Centralized versus decentralized operations

Early on, many large companies had departmental or unit-level DTP centers with each functioning on its own and no company-wide consistency or design standards. These fiefdoms became entrenched. People in departments liked the convenience of having DTP capabilities on their desktops, and managers liked having a department producing fabulous documents. Some DTP centers became hot properties, with territorial battles raging over who owned or had access to the capability. Anyone who tried to take it away saw the reaction.

Sometimes a decentralized setup will continue to make sense by allowing more flexibility, faster turnaround, and reducing bureaucracy. But the department may lose the corporation's bulk purchasing power. Less coordination and accountability may be costly in terms of productivity.

We've heard about highly trained engineers who start spending more time trying out fonts than on the content of their reports. DTP can be fun. But unless a person wants to switch jobs, in this kind of situation, engineers should probably restrict their graphic ambitions to after-hours experiments on non-company projects.

On the other hand, sometimes individual departments have developed an efficient process, enabling the people most in touch with the information to update their documents rapidly. Or giving people in departments some creative authority has resulted in unusual but successful publications that have produced more than the company would have gotten from publications constrained by company-wide standards. In such cases, even as the rest of the company centralizes, some departments might retain DTP capabilities. They could work with the center to standardize formats.

Centralization clarifies accountability and maximizes the company's clout with vendors, but can come at the price of less flexibility and a reduced sense of urgency in completing documents.

To centralize or decentralize? The argument never goes away. Sometimes it comes down to political clout—with DTP as a symbol of power. Sometimes MIS people, with little understanding of DTP, are brought into the power struggle. Or you, the inside or outside DTP consultant, may end up as the umpire. In ideal circumstances, it comes down to what's best overall for the corporation and its long-term goals.

Some specifics

The same approaches we outlined for entrepreneurs in 5. **Assembling Your Toolbox** apply to corporations. You may need bigger backup systems to handle many files, as well as archival capabilities with selective restore capabilities. Magneto-optical storage and tape backup will also be worth exploring. You'll also be looking at electronic mail, passwords and encryption for data, printer spoolers and file servers.

Local area networks (LANs) are essential to improve communications in a multiple-user DTP center. They make it easier to share and archive files, while keeping important data easily accessible to all network users.

LANs present challenges to ensure compatibility of equipment, software, and document formats. If you have an in-house MIS group to help with your LAN, that's a place to start, though even they may need some outside help. Otherwise, it's best to get a consultant who specializes in networking.

LANs vary according to how much traffic and how many people are on the network. The simplest one is SneakerNet, but corporations rarely find physically transporting floppy disks from computer to computer to be effective. Entry level LANs are small networks with about four to six users. They use low-cost, easy-to-install modular telephone cords. Macintosh AppleShare and PC PCnet are some "no-frills" but adequate software for entry-level networks.

If you have many more users, you may need a server and more sophisticated network software from companies like Novell or 3Com. Shielded coaxial cables and more elaborate networks like Ethernet will move data much more quickly and reliably; they also demand much more expertise to install and maintain. Even more tricky can be bridges and gateways, which allow incompatible devices to talk to one another, and geographically separated sites to connect.

Wireless technologies, from Motorola and other companies, are in place, but await Federal Communications Commission approval. They could replace hard-wired LANs in some circumstances.

Standards. Corporations may have graphic standards defining type and style for printed documents. If your company lacks such standards, the time to do it —budgeting time *and* money for it—is when you establish a DTP center. This way, your publications will reinforce the corporate identity and reflect its intentions rather than the personal agendas of the individuals who happen to have been producing documents.

You'll also need a company editorial style sheet for abbreviations, acronyms, titles, product names, similar to the one described in **Fig.** 7.7. While you're at it, you should work to establish computer file format standards for text and graphics to facilitate file exchanges as well as telecommunications exchange standards within a location and among various sites. The standards you select may influence your choice of hardware and software.

Personnel. In planning how you will staff your center, start with a clean slate when considering who is the best person for each job. Look at qualifications, experience, and training needs. You may need to hire new staff or simply reorganize and improve coordination of existing corporate personnel. The key question to ask is, "Who will have overall responsibility for the center?"

> We've been lucky because we've always managed to find good computer-oriented people. We don't do anything extraordinary: We just advertise in the newspaper classifieds. It's important for us to have people who have at least some sort of experience in graphic design work and who've been involved in work close to what our department does. They have to be very computer literate and know about production. Generally speaking, they are young, and early in their career paths. I don't try to kid anybody that I'm looking for someone who is going to stay in the job for life. One discussion that has been going on within Wiley over the last couple of years is over the value and worth of these jobs. How should they be priced? How should a salary and compensation be structured? It's easy to find people for $40,000 a year to do DTP. It's more of a trick to find someone for $25,000 who knows their stuff, can produce, be a team player, and has the enthusiasm and capability to learn. —*Paul Constantine*

Training. Because DTP is always changing and staff come and go, training will not only be a start-up cost, it will be a continuing expense. Money spent on equipment does not guarantee its effectiveness. Training costs money, not only for the classroom expenses, but also for the lost work time. Explore all the options presented in **1. Ways to learn it.** Be aggressive in leveraging your buying power. If you are pricing out training costs, look for discounted rates for training several people, and carefully compare on-site and their-site training programs.

The physical plant

Start by planning the work flow, and take into account any shared peripherals that will need to be accessible to many people. Start with your planned location, and its existing wiring, and lighting. Decide if you'll be running cabling along the floor, walls, or ceiling. A diagram of a floor plan will show you how much work you'll have to rearrange your workspace.

Keep ergonomics in mind. Operators should have no windows directly facing or right behind them. Tests show that most of the potentially dangerous emissions from video displays come from the rear of the monitor, so lining up desks or workstations one behind the other may be a bad idea. (See **6. Remember to protect your health.**) You'll need to keep electronic equipment out of direct sunlight. You'll also need to store paper properly. If it's exposed to too much humidity, it may jam in your printers.

If your center will be producing publications for the entire company, security may be an issue: The entire space might need to be secured from casual passersby. If the company is a nine-to-five operation, but you expect your center to be a place for much last-minute or round-the-clock work, you might give consideration to establishing a separate entrance from outside the building.

Costing it out

Costs associated with operating a DTP center include:

- Management and administration;
- Overhead for the space;
- Hardware, software, supplies, and service;
- Staff salaries and freelance costs.

Attach a cost estimate to each of your recommendations. To avoid sticker shock among top management, you could project a multi-phase schedule for acquiring equipment and expanding staff over the next 12 quarters. This way, you'll also be able to project cost savings over several years. It also makes cost savings easy to realize since they're spread out over several years. Fill out the checklist for current year, next year, and the following one.

Your company may have established purchasing agreements with vendors giving major cost savings. But these vendors may limit your choices, and they may be pushing certain equipment. Or worse, they may know nothing about DTP. Find out as soon as possible how flexibly you can work with a local dealer or a VAR, and whether you can order from the discount mail-order outfits. Get at least three vendors' prices. Be aggressive in asking for volume discounts.

Determine whether the volume of work justifies the cost of the DTP center. Demand is the key. You can quantify existing and forecasted demand from your analysis of "Where we are" and "Where we want to be." Keep in mind however, that establishing a center is similar to installing a copier. Work will ooze in from all sorts of unexpected places, so aim for more capacity.

Management will be looking hard at costs and justification: Avoid the temptation to project unrealistic cost saving through DTP. Take into full consideration the costs of training and of working out the kinks in operations. Remember what happened when word processing arrived? The scope and frequency of revisions to many documents rose from two or three to five to 10. After establishing a DTP center, you'll be tempted to work much harder to make publications look better. And if you start getting into more high-end production with color printing, you may throw out all your schedules. Don't expect to stick with your existing timetables for editing and production cycles.

Making it all work

When you get the go-ahead and are ready to start, take it in stages. As you phase in the new, keep your existing procedures in place for quite a while as a backup.

Operate the new or expanded center initially as a pilot program. Everyone will know it's a startup period, and you'll keep their judgments in abeyance.

Confirm all your wiring and cabling changes before the equipment arrives. It's sometimes difficult to coordinate vendors, but don't sign off on the electrical work until you know it's right. Otherwise, you may spend lots of time troubleshooting the wrong problems, especially for networking.

Startup is a period of training, adjusting jobs, and tracking mechanisms to ensure reliability and productivity. It's also a time to educate management. Too often, management expects instant confirmation of the wisdom of the DTP investment. They may want to put the just-installed tools and the new staff to unreasonable and premature tests. Learning DTP procedures and techniques takes time. If you don't spend enough time on training, the pressured staff will start off with awkward and time-consuming workarounds.

Don't avoid management, involve them. Give them a demo, show them the results, let them see where the money was spent. Stress the contribution of DTP design to your company's image.

As soon as you're ready, let your company know you exist, with some inside marketing and sales for the center. Help the word get out by producing high-visibility documents. Obviously, the first issue of a full-circulation in-house newsletter should profile and explain the center. Arrange for a high-level person to write a company-wide memo announcing the center.

At the same time, you will need to restrict the center's functions. If you choose to allow any personal use of the equipment, you'll have to strictly define guidelines. We've seen family Thanksgiving menus, directions to the summer cabin, and silly clip art on all kinds of documents. The issue is not only control of company resources, but also the danger to the equipment and corporate data that could result from unauthorized or inexpert use. Be very, very clear as to what the publishing setup is for and who gets to use it.

Once you're rolling, you need to produce. You'll be striving for:

- **Quality,** or you'll never gain credibility with management;
- **Service,** because departments need to see you as responsive;
- **Efficiency,** or cost overruns will be prohibitive and you'll be seen as unreliable.

Who does what

Analyze all the functions in the center and assign a person to perform each one:

- design
- writing
- production
- proofreading
- customer service
- vendor contact
- freelance contact
- printing buyer
- system administrator
- manager
- quality control
- distribution
- repairs
- utilization analysis

There's a lot to do. Of course, at a small center, one or two people may handle all of these functions, but spell it out. Put a name next to each function and circulate the list so everyone knows who does what.

You'll be looking for three types of personnel: permanent staff, temporary personnel, and freelancers. You'll need to have yourself covered for times when key people are sick, on vacation, or leave the company with little notice.

Your existing graphics production people will probably be able to learn to use DTP tools. That's usually easier than taking people who know all about computers and training them in the technical and aesthetic concepts of publishing.

Look for permanent staff by advertising in local papers and user group newsletters. Call the placement departments of local colleges with computer graphics or computer science departments and ask about work-study programs. Call temporary agencies *before* a crisis to find out what support they can offer. Note their rates and hours. Start to build a stable of freelancers, especially those with special expertise. Try them out on small projects to find the professional, dependable ones you can keep on call.

With freelancers, pay particular attention to whether they'll be working at home or at the center. The government regards anyone in your office as an employee and subject to taxes. Strictly speaking, freelancers should be working on their own equipment, not on your company's hardware. They'll need 1099 tax forms, so check with your personnel department on procedures for payment and taxes.

Establishing workflows

Develop a set routine for work flowing through the center. Even in a very small set-up, you'll need formal procedures. They'll make you, and everyone around you, more efficient and effective. Because corporate documents often need multiple reviews—by the originating department, legal, corporate communications, and top management—you'll need ways to keep jobs on track and on schedule. Companies with informal or inadequate procedures may find themselves going backward: getting back a proof incorporating new changes, but not reflecting the previous set of changes.

Organization can ease the production of even the most demanding technical documentation as it goes through multiple edits, redesigns, reorganizations, and reincarnations. It can protect you against slip-ups, such as that most typical error: failure to update a table of contents to reflect changes inside a document. In addition to the suggestions in **6. Backing up** and **7. Tracking and managing large jobs**, you'll need to create standard ways to handle all jobs that come in to the center:

- Establish a specific place for new jobs.
- Assign a job ticket (see **Fig. A2** on the following page).

TRACKING SHEET
(produce on wide page for large comment area)

Fig. A2
Job ticket

from Acanthus Associates

Name	Client	File Name	Graphics				
	Contact	Location 1	Page Size				
Date In	Address	Location 2	Page Orientation				
		Applications	Print Setup				
Date Out			Driver Required				
	Telephone	Fonts	Total Pages				
Due			Others				
Date	Things to do/Comments		Done	Operator	In	Out	Hours
	etc., down the page						

- Assign deadlines to each stage or facet of every project, with one person responsible for meeting that deadline. Assign an overall project manager for large jobs.
- Enter each job in a log book or computer-based tracking system. The tracking system should have two types of forms: job sheets and print orders. It should track just where work is: current, in a revision cycle, completed, or at the printer.
- Post a production board with erasable magic marker showing the status of each job.
- Put work in a folder with sealed sides. Chances are you've seen printers' job jackets—that's what we're talking about. Put the job ticket inside or on the front.
- Establish a specific place for jobs that are open—incomplete but not being actively worked on.
- Develop a procedure to archive completed jobs on paper and on disk or tape.
- Keep files for completed work by department, product, or outside client.
- Assign one person to be the primary contact for each job, and one person to be the liaison for printers and print brokers.
- Consider creating a center database. Maggie has helped develop formats to record and analyze the time spent on each job, software versions used, staff members involved, departmental assignment of charges for work, all the file names that make up the project, and to analyze costs and productivity.

Working efficiently in groups

The DTP center can have a different relationship to its customers than the independent DTPer. In theory, you are trying to increase efficiency and productivity company-wide. At every juncture, you could be asking, "Who should be doing this phase of the job?" If the originator of a publication can spend two hours preparing text to save the center four hours of cleanup, the company or institution benefits. On the other hand, every department has different levels of staff resources, and everyone is paid differently. Politics may intervene here. Some departments may be reluctant to take on more of the work in preparing publications.

In ideal circumstances, DTP center staff will find a way to establish and explain who is responsible for content, spelling, syntax, and computer formats. Staff will talk with each in-house client to straighten out responsibility and reduce finger-pointing later. A company-wide editorial style sheet should help improve the consistency of copy coming from all departments. (See **Fig. 7.7**.)

Beyond that basic starting point, you'll need to establish guidelines for the work process between the center and departmental clients and for the center's internal work process.

> People kept asking us for help. "This will take just a few minutes." "We have just a few changes." "Just a few lines of type, please." "Just one more." After a few months of this, I just wanted to punch them out. They weren't being nasty, simply unaware of what they were asking. We made a poster in our department. We hung it on a wall over the equipment so it was the first thing people would see when they walked in. "Wait a minute," I'd say, and point to the strange wallpaper. "We don't let that word in this room. Now what can I do for you?" People slowly got the message.   —*Joel Landy*

Although you'll have one person as the primary contact for each job, and the source of the work may also have a similar liaison person, more people will be involved on both ends. You'll need to establish who talks to whom, who is responsible for the entire copyediting and checking process, who decides whether the client or the center does revisions and corrections, and who assigns and monitors deadlines. You'll need to educate your departmental clients, so they understand the consequences of repeated revisions for meeting deadlines.

> Working in a company, you often deal indirectly with people giving deadlines. There may be several layers between you and the client. The

> people in the middle may not know what the project is about, but each
> may add a cushion by asking for it sooner than they need it. And they
> know the boss wouldn't mind getting it earlier. Getting the truth about
> deadlines is very important, but the people in the middle may be of no use
> in discovering the truth.   —*Joel Landy*

Within the center, you'll need to make sure staffers understand every step in the
production process—and don't skip any of them. Your institution will already
have ways of handling all these issues, established while contracting out publishing jobs. The establishment of the DTP center is an opportunity to re-think
the answers you already have and improve those that don't work well.

Special considerations for groups

The same issues of choosing platforms that individual DTPers face will also
come up in corporate centers. (See **5. PC versus Macintosh**.)

> What is going to be an issue in the corporate environment is who
> determines platforms. It really isn't the desktop publishing community
> inside corporations that determines the platform, it's everybody else.
> That is something I think people tend to overlook. For example, if you
> need to download stuff from the mainframe there are better ways to do it
> with an IBM than with a Macintosh. If you can download all of your sales
> statistics neatly into Excel and blast a beautiful graph inside of a minute
> with a couple of keystrokes, the issue of the Macintosh won't ever come
> up. The DTP shop will have to buy equipment compatible with "every-
> one else."   —*Susan Glinert Stevens*

DTP centers that frequently exchange files between PCs and Macs may be
tripped up occasionally by the uneven pace of software releases. During much
of 1990, many of these departments couldn't take advantage of the new features
of PageMaker 4 on the Mac because they needed to create files that could be
moved back to the PC, where Aldus was still only up to version 3.

Increasingly, software publishers are aiming for simultaneous release on all
platforms, but this remains only a goal. Releases for the Mac and MS-DOS
operating systems have their own schedules, as do those for Windows. OS/2
usually comes last. Until all your software is equalized, you can avoid the lowest-
common-denominator principle only at the cost of a less integrated operation.

Consider taking advantage of the latest electronic solutions. For instance, the
latest software category to emerge is **groupware**. That's software that enables
agglomerations of people, not necessarily in one place, to schedule, commu-

nicate and work together on common projects. One of its simplest forms is software that enables many people to annotate documents, adding their comments consecutively, so that at the end one person can see who suggested what and combine all the changes. One program for the Macintosh, MainstayMarkUp, uses the Post-it metaphor, with notes pasted onto particular parts of a document. Ashton-Tate FullWrite Professional and Microsoft Word for Windows have annotation capabilities. Broderbund For Comment for the PC allows a group to pass a disk around to different people, collecting their suggestions. Each can see the others' changes, cuts, and additions. Then the originator or editor can pick and choose what to accept. Farallon Annotator is an announced product that promises more advances in groupware.

> I define groupware as a range, from working on the same document from two different workstations to $30,000 document-management software. There's a low level of awareness in people running production teams that this kind of group effort—a distributive process concept—is possible, available, or efficient. But there is no question that it will come.
> —*Bob Mc Dowell*

Many of the industry-standard software packages are now able to accommodate more than one user working on different parts of a document at the same time. Using a local area network, a team can work on a FrameMaker document.

Another solution migrating down from high-end workstations is software that includes live links between page layout software and word processor, spreadsheet, and graphics files. With all files kept on a central server computer, changes in source files can be incorporated automatically in the page layout document. In some cases, the live links are bi-directional, so changes in the page layout document will be reflected back to the source files. (See **5. Your software starter kit.**)

These capabilities make coordination and tracking even more important as they make workgroup publishing a reality on desktop computers. New software is emerging to manage the flow of documents. Some packages include Odesta Document Management System for the Macintosh and VAX, and New Riders Desktop Manager for PC Ventura Publisher.

Another useful solution can begin as soon as the center has established a smooth relationship with one departmental customer. If one person in the department is interested and willing, the staff can work with that person to explain the style sheets and tags used for the department's regular publications. You can provide a printout sample of all of these elements and train the person to pre-format the text using codes that will turn into styles and tags. You don't have to include every single style you use. If you can show a person how to code just three levels of heads and subheads and two or three kinds of body type, you'll significantly speed the production process and reduce the center's costs. But you're asking for more work from the client, and you're asking them to clutter up their documents with keystrokes that will be distracting in early proofs. At the same time, you're also asking them to turn their writing and editing into a much more organized process, where they think more deeply about the characteristics and organization of their texts as they produce them. It only happens when you find a cooperative and enthusiastic person on the other end.

The approach to editing and production of one small book publishing company, New Riders, is summarized in *Managing Desktop Publishing*. (See **Appendix 2. Books on the business of graphics and DTP.**) Though it describes a process optimized for Ventura Publisher on the PC, the book has useful material for anyone.

Maggie gets calls from exasperated clients who say the work isn't getting out fast enough. Often management hasn't provided adequate tools: The PCs are too slow, or they haven't set up a file server, or network. The key to productivity in groups is efficient sharing of data. Without sufficiently powerful tools, the center cannot succeed.

Managing technical operations

The system administrator will be responsible for managing overall standards and efficiency, including:

- Naming data files and organizing them in folders or directories;
- Naming and organizing style sheets and tags, and updating and distributing them to staff and authors;
- Maintaining and upgrading software applications;
- Troubleshooting;
- Regularly backing up and archiving of current and past files.

This will be your center's key job and a crucial determinant of a smoothly running operation. Don't assign system administration as an afterthought. In a small center, it might be the same person as the center manager, or it might be a well-organized person or a computer expert from outside the department entirely. You can also retain a systems consultant on a monthly basis.

Set up rules for naming files and for documenting the work done on each file. Ideally, any center staffer should be able to sit down at any computer and locate and make sense of the files for jobs in progress. (See 7. **Name your files with care.**)

Post important hot line and service numbers.

Find ways to minimize unnecessary interruptions from callers and people walking in. Assign one person to handle this traffic.

You'll need to find ways to accommodate company employees who want to come to the center to work with you. Depending on the individual and the nature of the work, this collaboration can save time or be disruptive. If you have the space and budget, and if employees from other departments used to do their own DTP, you might want to set aside one workstation for visiting collaborators.

Cost tracking

Think of the center as a small business, because somewhere in your company someone is looking at the bottom line. You'll need to know how much each part of each job cost the center. (See 7. **Tracking your time**). And you'll need to track supplies, hardware, software upgrade costs, and personnel expenses.

For cost centers, you'll have to figure how to charge back departments for the work you do for them. Much of the discussion in 10. **Pricing and Bidding** will apply. You'll use an approach similar to that of the small DTP business. It's just that the numbers get larger.

Determine which department uses the center most often. Do this monthly so you're always prepared for management questions. You may want to lay the groundwork to go back and analyze the results of the center's work for particular departments or the entire company, compared to the "Where are we now" data you developed at the feasibility stage.

If the center isn't able to find and retain qualified and capable staff, management may see choosing software, staying up to date, and keeping the operation running as one large headache. Unless you've developed effective approaches to recruitment, training, job enrichment, incentives, and work management, your company may decide a center isn't worth the effort. (See 14. **Where will DTPers end up?**)

Getting a job at a corporate DTP center

If you're looking for a position in corporate DTP, start by looking in industrial and financial services corporations, publishing, design, communications, and advertising companies. If you're an artist or illustrator with a good command of drawing, computer-assisted design, color or illustration software, you'll have a good shot at finding full- or part-time work at practically any newspaper or magazine in the country. They're all increasing their use of computer graphics. In large companies that haven't centralized their DTP operations, you're likely to find centers in marketing, training, corporate communications, sales support, technical documentation, human resources, and public relations departments. Starting to work at a company through a temporary agency can be a good way to check it out. (See **11. Reducing your overhead**.)

Remember, too, that often your best way in will be to keep your ears close to the ground at your local computer user group meeting.

APPENDIX 2. RESOURCES

For the books and magazines listed, try your local bookstore, the national chain stores, college, business, and arts school libraries. For the specialized books we've given contact information; training centers and service bureaus are a good source for publications. You're also likely to find that any DTPer who's been around for some time will have many of these already. Some 800 numbers don't work in the state where the company is headquartered. If you don't get through, before searching too hard, ask a friend in another state to try the same number. Or call directory assistance at (800) 555-1212.

General business books

Hawken, Paul. *Growing a Business*. Simon & Schuster, 1988, $7.95. The New Age manual telling you how you can succeed in business and still feel good about yourself.

Peters, Thomas J., and Robert H. Waterman, Jr. *In Search of Excellence*. Warner Books, 1982, $9.95. The grandparent of the recent crop of books on business, it's still the best of the books emphasizing staying close to your customers, sticking to what you do well, and appreciating your employees.

Phillips, Michael, and Salli Rasberry. *Honest Business*. Random House, 1981, $7.00. Complements *Growing a Business*.

von Oech, Roger. *A Whack on the Side of the Head, How to Unlock Your Mind for Innovation*. Warner Books, 1988. $11.95. *A Kick In The Seat Of The Pants: Using Your Explorer, Artist, Judge, & Warrior to Be More Creative*. Harper Perennial, 1986, $9.95. Both are thought-provoking self-improvement books on finding out what you want to do and doing it.

Books on small business and working at home

Alarid, William, and Gustav Berle. *Free Help from Uncle Sam to Start Your Own Business (Or Expand the One You Have)*. Puma Publishing, 1989, $11.95. Discusses resources for government loans and counseling services.

Alvarez, Mark. *The Home Office Book: How To Set Up and Use an Efficient Personal Workspace in the Computer Age*. Goodwood Press, 1990, $14.95. Includes sample office layouts.

Bangs, Jr., David H. *The Start Up Guide, a One Year Plan for Entrepreneurship*, and *The Business Planning Guide, Creating a Plan for Success in Your Own Business*. Upstart Publishing Co., Dover, NH, 1987 and 1989, $18.95. Both have solid information, highly recommended.

Cohen, William A. *How to Make it Big as a Consultant*. AMACOM, Division of American Management Association, 1985, $19.95.

Edwards, Paul and Sarah. *Working from Home*. Jeremy P. Tarcher, Inc., (213) 273-3274, 1990, $14.95. It has lots of tips and resources.

Follett, Robert. *How to Keep Score in Business: Accounting and Financial Analysis for the Non-Accountant*. Mentor, 1980, $2.50. It will help you understand your books.

Harriman, Cynthia W. *The Macintosh Small Business Companion*. Brady Books, 1989, $24.95. Tells "open-collar workers" how to use their computer to make everyday work easier.

Holtz, Herman. *How to Succeed as an Independent Consultant*. John Wiley & Sons, 1988, $22.95. A thoughtful, comprehensive guide.

McQuowon, Judith. *Inc. Yourself, How to Profit by Setting Up Your Own Corporation*, revised edition. Macmillan, 1988, $19.95. The standard book on incorporating small businesses.

Namanworth, Phillip, and Gene Busnar. *Working for Yourself, A Guide to Success for People Who Work Outside the 9-5 World*. McGraw-Hill Paperbacks, 1985, $10.95. Solid advice on time management, financial matters, and marketing, as well as insights (some from Zen) on the psychology of success and developing good habits.

Sullivan, Nick. *Computer Power for Your Small Business: A Guide from Home-Office Computing*. American Management Association, 1990, $22.95. Covers PCs and Macintoshes.

Whitmyer, Claude, Salli Rasberry, and Michael Phillips. *Running a One-Person Business*. Ten Speed Press, 1989, $13.25 from PO Box 7123, Berkeley, CA 94707, (415) 845-8414. Advice about everything from time management to the pros and cons of hiring help.

The Whole Work Catalog. New Careers Center, 1515 23rd St., PO Box 297-CT, Boulder, CO 80306, (303) 447-1087. Lists resources on starting home businesses and alternative careers.

Small business resources

American Women's Economic Development Corporation (AWED), 60 East 42nd Street, New York, NY 10165, (212) 692-9100. AWED has training groups, seminars, and publications. Their consulting hotline costs $10 for 10 minutes, $35 for 90 minutes, (800) 222-2933 or (800) 442-2933.

Internal Revenue Service, pamphlet 583, *Record Keeping for Small Business*. Call (800) 424-3676 for forms; (800) 424-1040 taxpayer hotline for questions.

National Association for the Cottage Industry, PO Box 14850, Chicago, IL 60614, (312) 939-6490. Membership $45/year. Send SASE for free copy of newsletter.

National Association for the Self-Employed, 2328 Gravel Road, Ft. Worth, TX 76118, (800) 232-6273. Membership $48/year.

Service Corps of Retired Executives (SCORE), sponsored by the U.S. Small Business Administration, 1825 Connecticut Ave., Suite 503, Washington, DC 20009, (202) 653-6279, or through the SBA. Free local counseling by over 13,000 retired executives on starting a business and preparing a business plan.

U.S. Small Business Administration has an automated answer desk to provide information, (800) 368-5855. Ask for the SBA pamphlet, *Checklist for Starting a Small Business*. In addition to SCORE, above, the SBA sponsors Women's Network for Entrepreneurial Training to match up women starting businesses with experienced mentors. And the SBA runs a guaranteed loan program, in cooperation with private lenders, for small businesses.

Books on marketing and selling

Connor, Jr., Richard A., and Jeffrey P. Davidson. *Getting New Clients*. John Wiley & Sons, 1988, $15.95.

Davidson, Jeffrey P. *Marketing for the Home Based Business*. Bob Adams, 1990, $9.95.

Girard, Joe, with Robert Casemore. *How to Sell Yourself*. Warner Books, 1981, $10.95. A motivational book.

Hopkins, Tom. *How to Master the Art of Selling*. Warner Books, 1982, $12.95.

Johnson, Spencer, with Larry Wilson. *The One Minute Sales Person*. Avon Books, 1984, $5.00. Reduces the complexities of selling to easy-to-grasp concepts.

Phillips, Michael, and Salli Rasberry. *Marketing without Advertising*. Nolo Press, 1986, $14.00.

Sonnenberg, Frank K. *Marketing to Win, How You Can Build Your Client Base in the New Highly Competitive Service Economy*. Harper Business, 1990, $29.95.

Books on the business of graphics and DTP

Berst, Jesse. *Managing Desktop Publishing: How to Manage Files, Styles and People for Maximum Productivity.* New Riders Publishing, 1989, $9.95. Focuses on each stage of the DTP process and productivity-enhancing techniques, including MS-DOS and Ventura Publisher specifics.

Cochrane, D. *The Business of Art.* Watson-Gutpill, 1988, $19.95.

Crawford, Tad. *Legal Guide for the Visual Artist.* Allworth Press, 1989, $18.95. Provides information on copyrights and taxation, model contracts.

Crawford, Tad, and Eva Bruck. *Business and Legal Forms for Graphic Designers.* North Light Books, 1990, $19.95. Includes tear-out forms.

Crawford, Tad, and Arie Kopelman. *Selling Your Graphic Design and Illustration, the Complete Marketing, Business and Legal Guide.* St. Martin's Press, 1981, $17.95. Well presented treatment of selling in the field of graphic design; information is still current.

Davis, Sally Prince. *The Graphic Artist's Guide to Marketing and Self Promotion.* North Light Books, 1987, $15.95. Tips for self-promotion applicable to a DTPer.

Dynamic Graphics. *Designer's Guide to Outfitting the Studio.* Step-by-Step Publishing, 1990, $29.95, (800) 255-8800. About getting the equipment and organizing the workspace.

Entrepreneur Magazine's Guide to Desktop Publishing. Entrepreneur Group, 1990, $69.50 with money-back guarantee, (800) 421-2300. A loose-leaf format that covers basic issues.

Gold, Ed. *The Business of Graphic Design, a sensible approach to marketing and managing a graphic design firm.* Watson-Guptill Publications, 1985, $24.95. Includes profiles of 24 leading U.S. designers and their businesses.

Graphic Artists Guild, *Handbook of Pricing and Ethical Guidelines.* North Lights Books, 1987, $19.95. A bible for graphics freelancers.

Hoover, D. *Supporting Yourself as an Artist.* Oxford, 1985, $9.95.

Hudson, Howard Penn. *Publishing Newsletters—A Complete Guide to Markets, Editorial Content, Design, Subscriptions, Management, and Desktop Publishing.* The Newsletter Clearinghouse, 1988, $15.50. Available from The Clearinghouse, 44 W. Market St., PO Box 311, Rhinebeck, NY 12572, (914) 876-2081.

Jobs in Desktop Publishing, a brochure defining and describing DTP's job skills in terms of design, typography, system usage, production, and client interaction, produced by the School of Visual Communications, National Technical Institute for the Deaf, Rochester Institute of Technology. Free from Mary Bailey, Lyndon B. Johnson Building, PO Box 9887, Rochester, NY 14623.

Jones, Robert, *The Complete Guide to Corporate Desktop Publishing.* Cambridge University Press, 1988, $20.95.

Kelly, Kate. *How to Set Your Fees and Get Them.* Visibility Enterprises, 11 Rockwood Drive, Larchmont, NY 10538, (914) 834-0602, 1989, $17.50 including postage. An excellent guide to pricing services; for novices and veterans.

Klayman, T. *The Artist's Survival Manual.* Scribner's, 1987, $12.95.

Loftus, Michele. *How to Start and Operate a Home-Based Word Processing or Desktop Publishing Business.* Bob Adams, 1990, $9.95. Covers basic issues and complements this book. It's especially useful on the logistics of keeping your home and business lives going at the same time.

Michels, C. *How to Survive and Prosper as an Artist.* Henry Holt, 1988, $8.95.

Pennypacker, James S., and Deborah Weiss. *Desktop Publisher's Guide to Products and Services.* Fox Pond Communications, PO Box 3200, Maple Glen, PA 19002, (215) 643-5940, 1990, $27.95. A comprehensive listing of national software vendors, Northeastern service bureaus and DTP businesses, books, magazines, user groups, videos.

Sitarz, David. *The Desktop Publisher's Legal Handbook: A Comprehensive Guide to Computer Publishing Law.* Nova Publishing, Carbondale, IL 1989, $19.95.

Walker, Lisa, and Steve Blount. *Making Your Computer a Design and Business Partner: How to set up your own graphic computer system to increase the creativity and overall profitability of your design studio.* North Light Books, 1990, $27.95. Superb explanations of concepts, strategies, and tools, directed specifically at the designer making the transition to electronics.

Wilson, Lee. *Make It Legal.* North Light Books, 1990, $18.95. General book for graphic arts and copywriting fields.

DTP and graphics book clubs and sources

Get the latest catalogs from BUSINESS ONE IRWIN (708) 206-2700, North Light (800) 289-0963, Peachpit Press (800) 283-9444, Ventana (919) 942-0220, Verbum (619) 233-9977, Watson-Guptill (800) 526-3641, and other publishers specializing in graphic design.

Business and Computer Book Store, (800) 233-0233.

Dynamic Graphics Bookshelf, (800) 255-8800.

Electronic Publishing & Printing Book Store (offers additional discounts to National Association of Desktop Publishers members), PO Box 6500, Chicago, IL 60680.

Graphic Artist's Book Club works just like any book club, with a monthly newsletter, a main selection, and a highly-discounted initial special offer. PO Box 12526, Cincinnati, OH 45212-0526, (800) 937-0963.

PRINT Graphic Design Book Store, discounted prices on books and Pantone color specifiers, 6400 Goldsboro Road, Bethesda, MD 20817-9969, (800) 222-2654.

Tools of the Trade has catalogs for graphics, typography, and working with words, Box 12093 Seminar Post Office, Alexandria, VA 22304, (703) 823-1919.

U&lc Bookshop, 866 Second Ave., New York, NY 10017, (800) 634-9325.

Books on DTP and graphic design

Beach, Mark, Steve Shepro, Ken Russon, *Getting It Printed: How to Work with Printers and Graphic Arts Services to Assure Quality, Stay on Schedule, and Control Costs.* Coast to Coast Books, 1986, $29.50, 1115 SE Stephens St., Portland, OR 97214, (503) 232-9772.

Beach, Mark, Polly Pattison and Mary Pretzer, *Printed Media Outstanding Newsletter Designs.* Coast to Coast Books, (see above), 1990, $11. Includes 65 front page and inside spreads, with annotations, address above.

Black, Roger. *Roger Black's Desktop Design Power.* Bantam, 1990, $24.95. By a leading type and design expert.

Bolton, Francis X. *A Printer Looks at Desktop Publishing.* A forthcoming nuts-and-bolts book by publisher of the NY Personal Computer group's monthly magazine. For photocopies of informative articles, and an order form for the book, send $6 to Francis X. Bolton, 384A Fifth Street, Brooklyn, NY 11215, (718) 788-2282.

Burke, Clifford. *Type from the Desktop: Designing with Type and Your Computer.* Ventana, 1990, $23.85.

Bove, Tony, Cheryl Rhodes, Wes Thomas. *The Art of Desktop Publishing.* Bantam, 1990, $22.95. Newly revised overview.

Campbell, Alastair. *The Graphic Designer's Handbook.* Running Press, 1988, $19.65. Design from basic principles through final production; useful color charts.

Doty, David. *Basics of Desktop Publishing on the Macintosh.* The Page, PO Box 14493, Chicago, IL 60614, 1990, $10. Overview for beginners and consultants.

Gosney, Michael, and Linnea Dayton. *The Verbum Book of Electronic Page Design.* M&T Books, 1990, $29.95, from Verbum (see Specialized resources, below), project-oriented, for Mac and PC.

Gosney, Michael, Linnea Dayton and Janet Ashford. *The Verbum Book of PostScript Illustration.* M&T Books, 1990, $29.95 (see above).

Klepper, Michael. *The Illustrated Handbook of Desktop Publishing and Typesetting, Second edition.* Tab Books, 1990, $39.95. A standard reference covering the entire field. DTP Resource database for Macintosh or PC lists 1,300 resources such as software, publications, trade associations, $24.95. CD-ROM version has contents of the *Illustrated Handbook*, Resources database and 1,364 illustrations, $204 from Graphics Dimensions, 134 Cevershan Woods, Pittsford, NY 14534.

Koren, Leonard, and R. Wippo Meckler. *Graphic Design Cookbook.* Chronicle Books, 1989, $12.95. Design ideas for page layout, type treatment.

Laundy, Peter, and Massimo Vignelli, *Graphic Design Guide for Non-Profit Organizations*. American Institute of Graphic Arts, 1059 Third Avenue, New York, NY 10021, 1990, $10. Update of a 1980 book, now incorporating discussions of DTP.

McKenzie, Bruce G. *The Hammermill Guide to Desktop Publishing in Business*. Hammermill Papers, 1990, $24.95 plus handling, (800) 533-8669. A good place to find definitions of the basic vocabulary plus explanations of all of DTP's tools; it also covers cost-benefits, design basics, and introduces and explains paper—a good companion to *Pocket Pal*.

Manousos, Stephen and Scott Tilden, *The Professional Look: The Complete Guide to Desktop Publishing*. Venture Perspectives Press, 1990, $19.95 from 430 Stevens Creek Blvd, Suite 120, San Jose, CA 95129.

Meyerowitz, Michael, and Sam Sanchez. *The Graphic Designer's Basic Guide to the Macintosh*. Allworth Press, 1990, $19.95, (800) 289-0963. A comprehensive introduction, includes specifics on software and a glossary.

Miles, John. *Design for Desktop Publishing: A Guide to Layout and Typography on the Personal Computer*. Chronicle Books, 1987, $18.95.

Parker, Roger. *Looking Good in Print: Basic Design for Desktop Publishing*. Ventana, 1990, $23.95. *The Makeover Book*. Ventana, 1989, $23.55. *Newsletters from the Desktop*. Ventana, 1989, $23.95. And other books by this popular authority.

Pocket Pal, a graphic arts production handbook, 14th edition. International Paper Company, 1989, $6.25. Send check to Pocket Pal Books, PO Box 100, Church Street Station, New York, NY 10008-0100. An encyclopedic and low-priced introduction to graphics, type, and printing. The most recent update is by Michael Bruno and Frank Romano.

Publish Magazine, 1991 Technical Support Telephone Directory, 501 Second Street, San Francisco, CA 94107, (415) 442-1891, $15.95. Lists phone numbers, hours, and product support policies for 2,000 products from over 650 companies.

Romano, Frank J. *The TypEncyclopedia, A User's Guide to Better Typography*. RR Bowker, 1984, $24.95. Straightforward introduction to typography.

Shushan, Ronnie, and Don Wright. *Desktop Publishing by Design*. Microsoft Press, 1989, $19.95. Includes chapters on general principles of typography and design samples of grids and publications. Hands-on projects, Mac and PC PageMaker oriented.

Tufte, Edward. *The Visual Display of Quantitative Information*. Graphics Press, Box 430, Cheshire, CT 06410, 1983, $36 including postage. An indispensable starting point for infographics.

White, Jan V. *Graphic Design for the Electronic Age*. Watson Guptill, 1990, $24.95. *Editing by Design, A Guide to Effective Word and Picture Communication for Editors and Designers, 2nd edition*. R.R. Bowker, 1982, $34.95. *Great Pages*. Xerox, 1990, $12.95. And other books by this long-respected authority.

Will-Harris, Daniel, *TYPEStyle: How to Choose and Use Type.* Peachpit Press, 1990, $24.95.

Williams, Robin. *The mac is not a typewriter.* Peachpit Press, 1990, $9.95. An entertaining and well-presented series of 22 lessons to move from typewriter consciousness to typography.

Magazines and catalogs

Byte, 12 issues for $24.95 from PO Box 558, Hightstown, NJ 08520-9409. The most technically rigorous consumer computer magazine, with thoughtful articles on the implications of technology.

Computer Publishing (formerly *Electronic Publishing & Printing*), $35 for nine issues per year, free to qualified applicants, from PO Box 3066, Southeastern, PA 19398 or call (213) 455-1414.

Computer Shopper, $21.97 for 12 issues from PO Box 51020, Boulder, CO 80321-1020. The most do-it-yourself hackerlike publication. Worth reading for columns by PostScript guru Don Lancaster; listings of bulletin boards and user groups.

Desktop Communications, $24 for 6 bimonthly issues from PO Box 941745, Atlanta, GA 30341, glossy publication with a primary focus on corporate publishing and design.

Desktop Publisher, PO Box 3200, Maple Glen, PA 19002, monthly tabloid newsletter for mid-Atlantic DTPers, free to qualified applicants.

Desktop Publishing Buyer's Guide and Handbook, $28.95 for 12 issues from PO Box 318, Mt. Morris, IL 61054-8090, (800) 435-0715, is four of the 12 yearly issues of the *Computer Buyer's Guide and Handbook.* Includes reviews, articles, and useful surveys of street prices of equipment.

Entrepreneur, targeted to people starting and running small businesses, $19.97 for 12 issues from PO Box 50368, Boulder, CO 80321-0368 or call (800) 421-2300. See *Success,* below.

Font & Function, (800) 833-6687, free periodic type sampler from Adobe Systems.

Home Office Computing, $10.99 for 12 issues from PO Box 51344, Boulder, CO 80321-1344, offers advice to small computer-based businesspeople.

HOW, $41 for (800) 333-1115, case study orientation to graphic design and tools.

InfoWorld, PO Box 3014, Northbrook, IL 60065, (708) 564-0694, authoritative microcomputer weekly, free to qualified subscribers.

MacWeek, $95 per year or free to qualified subscribers from PO Box 1766, Riverton NJ 08077-7366, (609) 461-2100.

MacUser, $19.97 for 12 issues from (800) 622-8387.

Macworld, $24 for 12 issues from PO Box 51666, Boulder, CO 80321-16666.

PC Publishing, free to qualified subscribers, from PO Box 5050, Des Plaines, IL 60019-9162, or $36 for 13 issues from 650 South Clark Street, Chicago, IL 60605 for MS-DOS compatibles.

PC Week, free to qualified subscribers or $160 per year from (609) 428-5000.

Personal Publishing, $24 for 12 issues from PO Box 3019, Wheaton, IL 60189, hands-on approach.

PostScript Type Sampler, $81 from MacTography, (301) 424-3942, lists 3,000 typefaces.

PRINT, $49 for 12 issues from (800) 222-2654, magazine on graphic design.

Publish, $23.95 for 12 issues from PO Box 51966, Boulder, CO 80321. See their October buyer's guide, listing most major DTP products.

Quick Printing, The Information Source for Commercial Copyshops and Printshops, free to qualified subscribers, Coast Publishing, Zedcoast Center, 1680 SW Bayshore Blvd, Port St. Lucie, FL 34984, has ads for discount printers of labels, presentation folders, and other services.

Small Press: The Magazine for Independent/In-house Desktop Publishing, $35 for one year from (203) 226-6967.

Success: The Magazine for Today's Entrepreneurial Mind, 10 issues, $11.97, (800) 234-7324. If you're interested in this one, also take a look also at *Venture* and *Inc.* on your newsstand.

TypeWorld, twice monthly tabloid, $30/year, PO Box 2709, Tulsa OK 74101-2709, to some extent oriented to typesetters who have switched to DTP. Includes ads and articles on hardware and software interfaces between PC and conventional typesetting equipment.

Specialized resources

See also the publications of many of the user groups listed below.

Aldus Magazine, free to registered owners of FreeHand, Persuasion and PageMaker, $18 for six issues from 411 First Avenue South, Seattle, WA 98104-2871.

Before & After, $36 for six issues from Page Lab, 331 J Street, Suite 150, Sacramento, CA 95814-9671, informative and enjoyable nuts and bolts on design and software.

Bove & Rhodes Inside Report — On Desktop Publishing & Multimedia, 12 issues for $195 from PO Box 1289, Gualala, CA 95445.

Communications CONCEPTS, $97 for 12 issues from 2100 National Press Building, Washington, DC 20045.

Design Line Service for DTPers is a unique business. You join for $79, then fax pages to this service for critiques by professional graphic designers with ad agency experience, who fax you back their suggestions within two days, charging $45 to rework each page. Invision, 60 Dedham Avenue, Needham, MA 02192, (617) 444-4060. Much of their work involves solving typical problems for people not familiar with basic design principles.

Directions, $30 for quarterly publication from Wheeler-Hawkins, 23 East Fourth St, NY, NY 10003, (212) 533-9651, on DTP and multimedia.

In-House Graphics, 4550 Montgomery Avenue, Suite 700N, Bethesda, MD 20814.

Inside Word, $49 for 12 issues from Cobb Group, 9420 Bunsen Parkway, Suite 300, Louisville, KY 40220, (800) 223-8720, is one of many monthly newsletters with unique tips and how-to articles for word processing and other software.

JEFFE REPORT on Computer Graphics for Design, $135 for 10 issues from 45 Stephenson Terrace, Briarcliff Manor, NY 10510, (914) 741-2852.

MacPrePress, delivered weekly by fax for $250, (203) 227-2357, a newsletter by Steve Hannaford and Kathleen Tinkel.

Release 1.0, $495 for 12 issues plus the transcripts of the annual PC Forum from 375 Park Ave., Suite 2500, New York, NY 10152, (212) 758-3434. Leading authority, Esther Dyson, writes this newsletter for designers, vendors and marketers of software.

Seybold Report on Desktop Publishing, $192 for 12 issues from Seybold Publications, Inc., Box 644, Media, PA 19063, (215) 565-2480. Latest news, thorough reviews and comparisons of products. Good if you can't get to the Seybold Conference but want to know what goes on. Another newsletter for higher-end systems, the *Seybold Report on Publishing Systems*, $228 for 22 issues.

Step-by-Step Electronic Design: The How-To Newsletter for Desktop Designers, $48 for 12 issues from Dynamic Graphics, Inc., 16000 N. Forest Park Drive, Peoria, IL 61614-3592, (800) 255-8800, includes detailed production stages for jobs plus conceptual articles about ways of working and managing DTP. Also *Step by Step Graphics: The How-To Magazine for Visual Communicators*, more like *HOW* and not strictly for DTPers, $42 for six issues plus a *Designer's Guide*. Video tutorials on electronic design also available.

The Page, A visual guide to using the Macintosh in desktop publishing, $65 for 10 issues, $1 for a sample issue, $6 each for highly-recommended back issues from Box 14493, Chicago, IL 60614, (312) 348-1200, a very practical monthly tip sheet.

U & lc, quarterly design tabloid from International Typeface Corporation 2 Hammarskjold Plaza, New York, NY 10017, (212) 371-0699. Free to qualified subscribers, four to six month wait for subscription to be filled.

Ventura Professional, free to registered owners of software, $36 for 12 issues, $5 each for back issues, from 7502 Aaron Place, San Jose, CA 95139, (408) 227-5030, includes listing of local user groups.

Verbum, Journal of Personal Computer Aesthetics, $24 for four issues from PO Box 15439, San Diego, CA 92115-9868, a perceptive, future-oriented, arty quarterly showcase.

The WEIGAND Report on Desktop Publishing, Essential Information for Communicators, Desktop Publishers and Small Business Users, $128 for 20 issues from PO Box 647, Gales Ferry, CT 06335, combines tips with analysis of industry trends.

Trade shows and conferences

Trade show schedules vary. Many of the standard personal computer shows, such as MacWorld and PC Expo, will also be of interest. Check specialized magazines for the computer platform you use.

Computer Graphics, 817 Silver Spring Ave., #409, Silver Spring, MD 20910 (301) 587-4545, annually in New York City.

Corporate Electronic Publishing Systems, Cahners Exposition Group, 999 Summer St., Stamford, CT 06905, (203) 964-0000. Held in Chicago in the early spring.

Desktop, a periodic event sponsored by *Desktop Publisher* newspaper in Philadelphia, (215) 6433-5940.

Graph Expo, periodic, in New York and Los Angeles, sponsored by the Printing Industries of America, (703) 264-7208.

Lasers in Graphics, Electronic Publishing in the 90's, 1855 East Vista Way, Suite 1, Vista, CA 92084, (619) 758-9460, a very technical conference.

Magazine Publishing Congress, 911 Hope Street, Box 4232, Stamford, CT 06907-0232, (203) 358-9900, incorporating The Folio Show and Face to Face.

Multimedia Expo, American Expositions, Inc., 110 Greene Street, #703, New York, NY 10012, (212) 226-4141.

Seybold Seminars, PO Box 578, Malibu, CA 902675, (213) 457-5850, holds a spring conference in Boston and a fall conference in the San Francisco area to explore the latest trends in computer publishing and related topics. It's the most prestigious and most expensive trade show, where the industry gets together to talk about the future.

Type-X and Art-X, TypeWorld, PO Box 170, Salem, NH 03079, (603) 898-2822, Philadelphia in the spring.

User groups, trade groups, and professional organizations

Apple user groups: for locations, call (800) 538-9696. PC user groups: *Computer Shopper* magazine (see above) maintains one of the more complete lists. Also check with computer dealers and training centers.

Association for Development of Electronic Publishing Techniques (ADEPT), annual subscription to quarterly journal, $20, 360 N. Michigan Ave., Suite 111, Chicago, IL 60601, (312) 609-0577, a Chicago-based nationally oriented DTP user group.

Association for Multi Image, 8019 North Hines Avenue, Suite 401, Tampa, FL 33614, (813) 932-1692.

Association of Desktop Publishers, PO Box 881667, San Diego, CA 92168-1667, (619) 279-2116.

The Boston Computer Society, 1 Center Plaza, Boston, MA 02108, (617) 367-8080, many of its 30,000+ members find its publications worth reading even though they live far from Boston. The Macintosh monthly newsletter includes names and phone numbers of people to call for help with dozens of software packages.

Computer Professionals for Social Responsibility, PO Box 717, Palo Alto, CA 94302, (415) 322-3778, a national user group formed in 1982 for people involved in any way with computers to encourage discussion and education about the impact of computers on society. CPSR has local chapters in dozens of cities, and many projects including a Computers in the Workplace program.

Electronic Art Association, (603) 898-2822.

Graphic Artists Guild, 11 West 20th St., New York, NY 10011, (212) 463-7759, formed in 1967, with over 10 local chapters, a national newsletter, professional education programs, legal referral services, group insurance, and many other programs.

International Association of Business Communicators, 1 Hallidie Plaza, Suite 600, San Francisco, CA 954102, (415) 433-3400, a chapter-based organization with a newsletter and seminars.

National Association of Desktop Publishers (NADTP), Museum Wharf, 300 Congress St., Boston, MA 02210, (617) 426-2885, the leading trade association, offers publications, discounts on training, opportunities for networking.

National Composition and Prepress Association, 1730 North Lynn Street, Arlington, VA 22209, (703) 841-8165, has its roots in traditional typesetting, but is running programs about DTP.

NY Professional PostScript Users Group, 3058 Ann Street, Baldwin, NY 11510, an influential regional organization with a small newsletter reporting on the latest industry developments from the point of view of people who run imagesetting service bureaus. Worth reading wherever you live if you do much high-resolution work.

PageMaker User Group, PO Box 1410, Boston, MA 02205-8955, (800) 874-4113 ext. 25, national group sponsored by NADTP (see above).

Ventura User Groups: See listing for local groups in Ventura Professional magazine, above, in Specialized resources.

XPLOR International—The Association for Electronic Printing Professionals, (800) 669-7567, (213) 373-3633, aimed at high-end users.

DTP and layout tools and supplies

Desktop Publishing Corner, (800) 937-2387, sells hardware and software.

Font Shop, (800) 942-9110, discounts typefaces for Mac and PC.

Laser Press and Graphics, (800) 628-4517, sells hardware and software.

Mactography, (301) 424-3942, sells typefaces.

Midwest Publishing, (800) 621-1507, sells tools for pasteup, laser paper.

Office Supplies Wholesale Supply Company, (800) 962-9162.

Publisher's Toolbox, (800) 233-3898, sells hardware and software.

Publishing Perfection, (800) 782-5974, sells hardware and software.

Office and publishing supplies

Earth Care Paper, (608) 256-5522, for recycled paper.

Fidelity Graphic Arts, (800) 328-3034, for furniture and supplies.

Frank Eastern, (800) 221-4914, for office and computer furniture.

Paper Direct, (800) 272-7377, for their catalog of printer and DTP paper, or their $14.95 swatch selector of their complete line.

Viking, (800) 421-1222, for office products.

Visible, (800) 323-0628, for office and computer products.

Ergonomic furniture

Anthro Technology Furniture, (800) 325-3841.

Ergotron, (800) 888-8458.

Scandinavian Computer Furniture, (800) 722-6263.

Daisy Wheel Ribbon Co., (800) 266-5585. Wrist rests for your keyboard.

Discounts for new computers

Because they are mail order they've had to do better than most retailers on service, return policy, and technical support. Don't be restricted to this starting list.

CompuAdd, (800) 288-4445, MS-DOS.

Dell Computer Corporation, (800) 365-1460, MS-DOS.

Everex, (800) 821-0806, MS-DOS.

Northgate Computer Systems, (800) 548-1993, MS-DOS.

Maya Computer, (800) 541-2318, Macintosh. (You can also order this book through Maya.)

Resources for buying and selling used computers

Boston Computer Exchange Corp., Box 1177, Boston, MA 02103, (800) 262-6399 or (617) 542-4414; on CompuServe: GO BCE; on Delphi: BOCOEXCO; listings of prices and values appear weekly in P*C Week*, *ComputerWorld*, and *Computer Reseller News*.

Computer Brokerage Services, New York City, (800) 735-7856, mostly Macintosh-oriented.

Computer Classified Bluebook, $70/year from Jerry Nims, PO Box 3395, Reno, NV 89505.

Maya Computer, Waitsfield, VT, (800) 541-2318, Macintosh.

National Computer Exchange, New York City, (800) 359-2468, mostly PC-oriented. They sell a $69/year newsletter and a Computer Classified Blue Book listing prevailing prices.

Randall 5th, Dr. Alexander, and Steven J. Bennett. *Alex Randall's Used Computer Handbook*. Microsoft Press, 1990, $14.95. Randall is a co-founder of the Boston Computer Exchange.

INDEX